EXAM PRO

Criminal Law—Objective

What is *Exam Pro/Criminal Law—Objective*?

Exam Pro/Criminal Law—Objective is a study aid that helps law students prepare to take multiple-choice Criminal Law exams

How should *you* use *Exam Pro/Criminal Law—Objective* most productively?

You should first answer the specific subject matter multiple-choice questions in the first 16 chapters. Subsequently, you should try your hand at the mixed-subject tests in the final 3 chapters. In either case, after you've figured out your own answer to a question, then you should review the corresponding model answer and analysis provided to you in the second half of this book. *Don't look at the answer first!* Figure it out on your own first, then look at the answer.

Equally important, don't just look at what the ultimate answer is to each question in ***Exam Pro/Criminal Law—Objective***, *e.g.* "a," "b," "c," or "d" (and sometimes, we've only listed three possible answers; other times, we've included a fifth possible answer, an "e" possibility as well). You should focus your study also on precisely *why* each answer is incorrect and—*just as important!*—why the other answers are incorrect.

Note that the model answers in the back of this book are designed not only to show you the correct answer to each question, but also to provide you with the analysis you need to figure out what the right answer is in other questions on the same subject.

Preparation of this sort should provide you with a much better understanding of how to prepare for and to take a multiple choice Criminal Law exam ... and, hopefully, practice of this type will assist you in taking multiple choice exams in other law school subject areas as well.

What *Exam Pro/Criminal Law—Objective* offers *you*:

- ***Exam Pro/Criminal Law—Objective*** contains a total of 138 specific subject matter, multiple choice questions along with a detailed and thorough explanation of what is the correct answer to each of those questions, and what is not.

- ***Exam Pro/Criminal Law—Objective*** also contains 3 full, mixed-subject, multiple choice Criminal Law exams (25 questions each), along with a detailed and thorough explanation of what is the correct answer to each of those questions, and what is not. *That's an additional 75 questions to give you the practice that you need to be successful!*

Why ***Exam Pro/Criminal Law—Objective*** will work for *you*:

- ***Exam Pro/Criminal Law—Objective*** helps you anticipate and become familiar with similar questions that might appear on your own exams, and it gives you the tools to learn how to figure out the correct answer, and which answers are not—and cannot be—correct.

- ***Exam Pro/Criminal Law—Objective*** contains a range of multiple choice questions that cover most of the specific subject matter areas commonly tested on Criminal Law exams in U.S. law schools.

- ***Exam Pro/Criminal Law—Objective*** was co-authored by John M. Burkoff and Nancy M. Burkoff, each of whom is a respected and experienced law professor at the University of Pittsburgh. Professor John Burkoff has taught Criminal Law for many years and has published numerous books and articles in the criminal justice area. Professor Nancy Burkoff has taught Legal Analysis & Writing for years and has also published another book and articles in the criminal justice area.

Complementary Study Aids

Exam Pro/Criminal Law—Objective (West) is the companion volume to ***Exam Pro/Criminal Law—Essay*** (West). For law students who will be taking exams that may contain a combination of essay and multiple choice questions, using both books together can be extremely helpful. Many of the questions in this objective-questions study aid use the same (or similar) facts as questions found in the essay version. Accordingly, using both study aids together can help you see just how to answer *either* type of question, using exactly the same legal principles effectively for both types of questions.

Students should also consider acquiring ***Acing Criminal Law*** (West), also authored by Professor John M. Burkoff, as an additional study aid for preparing for a Criminal Law examination. This study aid features an innovative method of content organization. It uses a checklist format to lead students through questions they need to ask themselves to fully evaluate the legal problem they are trying to solve. It also synthesizes the material in a way that most students are unable to do on their own and assembles the different issues, presenting a clear guide to analysis that students can draw upon when writing their exams.

In the answers to questions found in both the ***Exam Pro/Criminal Law—Objective*** and ***Exam Pro/Criminal Law—Essay*** study aids, cross-references are made to the applicable chapters and sub-sections in ***Acing Criminal Law***.

Exam Pro/Criminal Law—Objective
from West

CRIMINAL LAW

By

John M. Burkoff

Professor of Law
University of Pittsburgh School of Law

and

Nancy M. Burkoff

Assistant Professor of Legal Writing
University of Pittsburgh School of Law

Exam Pro

WEST®

A Thomson Reuters business

Mat #40918180

610 Opperman Drive
St. Paul, MN 55123
1–800–313–9378

Printed in the United States of America

ISBN: 978–0–314–23296–0

Dedicated with love to
Amy & Sean, Dave & Emmy,
and Emma, Molly & Hannah

Table of Contents

QUESTIONS

SPECIFIC SUBJECT MATTER MULTIPLE CHOICE QUESTIONS

CHAPTER 1
JUSTIFICATIONS FOR CRIMINAL PUNISHMENT

The following facts apply to Questions 1–1 through 1–3 below:

Linda, who is twenty-four years old, was convicted of two counts of armed robbery. She held up two elderly men at knife point and took their wallets, which contained a total of $64. This is Linda's first criminal conviction. She is a single mother of two small children. She is unemployed, having recently lost her part-time secretarial job. The pre-sentence report that was prepared indicates that Linda has used narcotics in the past, but no longer does. Linda claims that she committed the robberies in order to obtain money to buy food for her children.

The sentencing judge has the discretion to sentence Linda to anything from probation to ten years in prison.

Question 1–1: Which of the following is true:

(a) The sentencing judge must consider the following rationales for the imposition of criminal punishment in deciding on a sentence: general deterrence; specific deterrence; incapacitation; rehabilitation; retribution; and the expression of community values.

(b) The sentencing judge must consider general deterrence, specific deterrence, incapacitation, rehabilitation, and retribution in deciding on a sentence, but need not consider the expression of community values.

(c) The sentencing judge must consider general deterrence, specific deterrence, incapacitation, rehabilitation, and the expression of community values in deciding on a sentence, but need not consider retribution.

(d) None of the above.

Question 1–2: Which of the following is most accurate:

(a) If the judge focuses upon the rationale of general deterrence in deciding on an appropriate sentence for Linda, she will be most concerned about ensuring that Linda "learns her lesson" and does not engage in criminal conduct in the future.

(b) If the judge focuses upon the rationale of specific deterrence in deciding on an appropriate sentence for Linda, she will be most concerned about ensuring that other people in Linda's specific situation do not engage in criminal conduct like Linda's in the future.

(c) If the judge focuses upon the rationale of specific deterrence in deciding on an appropriate sentence for Linda, she will be most concerned about ensuring that other people in Linda's specific situation do not engage in criminal conduct like Linda's in the future.

(d) None of the above.

Question 1–3: Which of the following is most accurate:

(a) If the judge considers the rationale of rehabilitation in deciding on an appropriate sentence for Linda, she must include some jail time to make sure that Linda has an opportunity while incarcerated to be rehabilitated.

(b) If the judge focuses upon the rationale of retribution in deciding on an appropriate sentence for Linda, a serious punishment may be warranted for Linda's offenses.

(c) If the judge focuses upon the rationale of expression of community values in deciding on an appropriate sentence for Linda, the punishment should be severe in order to reaffirm our strong abhorrence of this sort of antisocial behavior.

(d) All of the above.

Question 1–4: You are a legislative aide to a state legislator who is trying to decide whether or not to introduce a bill seeking to require veterinarians to report to the police any evidence they come across of "serious" cruelty to animals and to criminalize the failure of veterinarians to report such observations. Aside from the merits of this proposal as a matter of public policy, which of the following is most accurate:

(a) Whether this legislation would serve to generally deter veterinarians from failing to report such cruelty animals depends in large part on the certainty and severity of any proposed punishment.

(b) Passing legislation like this would likely serve the goals of specific deterrence and incapacitation.

(c) Neither the goals of rehabilitation nor retribution is a sensible justification for passing legislation like this.

(d) All of the above.

CHAPTER 2
ACTUS REUS

VOLUNTARY ACT

The following facts apply to Questions 2–1 and 2–2 below:

Sergio has a sleep disorder that causes him occasionally to wander around his home late at night and to make other movements without being aware that he is doing so. One night, Sergio, while sleepwalking in his living room, tripped over an electrical cord and fell onto and seriously injured a friend, Ilsa, who was sleeping on the living room couch.

Question 2–1: Which of the following is most accurate:

(a) Sergio did not commit a criminal act because his actions were involuntary since he was sleepwalking at the time he injured Ilsa.

(b) Sergio did commit a criminal act if but only if the crime with which he is charged is a strict liability offense.

(c) Both (a) and (b) are correct.

(d) Neither (a) nor (b) is correct.

Question 2–2: Which of the following is most accurate:

(a) If Sergio had realized that he possessed this sleep disorder, his actions which resulted in injuring Ilsa may not have been involuntary.

(b) Even if Sergio had realized that he possessed this sleep disorder, his actions which resulted in injuring Ilsa were still involuntary.

(c) If Sergio's sleepwalking on the night in question was shown not to have been a direct result of his sleep disorder, but resulted instead from drunkenness resulting from the fact that he had drunk a great quantity of tequila before going to bed, his actions were still involuntary.

(d) Both (b) and (c) are correct, and (a) is incorrect.

Question 2–3: Maria was driving her car at a lawful rate of speed down a crowded, residential street when she suffered an unprovoked seizure, lost consciousness, and the car careened out of control, hitting and killing a small child who was playing in her front yard. Maria had never had a seizure previously and her doctors have not been able to determine for sure why she had this one. Which of the following is most accurate:

(a) Maria did not commit a criminal act because her act of losing control of the car was involuntary.

(b) Maria committed a criminal act because people are responsible for the proximate consequences of their own medical conditions.

(c) Maria committed a criminal act because an act is not involuntary when it is the product of a person's external body movement.

(d) Both (b) and (c) are correct, and (a) is incorrect.

POSSESSION

The following facts apply to Questions 2–4 and 2–5 below:

Estelle was driving her car on an interstate highway, when she was stopped by a state trooper for speeding. After asking Estelle for her driver's license and car registration, the trooper believed from her slurred speech that she was drunk and had her get out of the car and perform some simple sobriety tests, all of which she failed. Estelle was then arrested for driving while intoxicated. Her car was subsequently towed to an impound lot and an inventory search of its contents was performed.

The inventory search turned up two, small baggies containing crack cocaine, both of which were found inside a backpack that was in the trunk of the car. The backpack belonged to Estelle's friend, Thomas.

Question 2–4: Assume that Estelle did not know that Thomas had left crack cocaine in his backpack in her car. Which of the following is most accurate:

(a) Estelle is nonetheless guilty of possession of narcotics because the narcotics were in her car.

(b) Estelle is nonetheless guilty of possession of narcotics due to the doctrines of joint and constructive possession.

(c) Both of the above are true.

(d) None of the above is true.

Question 2–5: Assume that Estelle did know that Thomas had left crack cocaine in his backpack in her car, but it was not her cocaine and she had no plans to use any of it. Which of the following is most accurate:

(a) Estelle is guilty of possession of narcotics because the narcotics were in her car.

(b) Estelle is guilty of possession of narcotics because she had control over them.

(c) Both of the above are true.

(d) None of the above is true.

The following facts apply to Questions 2–6 and 2–7 below:

Doc and Andrea were at home asleep in bed in their second-floor bedroom when police officers executed a search warrant on their house, looking for stolen jewelry. During the course of the search, the executing officers discovered a growing marijuana plant in plain view on the kitchen table downstairs. When the marijuana was found, Doc and Andrea were nowhere near it; they were both still upstairs in their bedroom. The officers did not know whose marijuana plant it was, but arrested both Doc and Andrea for possession of marijuana.

Question 2–6: Assume that the marijuana belonged only to Doc, not to Andrea, but that Andrea knew that the marijuana was there. Which of the following is most accurate:

(a) Doc can be found guilty of possession of marijuana, but Andrea cannot.

(b) Both Doc and Andrea can be found guilty of possession of marijuana.

(c) Neither Doc nor Andrea can be found guilty of possession of marijuana because they were not in control of it at the time that it was seized.

(d) Neither Doc nor Andrea can be found guilty of possession of marijuana because, although they were in control of the marijuana, two people cannot both be convicted of possessing only a single contraband item.

Question 2–7: Assume that the prosecution discovers that the marijuana was left at the house by Doc's and Andrea's friend, Annie, who told the couple that she would return and pick it up the next day. Which of the following is most accurate:

(a) Neither Doc nor Andrea cannot be found guilty of possession of Annie's marijuana because they were not in control of it at the time that it was seized.

(b) Neither Doc nor Andrea can be found guilty of possession of Annie's marijuana because, although they were in control of the marijuana, they cannot be convicted of possessing another person's contraband.

(c) Doc and Andrea can be found guilty of possession of Annie's marijuana.

(d) Answers (a) and (b) are both true, and answer (c) is not true.

OMISSIONS

Question 2–8: Deidre believed that her next-door neighbor, Olivia, was mistreating her—Olivia's—two children, Dorita and Ella, who were two and three years old respectively. Deidre had heard rumors from some of her other neighbors that Olivia often locked the children in a small, unheated room for hours at a time, without food or access to a toilet. She had also heard screams from the children late at night from time to time. And while she had rarely seen the children outside their home, on the few occasions when Deidre had spotted them, they both looked to her to be excessively gaunt and malnourished.

Ella subsequently died of complications from an untreated kidney infection. An investigation that followed resulted in criminal charges being filed against Olivia for child abuse of both Dorita and Ella. Which of the following is most accurate:

(a) Deidre can be prosecuted successfully as Olivia's accomplice for failing to report to the authorities her belief that the children were being abused.

(b) Deidre cannot be prosecuted successfully as Olivia's accomplice for failing to report to the authorities her belief that the children were being abused.

(c) Deidre can be prosecuted successfully as Olivia's accomplice for failing to report to the authorities her belief that child abuse was taking place, but only with respect to Ella.

(d) Deidre can be prosecuted successfully as Olivia's accomplice for failing to report to the authorities her belief that child abuse was taking place, but only if it can be proved that she actually knew about Ella's kidney infection.

Question 2–9: Bill, a summer lifeguard at a municipal swimming pool, failed to notice that Cindy, a six-year old child who was swimming in the crowded pool, had slipped off the flotation devices that had been on her arms, and was drowning. Bill failed to notice this because he was preoccupied with flirting with two young women wearing skimpy swimsuits who were standing next to him, busy flirting with him. By the time Bill was finally alerted by others to Cindy's distress and jumped into the water to rescue her, it was too late. Cindy never regained consciousness.

Bill has been charged with involuntary manslaughter in the death of Cindy. His defense counsel claims that he is not guilty of these charges, *inter alia*, because he committed no criminal act. Rather, Bill simply failed to act—an omission, which is not deemed to be culpable in criminal law. Which of the following is most accurate:

(a) Bill's failure to act does not satisfy the actus reus element of involuntary manslaughter.

(b) Bill's failure to act satisfies the actus reus element of involuntary manslaughter.

(c) Bill's failure to act satisfies the actus reus element of involuntary manslaughter, but only if he was related to Cindy.

(d) Bill's failure to act satisfies the actus reus element of involuntary manslaughter, but only if a statute created a duty for lifeguards to act to save distressed swimmers.

CHAPTER 3
MENS REA

DISTINGUISHING MENS REA ELEMENTS

Question 3–1: Sandy knew that the brakes on his truck were failing. He simply did not have the money to get them repaired for a couple of weeks, until after he got paid. Finally, payday came and Sandy had enough money in the bank to take his truck to a service station for repair. Unfortunately, on his way to the service station, his brakes failed completely as he tried to come to a complete stop at a red light and he rolled right through the intersection and smashed into the passenger side of a car, killing the front-seat passenger, Tim.

Sandy has been charged with first degree murder. In the jurisdiction where these events took place, first degree murder has a mens rea element of "purposeful" conduct, i.e. to be guilty of first degree murder, the prosecution must prove, *inter alia*, that the accused had the "conscious object to cause" the resulting death of the victim. Which of the following is most accurate:

(a) Sandy acted purposefully in killing Tim.

(b) Sandy did not act purposefully in killing Tim.

(c) Sandy did not act purposefully in killing Tim if but only if it is true that he did not have the money to repair the truck's brakes prior to the accident.

(d) Sandy did not act purposefully in killing Tim if but only if his actions were reckless.

Question 3–2: Diana anonymously telephoned a false bomb threat to a public high school. The school was evacuated and searched top to bottom, but, of course, nothing was found as there was no bomb there. Diana's role in making the call was discovered when her brother overheard her talking about it with one of her friends, and he turned her in for the

$1,000 reward money. Diana was subsequently arrested and charged with the criminal offense of recklessly endangering another person.

In the jurisdiction where these events took place, this offense is defined as follows: "A person is guilty of recklessly endangering another person where he or she recklessly engages in conduct which places or may place another person in danger of death or serious bodily injury."

Recklessness is defined in this jurisdiction the same way it is defined in the Model Penal Code: "A person acts recklessly with respect to a material element of an offense when he consciously disregards a substantial and unjustifiable risk that the material element exists or will result from his conduct. The risk must be of such a nature and degree that, considering the nature and purpose of the actor's conduct and the circumstances known to him, its disregard involves a gross deviation from the standard of conduct that a law-abiding person would observe in the actor's situation." Which of the following is most accurate:

(a) Diana is guilty of recklessly endangering another person.

(b) Diana is not guilty of recklessly endangering another person because no one was actually placed in danger of death or serious bodily injury.

(c) Diana is not guilty of recklessly endangering another person because she did not consciously intend to harm anyone.

(d) Answers (b) and (c) are both true, but answer (a) is not true.

The following facts apply to Questions 3–3 and 3–4 below:

Larry, who lived in Detroit, was out of town on a business trip for a week in February. While he was gone, he let two of his friends, Dan and Candy, use his house. He did not tell them, however, that the furnace in his home was an old one, and that he knew that it was not working well, that it did not produce enough heat, and that the house stayed too cold. As a result, Larry had scheduled a furnace repair person to come and look at it the week after he returned to town to let him know if it could be repaired, or if he needed to replace it.

While he was gone and Dan and Candy were living in the house, carbon monoxide leaked from the furnace late one evening. Dan never woke up, but Candy woke up, nauseous and lightheaded, and feeling that her heart was beating funny. She dragged Dan, who was unresponsive, out of the house and called 911. The Fire Department arrived and discovered the leak. Dan was rushed to the hospital, but he subsequently died there of carbon monoxide poisoning.

Question 3–3: Assume that Larry has been charged with second degree murder of Dan for failing to tell Dan and Candy that he wondered if his furnace might be leaky. Second degree murder in this jurisdiction contains a mens rea element of recklessness. Recklessness is defined in this jurisdiction the same way it is defined in the Model Penal Code: "A person acts recklessly with respect to a material element of an offense when he consciously disregards a substantial and unjustifiable risk that the material element exists or will result from his conduct. The risk must be of such a nature and degree that, considering the nature and purpose of the actor's conduct and the circumstances known to him, its disregard involves a gross deviation from the standard of conduct that a law-abiding person would observe in the actor's situation."

Which of the following is most accurate:

(a) Larry is probably guilty of second degree murder.

(b) Larry is probably not guilty of second degree murder because there is no evidence that he actually intended to harm Dan.

(c) Larry is probably not guilty of second degree murder because he did not actually know that his furnace was leaky and posed a risk of harm to others.

(d) Answers (b) and (c) are both true, but answer (a) is not true.

Question 3–4: Assume that Larry has been charged with involuntary manslaughter of Dan for failing to tell Dan and Candy that he suspected that his furnace might be leaky. Involuntary manslaughter murder in this jurisdiction contains a mens rea element of criminal negligence. Criminal negligence is defined in this jurisdiction the same way it is defined in the Model Penal Code: "A person acts negligently with respect to a material element of an offense when he should be aware of a substantial and unjustifiable risk that the material element exists or will result from his conduct. The risk must be of such a nature and degree that the actor's failure to perceive it, considering the nature and purpose of his conduct and the circumstances known to him, involves a gross deviation from the standard of care that a reasonable person would observe in the actor's situation."

Which of the following is most accurate:

(a) Larry is probably guilty of involuntary manslaughter.

(b) Larry is probably not guilty of involuntary manslaughter because there is no evidence that he actually intended to harm Dan.

(c) Larry is probably not guilty of involuntary manslaughter because he did not actually know that his furnace was leaky and posed a risk of harm to others.

(d) Larry is probably not guilty of involuntary manslaughter because his failure to inform Dan and Candy of the risk of harm was not a gross deviation from the standard of care that a reasonable person would have observed in his situation.

(e) Answers (b), (c), and (d) are all correct, and answer (a) is incorrect.

STRICT LIABILITY

Question 3–5: Tony, who is twenty-two years old, had sexual intercourse with a fifteen year-old girl, Lizzie, who he met at a concert. Her parents subsequently discovered that Lizzie had had sex with Tony and alerted the police. Tony has been arrested and charged with the crime of statutory rape.

Statutory rape in this jurisdiction is committed when "a person engages in sexual intercourse with a complainant who is less than sixteen years of age and that person is four or more years older than the complainant."

Tony argues that he is not guilty of this offense as Lizzie was physically very mature and looked to be much older than sixteen years of age. He also notes that he had seen that she had a driver's license in her wallet, and he knew that the minimum age for a driver's license in that jurisdiction is sixteen. (The license was a fake.) Which of the following is most accurate:

(a) Tony is guilty of statutory rape.

(b) Tony is not guilty of statutory rape because Lizzie reasonably appeared to be at least sixteen years old.

(c) Tony is not guilty of statutory rape because he honestly and reasonably believed that Lizzie was at least sixteen years old.

(d) Both answers (b) and (c) are true, and answer (a) is untrue.

Question 3–6: Stewart runs a small bed-and-breakfast which has only six guest rooms. During a regular, periodic inspection undertaken by the state licensing agency that oversees the operation of such establishments, Stewart was cited under a criminal statute for three separate violations for having available for use three old, antique cribs that contained lead-based paint.

The statute in question made it a petty misdemeanor punishable by a fine of up to $1,000 for an operator of an inn or bed-and-breakfast to "offer or provide for use or otherwise place in the stream of commerce, on or after the effective date of this act, a full-size or non-full-size crib that is unsafe for any infant using the crib because" of a number of specified, unsafe conditions, including the presence of lead-based paint.

Stewart explained to the regulatory agency that he had no idea that the cribs contained lead-based paint and that he would immediately have them stripped and repainted. The regulatory agency responded that the paint needed to be removed as he described, but added that he would still be prosecuted and subject to a criminal fine of $3,000. Which of the following is most accurate:

(a) Stewart is not likely to be convicted of these offenses because he had no knowledge of the presence of lead-based paint.

(b) Stewart is not likely to be convicted of these offenses because he did not intentionally or recklessly violate this statute.

(c) Both (a) and (b) are true.

(d) Stewart is likely to be convicted of these offenses.

Question 3–7: A manufacturer has released five times the permitted amount of dangerous gas into the air, in violation of a state criminal environmental statute. Courts in this jurisdiction have construed this statute as strict liability. Which of the following is most accurate:

(a) The manufacturer cannot be convicted of violating the statute if it can show that it did not know the gas was being emitted.

(b) The manufacturer has a strong defense that it was not aware of the statutory requirements and did not intend to violate the law.

(c) The manufacturer has no possible mens rea defense in these circumstances.

(d) Answers (a) and (b) are true, and answer (c) is untrue.

INTOXICATION & DRUGGED CONDITION

Question 3–8: Kenneth has been charged with the crime of rape. The applicable rape statute in this jurisdiction provides as follows: "A person commits the crime of rape when he or she engages in sexual intercourse with another person by forcible compulsion."

Kenneth admits that he had sexual intercourse with Susan by forcible compulsion. But he argues that he was heavily intoxicated at the time and, as a result, he had no idea what he was doing. Which of the following is most accurate:

(a) Kenneth is not likely to be convicted of rape because he did not have the mens rea required to establish the commission of that offense at the time the sexual intercourse took place.

(b) Kenneth is not likely to be convicted of rape because he was unconscious at the time of the sexual intercourse due to heavy intoxication.

(c) Kenneth is likely to be convicted of rape because intoxication is not a good defense to the crime of rape.

(d) Kenneth is likely to be convicted of rape because even though intoxication can be a good defense to the crime of rape, there is not enough evidence that Kenneth was sufficiently intoxicated to make out that defense.

The following facts apply to Questions 3–9 and 3–10 below:

Keisha is addicted to crack cocaine. One evening, after smoking crack and drinking heavily for hours at a friend's apartment, Keisha got into her car and began to drive home. Unsurprisingly, her driving was extremely erratic. She kept swerving and crossing the center line and braking unexpectedly. Eventually, her erratic driving was observed by a police officer who put on his siren and lights and tried to pull her over.

Keisha would not pull over, however. Instead, she sped away and tried to lose the pursuing police car. Eventually, a number of police cars joined the chase which ended only after Keisha completely lost control of her car and ran into and over two pedestrians, killing both of them.

Question 3–9: Keisha has been charged with two counts of first degree murder in the deaths of the two pedestrians. Her defense is that she was both intoxicated and in a drugged condition when she hit and killed them. Which of the following is most accurate:

(a) Voluntary intoxication or drugged condition is a good defense for Keisha with respect to these first degree murder charges because she did not have the mens rea required to establish the commission of these offenses at the time the deaths occurred.

(b) Voluntary intoxication or drugged condition is not a good defense to first degree murder charges.

(c) A voluntary intoxication or drugged condition defense to first degree murder charges will not work for Keisha in these circumstances because she could have reasonably anticipated that someone might be killed or injured when she sped away from the police officers.

(d) Answers (b) and (c) are both correct, and answer (a) is incorrect.

Question 3–10: Keisha has been charged with two counts of involuntary manslaughter in the deaths of the two pedestrians. Her defense is that she was both intoxicated and in a drugged condition when she hit and killed them. Which of the following is most accurate:

(a) Voluntary intoxication or drugged condition is a good defense for Keisha with respect to these involuntary manslaughter charges because she did not have the mens rea required to establish the commission of these offenses at the time the deaths occurred.

(b) Voluntary intoxication or drugged condition is not a good defense to involuntary manslaughter charges.

(c) A voluntary intoxication or drugged condition defense to involuntary manslaughter charges will not work for Keisha in these circumstances because she was not sufficiently intoxicated or drugged.

(d) Answers (b) and (c) are both correct, and answer (a) is incorrect.

Question 3–11: Harley drank a fifth of Jack Daniels whiskey and—although he does not remember a thing—set fire to and burned up his neighbor's garage while he was intoxicated. He has been charged with arson.

Arson is defined in this jurisdiction as "starting a fire or causing an explosion with the purpose of destroying a building or occupied structure of another."

Harley plans to defend against the arson charge by proving that he was so intoxicated that he did not possess the mens rea for arson. Which of the following is most accurate:

(a) Harley is not likely to be convicted of arson because he did not have the mens rea required to establish the commission of that offense at the time the burning took place.

(b) Harley is not likely to be convicted of arson because he was unconscious at the time the burning took place due to heavy intoxication.

(c) Harley is likely to be convicted of arson because intoxication is not likely to be a good defense to the crime of arson.

(d) Harley is likely to be convicted of arson because even though intoxication can be a good defense to the crime of arson, there is not enough evidence that Harley was sufficiently intoxicated to make out that defense.

CHAPTER 4
MISTAKE

MISTAKE OF FACT

The following facts apply to Questions 4–1 and 4–2 below:

Donald pointed a gun at the head of his friend, Edward, and pretended that he was going to shoot him. Donald did not really intend to shoot Edward. He just wanted to scare him, and he thought the gun was unloaded. He had seen another one of his friends, the owner of the gun, remove all of the bullets from the gun. Or so he thought. This friend even told Donald that "the gun's unloaded now."

In fact, however, the friend and Donald were both mistaken. Although bullets had been removed, there was still one bullet left in the firing chamber of the gun. So when Donald pulled the trigger and thought that he was pretending to shoot his friend, Edward, he *actually* shot him in the head, killing Edward instantly.

Question 4–1: Donald has been charged with first degree murder. In the jurisdiction where these events took place, first degree murder has a mens rea element of "purposeful" conduct, i.e. to be guilty of first degree murder, the prosecution must prove, *inter alia*, that the accused had the "conscious object to cause" the resulting death of the victim.

Donald's defense counsel argues that he is not guilty of first degree murder because he mistakenly thought the gun was unloaded. Which of the following is most accurate:

(a) Donald is guilty of first degree murder.

(b) Donald is not guilty of first degree murder because he did not consciously intend to kill Edward as he reasonably and mistakenly believed the gun was not loaded.

(c) Donald is not guilty of first degree murder because a person cannot be found guilty of any homicide crime where he or she did not actually intend to kill the victim.

(d) Both (b) and (c) are true, and (a) is untrue.

Question 4–2: Donald has been charged with involuntary manslaughter. In the jurisdiction where these events took place, involuntary manslaughter has a mens rea element of gross negligence, i.e. to be guilty of involuntary manslaughter, the prosecution must prove, *inter alia*, that the accused should have been aware of a substantial and unjustifiable risk that the victim would die as a result of his or her conduct.

Donald's defense counsel argues that he is not guilty of first degree murder because he mistakenly thought the gun was unloaded. Which of the following is most accurate:

(a) Donald is guilty of involuntary manslaughter.

(b) Donald is not guilty of involuntary manslaughter because he did not consciously intend to kill Edward as he reasonably and mistakenly believed the gun was not loaded.

(c) Donald is not guilty of first degree murder because a person cannot be found guilty of any homicide crime where he or she did not actually intend to kill the victim.

(d) Donald is not guilty of involuntary manslaughter because he should not have been aware of a substantial and unjustifiable risk that Edward would die as a result of his conduct.

Question 4–3: Cyril was a die-hard Pittsburgh Steelers fan. His friend, Abe, was a devoted Cleveland Browns fan. As a result of the two football teams' long-standing rivalry, Cyril and Abe often fought with each other about which football team was the better one.

One evening, the two friends watched the Steelers play the Browns on TV at Cyril's house. Cyril was wearing his Steelers jersey and Abe was wearing his Browns jersey. The Steelers lost the game in the last few seconds of the fourth quarter as a result of a bad call by one of the referees, and Cyril was steaming mad. Unwisely, Abe took that opportunity at that moment to taunt Cyril, casting aspersions on the manhood of the Steelers' quarterback, Cyril's favorite player. Enraged, Cyril screamed at Abe, "I've had it! You're going to die now!" And with that, Cyril rushed into the kitchen, grabbed a butcher's knife and came after Abe.

Abe took off running, out the door and down the street, with Cyril in hot pursuit. After a chase of four blocks through crowds of people out on the street, Cyril realized that he was not going to catch up with Abe. So he stopped and threw the knife at the back of Abe's retreating Browns' jersey. Unfortunately, the person wearing the Browns jersey who was actually stabbed in the back was not Abe, but a complete stranger, Brian. Brian was badly injured by the knife wound, although he survived.

Cyril has been charged with the attempted murder of Brian. In the jurisdiction where these events took place, in order to establish attempted murder, the prosecution must establish that the accused had the intent to commit the crime of first degree murder. Cyril argues that he is not guilty of the crime of attempted murder because he intended to kill Abe not Brian. The only reason he threw his knife at Brian was that he honestly and reasonably believed that Brian was Abe as they were both running the same direction in a Cleveland Browns football jersey. Which of the following is most accurate:

(a) Cyril is guilty of first degree murder.

(b) Cyril is not guilty of first degree murder because he did not consciously intend to kill Brian as he reasonably and mistakenly believed that Brian was Abe.

(c) Cyril is not guilty of first degree murder because a person cannot be found guilty of any homicide crime where he or she did not actually intend to kill the victim who actually died.

(d) Both (b) and (c) are true, and (a) is untrue.

Question 4–4: Frank had sexual intercourse with Maya even though Maya kept saying "no" to him as he removed her clothes, pushed her onto the living room sofa, and subsequently penetrated her. Afterwards, when Maya tearfully asked him why he did not stop even though she kept saying "no," Frank responded: "Did you really mean that? I really didn't think that you did. I thought you meant me to keep on doing what I was doing since you didn't push me away."

The rape statute in this jurisdiction provides that "[a] person commits the crime of rape when that person engages in sexual intercourse with a complainant without the complainant's consent." Which of the following is most accurate:

(a) Frank is not guilty of rape because he honestly and reasonably believed that Maya meant for him to proceed with sexual intercourse.

(b) Frank is not guilty of rape because he did not consciously intend to have sex with Maya without her consent.

(c) Frank is guilty of rape.

(d) Both (a) and (b) are true, and (c) is untrue.

MISTAKE OF LAW

The following facts apply to Questions 4–5 and 4–6 below:

Cheech was growing a small marijuana patch in his backyard garden. A neighbor observed the marijuana, alerted the police, and Cheech was arrested. He has been charged with possession of narcotics.

Question 4–5: If Cheech can convince a jury that he honestly believed that it was not against the law to grow a small amount of marijuana for one's own personal use in that jurisdiction, would that be a good defense?

(a) Yes, but only if the possession of narcotics statute in his jurisdiction is a strict liability statute.

(b) Yes, but only if his belief was a reasonable one.

(c) No, it would not be a good defense.

(d) Yes, but only if the possession of narcotics statute in his jurisdiction includes a mens rea element of purposeful, intentional, or knowing behavior.

Question 4–6: If Cheech can convince a jury that he honestly and reasonably believed that the marijuana plants growing in his garden were actually oregano, would that be a good defense?

(a) Yes, but only if the possession of narcotics statute in this jurisdiction is a strict liability statute.

(b) Yes, it would be a good defense with respect to any mens rea element, but only if his belief was a reasonable one.

(c) No, it would not be a good defense.

(d) Yes, but only if the possession of narcotics statute in his jurisdiction includes a mens rea element.

Question 4–7: Sylvie was arrested by a local police officer for walking her dog, Trixie, in a park near her home without Trixie being on a leash. The criminal statute under which she was arrested provides that "[n]o dog shall be permitted except on leash within any park or wildlife management area except in accordance with the rules and regulations promulgated by the Commissioner of Conservation and Natural Resources, and whoever shall be the owner of any dog at large within any park or wildlife management area, knowing that this conduct is unlawful, shall be guilty of a misdemeanor."

When she was arrested, Sylvie told the arresting officer that she did not know that she needed to have Trixie on a leash. The officer responded, "I'm sorry, but that's irrelevant, ma'am. Ignorance of the law is no defense." Assuming that Sylvie's statement that she did not know that she needed to have Trixie on a leash is truthful, is that a defense?

(a) No, it is not a good defense.

(b) Yes, but only if her belief was a reasonable one.

(c) Yes, it is a good defense.

(d) Yes, but only if the statute also includes a mens rea element of purposeful, intentional, or knowing behavior.

CHAPTER 5
CAUSATION

Question 5–1: Celia shot Barry in the chest after a heated domestic dispute. The gunshot wound was a serious one and Barry would have died from it in a few hours, at most. But Barry actually died as a result of a traffic accident when the ambulance driver rushing him to the hospital, Lewis, recklessly decided to drive the wrong way down a one-way street and smashed headfirst into an oncoming car. Barry was killed when the ambulance burst into flames after the crash.

Celia and Lewis have both been charged with homicide offenses relating to the death of Barry. Each of them is defending on the ground that the other one "caused" Barry's death. Which of the following is true:

(a) Celia and Lewis each caused Barry's death.

(b) Only Celia caused Barry's death.

(c) Only Lewis caused Barry's death.

(d) Neither Celia nor Lewis caused Barry's death.

Question 5–2: On October 1, 2007, Eileen ran a red light in her car and hit Jay who had entered a crosswalk lawfully when the "WALK" sign came on. Jay was severely injured. Due to the severity of his injuries, he remained hospitalized until he finally died on October 3, 2008, due to complications arising out of the original injuries.

Eileen has been charged with the crime of involuntary manslaughter. Her defense counsel claims that Eileen was not the cause of Jay's death due to the length of time that passed between the time that she struck him with her car and the date of Jay's actual death. Which of the following is true:

(a) Under the causation rules applicable in every U.S. jurisdiction, Eileen caused Jay's death.

(b) Eileen caused Jay's death whether or not this jurisdiction uses the common law "year and a day rule."

(c) Under the causation rules applicable in every U.S. jurisdiction, Eileen did not cause Jay's death.

(d) Eileen did not cause Jay's death, but only if this jurisdiction uses the common law "year and a day rule."

Question 5–3: After a drug deal went wrong, George shot Rudolfo twice in the abdomen, gravely wounding him. Rudolfo was rushed to the hospital.

While he was still unconscious, Rudolfo was placed on a gurney and wheeled into an X-ray room. A hospital employee then sat him up at an angle but failed to secure him to the gurney before lowering a side rail. As a result, Rudolfo fell off of the gurney, breaking his neck at the fifth and sixth vertebrae. This break resulted in Rudolfo dying almost instantaneously as a result of spinal shock.

George has been charged with first degree murder in the shooting of Rudolfo. His defense counsel has argued, however, that George did not cause Rudolfo's death due to the intervening negligence of the hospital employee who failed to secure him to the gurney while he was being x-rayed, resulting in his fall and subsequent death. Which of the following is most accurate:

(a) The fact-finder will probably find that George did not cause Rudolfo's death because the hospital employee's negligence broke the causal chain.

(b) The fact-finder will probably find that George did not cause Rudolfo's death because the hospital employee was the only proximate cause of Rudolfo's death.

(c) The fact-finder will probably find that George caused Rudolfo's death.

(d) Answers (a) and (b) are correct, and answer (c) is incorrect.

Question 5–4: Andy was shot multiple times by Keith as he resisted Keith's attempt to take his wallet and briefcase from him at gunpoint. Andy was rushed to the hospital. When he arrived, his heart was still beating, but it was concluded by the medical staff that he had suffered irreversible brain damage and loss of brain function. This was established, *inter alia*, by Andy's inability to breathe on his own, by the absence of other vital reflexes, by his lack of responsiveness to stimuli, by the absence of muscle activity, and by a flat electroencephalogram (measuring brain wave activity).

Andy's wife, who had rushed to the hospital after she heard that he had been shot, ultimately agreed to let the doctors discontinue the artificial ventilation that was keeping his heart going so that his organs could be used as transplants in other people. The doctors discontinued the ventilation, and Andy died.

Keith was charged with first degree murder in Andy's death. He argues in his defense that the doctors who disconnected the ventilator were the cause of Andy's death, not his actions in shooting Andy. Which of the following is most accurate:

(a) The fact-finder will probably find that Keith did not cause Andy's death because the doctor's act of discontinuing ventilation broke the causal chain.

(b) The fact-finder will probably find that Keith did not cause Andy's death because the hospital doctors were the only proximate cause of Rudolfo's death.

(c) The fact-finder will probably find that Keith caused Andy's death.

(d) Answers (a) and (b) are correct, and answer (c) is incorrect.

Question 5–5: Bianca was standing at the rail on the top deck of a ferry boat, smoking and talking to her friends, while the ferry crossed a long expanse of water. At one point, Bianca flicked her half-smoked cigarette overboard. But, because of the strong wind generated by the ferry boat's motion, the cigarette was blown right back onto the boat and onto a lower deck, and it was still lit and burning.

The cigarette landed in a pail of cleaning liquid that was being used by a crew member to clean woodwork, and it immediately ignited that liquid. The ensuing fire on the ferry boat ended up engulfing the entire boat in flames, causing many injuries, including the deaths of two passengers, Bernard and Penny, who jumped in the water to escape the burning boat and drowned.

Bianca has been charged with two counts of involuntary manslaughter in the deaths of Bernard and Penny. Her defense counsel claims that Bianca could not have anticipated the strong wind that caught her cigarette and blew it back onto the boat and that, accordingly, she was not criminally responsible for their deaths. Which of the following is most accurate:

(a) The fact-finder will probably find that Bianca did not cause Bernard's and Penny's deaths because the wind blowing the cigarette back onto the boat was an action that broke the causal chain.

(b) The fact-finder will probably find that Bianca did not cause Bernard's and Penny's deaths because the fact that the wind blew the cigarette back onto the boat was causing those deaths was a result that was too remote or accidental.

(c) The fact-finder will probably find that Bianca caused Bernard's and Penny's deaths.

(d) Answers (a) and (b) are correct, and answer (c) is incorrect.

CHAPTER 6
ACCOMPLICE LIABILITY

Question 6–1: Moments after their college football team won a prestigious New Year's Day bowl game, Arlen and Woody pushed an old, dilapidated couch into the street in front of their apartment building and set it on fire. Hundreds of other college students poured into the streets, many of them chanting and yelling and screaming near or around the flaming couch.

As the flames began to spread from the couch to other trash littering the street, the fire department and the police arrived at the scene. The firemen extinguished the burning flames, and the police officers arrested a number of college students who were in the street, chanting around the burning couch.

Arlen and Woody were among those arrested and they were charged with the criminal offense of arson endangering property. Both of them quickly hired criminal defense counsel who negotiated a plea agreement with the prosecutor's office, resulting in pleas of guilty by both Arlen and Woody to the lesser offense of disorderly conduct.

Ellie and Miranda were also arrested at the scene as both were standing right next to the burning couch when the police arrived. They were each charged with being accessories to the crime of arson endangering property. Although each of them has also been offered the chance to plead guilty to the lesser offense of disorderly conduct, they claim that they did nothing wrong and have declined to consider any plea agreement. Which of the following is most accurate:

(a) Ellie and Miranda were complicit in the crime of arson endangering property.

(b) Ellie and Miranda were not complicit in the crime of arson endangering property because there is no proof that they intended to assist another person in committing a crime.

(c) Ellie and Miranda were not complicit in the crime of arson endangering property because there is no proof that they actively assisted another person in committing a crime.

(d) Answers (b) and (c) are correct, and answer (a) is incorrect.

Question 6–2: Darius, an undercover agent in his 20's working in plain clothes for the local police force, was trying to identify the major narcotics sellers in a high-crime area of the city. He hung out for a few weeks outside a check-cashing store where a lot of other young, unemployed males roughly his age hung out and began to befriend them.

Eventually, he asked some of the young men he had met where he could get an "eight ball" (meaning, in that setting, one-eighth of an ounce of crack cocaine). Reluctant at first to talk to him about it, eventually one of the young men, Ernesto, told him that he should probably stop by and see DeJuan, who lived three blocks away "in the gray house on Dinwiddie Street."

Darius contacted DeJuan and made three different controlled buys of crack cocaine from him. Subsequently, DeJuan was arrested for sale of narcotics and Ernesto was also arrested as an accomplice in those sales. Which of the following is most accurate:

(a) Ernesto was complicit in the crime of sale of cocaine.

(b) Ernesto was not complicit in the crime of arson endangering property because there is no proof that he intended to assist DeJuan in selling cocaine.

(c) Ernesto was not complicit in the crime of arson endangering property because there is no proof that he actively assisted DeJuan in selling cocaine.

(d) Answers (b) and (c) are correct, and answer (a) is incorrect.

The following facts apply to Questions 6–3 and 6–4 below:

Kailee and Diem were both accused of shoplifting. They were each arrested when a department store detective watched the two of them together looking at scarves, and then saw Diem put a Hermes scarf in her purse while Kailee simply looked around to see if anyone was watching them.

Question 6–3: Diem was tried first and after a three-hour trial, she was acquitted by a jury. Kailee's defense attorney has now moved to dismiss the charges against Kailee due to the prior acquittal of Diem, arguing that since a jury has concluded that no crime was committed, Kailee cannot be tried or convicted for a crime that did not occur.

Is this a good defense? Assuming that this jurisdiction follows the approach to complicity followed by a majority of U.S. jurisdictions, which of the following is most accurate:

(a) This is a good defense for Kailee because Diem was acquitted, hence a jury determined that no crime was committed.

(b) This is not a good defense for Kailee because her culpability does not depend on Diem's culpability.

(c) This is a good defense for Kailee because she did not actually take the scarf.

(d) Answers (a) and (c) are correct, and answer (b) is incorrect.

Question 6–4: Kailee was charged with aiding and abetting Diem in the act of shoplifting. Which of the following is most accurate:

(a) Kailee was complicit in the crime of shoplifting.

(b) Kailee was not complicit in the crime of shoplifting because there is no proof that she intended to assist Diem in committing the crime.

(c) Kailee was not complicit in the crime of shoplifting because there is no proof that she actively assisted Diem in committing the crime.

(d) Answers (b) and (c) are correct, and answer (a) is incorrect.

Question 6–5: Vinny runs a pawn shop. He has been arrested as an accomplice in the burglary of three different residences after the police discovered a number of items stolen from those homes for sale in his store.

Vinny has admitted that when he purchased these items very cheaply from someone he had never met before, he suspected that they may have been stolen. But he did not know that for sure. He claims not to have known anything about the burglaries in question.

If Vinny is telling the truth, is he an accomplice in these burglaries? Which of the following is most accurate:

(a) Vinny was complicit in these three burglaries.

(b) Vinny was not complicit in these burglaries because there is no proof that he intended to assist the burglars in committing the crimes.

(c) Vinny was not complicit in these burglaries because there is no proof that he actively assisted the burglars in committing the crimes.

(d) Answers (b) and (c) are correct, and answer (a) is incorrect.

Question 6–6: Claire agreed to work as a "lookout" for Eddie, a marijuana salesman. Claire's job was simply to sit on the front stoop of the building where Eddie sold his wares. If she saw a police officer or someone who looked like he or she might be an undercover officer coming near the building, she was to bang on a garbage can lid to alert Eddie inside of the possible danger to him.

Claire did not do a very good job as a lookout. She saw nothing suspicious about the undercover agent who came to the door, went inside, bought marijuana from Eddie, and then arrested him. As a result, she did not bang on the garbage can lid. She did nothing.

Is Claire an accomplice in Eddie's sale of marijuana? Which of the following is most accurate:

(a) Claire was not an accomplice in Eddie's sale of marijuana because there is no proof that she intended to assist him in making these sales.

(b) Claire was not an accomplice in Eddie's sale of marijuana because there is no proof that she actively assisted him in making these sales.

(c) Claire was an accomplice in Eddie's sale of marijuana.

(d) Answers (a) and (b) are correct, and answer (c) is incorrect.

The following facts apply to Questions 6–7 and 6–8 below:

David was recruited by some of his friends to take part in a bank robbery. Each of the five young men who became involved in the bank robbery plot was assigned a specific role to prepare for it. David's job prior to the robbery was to scout the scene of the crime and to prepare an accurate drawing of where all of the bank employees, including the guards, were likely to be sitting or standing on the Tuesday morning when the robbery was planned to take place. On the day of the robbery, David's assigned job was to stay in the car during the robbery and serve as a getaway driver.

David visited the bank half a dozen times in order to figure out where all of the employees were likely to be. He then put together on his computer a detailed drawing of their likely positions. The other four would-be bank robbers had different preparatory tasks, and all of them accomplished their assigned jobs and began meeting to do the actual planning.

Two weeks before the bank robbery was to take place, David began regretting his decision to get involved in the robbery. As a result, he told the others that he was no longer going to be a part of the crime. Although reluctant at first to let him leave the group, the rest ultimately agreed when he swore that he would not tell anyone what the group was up to. The remaining four robbers found another friend to join the group as the getaway driver and the bank robbery went on just as planned. The group got away with over $24,000 in cash.

Unfortunately for the new group of robbers, however, their identity was ultimately discovered. They were all arrested and charged with the crime of bank robbery. One of the robbers decided to plead guilty and cooperate with the government in exchange for a lesser charge, and that robber informed the authorities of David's earlier role in the plot. David has now been charged as an accomplice to bank robbery.

Question 6–7: Without regard to any defense he may have due to his withdrawal from the planning (*see* Question 6–8), was David an accomplice to the bank robbery that took place without him? Which of the following is most accurate:

(a) David was not an accomplice in the bank robbery because there is no proof that he intended to assist the others in committing this crime.

(b) David was not an accomplice in the bank robbery because there is no proof that he actively assisted the others in committing this crime.

(c) David was an accomplice in the bank robbery.

(d) Answers (a) and (b) are correct, and answer (c) is incorrect.

Question 6–8: David's criminal defense counsel argues that even if he was at one time planning to be an accomplice in this bank robbery, he was nonetheless not guilty when the crime actually occurred as he had withdrawn from the robbery plan and did not participate in it. Withdrawal from or renunciation of a criminal plan is recognized as a good defense for an accused in this jurisdiction under the conditions set forth in the Model Penal Code. Is this a good defense in this case for David? Which of the following is true:

(a) This is a good defense for David in these circumstances.

(b) This is not a good defense for David in these circumstances because his withdrawal was not voluntary.

(c) This is not a good defense for David in these circumstances because his withdrawal was not complete.

(d) None of the above.

The following facts apply to Questions 6–9 and 6–10 below:

Diane agreed to help her daughter, Megan, steal coins from parking meters. Diane would "stuff" the coin slots of forty or fifty meters so that coins inserted in the slots in those meters would stay flush with the slot and not fall into a catchment area lower in the meter. Then, a few hours later, after motorists had inserted a number of coins into these "stuffed meters," Megan would show up and hook and pull the coins out with bent paperclips. She could remove the coins from a meter in this fashion in less than ten seconds. Diane and Megan shared the proceeds that they obtained by stealing from these meters.

One afternoon, however, when Megan was retrieving coins from one of the stuffed meters, a motorist returning to his motorcycle, Bruce, noticed what she was doing and yelled at her to stop, that he was calling the police. Megan responded, "no, you don't," and ran straight at Bruce and hit him on the head with her bag of coins stolen from prior stuffed meters. The blow to the head knocked Bruce unconscious, although he recovered fully—other than bruising and a headache—after he regained consciousness.

Question 6–9: Diane and Megan have been arrested and charged with the assault on Bruce. Megan has pleaded guilty to this charge in exchange for the prosecutor's agreement to recommend to the sentencing judge that she receive a suspended sentence. Megan also agreed to reimburse the Parking Authority for all of the money that she and Diane stole from the parking meters, and to testify against Diane at Diane's trial for assault.

Diane claims that she had nothing at all to do with the Megan's assault on Bruce and wasn't even present at the scene when the assault occurred. Is this a good defense for Diane? Which of the following is most accurate:

(a) Diane was not an accomplice in the assault because there is no proof that she intended to assist Megan in committing this crime.

(b) Diane was not an accomplice in the assault because there is no proof that she actively assisted Megan in committing this crime.

(c) Diane is guilty of the assault as an accomplice.

(d) Answers (a) and (b) are correct, and answer (c) is incorrect.

Question 6–10: Diane has been charged with the theft of parking meter coins. Megan was not charged with this crime as part of the same plea agreement outlined above in Question 6–9, as a result of which she pled guilty to the assault on Bruce. Which of the following is most accurate:

(a) Diane was not an accomplice in the theft because there is no proof that she intended to assist Megan in committing this crime.

(b) Diane is guilty of the theft as an accomplice.

(c) Diane was not an accomplice in the theft because there is no proof that she was ever present at the scene when the coins were stolen.

(d) Answers (a) and (c) are correct, and answer (b) is incorrect.

CHAPTER 7
VICARIOUS LIABILITY

Question 7–1: Manny owned a small business, Manny's Bar & Grill. Since Manny's establishment was located in a strip mall only one-quarter mile from a rural college campus, a great deal of his business resulted from college students coming to the bar and drinking in the evenings.

Manny stressed to his regular bartender, Cherie, that she was to take care not to serve alcohol to any underage patrons because Manny could lose his liquor license for Manny's Bar & Grill if the state Alcohol Enforcement Agency (AEA) discovered that minors were being served alcoholic beverages on his premises.

One evening, however, AEA agents arrived at Manny's Bar & Grill during an unannounced inspection, and discovered that five underage college students were drinking beer. When questioned about this fact, Cherie admitted that she knew these five were minors but she served them anyway because they "were great tippers." Manny was not present on the premises when any of this occurred.

State law makes it a strict liability crime for any person to furnish alcohol to minors and further provides that liquor licensees are vicariously liable for the acts of their employees. Both Manny and Cherie have each been charged with five counts of that criminal offense, one for each of the minors served.

Manny argues that he did nothing wrong, that it was Cherie who served these five minors, not him. He wasn't even around when these offenses took place. Which of the following is most accurate:

(a) Manny is likely to be found guilty of furnishing alcohol to minors.

(b) Manny is not likely to be found guilty of furnishing alcohol to minors because he was not present in the bar when the crimes took place.

(c) Manny is not likely to be found guilty of furnishing alcohol to minors because Cherie committed the crimes and he did not assist her in their commission.

(d) Answers (b) and (c) are correct, and answer (a) is incorrect.

Question 7–2: Jimmy is the CEO of Stick–To–It Enterprises, a company that manufactures peanut butter and other peanut-related products. Some of the peanut products distributed by Stick–To–It Enterprises in January of 2009 have caused food poisoning in young children and were recalled by the Food and Drug Administration.

It is a crime in the jurisdiction where Stick–To–It Enterprises is located to distribute such tainted food products. The District Attorney in this jurisdiction has asked you, an Assistant District Attorney, whether it is possible to prosecute Jimmy for this crime, or whether any criminal prosecution would have to be limited to a prosecution only of Stick–To–It Enterprises. What is your response? Which of the following is most accurate:

(a) Jimmy may be personally prosecuted for distributing tainted food products whether or not he had the power to prevent this distribution from occurring.

(b) Jimmy may not be personally prosecuted for distributing tainted food products if it can be demonstrated that he lacked the power to prevent this distribution from occurring.

(c) Jimmy may not be personally prosecuted for distributing tainted food products because the acts of Stick–To–It Enterprises are not attributable to him unless he knew about and ratified them.

(d) Answers (b) and (c) are correct, and answer (a) is incorrect.

Question 7–3: Gary, a driver of a package delivery truck, learned one morning that his wife of twenty-one years was leaving him and their two children and moving to Mexico with her hair dresser to open a tacqueria. Understandably upset, Gary spent his lunch hour drinking heavily.

When Gary got back in his truck, he was very intoxicated and he drove erratically. At one point, he started crying, and when he did, his truck veered off the road and he hit a pedestrian who was walking her dog. The pedestrian was badly injured and her dog was killed. Gary has been charged with the crimes of reckless driving and aggravated assault.

Wayne is Gary's supervisor at the package delivery company. On the theory that Wayne was responsible for Gary's actions since he was Gary's supervisor, the District Attorney is also considering filing charges against Wayne. She has asked you, an Assistant District Attorney, whether that is possible, whether criminal charges can be filed against Wayne based on Gary's conduct in these circumstances. What is your response? Which of the following is most accurate:

(a) Wayne cannot be held responsible at criminal law for Gary's actions under any circumstances.

(b) Wayne can be held responsible at criminal law for Gary's actions if he had the power to supervise Gary's actions while working for the company.

(c) Wayne can be held responsible at criminal law for Gary's actions if he knew that Gary had previously imbibed alcohol at lunch and had driven recklessly while intoxicated on the job.

(d) Answers (b) and (c) are correct, and answer (a) is incorrect.

CHAPTER 8
ATTEMPT

ACTUS REUS

Question 8–1: Robbie decided that she would rob a neighborhood convenience store in order to obtain enough money to buy herself some new clothes and a new mobile telephone. Robbie had been in this convenience store many times previously and she knew that there was only one clerk-cashier working there after 9:00 p.m. She also knew that the security camera in the store had been broken for at least three months. So Robbie decided that she would rob the store the next evening, some time around 10:00 p.m.

However, the next morning, Robbie unwisely told Aleesha, her roommate, all about her robbery plan. As soon as Robbie left the room, Aleesha immediately called the neighborhood police precinct, and warned the desk sergeant who answered the phone exactly what Robbie planned to do that evening. In the early afternoon, as a result of this tip, two police officers arrived at Robbie's and Aleesha's apartment and arrested Robbie. She was subsequently charged with attempted robbery of the convenience store.

Can Robbie be prosecuted successfully for attempted robbery of the convenience store on these facts? Which of the following is most accurate:

(a) Robbie can be prosecuted successfully for attempted robbery of the convenience store.

(b) Robbie cannot be prosecuted successfully for attempted robbery of the convenience store because she never actually entered the store.

(c) Robbie cannot be prosecuted successfully for attempted robbery of the convenience store because she merely prepared for the robbery and went no further.

(d) Answers (b) and (c) are correct, and answer (a) is incorrect.

Question 8–2: Omar and Franklin decided to burn down a failing business—a dry cleaners—located in a building that they owned. Their plan was to make a claim for the insurance proceeds on the burned building. Neither of them wanted anyone to get hurt in the fire, however, so they planned to burn the building that housed the dry cleaning shop in the very early morning, a time when no one would be around the commercial area where the building was located.

Omar purchased gasoline to pour on the shop floor to be burned. Franklin purchased fuses and other accelerant materials to help ignite the gasoline from a distance. As they were spreading these various materials around the shop in the middle of the night, working only by flashlight, a passing police officer happened to see the light beams from their flashlights from outside the shop front window, and he called for other police officers to come to the scene as backup to assist him in stopping what he thought was a burglary in progress.

The other officers arrived at the scene and joined the first officer outside on the sidewalk. All together, they broke into the dry cleaners shop, yelling "Freeze! Police Officers!", with their guns at the ready. Inside, they discovered the shop owners, Omar and Franklin, just about to light the fuses to start the fire to burn down the shop. Omar and Franklin were immediately arrested and subsequently they were each charged with the crime of attempted arson.

Can Omar and Franklin be prosecuted successfully for the attempted arson of the building housing the dry cleaning shop? Which of the following is most accurate:

(a) Omar and Franklin can be prosecuted successfully for attempted arson.

(b) Omar and Franklin cannot be prosecuted successfully for attempted arson because they did not commit the last proximate act before starting a fire.

(c) Omar and Franklin cannot be prosecuted successfully for attempted arson because they merely prepared for the arson, but never actually lit the fuses.

(d) Answers (b) and (c) are correct, and answer (a) is incorrect.

The following facts apply to Questions 8–3 and 8–4 below:

Bobbie decided that she would rob a neighborhood convenience store in order to obtain enough money to buy herself some new clothes and a new mobile telephone. Bobbie had been in this particular store many times previously and she knew that there was only one clerk-cashier working there after 9:00 p.m. She also knew that the security camera in the store had been broken for at least three months. So she decided that she would rob the store the next evening, some time around 10:00 p.m. To accomplish the robbery, Bobbie purchased a gun—illegally—from a friend of her brother's.

However, the next morning, Bobbie unwisely told Latesha, her roommate, about her robbery plan. Latesha immediately called the neighborhood police precinct, and warned the desk sergeant who answered the phone about what Bobbie apparently planned to do that evening. In the early afternoon, two police officers arrived at Bobbie's and Lateesha's apartment and arrested Bobbie. She was subsequently charged with the crime of attempted robbery of the convenience store.

Question 8–3: Can Bobbie be prosecuted successfully for attempted robbery of the convenience store on these facts? The jurisdiction in which these events took place uses the majority (and Model Penal Code) approach to determining when the actus reus element of an attempt is satisfied. Which of the following is most accurate:

(a) Bobbie can be prosecuted successfully for attempted robbery of the convenience store.

(b) Bobbie cannot be prosecuted successfully for attempted robbery of the convenience store because she never actually entered the store.

(c) Bobbie cannot be prosecuted successfully for attempted robbery of the convenience store because she merely prepared for the robbery and went no further.

(d) Answers (b) and (c) are correct, and answer (a) is incorrect.

Question 8–4: Can Bobbie be prosecuted successfully for attempted robbery of the convenience store on these facts? The jurisdiction in which these events took place uses the minority (and common law) approach to determining when the actus reus element of an attempt is satisfied. Which of the following is most accurate:

(a) Bobbie can be prosecuted successfully for attempted robbery of the convenience store.

(b) Bobbie cannot be prosecuted successfully for attempted robbery of the convenience store because she never took a substantial step toward actually committing the robbery.

(c) Bobbie cannot be prosecuted successfully for attempted robbery of the convenience store because she did not come close to actually committing the robbery.

(d) Answers (b) and (c) are correct, and answer (a) is incorrect.

MENS REA

Question 8–5: Late one night, as she was walking back to her apartment from the bus stop along a deserted and poorly lit city block, Susan was grabbed from behind by a stranger and dragged into an alleyway. She screamed, but apparently no one heard her.

Susan's attacker pulled her purse away from her and then yelled at her, "Turn around," pushing her and trying to get her to turn away from him and to face the building wall instead. Terrified, Susan, started to turn around but, as she turned, she managed to rake her fingernails across her attacker's face, drawing blood. While he screamed in pain, Susan then managed to break his grip on her and run away from him. As she began to run, he grabbed after her and, in the process, he ripped and tore her blouse in the process.

Susan raced from the alley to her apartment and called 911. The police quickly responded to her call, and they managed to quickly find and apprehend her attacker, George. George was subsequently charged with a number of criminal offenses including assault, kidnaping, robbery, and attempted rape.

On these facts alone, is there enough evidence to convict George of the crime of attempted rape? Which of the following is most accurate:

(a) George can be prosecuted successfully for the attempted rape of Susan.

(b) It is not likely that George can be prosecuted successfully for attempted rape because there is not enough evidence that he satisfied the act element of attempted rape.

(c) It is not likely that George can be prosecuted successfully for attempted rape because there is not enough evidence that he had the specific intention to sexually assault Susan.

(d) Answers (b) and (c) are correct, and answer (a) is incorrect.

Question 8–6: Dwight entered a bank just before closing time, and he pulled on a ski mask as he walked through the door. He then sprinted over to the one teller window that was still open and handed the teller a note which read:

THIS IS A ROBBERY

PUT BIG BILLS (20s, 50s & 100s) IN BAG

DON'T SCREAM OR ALERT ANYONE OR I'LL SHOOT YOU

The teller instantly complied with the demand in Dwight's note. But, as he was stuffing a bag full of cash to hand over, he also surreptitiously triggered a silent alarm with his foot.

The silent alarm alerted the police that a robbery was in progress. Three police cars responded and arrived on the scene just as Dwight was leaving the bank, pulling off his ski mask, carrying the bag which was bulging with cash. Ignoring the police officers' screams at him to drop the bag and to surrender, Dwight instead pulled a gun out of his jacket pocket and fired twice at one of the officers, the closest one to him (missing him, fortunately). Another officer responded to Dwight's shots by returning fire, wounding Dwight, who immediately dropped to the ground and dropped his gun. At that point, the other police officers ran over and cuffed and arrested him.

Dwight has now been charged with armed robbery and attempted murder.

On these facts, can Dwight be prosecuted successfully for the crime of attempted murder? Which of the following is most accurate:

(a) Dwight can be prosecuted successfully for the attempted murder.

(b) It is not likely that Dwight can be prosecuted successfully for attempted murder because the shots he fired hit no one.

(c) It is not likely that Dwight can be prosecuted successfully for attempted murder because there is insufficient evidence that he intended to kill one of the police officers.

(d) None of the above.

Question 8–7: Gloria was angry at her husband, Mario, because Mario watched soccer games on television for hours and hours on end, ignoring her. She yelled and screamed at him for nearly an hour about this and other problems with their marriage, and was largely ignored. So when Mario left the living room and his television set to take a short bathroom break, Gloria maneuvered their large flat-screen television set—Mario's favorite possession—to the living room window and shoved it outside.

Gloria and Mario lived on the tenth floor of an apartment building in an urban area. So when Gloria shoved the television set out their window, it fell all ten stories, smashing on the ground less than a foot from a passing pedestrian, Yves. Had the set fallen one foot farther away, it would have landed right on top of Yves, and would surely have killed him or injured him severely. As it happened, however, Yves was unhurt. Angry and upset, of course. But completely unhurt.

Gloria has been charged with the crime of attempted murder of Yves. Can she be successfully prosecuted for this offense? Which of the following is most accurate:

(a) Gloria can be prosecuted successfully for the attempted murder.

(b) It is not likely that Gloria can be prosecuted successfully for attempted murder because she did not intend to kill anyone.

(c) It is not likely that Gloria can be prosecuted successfully for attempted murder because she did not take a substantial step toward killing Yves.

(d) Answers (b) and (c) are both true, but answer (a) is false.

Question 8–8: Doria was angry at her husband, Martin, because Martin watched soccer games on television for hours and hours on end, ignoring her. She yelled and screamed at him for nearly an hour about this and other problems with their marriage, and was largely ignored. So when Martin left the living room and his television set to take a short bathroom break, Doria maneuvered their large flat-screen television set—Martin's favorite possession—to the living room window and shoved it outside.

Doria and Martin lived on the tenth floor of an apartment building in an urban area. So when Doria shoved the television set out their window, it fell all ten stories, smashing on the ground less than a foot from a passing pedestrian, Yves. Had the set fallen one foot farther away, it would have landed right on top of Yves, and would surely have killed him or injured him severely. As it happened, however, Yves was unhurt. Angry and upset, of course. But completely unhurt.

Doria has been charged with the crime of attempted involuntary manslaughter of Yvette. Can she be successfully prosecuted for this offense? Which of the following is most accurate:

(a) Doria can be prosecuted successfully for attempted involuntary manslaughter.

(b) It is not likely that Doria can be prosecuted successfully for attempted murder because she did not act recklessly or with criminal negligence.

(c) It is not likely that Doria can be prosecuted successfully for attempted murder because she did not take a substantial step toward killing Yves.

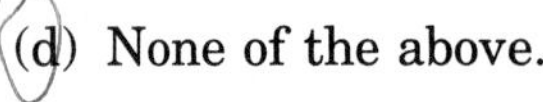

(d) None of the above.

ABANDONMENT

Question 8–9: A young mother, Violet, was shopping in a suburban shopping mall and tending to her crying, six-month old daughter who was in a stroller. Violet was careless, however, about where she put her purse.

Distracted by her daughter's crying, Violet placed the purse on the ground behind her back, in a spot where she couldn't see it.

Darius, just hanging around out at the mall and watching all of this, saw an opportunity in Violet's inattention. He quietly crept up behind her, and quickly grabbed her purse and walked away. But, after no more than thirty seconds had passed, Darius regretted what he had done so hastily and without really thinking about it. So he turned right around and took Violet's purse right back to where he had taken it from, behind Violet, who was still tending to her daughter. In fact, she never noticed that her purse had been taken by Darius, or that it had been returned.

However, Darius' actions were observed. They were viewed and recorded in their entirety by members of the mall security force on security cameras. As a result, Darius was apprehended and arrested, and he was subsequently prosecuted for purse-snatching.

Darius' defense counsel has raised the defense of abandonment, that Darius cannot be convicted of this offense because he did not complete it since he successfully abandoned its commission. Will defense counsel be successful in making this defense on Darius' behalf on these facts? Which of the following is most accurate:

(a) Darius can be prosecuted successfully for purse-snatching.

(b) Darius cannot be prosecuted successfully for purse-snatching because he returned Violet's purse voluntarily.

(c) Darius cannot be prosecuted successfully for purse-snatching because Violet never even noticed that her purse was missing.

(d) Answers (b) and (c) are true, and answer (a) is untrue.

Question 8–10: Barby and Harvey were grocery shopping at Hawthorne supermarket. But, while they were putting some larger grocery items into their shopping cart, they were also surreptitiously (they thought) stuffing some smaller and more expensive items into Barby's over-sized purse.

As Barby and Harvey pushed their cart into the checkout lane, Harvey glanced around and noticed that there was a security guard stationed at the exit door of the supermarket and that he was glancing into shoppers' purses and bags as they left. Harvey quickly pointed this out to Barby, who then left the checkout line before they got to the cashier, and put all of the supermarket items that were in her purse back on a shelf.

However, all of Barby and Harvey's actions were observed by a supermarket staff member who was watching them with a security camera. As a result, they were both arrested as they left the store with the grocery items which they had bought, and both of them were subsequently charged with the crime of attempted retail theft of the items that had been in Barby's purse.

Barby's and Harvey's defense counsel has raised the defense of abandonment (a valid defense in this jurisdiction to attempt offenses), that they cannot be convicted of the crime of attempted retail theft because they abandoned commission of the offense. Will defense counsel be successful in making this defense on Barby and Harvey's behalf on these facts? Which of the following is most accurate:

(a) Barby and Harvey can be prosecuted successfully for attempted retail theft.

(b) Barby and Harvey cannot be prosecuted successfully for attempted retail theft because they returned the groceries in question voluntarily.

(c) Barby and Harvey cannot be prosecuted successfully for attempted retail theft because they never actually took the groceries in question out of the store.

(d) Answers (b) and (c) are true, and answer (a) is untrue.

IMPOSSIBILITY

Question 8–11: Bruce sold what he thought was cocaine to an undercover agent. In fact, it wasn't cocaine at all. It was quinine, a natural white crystalline alkaloid. It is perfectly lawful to possess or sell quinine.

Bruce was arrested and charged with the crime of attempted sale of cocaine. Bruce's defense counsel plans to argue that he cannot be convicted of this crime for the act of selling quinine because it is perfectly lawful to possess or sell quinine.

Is this a good defense? This jurisdiction follows the Model Penal Code approach to the defense of impossibility. Which of the following is most accurate:

(a) No, this is not a good defense because this is a case involving factual impossibility rather than legal impossibility.

(b) No, this is not a good defense because Bruce intended to sell cocaine, not quinine.

(c) Yes, this is a good defense because Bruce did not commit a crime since it is lawful to possess or sell quinine.

(d) Answers (a) and (b) are correct, but answer (c) is incorrect.

Question 8–12: Bryce sold what he knew to be quinine to an undercover agent, lying to the agent and telling her that it was really cocaine. Quinine is a natural white crystalline alkaloid. It is perfectly lawful to possess or sell quinine.

Bryce was arrested and charged with the crime of attempted sale of cocaine. Bryce's defense counsel plans to argue that he cannot be convicted of this crime for the act of selling quinine because it is perfectly lawful to possess or sell quinine.

Is this a good defense? This jurisdiction follows the Model Penal Code approach to the defense of impossibility. Which of the following is most accurate:

(a) No, this is not a good defense because this is a case involving factual impossibility rather than legal impossibility.

(b) No, this is not a good defense because Bryce pretended to sell cocaine, not quinine.

(c) Yes, this is a good defense because Bryce did not commit this crime since he did not actually intend to sell cocaine.

(d) Answers (a) and (b) are correct, but answer (c) is incorrect.

Question 8–13: Mary Lou's brother was on trial for the crime of sexual assault. Mary Lou was distraught. She believed that her brother had not committed the crime for which he was standing trial, but she was concerned that the trial was not going well and that the jury might convict him anyway. So, at a lunch break during her brother's trial one day, Mary Lou followed a group of jurors to the restaurant where they were having lunch. When one of the women went to the restroom by herself, Mary Lou followed after her and—with no one else around—and a faucet running to make it difficult for anyone to overhear what she was saying, she offered to pay this juror $10,000 if she would vote to acquit her brother during jury deliberations.

Unfortunately for Mary Lou, the woman to whom she offered the money was not a juror at all, but actually she was a court official who had accompanied the group of jurors to lunch. Mary Lou was subsequently arrested and charged with the crime of attempted jury tampering.

Mary Lou's defense counsel plans to argue that she cannot be convicted of attempted jury tampering because the woman she approached was not actually a juror at all. Is this a good defense? This jurisdiction follows the Model Penal Code approach to the defense of impossibility. Which of the following is most accurate:

(a) Yes, this is a good defense because it involves legal impossibility rather than factual impossibility.

(b) No, this is not a good defense because Mary Lou intended to bribe a juror even though the person to whom she offered money was not a juror.

(c) Yes, this is a good defense because Mary Lou did not commit this crime since she did not actually bribe a juror.

(d) Answers (a) and (c) are correct, but answer (b) is incorrect.

CHAPTER 9
CONSPIRACY

UNILATERAL-BILATERAL

Question 9–1: Hamilton approached Sonia and asked her if she would assist him in bringing a load of marijuana up from Fort Lauderdale. He told her that he would be driving down to Fort Lauderdale the next day in a rented truck and all that he needed for her to do was to split the driving each way with him. In exchange for her help, Hamilton told Sonia that he would give her two pounds of marijuana that she could either keep or sell.

Sonia told Hamilton that she agreed to help him drive down and back with the marijuana. But she was actually feigning agreement. She actually wanted no part of his plan. She told him that she agreed only because she was afraid of Hamilton, and afraid that if she did not appear to agree with his request, that he might hurt her or her family.

Sonia initially thought she would just run away before Hamilton picked her up to drive to Ft. Lauderdale. But she decided instead simply to alert the police to Hamilton's plan. After much discussion with police officers in the Narcotics Unit, she was asked if she would help them arrest Hamilton and send him to prison by going ahead and driving to Florida with him and picking up the marijuana. The plan was that Hamilton would be arrested the moment that they arrived back home with the marijuana.

And that is precisely what happened. Hamilton and Sonia drove to Fort Lauderdale in Hamilton's rental truck. Hamilton picked up the marijuana there, and they both loaded it into the back of the truck. They then both drove back home, and Hamilton was arrested by the police as soon as they arrived there with the marijuana.

Hamilton has now been charged with possession of marijuana with intent to distribute and with conspiracy to distribute marijuana. Based solely on his complicity with Sonia:

(a) In a bilateral conspiracy jurisdiction, Hamilton is guilty of the crime of conspiracy to distribute marijuana.

(b) In a unilateral conspiracy jurisdiction, Hamilton is guilty of the crime of conspiracy to distribute marijuana.

(c) Both of the above.

(d) None of the above.

Question 9–2: Jon and his twenty-one year old daughter, Elizabeth, had consensual sexual intercourse with one another on several occasions and this fact came to the attention of the local District Attorney. The DA then charged them both with conspiracy to commit the crime of incest. The crime of incest in this jurisdiction includes any form of sexual contact, whether or not it is consensual, between a parent and his or her child. Which of the following is true:

(a) Jon and Elizabeth are both guilty of the criminal offense of conspiracy to commit incest whether or not this is a unilateral or bilateral conspiracy jurisdiction.

(b) Neither Jon nor Elizabeth is guilty of the criminal offense of conspiracy to commit incest whether or not this is a unilateral or bilateral conspiracy jurisdiction.

(c) Jon is guilty of the criminal offense of conspiracy to commit incest whether or not this is a unilateral or bilateral conspiracy jurisdiction, but Elizabeth is not.

(d) In a unilateral conspiracy jurisdiction, Jon and Elizabeth are guilty of the criminal offense of conspiracy to commit incest, but in a bilateral conspiracy jurisdiction, neither are guilty.

AGREEMENT

Question 9–3: Moe, Larry, and Curly, nearing retirement age and without enough money or assets to retire comfortably, decided to engage in a robbery spree. They figured that they would pull off a number of robberies all at once and, if they were successful, they could all retire comfortably with no problem at all. And, if they were unsuccessful, at least they would have a place to live and food to eat in their old age—in prison.

Following up on their plan, in the course of only four and one-half hours, the three of them, Moe, Larry, and Curly, acting together, held up a laundromat, a neighborhood branch bank, a gas station, and three separate pedestrians. These six robberies netted the trio a grand total of $4,655.24, not nearly enough to meet their retirement plan goal.

But, there is some chance that their alternate retirement plan—room and board in prison—might work out for them. Moe, Larry, and Curly were quickly arrested and each of them was charged with six separate conspiracies: conspiracy to rob the laundromat; conspiracy to rob the bank; conspiracy to rob the gas station; and three separate conspiracies relating to each of the pedestrians who they held up. Which of the following is true:

(a) Moe, Larry, and Curly are not guilty of the six separate conspiracy offenses.

(b) Moe, Larry, and Curly are guilty of the six separate conspiracy offenses.

(c) Moe, Larry, and Curly are not guilty of a single overarching conspiracy to commit six criminal offenses.

(d) Moe, Larry, and Curly are guilty of a single overarching conspiracy to commit six criminal offenses.

(e) None of the above.

Question 9–4: Don and Ron robbed a bank. They both entered the bank together. Then, while Don stood in the bank doorway and brandished a firearm, making sure that no one entered or left the bank, and that no one inside the bank attempted to stop the robbery, Ron went to the teller windows and collected cash from the cash drawers.

On these facts alone, which of the following is true:

(a) Don and Ron are guilty of the crime of conspiracy to commit bank robbery in a jurisdiction that has a criminal conspiracy offense in its crime code.

(b) Don and Ron are guilty of the crime of conspiracy to commit bank robbery only in a jurisdiction that has a unilateral criminal conspiracy offense in its crime code.

(c) Don and Ron are not guilty of the crime of conspiracy to commit bank robbery in a jurisdiction that has a criminal conspiracy offense in its crime code.

(d) None of the above.

MENS REA

Question 9–5: Fred told Ginger, his roommate, not to hang around their apartment from 6:00 p.m. until midnight on the next evening because

Fred was expecting delivery of a large quantity of cocaine then and some of his friends were going to come over to help him cut and package it for distribution to others. By midnight, Fred told Ginger, the cocaine would have all been cut, packaged, and distributed and everyone would have left the apartment and she could return home.

Ginger was not happy about the fact that her roommate was involved in this cocaine distribution scheme. Nor was she happy, to say the least, about the fact that her apartment was going to be used as a venue for such criminal acts. Nonetheless, she stayed away from the apartment until well after midnight the next evening.

When she did return home, Ginger found yellow police tape blocking entry through the front door and scores of police officers swarming all over the place. "Hey, what's going on?," she asked one of the officers. "What are you doing in my apartment?" "Your apartment?," the officer responded. "Did you know that your roommate, Fred, was distributing cocaine?" "Sure, I knew," Ginger replied, "but I had nothing to do with it. That was his world. It had nothing to do with me. I stayed out of it. And I tried to get him to stop it. But he wouldn't listen to me."

Ginger was subsequently arrested and charged—along with Fred and three of Fred's accomplices in cutting and bagging the cocaine—with the crime of conspiracy to distribute narcotics. Which of the following is true:

(a) Ginger is guilty of the crime of conspiracy to distribute narcotics.

(b) Ginger is not guilty of the crime of conspiracy to distribute narcotics because she clearly did not commit a conspiratorial act.

(c) Ginger is guilty of the crime of conspiracy to distribute narcotics because she clearly did not possess a conspiratorial intent.

(d) Ginger is not guilty of the crime of conspiracy to distribute narcotics because she clearly did not commit a conspiratorial act nor did she possess a conspiratorial intent.

Question 9–6: Abdul was driving his convertible in a residential area where the speed limit was 25 miles per hour. Mariyah was sitting next to him, in the passenger seat. Abdul had the radio on extremely loud. It was blasting away, so loud that a number of pedestrians yelled at him to turn the volume down. Abdul ignored them. And when he did, Mariyah teased him, turning toward him, smiling, and yelling at him so that she could be heard over the blaring music: "Hey, baby, can you play that thing any louder?"

Abdul laughed, and responded by turning up the radio even louder. As loud as it would go. It was so loud in fact that neither Abdul or

Mariyah heard the siren of the ambulance as it rapidly approached their car from a cross street to their right, speeding toward a hospital. But, at the very last second, Abdul saw the ambulance coming right at him out of his peripheral vision, and he swerved his car onto the sidewalk to avoid being rammed by it on the front passenger side. The ambulance driver swerved to avoid Abdul's car at the very same moment. And—as luck would have it—the two vehicles missed each other by a matter of inches. The ambulance never stopped, and no one in either vehicle was seriously hurt by the mishap.

The ambulance driver, however, radioed the license plate number of Abdul's car to the police. Abdul and Mariyah were soon pulled over and arrested. They were subsequently charged with the crime of conspiracy to commit reckless driving. Which of the following is true:

(a) Abdul and Mariyah are both guilty of the crime of conspiracy to commit reckless driving.

(b) In a unilateral conspiracy jurisdiction, Abdul is guilty of the crime of conspiracy to commit reckless driving, but Mariyah is not.

(c) In a unilateral conspiracy jurisdiction, Mariyah is guilty of the crime of conspiracy to commit reckless driving, but Abdul is not.

(d) Neither Abdul nor Mariyah is guilty of the crime of conspiracy to commit reckless driving.

OVERT ACT

Question 9–7: Xavier, Yarone and Zeb decided that they would rob a local clothing store. They talked about committing a robbery somewhere for about forty minutes one morning while they were sitting together in their neighborhood coffee shop, just talking, gossiping, planning a robbery, and drinking coffee. The three friends finally decided that they would rob the clothing store down the block, some time during the next week or two.

But none of the three of them ever did a single thing after that discussion about actually carrying out the robbery plan, except that Zeb—unbeknownst to Xavier and Yarone—stood outside the clothing store in question the next afternoon after the three of them had had this discussion. Zeb just wanted to watch and see what time the store manager locked up and left for the evening.

On these facts only, which of the following is true:

(a) Xavier, Yarone and Zeb are all guilty of the crime of conspiracy to rob the clothing store.

(b) Xavier, Yarone and Zeb are all not guilty of the crime of conspiracy to rob the clothing store.

(c) Zeb is guilty of the crime of conspiracy to rob the clothing store in a unilateral conspiracy jurisdiction, but Xavier and Yarone are not guilty.

Question 9–8: Javier, Barone and Deb decided that they would rob a local clothing store. They talked about committing a robbery somewhere for about forty minutes one morning while they were sitting together in their neighborhood coffee shop, just talking, gossiping, planning a robbery, and drinking coffee. The three friends finally decided that they would rob the clothing store down the block, some time during the next week or two.

But none of the three of them ever did a single thing after that discussion about actually carrying out the robbery plan. Nothing at all.

On these facts only, which of the following is *not* true, i.e. which is false:

(a) In a jurisdiction requiring proof of an overt act in order to establish a conspiracy, Javier, Barone and Deb are all guilty of the crime of conspiracy to rob the clothing store.

(b) In a jurisdiction requiring proof of an overt act in order to establish a conspiracy, Javier, Barone and Deb are all not guilty of the crime of conspiracy to rob the clothing store.

(c) In a jurisdiction not requiring proof of an overt act in order to establish a conspiracy, Javier, Barone and Deb are all guilty of the crime of conspiracy to rob the clothing store.

RENUNCIATION & WITHDRAWAL

Question 9–9: Manny, Doug and Charlie were roommates and they lived next door to an elderly widow, Frances. Doug often did odd jobs for Frances and she paid him ten dollars an hour for his services. Frances had almost no cash on hand so she always paid Doug by writing him a check. Since Doug came inside Frances' house to be paid, he knew just where she kept her checkbook.

Doug suggested to his two roommates that they steal a few checks from Frances' checkbook, forge her signature on them, cash them, and make themselves a few hundred dollars. "Believe me, the old bat will never miss them," he told the others, "she has no idea which checks she's written and she doesn't keep a running balance of how much money is in her account. I know. I've seen her check register a dozen times."

Manny and Charlie agreed to help Doug accomplish this plan. Manny was to create a diversion in their front yard while Frances had her front door open. Doug was then going to dash inside and quickly tear out a few checks from her checkbook. And Charlie, who had the best and the most feminine-looking penmanship, was to forge Frances' signature on the stolen checks, using her signature on a check she had written to Doug but that he had not yet cashed as a model.

Charlie began practicing making Frances' signature. But before he finally mastered it, he decided that he couldn't go through with the plan after all. Charlie felt too guilty about robbing Frances. So he told Doug that he was pulling out of the plan, that he wouldn't help. But Doug threatened to hurt him if he backed out, so he told Doug that he would still go through with his part of the plan.

In fact, despite what he told Doug, Charlie had decided not to continue as a participant in this plan. He didn't want to take Frances' money. So he went to the local police station and he confessed everything to one of the detectives there.

As a result of Charlie's confession, Manny, Doug and Charlie have each been charged with conspiracy to commit theft and to pass bad checks. Which of the following is true:

(a) Manny, Doug and Charlie are all guilty of conspiracy to commit theft and to pass bad checks.

(b) Manny, Doug and Charlie are all not guilty of conspiracy to commit theft and to pass bad checks.

(c) Doug is guilty of conspiracy to commit theft and to pass bad checks, but Manny and Charlie are probably not guilty.

(d) Manny and Doug are guilty of conspiracy to commit theft and to pass bad checks, but Charlie is probably not guilty.

Question 9–10: Bouvier, Darren and Zeke decided that they would rob a local clothing store. They talked about committing a robbery somewhere for about forty minutes one morning while they were sitting together in their neighborhood coffee shop, just talking, gossiping, planning a robbery, and drinking coffee. The three friends finally decided that they would rob the clothing store down the block, some time during the next week or two.

But none of the three of them ever did a single thing after that discussion about actually carrying out the robbery plan. Nothing at all.

Ten years after this robbery planning took place, one of the three, Zeke, mentioned the plan to a friend of his, who—unfortunately—happened to be an undercover agent working for the police. This undercover agent quickly reported the robbery plan to his police supervisor. As a result of this information, Bouvier, Darren and Zeke were arrested and each of them was charged with the crime of engaging in a conspiracy to rob the clothing store. On these facts only, which of the following is true:

(a) In a jurisdiction requiring proof of an overt act in order to establish a conspiracy, Bouvier, Darren and Zeke are all probably guilty of the crime of conspiracy to rob the clothing store.

(b) In a jurisdiction requiring proof of an overt act in order to establish a conspiracy, Bouvier, Darren and Zeke are all probably not guilty of the crime of conspiracy to rob the clothing store.

(c) In a jurisdiction not requiring proof of an overt act in order to establish a conspiracy, Bouvier, Darren and Zeke are all probably guilty of the crime of conspiracy to rob the clothing store.

UNKNOWN CO-CONSPIRATORS

Question 9–11: Nora supplied crack cocaine to Marcus who—Nora knew—supplied it to someone else to actually sell to customers. But Nora had no idea who it was exactly that Marcus gave the crack to for ultimate sale. In fact, it was Eddie. Eddie, in turn, had no idea from whom Marcus got the crack cocaine that he gave to him.

Eddie was arrested by the police for the sale of narcotics. During interrogation following his arrest, Eddie revealed that Marcus was his supplier. Marcus was then arrested and he subsequently revealed to the police that Nora was his supplier.

Nora, Marcus, and Eddie have each been charged with a single conspiracy: conspiracy to distribute narcotics. Nora's defense counsel, Leah, has moved to dismiss this charge against Nora, arguing that Nora can be charged with a conspiracy with Marcus and Marcus can be charged with a conspiracy with Eddie, but that Nora and Eddie cannot be charged as co-conspirators in the same conspiracy because Nora and Eddie don't—and never did—know one another. Which of the following is most accurate:

(a) Nora needed to know who her alleged co-conspirator, Eddie, was in order for a conspiracy to exist with him.

(b) On these facts, Nora, Marcus, and Eddie may not properly be charged with a single count of conspiracy to distribute narcotics.

(c) Both of the above.

(d) None of the above.

CHAPTER 10
SOLICITATION

Question 10–1: Lucas and Charlie were sitting together at their neighborhood bar on a Friday night after a tough work week, just drinking and talking and watching sports on the barroom television set. After a few beers, Lucas began to complain about his wife and how much she nagged him and disapproved of all of his friends.

"Man, sometimes I just wish she were dead," Lucas said to Charlie, "you know what I mean?" Charlie responded: "Hey, you want me to knock her off for you? I'd do it for a case of beer. Really. Nope. You know what, buddy? For you, Lucas, my friend, I'd do it for a cold six-pack!" Lucas replied: "It's a deal, brother!" And both Lucas and Charlie laughed uproariously, and kept right on drinking.

Is Lucas guilty of the crime of soliciting Charlie to murder Lucas' wife? Which of the following is most accurate:

(a) No, Lucas is not guilty of the crime of soliciting Charlie to murder his wife because there is not enough evidence that he wasn't joking.

(b) No, Lucas is not guilty of the crime of soliciting Charlie to murder his wife because there is not enough evidence that he was serious about this solicitation.

(c) Yes, Lucas is guilty of the crime of soliciting Charlie to murder his wife.

(d) Answers (a) and (b) are correct, and answer (c) is incorrect.

Question 10–2: Lolita approached Clyde, an out-of-town visitor, who was out taking a walk in a downtown urban area one evening. Lolita asked Clyde whether he "was looking for a date?" When Clyde naively responded by asking her what she meant by that, Lolita then graphically described to him a menu of more than a dozen various sex acts that she would be willing to perform on or with or in front of him in exchange for differing amounts of money. This list included supposed forms of sexual activity that Clyde did not even realize were physically possible.

Clyde was stunned. He was not able to say anything in response to Lolita's catalogue of proffered services. Lolita filled in the silence by adding, "Come on, baby. What I'm offering you is more than worth the money." Instead of responding, Clyde just turned around and walked away.

This conversation was overhead by an undercover police officer who was standing nearby. Lolita was immediately arrested and she was subsequently charged with the offense of solicitation to commit prostitution. Lolita's defense counsel, Vladimir, has argued that Lolita did not commit this particular crime because no sexual activity ever took place between Lolita and Clyde.

Is Vladimir correct? Did Lolita in fact commit the crime of solicitation to commit prostitution? Which of the following is most accurate:

(a) No, Lolita is not guilty of the crime of soliciting Clyde to participate in an act of prostitution because no sexual activity ever took place between Lolita and Clyde.

(b) No, Lolita is not guilty of the crime of soliciting Clyde to participate in an act of prostitution because there is not enough evidence that she was serious about this solicitation.

(c) Yes, Lolita is guilty of the crime of soliciting Clyde to participate in an act of prostitution.

(d) Answers (a) and (b) are correct, and answer (c) is incorrect.

The following facts apply to Questions 10–3 and 10–4 below:

Gordon was standing trial in state court for sale of marijuana to an undercover informant. Gilda, Gordon's wife, decided to make sure that Gordon was not convicted of this offense by bribing one of the jurors to vote to acquit Gordon during jury deliberations.

As part of this plan, Gilda followed one of the jurors to a local restaurant during the lunch break. When the juror left the table and went into the restroom, Gilda followed her and whispered into a locked toilet stall: "Psssst. Hey, I know you're in there and I know you're one of the jurors in the marijuana case going on down at the courthouse. If you're willing to vote to acquit the guy on trial, Gordon, who's a good guy, I know someone who can get you $10,000 in cash." The woman inside the stall responded, "Okay. You're on. It's a deal. I'll take the ten grand, but only if you give me $100 right now" Gilda agreed.

The toilet then flushed, and the occupant of the stall, Hermione, emerged. Gilda realized immediately that Hermione wasn't the juror she had followed into the restroom. In fact, Hermione wasn't a juror at all. The real juror in Gordon's trial soon emerged from a different toilet stall, washed her hands, glared at Gilda, and left the restroom.

Hermione turned to Gilda and said "So where's my money? Where's my hundred bucks?" Gilda responded, "Go f* * * yourself. You're no juror." Gilda then left the restroom, trying (unsuccessfully) to catch up to the real juror who had just left.

Question 10–3: On the basis of these facts and without considering any possibility of a renunciation defense (*see* Question 10–4), is Gilda guilty of the crime of solicitation of Hermione to commit a crime? Which of the following is most accurate:

(a) No, Gilda is not guilty of soliciting criminal activity because Hermione was not really a juror and could not be bribed to do anything wrong.

(b) No, Gilda is not guilty of soliciting criminal activity because there is not enough evidence that she was serious about this solicitation.

(c) Yes, Gilda is guilty of the crime of soliciting criminal activity despite the fact that Hermione was not really a juror.

(d) None of the above.

Question 10–4: If this jurisdiction permits such a defense, does Gilda possess a tenable renunciation defense to the charge that she solicited Hermione to commit a criminal offense? Which of the following is most accurate:

(a) Gilda can be prosecuted successfully for soliciting Hermione to commit a criminal offense.

(b) No, Gilda cannot be prosecuted successfully for soliciting Hermione to commit a criminal offense because she completely abandoned her plan to bribe a juror.

(c) Gilda cannot be prosecuted successfully for soliciting Hermione to commit a criminal offense because they she voluntarily abandoned her plan to bribe a juror.

(d) Answers (b) and (c) are true, and answer (a) is untrue.

CHAPTER 11
ASSAULT

Question 11–1: Ellen and Chloe were roommates, living together in a small, two-bedroom apartment. Ellen has an "odd" sense of humor, and she decided to play a practical joke on Chloe by running into Chloe's bedroom in the middle of the night, screaming at the top of her lungs, and pointing a gun at her. The gun that Ellen decided to use for this purpose was a real pistol, but Ellen made sure that it was unloaded. And it was.

Ellen went through with the joke just as she had planned. Chloe was in a deep sleep when Ellen turned on the overhead light, burst in to Chloe's bedroom, screaming and brandishing the pistol in the air. As a direct result of these actions on Ellen's part, she scared Chloe so thoroughly that Chloe immediately dressed and left the apartment and refused to come back—or even to talk to Ellen—ever again. However, other than being severely frightened by Ellen's "joke," Chloe was not harmed physically or mentally in any other way as a result of this bizarre episode.

Ellen has been charged with criminal assault on Chloe as a result of her actions as described above. Her defense counsel argues that this was just a joke and that no one was harmed and that, accordingly, Ellen did not commit a criminal act. Is defense counsel correct in this contention? Which of the following is most accurate:

(a) Ellen criminally assaulted Chloe.

(b) Ellen did not criminally assault Chloe because Ellen's actions were not intended to actually harm Chloe.

(c) Ellen did not criminally assault Chloe because Ellen's actions did not actually harm Chloe.

(d) Answers (b) and (c) are correct, and answer (a) is incorrect.

Question 11–2: Henry was visiting his grandmother, Henrietta, at the assisted-living facility where she lived. Having forgotten to bring in the box of candy that he had brought Henrietta as a gift, Henry dashed out to his car which was parked in the parking lot, retrieved the candy, and carried it back into the facility.

In his delight at being able to give Henrietta such a terrific gift that he knew she would like (Henrietta loved chocolates), Henry exuberantly burst into the room, yelling "Ta-da! Look what I brought you, Nana! Chocolates! Your favorite!," holding the box of candy out in front of him.

Unfortunately, Henry had burst into the wrong room, the room next door to his grandmother, surprising and frightening Marielle, the resident who lived there. Marielle was 91 years old and often very confused. She had no relatives or anyone else who visited her, and she was a diabetic who did not and could not eat chocolate. Marielle had absolutely no idea what was going on when Henry burst in to her room, yelling about chocolates, and she immediately started screaming with fear, causing attendants in the facility to dash into her room to calm her down. Henry apologized repeatedly and then quickly left to go next door.

Marielle insisted on filing a criminal complaint against Henry ("that scary young man") for assault. On these facts, is Henry actually guilty of the crime of assault? Which of the following is most accurate:

(a) Henry criminally assaulted Marielle.

(b) Henry did not criminally assault Marielle because his actions were not intended to place Marielle in fear of an imminent battery.

(c) Henry did not criminally assault Marielle because any fear that Marielle may have had arising out of Henry's actions was unreasonable.

(d) Answers (b) and (c) are correct, and answer (a) is incorrect.

Question 11–3: Dennis ran up to Brenda, who was sitting by herself on a park bench, and—pulling a gun out of his pocket—demanded that she give him her purse, her necklace, and her watch. Brenda, was—unsurprisingly—absolutely terrified. She immediately took off her necklace and her watch, and she handed both of them to Dennis, along with her purse.

Dennis then ran away with all three of these items, but he was soon apprehended by the police. Dennis has now been charged in state court with two criminal offenses: one count of armed robbery and one count of battery. All of these events took place in a jurisdiction which continues to use the common law definition of battery in its Crimes Code. Which of the following is most accurate:

(a) Dennis is not guilty of battery because he did not touch Brenda.

(b) Dennis is guilty of battery.

(c) Dennis is not guilty of battery because he did not injure Brenda.

(d) Answers (a) and (c) are correct, and answer (b) is incorrect.

Question 11–4: Sierra, a law student, was extremely upset by the C+ grade that she received from her Criminal Law professor, John, on her Criminal Law final examination. After meeting with John and reviewing all of her answers and listening to his detailed (and very unflattering) analysis of all of the alleged deficiencies in her answers, Sierra's upset turned to pure anger.

"You know what? This is the most unfair grade I have ever received in my whole academic career," Sierra thundered at John, "I don't know why in the world they keep you on this faculty!" "And," Sierra hissed back at John, as she stomped out of his office, slamming the door behind her, "you better watch your back, mister! Some day, some day when you least expect it, some day, I'll be a lawyer and then I'll get my revenge! You'll see!"

John, shaken, immediately telephoned his former student, Abbie, who had recently been elected the local District Attorney. "Hey, you won't believe what just happened. I was just threatened by one of my own students," he told Abbie, and then he recounted exactly what had transpired in his office. "You've got to do something about this. Charge her with assault."

Abbie did exactly that. She charged Sierra with the crime of assault on John. Is Sierra likely to be convicted of assault on the basis of these facts? Which of the following is most accurate:

(a) Sierra criminally assaulted John.

(b) Sierra did not criminally assault John because her actions were not intended to place Marielle in fear of an imminent battery.

(c) John's fear of an imminent battery arising out of Sierra's actions was reasonable.

(d) Answers (b) and (c) are correct, and answer (a) is incorrect.

CHAPTER 12
SEX CRIMES

USE OF FORCE OR ABSENCE OF CONSENT

Question 12–1: Calvin was Crystal's boss. Crystal became very uncomfortable when—for a two-week period—Calvin constantly flirted with her and made suggestive comments to her about her body and her clothing. But despite her discomfort, Crystal never said anything to Calvin about his actions. Crystal had absolutely no sexual or romantic interest in Calvin, and she simply tried to ignore him when he did this. She hoped that he would lose interest in her after some time had passed and she had not responded positively to his unwanted attentions.

Calvin did not stop, however. One day, in fact, Calvin approached Crystal in the hallway, and said to her: "Look, you've been playing hard to get for too long now. We need to move our relationship to another stage. And there is a really good reason for you to give me what you know that I want. And what you want, too. If you sleep with me tonight, I'll make sure that you receive a $500 a month raise. Sex with me *and* six grand a year. You can't beat that! What do you say?"

Crystal ultimately agreed to come over to Calvin's apartment that evening and have sex with him, and that is exactly what she did. The next morning, Crystal felt horrible and ashamed and upset about what she had done, and after thinking and worrying about it for a couple of days, she eventually reported everything that had occurred to the local police department.

Calvin was subsequently charged with the rape of Crystal on the basis of these facts. Is he likely to be convicted of this criminal offense? Which of the following is most accurate:

(a) Calvin is likely not to be found guilty of raping Crystal because Crystal only had sex with him because she knew that her failure to do so would lead to negative employment consequences.

(b) Calvin is likely not to be found guilty of raping Crystal because he did not force her to have sex with him and Crystal consented to the intercourse.

(c) Calvin is likely to be found guilty of raping Crystal.

(d) Answers (a) and (b) are correct, and answer (c) is incorrect.

Question 12–2: At the end of a long evening, Lloyd asked his date, Mandy, to come up to his apartment and have sexual relations with him. Mandy said "No." After Lloyd repeated his request three more times, she continued to say "No" in response to Lloyd's request every time he asked.

Finally, Lloyd asked her to have sex with him again, and Mandy did not say "no." Instead, she said simply: "Please take me home. I'm tired and I want to go home." But, instead of taking Mandy home, Lloyd drove her to his apartment, ripped her clothes off, threw her on his bed, and had sexual intercourse with her. Mandy did not resist him. She was passive throughout the episode, and quickly dressed and left his apartment as soon as he rolled off of her.

The next day, Mandy reported Lloyd to the police, and he was subsequently charged with rape. Lloyd's defense counsel has argued that Lloyd did not rape Mandy because she did not say "No" the final time that Lloyd asked her to have sex with him, and he thought that her silence indicated her acquiescence. Defense counsel also argues that the fact that Mandy did not resist Lloyd physically as the sex act was taking place led Lloyd to believe that she was agreeing to have sexual intercourse with him.

Is Lloyd likely to be convicted of the rape of Mandy? Which of the following is true:

(a) Lloyd is likely not to be found guilty of raping Mandy because Mandy did not resist him when they had intercourse.

(b) Lloyd is likely not to be found guilty of raping Mandy because he did not force her to have sex with him.

(c) Lloyd is likely to be found guilty of raping Mandy.

(d) Lloyd is likely not to be found guilty of raping Mandy because Mandy consented to the intercourse.

Question 12–3: Conan and Margie were kissing and hugging on the couch in the living room of Margie's apartment. Eventually, Conan started removing Margie's clothing, and Margie helped him with this, as well as helping him remove his own clothing. Conan asked Margie: "Are you sure this is okay?" Margie responded: "I'm sure. I want you as much as you want me."

Hearing that, Conan got up from the couch and put on a condom. But, just as he returned to the couch but before he actually had sexual intercourse with Margie, Margie sat up and cried out: "No. No. Stop it, Conan. You've got to stop. I'm so sorry. I can't do this now. I thought I could, but I can't. Not now." Conan moaned and replied: "I can't stop now, baby. It's too late. I know you want me."

Margie tried to get up from the couch and put her clothes back on, but Conan grabbed her by both arms, threw her back on the couch, and immediately had sexual intercourse with her as she cried, but didn't resist him. After he had finished, Conan said: "I'm really sorry, Margie. I really am. I just couldn't stop after we'd gone that far. It was too late, honey."

Did Conan commit the crime of rape with Margie? Which of the following is most true:

(a) Conan is likely not to be found guilty of raping Margie because Margie consented to the intercourse.

(b) Conan is likely not to be found guilty of raping Margie because Margie did not resist him when they had intercourse.

(c) Conan is likely not to be found guilty of raping Margie because he did not force her to have sex with him.

(d) Conan is likely to be found guilty of raping Margie.

Question 12–4: Rodney and Desiree drove to another city, three hours away, to spend a long holiday weekend together. They arrived at a mutual friend's—Darell's—one-bedroom apartment where they planned to stay. They had each brought a sleeping bag with them and they unrolled and slept in them on Darell's living room floor.

In the middle of the night, Rodney took off his pajamas and stealthily climbed out of his sleeping bag and into Desiree's, while she was still sleeping. He pulled up her nightgown, and began to have sexual intercourse with her. Desiree woke up as Rodney penetrated her. She writhed and squirmed underneath him while screaming at him to stop. When he didn't stop immediately, she started scratching his face with her fingernails and pulling his hair. In response, Rodney quickly rolled off of her and yelled at her: "Hey, why the f* * * did you do that, Desiree? You knew we were going to f* * *. You came with me on this road trip. What did you expect?" Desiree jumped up and ran into Darell's bedroom, locked the door, and called the police.

Rodney was subsequently arrested and charged with rape. Rodney's defense counsel has argued that Rodney is not guilty of raping Desiree because he honestly believed that Desiree had consented to have sex with him when she agreed to accompany him on their road trip together.

All of these events took place in a jurisdiction where the crime of rape is defined as follows: "A person commits rape when the actor has sexual intercourse with another person without the victim's consent." On these facts, is Rodney likely to be convicted of the rape of Desiree? Which of the following is most accurate:

(a) Rodney is likely not to be found guilty of rape because Desiree implicitly consented to have intercourse with him when she accompanied him on a trip where she knew they would be spending the night together in the same apartment.

(b) Rodney is likely not to be found guilty of raping Desiree because Desiree did not resist him until after he had already penetrated her.

(c) Rodney is likely to be found guilty of raping Desiree.

(d) Answers (a) and (b) are true, and answer (c) is false.

SPOUSAL RAPE

The following facts apply to Questions 12–5 through 12–7 below:

Arnold's wife, Helen, refused to have sex with him. "You're my wife, dammit! I have the right to have sex with you whenever I want it!," Arnold thundered at her. "Go f* * * yourself," Helen replied. Hearing that, Arnold grabbed Helen, threw her on the bed, and had sexual intercourse with her forcibly.

Question 12–5: Helen immediately called the police after Arnold let her up from the bed. Arnold was arrested, and has now been charged with rape. His defense counsel argues that a husband cannot be convicted of raping his wife. Is his defense counsel correct? Can Arnold be convicted of rape on these facts? In this jurisdiction, the common law rules relating to spousal rape still apply. Which of the following is most accurate:

(a) Arnold is not guilty of rape because Helen is his wife.

(b) Arnold is guilty of raping Helen because she did not consent to have intercourse with him.

(c) Arnold is guilty of raping Helen because he forced her to have intercourse with him.

(d) Answers (b) and (c) are true, and answer (a) is false.

Question 12–6: Helen immediately called the police after Arnold let her up from the bed. Arnold was arrested, and has now been charged with rape.

His defense counsel argues that a husband cannot be convicted of raping his wife. Is his defense counsel correct? Can Arnold be convicted of rape on these facts? In this jurisdiction, the common law rules relating to spousal rape have been repealed or otherwise rejected entirely. Which of the following is most accurate:

(a) Arnold is not guilty of rape because Helen is his wife.

(b) Arnold is guilty of raping Helen.

(c) Arnold is not guilty of rape because rape of a spouse can only be punished as aggravated assault, not as a sex crime.

(d) Answers (a) and (c) are true, and answer (b) is false.

Question 12–7: Helen immediately called the police after Arnold let her up from the bed. Arnold was arrested, and has now been charged with the crime of spousal rape. In this jurisdiction, spousal rape is a separate crime from rape, the latter only applying to non-spousal victims. The spousal rape statute enacted in this jurisdiction, borrowing from the common law, requires, *inter alia*, that in order to establish the crime of spousal rape, the spousal victim must have made a "fresh complaint." Other than that difference (and a difference in severity of sentence), the spousal rape statute is the same as the rape statute. Which of the following is most accurate:

(a) Arnold is not guilty of spousal rape because Helen is his wife.

(b) Arnold is not guilty of spousal rape because Helen did not make a "fresh complaint."

(c) Arnold is guilty of the offense of spousal rape.

(d) Arnold is not guilty of rape.

(e) Answers (c) and (d) are correct, but answers (a) and (b) are incorrect.

STATUTORY RAPE

Question 12–8: Mike, who is 22 years old, had sexual intercourse with Alicia, who was only 15 years old at the time. Alicia was more than willing to engage in sexual intercourse with Mike. In fact, it was her idea.

At first, Mike was reluctant to have sex with her, arguing that she was too young and that they should wait until she was at least one year older. But Alicia persisted. Ultimately, she simply took off all of her clothes in front of him and threw herself at him. One thing then led to another, and they had intercourse. Four times.

Alicia's mother, Joyce, discovered that Mike and Alicia had had intercourse when she overheard Alicia talking about her experience on the telephone with one of her friends. Joyce then called the police and told them what had taken place.

After the police interviewed Alicia, who told them that she loved Mike and admitted that she had willingly had sex with him, Mike was arrested. He was subsequently charged with statutory rape.

What is the likelihood that Mike will be convicted of this offense? The "age of consent" in this jurisdiction is 16. Which of the following is most accurate:

(a) Mike is not likely to be found guilty of statutory rape because Alicia consented to have sexual intercourse with him.

(b) Mike is not likely to be found guilty of statutory rape because it was not his idea to have sex with Alicia, in fact he urged her to wait until she was older.

(c) Mike is likely to be found guilty of statutory rape.

(d) Answers (a) and (b) are correct, but answer (c) is incorrect.

Question 12–9: Spike, who is 22 years old, had anal sex with Edward, who was only 15 years old at the time of their encounter.

Although Spike and Edward had just met that same evening at an outdoor concert, Edward was more than willing to have sex with Spike. In fact, it was his idea. At first, Spike was reluctant to have sex with Edward, thinking that he looked like he was too young.

But after he said that to him, Edward showed Spike his driver's license which stated that Edward was 16. Spike knew—correctly—that the age of consent in that jurisdiction was 16 years of age. So when Edward took off all of his clothes in front of him and then threw himself at him, one thing quickly led to another, and the two of them engaged in sexual activity. Four times.

As it turned out, however, the driver's license Edward showed Spike was fake. As noted previously, he was only 15 years old, one year under the age of consent, 16. Edward's mother, Joy, discovered that Spike and Edward had had intercourse when she overheard Edward talking about his experience on the telephone with one of his friends. Joy then called the police and told them what had taken place.

When the police interviewed Edward, he freely admitted that he had willingly had sex with Spike, and he was arrested. Spike was subsequently charged with the crime of statutory rape.

"Sexual intercourse" is defined in this jurisdiction as "vaginal penetration as well as cunnilingus, fellatio or anal intercourse between persons." What is the likelihood that Spike will be convicted of this offense? Which of the following is most accurate:

(a) Spike is not likely to be found guilty of statutory rape because Edward consented to have sexual intercourse with him.

(b) Spike is not likely to be found guilty of statutory rape because he honestly and reasonably believed that Edward was 16 years old.

(c) Spike is likely to be found guilty of statutory rape.

(d) None of the above.

CHAPTER 13
HOMICIDE

FIRST DEGREE MURDER

Question 13–1: Sid was an electrician, one of many workers who were working for a general contractor on a very big construction project, the construction of a large civic auditorium. One day, when Sid was installing a very large and heavy light fixture in the central hallway of the building under construction, he did a very sloppy and slipshod job of securing the fixture to the ceiling.

A co-worker, Amir, who was helping him attach the fixture, both of them high above the floor on a scaffold, told him: "Hey, Sid, that light's gonna fall. You got to at least support it better somehow before we secure it or somebody's gonna get conked pretty good when it lets go." "Nah," Sid replied, "don't worry about it. I know it's loose. I know. I know. But it's good enough for tonight. I got to get home. I got something to do. I don't have the time to work on this any more today. We'll get it fixed up right tomorrow morning." Soon thereafter, Sid and Amir left the work site without taking any additional steps to secure or support the light fixture.

The next morning, as Sid and Amir were climbing the scaffolding to get back to the ceiling to resume work on the fixture, the fixture fell from the ceiling, crashing into and through the scaffolding, striking Amir forcefully on its way to the floor. Amir was critically injured, and he subsequently died from the injuries he received as a result of being struck directly by the fixture and his subsequent fall to the floor.

Sid has been charged with first degree murder in the death of Amir. Which of the following is true:

(a) Sid is guilty of first degree murder in the death of Amir because he knew the fixture could fall.

(b) Sid is guilty of first degree murder in the death of Amir because he was reckless in not repairing the fixture before he left for the evening.

(c) Sid is guilty of first degree murder in the death of Amir because he was criminally negligent in not repairing the fixture before he left for the evening.

(d) None of the above.

Question 13–2: Marcos and Lacey, husband and wife, were sitting at their kitchen table late one evening, arguing angrily with one another about their family finances. Lacey had recently lost her job and she was still looking for a new one. As a result, she wanted to economize dramatically in all family spending, at least until she was back at work again and bringing home a regular paycheck.

Marcos, on the other hand, thought that Lacey would get another job soon and he argued that, until she did, their family's continuing quality of life was more important than keeping their savings account intact. More specifically, Marcos wanted to dip into their savings to pay for a trip for them to take their two kids to Disney World for a few days. Lacey thought that it was absolutely ridiculous to take a vacation like that when it would so heavily deplete their savings at a time when she was unemployed.

Their argument raged on and on. Each of them got really carried away arguing with one another. And each of them got progressively angrier and angrier. As their arguments got more heated, they each began screaming at one another as well.

Eventually, still screaming, Marcos bolted upright and walked over to the kitchen counter, picked up the toaster oven, and heaved it in Lacey's direction. It missing her by two feet, sailing over head, and smashing against the back wall. Lacey then jumped up and picked up a dinner plate that had been sitting on the counter and threw it at Marcos, missing him by a good foot and smashing it against the wall. After another five minutes of exchanging heated epithets back and forth, Lacey simply stomped out the kitchen door and went into the back yard, fuming about what was happening and muttering loudly about Marcos.

After another five minutes had passed, Lacey stomped back into the kitchen, slamming the kitchen door behind her. She began yelling once again at Marcos, who was still sitting at the kitchen table at that point, his head in his hands. Lacey headed toward the knife rack on the kitchen wall. "Look," Marcos began to say to Lacey, head still in hands, not looking up, "I'm sorry I overacted just a little bit there. I shouldn't have thrown anything at you, I know, but you're being so irrational that ..." Before Marcos could finish this sentence, however, Lacey screamed at him, "I'm irrational? I'm irrational? You son of a bitch! Is this irrational?" And saying that, she quickly grabbed a long, serrated kitchen knife from the rack and lunged right at him, stabbing him in his back three times.

The family did not go to Disney World. Marcos subsequently died as a result of these stab wounds.

Lacey has now been charged with first degree murder in the killing of Marcos. Which of the following is the most accurate statement:

(a) On these facts, Lacey cannot be found guilty of first degree murder in the death of Marcos because she clearly did not act maliciously.

(b) On these facts, Lacey cannot be found guilty of first degree murder in the death of Marcos because she clearly did not act with premeditation and deliberation.

(c) On these facts, Lacey cannot be found guilty of first degree murder in the death of Marcos because this was clearly an impulsive killing.

(d) All of the above.

(e) On these facts, Lacey could be found guilty of first degree murder in the death of Marcos.

Question 13–3: Amos decided to celebrate his twenty-first birthday by shooting his rifle into the air twenty-one times. Of course, what goes up, must come down. One of the bullets that he shot into the air in this celebratory fashion fell to earth and hit four year-old Tommy in the top of his head, killing him instantly. Tommy was more than a quarter mile away from where Amos shot his rifle into the air and was not visible to Amos as he shot.

Amos has been charged with first degree murder in the shooting death of Tommy. Which of the following is the most accurate statement:

(a) On these facts, Amos cannot be found guilty of first degree murder in the death of Tommy because he clearly did not act maliciously.

(b) On these facts, Amos cannot be found guilty of first degree murder in the death of Tommy because he clearly did not act with premeditation and deliberation.

(c) Both of the above.

(d) On these facts, Amos could be found guilty of first degree murder in the death of Tommy.

Question 13–4: Chris and Alexander robbed a downtown bank. Chris took money from the bank tellers' desks while Alexander, visibly armed with an automatic pistol, ordered all of the people in the bank to get down on the floor and put their hands on top of their heads.

As Chris and Alexander were leaving the bank, Chris carried a bag full of money and Alexander kept his weapon trained on the people who were still huddled on the floor, yelling at them to "keep down." But one of the people on the floor, Anthony, the bank security guard, started to rise up just as Chris and Alexander were almost out of the door of the bank. Alexander saw Anthony rise out of the corner of his eye, wheeled around, and immediately shot him. The bullet killed Anthony instantly. Which of the following is the most accurate statement:

(a) On these facts, Alexander cannot be found guilty of first degree murder in the death of Anthony because he clearly did not act maliciously.

(b) On these facts, Alexander cannot be found guilty of first degree murder in the death of Anthony because he clearly did not act with premeditation and deliberation.

(c) Both of the above.

(d) On these facts, Alexander could be found guilty of first degree murder in the death of Anthony.

SECOND DEGREE MURDER

Question 13–5: Glenna cajoled and bullied Lidia into "playing" a "game" of "Russian roulette" with her. Russian roulette is an activity where only one bullet is put into the chamber of a gun, the chamber is spun, and each "player" aims the gun at his or head and pulls the trigger.

In Russian roulette, the person pulling the trigger has a chance of shooting a bullet into his or head equal to one in however many bullets the firing chamber would ordinarily hold. In this particular case, however, Glenna didn't tell Lidia that she had actually taken—she thought—all of the bullets out of the gun's firing chamber. Glenna told Lidia instead that the gun was loaded with one—but only one—bullet. Glenna intended to mislead Lidia because she wanted to see how courageous (stupid?) Lidia was. But she thought that the gun was unloaded because she did not want to really take any risk that she or Lidia would actually shoot themselves.

Unfortunately, although she thought that she had unloaded the gun entirely, Glenna in fact had failed to take all of the bullets out of the firing chamber. One bullet remained in the firing chamber, just as Glenna had told Lidia, but not what she actually believed was the case.

Lidia went first, aimed the gun at her head, and pulled the trigger. The one bullet in the firing chamber fired into her head. She died instantaneously.

Glenna has been charged with them murder of Lidia on the basis of this episode. Her defense counsel has argued that Glenna is not guilty of murder because she honestly thought that the gun was unloaded and, as a result, she did not believe that there was any risk that Lidia would be hurt or killed. Which of the following is true:

(a) Glenna is likely to be convicted of murder on these facts.

(b) Glenna is not likely to be convicted of murder because she honestly thought that the gun was unloaded.

(c) Glenna is not likely to be convicted of murder because Lidia assumed the risk that she might die playing Russian Roulette.

(d) None of the above.

Question 13–6: Bernie was driving his BMW convertible down a suburban, residential street where the speed limit was 25 miles per hour. Bernie was driving at 40 miles per hour—fifteen miles per hour over the speed limit—but he did not see anyone in, around, or near the street and the weather was good, so he saw no need or reason to slow down.

Unfortunately, 7 year-old, Joshua, playing a game of hide-and-seek with some friends and not looking where he was going, dashed right out into the street in front of Bernie's car. Bernie didn't see Joshua until he was right in front of the car since he emerged from behind some dense foliage that grew right up to the edge of the roadway.

Bernie braked as soon as he saw Joshua, but it was already too late. He ran right over him. Joshua subsequently died of the internal injuries he suffered as a result of being struck and run over by Bernie's car.

Bernie has been charged with the murder of Joshua. Which of the following is true:

(a) Bernie is likely to be convicted of murder on these facts.

(b) Bernie is not likely to be convicted of murder because Joshua assumed the risk that he might die or be seriously injured when he emerged from the foliage at the edge of the roadway.

(c) Bernie is not likely to be convicted of murder because he did not act maliciously.

(d) None of the above.

Question 13–7: Cy was an electrician, one of many workers who were working for a general contractor on a very big construction project, the construction of a large civic auditorium. One day, when Cy was installing a very large and heavy light fixture in the central hallway of the building under construction, he did a very sloppy and slipshod job of securing the fixture to the ceiling.

A co-worker, Amos, who was helping him attach the fixture, both of them high above the floor on a scaffold, told him: "Hey, Cy, that light's gonna fall. You got to at least support it better somehow before we secure it or somebody's gonna get conked pretty good when it lets go." "Nah," Cy replied, "don't worry about it. I know it's loose. I know. I know. But it's good enough for tonight. I got to get home. I got something to do. I don't have the time to work on this any more today. We'll get it fixed up right tomorrow morning." Soon thereafter, Cy and Amos left the work site without taking any additional steps to secure or support the light fixture.

The next morning, as Cy and Amos were climbing the scaffolding to get back to the ceiling to resume work on the fixture, the fixture fell from the ceiling, crashing into and through the scaffolding, striking Amos forcefully on its way to the floor. Amos was critically injured, and he subsequently died from the injuries he received as a result of being struck directly by the fixture and his subsequent fall to the floor.

Cy has been charged with second degree murder in the death of Amos. Which of the following is most accurate:

(a) Cy can be convicted of murder on these facts.

(b) Cy cannot be convicted of murder on these facts because he was not reckless.

(c) Cy cannot be convicted of murder on these facts because he did not act maliciously.

(d) Both (b) and (c) above.

Question 13–8: Althea was very depressed. And for good reason. Her husband had recently left her for another woman, Althea's best friend. Both of her children were narcotics addicts. Half of her friends on Facebook had recently de-friended her. And her dog had fleas and they had spread throughout her studio apartment. Althea just plain couldn't take any more. She decided to end it all.

Althea took the elevator to the top—fourth—floor of her favorite, downtown department store. She then snuck into a restricted, employees-only area and found and managed to pry open the door to the roof. Once there, Althea walked to the edge of the roof, climbed up and stood on the precipice, and looked down at all the people hurrying along on the sidewalk below. She debated whether or not to actually jump. Finally, she decided she'd had enough. She jumped.

Althea did not die from her fall, however. Her descent was slowed, first, by striking the ledge one floor underneath where she stood, then by hitting the large awning above the ground-floor, department-store windows, and finally, by striking a pedestrian, Paige, who had just left the department store and was standing on the sidewalk below.

Althea did suffer a concussion, serious internal injuries, a broken hip, a broken arm and wrist and numerous lacerations. But, tragically, Paige was struck on the head by Althea's falling body. Althea's weight and momentum smashed Paige to the sidewalk and she suffered numerous severe injuries, including a fractured skull, which ultimately led to her death.

After recovering from her own injuries, Althea has been charged with murder in the death of Paige. Which of the following is most accurate:

(a) Althea cannot be convicted of murder on these facts because she was not reckless.

(b) Althea cannot be convicted of murder on these facts because she did not act maliciously.

(c) Both (a) and (b) above.

(d) Althea can be convicted of murder on these facts.

FELONY MURDER

Question 13–9: Lamar and Ray, sitting on stools adjacent to one another at their neighborhood tavern and drinking beer, argued vociferously with one another about which of their favorite National Football League teams was the better team. Lamar, an ardent Dallas Cowboys fan, could not believe that anyone else could possibly believe for one moment that the Baltimore Ravens were a better team than the Cowboys. Yet, that was exactly the position that Ray advocated. At length and in lengthy statistical detail.

After the argument raged back and forth for the better part of half an hour, Ray muttered, "You're just an idiot. There's no talking sense to a Cowboys fan," at Lamar, and he turned away from him and back to his beer. Enraged, Lamar grabbed his own beer bottle, held it tightly by the neck of the bottle, and slammed it against the bar top, smashing off the bottom of the bottle, leaving a dangerous jagged edge. (Lamar had seen this maneuver accomplished in a movie, but was pretty surprised that it actually worked in real life.) Lamar then immediately rammed the jagged edge of the bottle into Ray's neck, twisting it brutally, and yelling, "Take that birdie boy!"

Unfortunately, the resulting neck wound severed Ray's carotid artery, spraying blood everywhere, and killing him in a matter of seconds. Lamar was subsequently arrested and charged with felony murder. The underlying felony the prosecution has cited as the basis for this charge was the aggravated assault on Ray with the jagged edge of the bottle. Which of the following is most accurate:

(a) Lamar is not likely to be convicted of felony murder on these facts because he did not commit a felony.

(b) Lamar is not likely to be convicted of felony murder on these facts because aggravated assault is not an adequate predicate felony.

(c) Both (a) and (b) above.

(d) Lamar is likely to be convicted of felony murder on these facts.

Question 13–10: Jayden kidnaped ten year-old Aiden, the child of a wealthy couple who lived in a neighboring town. He sent an anonymous ransom note to Aiden's parents. Jayden threatened in the note that if the parents did not pay $80,000 in cash within forty-eight hours, he would kill Aiden.

Jayden never intended to actually harm Aiden. He simply made the threat in the ransom note to increase the chances that the ransom would be paid by frightening Aiden's parents. In fact, the entire time that Jayden held Aiden as a hostage, he was very well treated and he was not harmed in any way.

Aiden's parents did pay the ransom that was demanded within the deadline period. They had a courier drop $80,000 in unmarked $20 bills in a sealed package at a location designated by Jayden. After collecting the money, Jayden put Aiden in his car to drive him to a convenience store located ten miles away, from which Aiden could call his parents to come and pick him up.

Unfortunately, on the way to the convenience store, Jayden was in a traffic accident. A drunk driver, Addison, ran a red light and smashed into Jayden's car on the passenger side. The accident was entirely Addison's fault. Jayden was not at fault at all. Aiden was sitting in the passenger seat when the accident occurred, and was killed immediately by the impact.

When the police arrived at the accident scene, they recognized Aiden's body immediately and Jayden, who had been pinned to his seat, was arrested. He was subsequently charged with kidnaping and felony murder in the death of Aiden. Jayden's defense counsel concedes that he was guilty of kidnaping, but argues that Addison killed Aiden, not Jayden. As a result, defense counsel argues further, Jayden is not guilty of felony murder. Which of the following is most accurate:

(a) Jayden is not likely to be convicted of felony murder on these facts because the underlying felony had been completed at the time of Aiden's death.

(b) Jayden is not likely to be convicted of felony murder on these facts because kidnaping is not an adequate predicate felony.

(c) Jayden is not likely to be convicted of felony murder on these facts because his actions were not causally related to Aiden's death.

(d) None of the above.

(e) Answers (a), (b), and (c) are all true.

Question 13–11: Jack and Owen robbed a jewelry store in a suburban mall at gunpoint. After the robbery, they ran to their car, a red Ford Taurus, which was parked in the mall parking lot, and drove away at high speed.

By the time the police arrived at the scene, their vehicle was nowhere in sight. Witnesses in the parking lot reported the color and make of the car to the police, and also reported that the license plate number on the vehicle began with the letters "RTC." The police put out an all-points bulletin for all law enforcement officers in the region to be on the lookout for vehicles matching this description.

Two days after the robbery, a red Ford Taurus with the license plate "RTC–556" was spotted by a police officer about twelve miles from the mall where the robbery had taken place. The officer radioed for assistance, then put on his lights and siren and tried to get the driver of the car to pull over. Instead, the driver of the car, who turned out to be Jack, tried to get away, accelerating and leading the officer on a high-speed chase lasting for ten minutes and nearly seven miles. The chase ended only when Jack, driving erratically and way too fast for the area and conditions, slammed into a car that was backing out of a residential driveway. The driver of that car, Anna, was killed instantly upon impact.

Jack and Owen have each been charged with felony murder in the death of Anna. The triggering felony used by the prosecution as the basis for the felony murder charge was the robbery of the jewelry store two days earlier. Owen was not in the vehicle when it was spotted or at the time of the high speed chase or when it struck Anna's car. Which of the following is most accurate:

(a) Jack and Owen are not likely to be convicted of felony murder on these facts because the underlying felony had been completed at the time of Anna's death.

(b) Jack and Owen are not likely to be convicted of felony murder on these facts because robbery is not an adequate predicate felony.

(c) None of the above.

(d) Answers (a), (b) are both true.

VOLUNTARY MANSLAUGHTER

Question 13–12: Doris returned home four hours early from an out-of-town trip, having caught an earlier flight when her meeting was cancelled. As she entered her home, she heard strange noises coming from the upstairs bedroom. "Fred," she called out, yelling her husband's name, "Fred, is that you?"

Receiving no answer in response to her shout, Doris quietly ascended the staircase and, continuing to hear the same noises coming from the bedroom, she cracked the bedroom door open just slightly and peered inside. What she saw was her husband and two other men, each of them naked except that the two men other than her husband were partially clothed in furry animal costumes. All three of the men were engaged in sexual activity with one another. "Oh my sweet Lord!," Doris screamed, "What the f* * * are you doing, Fred?" But, engrossed in their activities, none of the three even heard her. They continued in their activities undeterred.

Shocked, appalled, and disgusted, Doris ran downstairs to the dining room and retrieved her pistol from the bottom drawer of the china cabinet. She then ran right back upstairs, ran into the bedroom, and shot her husband, Fred, once right in the head. Fred died instantly.

Doris has been charged with murder with respect to the killing of her husband, Fred. Doris' defense counsel has argued that this charge should be mitigated to voluntary manslaughter and has made that the basis of Doris' defense. Which of the following is most accurate:

(a) Doris is not likely to be able to make a successful mitigating voluntary manslaughter defense on these facts because she did not act as a result of a sudden and intense passion.

(b) Doris is not likely to be able to make a successful mitigating voluntary manslaughter defense on these facts because any provocation by her husband was not so serious that it would create passion in a reasonable person.

(c) Both of the above are true.

(d) Doris is likely to be able to make a successful mitigating voluntary manslaughter defense on these facts.

Question 13–13: Lashawn and Raheem, sitting on stools adjacent to one another at their neighborhood tavern and drinking beer, argued vociferously with one another about which of their favorite National Football League teams was the better team. Lashawn, an ardent Dallas Cowboys fan, could not believe that anyone else could possibly believe for one moment that the Baltimore Ravens were a better team than the Cowboys. Yet, that was exactly the position that Raheem advocated. At length and in lengthy statistical detail.

After the argument raged back and forth for the better part of half an hour, Raheem muttered, "You're just an idiot. There's no talking sense to a Cowboys fan," at Lamar, and he turned away from him and back to his beer. Enraged, Lashawn grabbed his own beer bottle, held it tightly by the neck of the bottle, and slammed it against the bar top, smashing off the bottom of the bottle, leaving a dangerous jagged edge. (Lashawn had seen this maneuver accomplished in a movie, but was pretty surprised that it actually worked in real life.) Lashawn then immediately rammed the jagged edge of the bottle into Raheem's neck, twisting it brutally, and yelling, "Take that birdie boy!"

Unfortunately, the resulting neck wound severed Raheem's carotid artery, spraying blood everywhere, and killing him in a matter of seconds. Lashawn was subsequently arrested and charged with first degree murder. Lashawn's defense counsel has argued that this charge should be mitigated to voluntary manslaughter and has made that the basis of Lashawn's defense. Which of the following is most accurate:

(a) Lashawn is not likely to be able to make a successful mitigating voluntary manslaughter defense on these facts because he did not act as a result of a sudden and intense passion.

(b) Lashawn is not likely to be able to make a successful mitigating voluntary manslaughter defense on these facts because any provocation by Raheem was not so serious that it would create passion in a reasonable person.

(c) Both of the above are true.

(d) Lashawn is likely to be able to make a successful mitigating voluntary manslaughter defense on these facts.

Question 13–14: [Note: this question is based on the same facts as Question 15–10.] Wyatt, a first-year law student, moved into a new studio apartment near his Law School just in time for school to start. The apartment and the Law School were both located in a downtown, urban area with high crime rates. Wyatt was from a rural area in another state and was more than a little apprehensive about walking in his new neighborhood at night. As much as he could, he tried not to go out in the evenings.

One evening during his third week of school, however, Wyatt had to stay late at the law school for a meeting of his first-year section. Knowing that he was going to have to return home late that evening and, still apprehensive even after having lived in the neighborhood for nearly a month, Wyatt put his handgun in his backpack and took it to school with him. He was not licensed to carry this gun in the state in which he now resided.

Walking home from school late that evening, Wyatt kept looking around anxiously and walking as fast as he could. After a couple of minutes, he could hear footsteps behind him, which made him walk even faster. As he picked up his pace, the footsteps behind him came quicker. Wyatt broke into a run. The quickening footsteps behind him indicated that the person following him was running as well.

Wyatt wheeled around, reaching inside his backpack for his gun at the very same moment. As he wheeled around, Wyatt could see that a young boy (who turned out to be Levi) was chasing after him, carrying what looked to be a large, brightly multi-colored, plastic "weapon" in his hands. That "weapon" was actually a massive squirt gun, commonly called a "super soaker." But Wyatt did not know what the "weapon" actually was. He had never seen a super soaker or a squirt gun of that size. Terrified, Wyatt fired three shots at Levi's chest, just after Wyatt pulled the trigger on his super soaker and doused Wyatt with water. Levi subsequently died from the bullet wounds.

Wyatt has been charged with murder. Wyatt's defense counsel, Katherine, referred to him by his Criminal Law professor, has argued that since Wyatt thought that Levi was going to shoot him, the most serious homicide offense of which he could be found guilty is voluntary manslaughter. Which of the following is most accurate:

(a) If the fact-finder accepts the facts set out above, Wyatt killed Levi as a result of a sudden and intense passion.

(b) If the fact-finder accepts the facts set out above, Wyatt's act of killing Levi was a result of provocation by Levi that was not so serious that it would create passion in a reasonable person.

(c) If the fact-finder accepts the facts set out above, Wyatt cannot likely be convicted of a homicide offense more serious than voluntary manslaughter.

(d) All of the above are true.

INVOLUNTARY MANSLAUGHTER

Question 13–15: Colin owned a power chain saw which began to give him some serious problems. When he was cutting with it, he started to get some resistance from the cutting chain which caused the saw to violently kick upward and sometimes it made his hand slip from the handle and the cutting chain jerk toward his arm and chest. Although Colin was never actually injured on these occasions, using this saw began to make him very nervous and so he decided to buy a new one. He threw the old power saw on top of a pile of old tools in the corner of his garage.

About a year after this occurred, Colin and Lydia, Colin's wife, had a "yard sale" one weekend, where they offered for sale at very cheap prices a number of used and personal items they wanted to discard. Among the items they offered for sale was Colin's old power saw. "Hey," Lydia said to Colin, when she saw the saw on one of their folding tables, offered for sale, "isn't that saw of yours broken?" "Nah," Colin responded, "it still works. It's just a little screwed up. That's all. Everyone knows that the stuff you buy at a yard sale is a little screwed up."

Lydia sold the old power saw to a neighbor, Garrett, for five dollars. Garrett tried to use the saw that very same afternoon. When he did, the saw immediately kicked back at him violently, the same way that it had when Colin used it. But, unlike Colin, Garrett was severely injured as a result of the kickback. Garrett's hand accidentally engaged the rapidly moving cutting chain as it kicked back, and the hand was severed. Garrett immediately passed out, and he ultimately died from the subsequent unchecked blood loss.

Colin has now been charged with involuntary manslaughter due to his role in the sale of his defective power saw to Garrett, the use of which resulted in Garrett's death. Which of the following is true:

(a) Colin is likely to be convicted of involuntary manslaughter on these facts.

(b) Colin is not likely to be convicted of guilty of involuntary manslaughter because Garrett assumed the risk that he might die or be seriously injured when he used the used power saw.

(c) Colin is not likely to be convicted of guilty of involuntary manslaughter because he did not act criminally negligently.

(d) None of the above.

Question 13–16: Bonnie was driving her BMW convertible down a suburban, residential street where the speed limit was 25 miles per hour.

Bonnie was driving at 40 miles per hour—fifteen miles per hour over the speed limit—but she did not see anyone in, around, or near the street and the weather was good, so she saw no need or reason to slow down.

Unfortunately, 7 year-old, Josiah, playing a game of hide-and-seek with some friends and not looking where he was going, dashed right out into the street in front of Bonnie's car. Bonnie didn't see Josiah until he was right in front of the car since he emerged from behind some dense foliage that grew right up to the edge of the roadway.

Bonnie braked as soon as she saw Josiah, but it was already too late. She ran right over him. Josiah subsequently died of the internal injuries he suffered as a result of being struck and run over by Bonnie's car.

Bonnie has been charged with involuntary manslaughter in the death of Josiah. Which of the following is true:

(a) Whether Bonnie will be convicted of involuntary manslaughter on these facts turns on whether she should have been aware of a substantial and unjustifiable risk that death or serious bodily injury might occur as a result of her speeding in this residential neighborhood.

(b) Bonnie is not likely to be convicted of guilty of involuntary manslaughter because Josiah assumed the risk that he might die or be seriously injured when he emerged from the foliage at the edge of the roadway.

(c) Whether Bonnie will be convicted of involuntary manslaughter on these facts turns on whether she acted maliciously in taking a substantial and unjustifiable risk that death or serious bodily injury might occur as a result of her speeding in this residential neighborhood.

(d) None of the above.

Question 13–17: Ty was an electrician, one of many workers who were working for a general contractor on a very big construction project, the construction of a large civic auditorium. One day, when Ty was installing a very large and heavy light fixture in the central hallway of the building under construction, he did a very sloppy and slipshod job of securing the fixture to the ceiling.

A co-worker, Amy, who was helping him attach the fixture, both of them high above the floor on a scaffold, told him: "Hey, Ty, that light's gonna fall. You got to at least support it better somehow before we secure it or somebody's gonna get conked pretty good when it lets go." "Nah," Ty replied, "don't worry about it. I know it's loose. I know. I know. But it's good enough for tonight. I got to get home. I got something to do. I don't have the time to work on this any more today. We'll get it fixed up right tomorrow morning." Soon thereafter, Ty and Amy left the work site without taking any additional steps to secure or support the light fixture.

The next morning, as Ty and Amy were climbing the scaffolding to get back to the ceiling to resume work on the fixture, the fixture fell from the ceiling, crashing into and through the scaffolding, striking Amy forcefully on its way to the floor. Amy was critically injured, and she subsequently died from the injuries she received as a result of being struck directly by the fixture and her subsequent fall to the floor.

Ty has been charged with involuntary manslaughter in the death of Amy. Which of the following is true:

(a) Ty is likely guilty of involuntary manslaughter in the death of Amy because he knew the fixture could fall.

(b) Ty is likely guilty of involuntary manslaughter in the death of Amy because he acted maliciously in not repairing the fixture before he left for the evening.

(c) Ty is likely guilty of involuntary manslaughter in the death of Amy because he was criminally negligent in not repairing the fixture before he left for the evening.

(d) None of the above.

CHAPTER 14
THEFT

TRADITIONAL THEFT CRIMES

Question 14–1: Miles borrowed Kate's television set for the weekend because his was broken. Miles wanted to watch a couple of important football games over the weekend and he knew that Kate, a co-worker, was going to be out of town and wouldn't be using her set anyway. Kate was perfectly agreeable to lending her television set to Miles. But, she made him "swear" to her that he would return it some time on Monday, in time for her to watch her favorite television program that was broadcast on Monday evenings. Miles told Kate that that was no problem. He would return the set first thing Monday morning, before Kate left for work.

Miles had every intention of returning Kate's television on Monday morning. But on Saturday morning, he received a call from his father, who lived a four-hour drive away with his mother. His father told him that Miles' mother had been hospitalized, and Miles immediately packed a suitcase and drove four hours to the hospital to join them at the hospital. He never gave any thought to Kate's television as he was preoccupied with his mother's illness.

As a result, Miles did not talk to Kate or return her television set on Monday morning as he had agreed. Miles did not even return from visiting his parents until Thursday night, after his mother was released from the hospital on Thursday morning.

However, on Wednesday morning, after Miles had not returned her television set and she had not heard anything from him and he had not showed up for work, Kate called the police and accused Miles of stealing her television set. She subsequently went down to the station house and filed a criminal complaint against him.

Is Miles guilty of a common law or traditional theft crime in these circumstances? Which of the following is most accurate:

(a) Miles is guilty of larceny, but is not guilty of larceny by trick.

(b) Miles is not guilty of any common law or traditional theft crime.

(c) Miles is guilty of false pretenses, but is not guilty of embezzlement.

(d) Miles is guilty of larceny and false pretenses, but is not guilty of larceny by trick or embezzlement.

Question 14–2: Heinrich saw a notice on a supermarket bulletin board in which Laura and Michelle offered to come and clean up people's basements for a very reasonable price. Heinrich contacted Laura and Michelle and arranged for them to spend one morning later in the week cleaning out his very cluttered and filthy basement.

Laura and Michelle worked furiously for four hours in Heinrich's basement without taking a break. They took out and discarded all of the trash and broken items. They straightened up and organized all of the remaining, unbroken items that Heinrich told them to keep there. When all of that was accomplished, they then swept up and mopped the basement floor and, finally, dusted all of the shelves and the basement walls.

After they had completed all of this work, Laura and Michelle went to Heinrich to be paid the $80.00 he had agreed to pay them ($10 an hour for each of them). Laughing at them, Heinrich refused to pay them anything at all and threatened them if they didn't leave his premises immediately.

Laura and Michelle have filed a criminal complaint against Heinrich with the local police. The jurisdiction in which the foregoing took place still uses the common law larceny offense. Did Heinrich commit larceny in these circumstances? Which of the following is true:

(a) Heinrich is guilty of larceny.

(b) Heinrich is not guilty of larceny because he did not take any personal property.

(c) Heinrich is not guilty of larceny because Laura and Michelle had not contracted with him in writing.

Question 14–3: Dee Dee loaned Inga her whole CD collection for Inga to take with her on a two-week long road trip from New Hampshire to California, and back again. When Inga returned from the trip, she promptly returned the CDs to Dee Dee. The CDs were stored in three bulky storage albums.

But when Dee Dee paged through the albums after they were returned to her, she discovered that twelve of her very favorite CDs were missing. Dee Dee called Inga and asked her what had happened to the missing CDs. Inga responded: "Look, Dee Dee, you never use those CDs any more. You know that. You have all of that same exact music on your iPod now. My friend Connie in San Francisco has an amazing CD collection. When I asked to borrow your CDs, I knew that there were a few of them that I wanted to give to her for her collection. So I gave them to her. Twelve lousy CDs, Dee Dee. Come on, it's no big deal. Get over it."

Dee Dee did not get over it. She filed a criminal complaint against Inga with the local police. The jurisdiction in which the foregoing took place still uses the common law larceny offense. Did Inga commit the crime of larceny in these circumstances? Which of the following is true:

(a) Inga is not guilty of larceny because she did not "break bulk."

(b) Inga is not guilty of larceny because she did not take any personal property of Dee Dee's.

(c) Inga is not guilty of larceny because she is guilty of larceny by trick instead.

(d) None of the above.

Question 14–4: Colette was sitting on a park bench on a warm Sunday afternoon, reading a book and watching scores of joggers, walkers, and bicyclists go by. All of a sudden, a splash of bright color under the bench she was sitting on caught her eye. Putting down her book, she peered under the bench and discovered a bright pink and orange, patterned silk scarf. She hadn't seen the scarf when she first sat down because it was laying underneath—and was largely obscured by—a couple of empty beer cans and some other trash.

Colette picked up the scarf. Underneath it, she also saw two wadded-up five dollar bills underneath some other refuse. Putting the scarf and the ten dollars in her purse, Colette hummed to herself, almost inaudibly, just under her breath: "Finders keepers. Losers weepers."

Looking around then to make sure that no one had seen her put these items into her purse, Colette then quickly left the park and took the scarf and the money home. The scarf turned out to be an expensive vintage Hermes scarf worth hundreds of dollars. Colette was absolutely delighted with it, and she wore it often, although never in the park where she had found it.

Was Colette guilty of the crime of common law larceny in taking and keeping the scarf and the two five dollar bills? Which of the following is true:

(a) Colette is guilty of larceny for taking and keeping the scarf and the two five dollar bills.

(b) Colette is not guilty of larceny for taking and keeping the scarf or the two five dollar bills.

(c) Colette is guilty of larceny for taking and keeping the scarf, but not for taking and keeping the two five dollar bills.

(d) None of the above.

MERGER OF THEFT CRIMES

Question 14–5: Jimmy was charged with and prosecuted for the crime of theft by unlawful taking. This charge resulted from the discovery that he was in possession of sixteen pieces of antique furniture that had been stolen from a local upscale hotel, the Delmonico.

At trial, however, witnesses testifying in the prosecution's case in chief offered no testimony that Jimmy himself had actually taken any of the furniture from the hotel. Instead, the evidence adduced in the prosecution's case established clearly instead that Jimmy had purchased all of the pieces of furniture in question from his friend, Emil, knowing full well that Emil and some of his buddies had stolen them from the Delmonico.

At the end of the prosecution's case, Jimmy's defense counsel, Bridget, moved to dismiss the theft charge against Jimmy on the basis of failure of proof. "The prosecution has simply failed to establish the elements of the crime of theft by unlawful taking. That was what he was charged with and the prosecution has not proved he committed that crime. It's just that simple, Your Honor," Bridget argued to the trial judge, adding that "[t]he fact that the prosecution may have made out the elements of an entirely different crime—the crime of receiving stolen property—is simply irrelevant. Jimmy wasn't charged with that crime."

Is Bridget's argument correct? The jurisdiction in which Jimmy is being tried uses the Model Penal Code's approach to proof of theft crimes, not the common law approach. How should the trial judge rule? Should the theft charge be dismissed against Jimmy? Which of the following is most accurate:

(a) Jimmy is guilty of theft.

(b) Jimmy is not guilty of theft because the prosecution did not prove that Jimmy was guilty of the theft offense with which he was charged.

(c) Jimmy is not guilty of theft because the prosecution did not prove that Jimmy personally took the furniture from the Delmonico.

(d) Answers (b) and (c) are true, and answer (a) is false.

CHAPTER 15
JUSTIFICATION DEFENSES

SELF DEFENSE

Question 15–1: Wade and Gabe were each separately attending the same football game. Wade was a rabid fan of the home team. He was wearing that team's colors and a replica of the home team's quarterback's jersey. Gabe was a rabid fan of the visiting team. He was decked out in that team's colors, including having had his face painted with his team's emblem on it.

As the game went on, Wade and Gabe each cheered loudly when their team made a good play. And each of them booed just as loudly when the other team made a good play. Because each of them was such a fanatical fan and because they were sitting just a few seats away from one another, eventually, they began to yell insults at one another as well. At first, the insults were just in good fun. But, after a little while, their comments began to become more pointed, more personal, and entirely mean-spirited.

As the game was nearing its end, Wade finally stood and turned around in his seat to face Gabe directly and pointed at him and called him an obscene and offensive name. When Gabe didn't respond to this insult, Wade then stood back up and threw his seat cushion at Gabe, narrowly missing hitting him in the head.

Gabe, enraged by Wade's actions, yelled, "Okay! Okay! I'm just going to have to kill that little f* * ***!" And he rushed toward Wade, fuming, with his fists balled up like he was about to slug him. Just before he reached Wade, however, three of Gabe's friends grabbed and restrained him forcibly. While Gabe was restrained by his friends, Wade picked up a long, plastic stadium horn that he had brought with him to the game and swung it wildly and forcefully at Gabe's head, striking him and resulting in a nasty gash.

Wade was immediately taken out of the stadium by security officers and turned over to the local police. He has been charged with assault as a result of his actions in striking Gabe with the stadium horn. Wade's defense counsel, Haley, has argued, however, that Wade's actions were completely justified as he was acting in self defense in response to Gabe's attempted attack on him.

Is Haley correct? Does Wade have a good self defense argument in these circumstances? Which of the following is most accurate:

(a) Wade has a good self defense argument.

(b) Wade does not have a good self defense argument because Wade was the aggressor in this situation.

(c) Wade does not have a good self defense argument because it was unnecessary to strike Gabe in order to repel his threatened attack.

(d) Answers (b) and (c) are true, and answer (a) is false.

Question 15–2: Amanda received a text message from her best friend, Lacey. Lacey told her in the message that she had just heard that their mutual acquaintance, Sara, was telling other people that she was going to break both of Amanda's arms. Amanda and Lacey both knew that Sara was boiling mad at Amanda because Amanda was now in a serious relationship with Sara's former boyfriend, Hank. Hank had left Sara for Amanda, and Sara was not happy about it. To say the least.

Amanda also knew that Sara had been convicted of assault on a prior occasion so she took this threat from her very seriously. In fact, she called Sara to try to calm her down about the situation, but Sara just hung up on her. Amanda then asked Hank to talk to Sara, and he did. But when Hank and Sara talked, Sara repeated her threats against Amanda. She confirmed that she planned to surprise Amanda one day when she least expected it and break both of her arms with a baseball bat.

Amanda was genuinely terrified. She decided that the only way that she could protect herself from Sara was to take the offensive. Her plan was to scare Sara so much that she would be too afraid of what might happen to her to risk hurting Amanda. As a result, with Lacey's and Hank's assistance, Amanda ambushed Sara, surprising her as she was coming home late one night. While Lacey and Hank restrained Sara, Amanda broke Sara's left wrist with a baseball bat, warning her at the same time to leave her alone or "next time, I'll break your other wrist and both of your kneecaps!"

Amanda has been charged with assault as a result of her actions in breaking Sara's wrist with a baseball bat. Amanda's defense counsel, Zachary, has argued, however, that Amanda's actions were justified as she was acting in self defense in response to Sara's wholly believable threats to break both of Amanda's arms.

Is Zachary correct? Does Amanda have a good self defense argument in these circumstances? Which of the following is most accurate:

(a) Amanda has a good self defense argument.

(b) Amanda does not have a good self defense argument because Amanda was the aggressor in this situation.

(c) Amanda does not have a good self defense argument because Sara's threatened attack on her was not imminent.

(d) Answers (b) and (c) are true, and answer (a) is false.

Question 15–3: While walking home alone late one evening, Marcel was accosted by Carl, who jumped out at him unexpectedly from a dark alley. Carl grabbed Marcel by his arm and shouted at him: "Give me your wallet! Now! Right now!"

Marcel reached into his pocket. But instead of pulling out his wallet, he pulled out a knife instead and stabbed Carl three times in the chest. Carl subsequently died as a result of complications resulting from internal bleeding caused by the stab wounds.

Marcel has been charged with second degree murder as a result of his stabbing of Carl and Carl's subsequent death. Marcel's defense counsel, Ursula, has argued, however, that Marcel's actions were completely justified as he was acting in self defense in response to being physically accosted by Carl in a robbery attempt.

Is Ursula correct? Does Marcel have a good self defense argument in these circumstances? Which of the following is most accurate:

(a) Marcel has a good self defense argument.

(b) Marcel does not have a good self defense argument because Marcel was the aggressor in this situation.

(c) Marcel does not have a good self defense argument because Carl did not threaten him with deadly force.

(d) Answers (b) and (c) are true, and answer (a) is false.

The following facts apply to Questions 15–4 and 15–5 below:

Vanna was extremely angry—boiling mad, in fact—at her boyfriend, Pat. Pat had forgotten to pick her up after work, and that was the third time in just two weeks that he had done that to her. Vanna took the bus home. When she got there, she immediately left a voicemail on Pat's mobile phone telling him that she had had more than enough of his thoughtlessness and that, as far as she was concerned, their relationship was over. Finished.

Later that evening, Vanna heard a knock on her apartment door. When she opened the door, there was Pat, smiling and holding out a six-pack of beer. "Hey, baby," he said to Vanna, "no reason to be so steamed at me. Come on, honey. I was just busy. You know. I've got stuff going on. You know. Whatever. So it's no big deal, angel. Really. Here. Here, I brought you a six-pack of your favorite beer, Corona Light!" As Pat held out the bottles of beer to her, grinning ear to ear, Vanna reared back and smacked him as hard as she could, sending both Pat and the beer flying.

As Pat tried to get up, Vanna ran over and started kicking him violently. "Corona Light! I don't even like Corona Light! You know that, you piece of s* * *! That's f* * ** * * Debbie that drinks Coronas, you a* * ** * *!"

Pat, furious and in pain, struggled to get up in the face of Vanna's repeated kicks. When he finally managed to get to his feet, he shoved her violently across the room and into the far wall, which she hit and crumpled to the ground. "Alright, that's it, b* * **! You've pushed me too far!," Pat snarled at her, "[s]o you can leave me, b* * **. Good f* * ** * * riddance! But you'll remember me. 'Cause I'm going to cut up your pretty face before I go!" Pat then pulled a switch-blade knife out of his jacket pocket and, opening and extending the blade, he started slowly walking toward Vanna.

Vanna, terrified, quickly scrambled over to a nearby drawer where she kept her pistol. She grabbed it from the drawer and, just as Pat had almost reached her with his knife outstretched and pointed at her face, she shot him twice in his face.

Pat died as a result of these gunshot wounds. Vanna was subsequently charged with second degree murder as a result of her shooting and killing of Pat. Her defense counsel, Gina, has argued, however, that Vanna's actions were justified as she was acting in self defense in response to Pat's threatened attack on her with a knife.

Is Gina correct? Does Vanna have a good self defense argument in these circumstances?

Question 15–4: Which of the following is most accurate:

(a) Vanna does not have a good self defense argument because she did not have the right to use deadly force.

(b) Vanna does not have a good self defense argument because she was the aggressor in this situation.

(c) Vanna does not have a good self defense argument because it was not reasonable to believe that Pat posed an immediate threat to her.

(d) All of the above.

(e) None of the above.

Question 15–5: The jurisdiction in which this occurred has a "retreat requirement" similar to that found in the Model Penal Code as part of its self-defense law. Which of the following is most accurate:

(a) Vanna does not have a good self defense argument because she should have and could have retreated before using deadly force against Pat.

(b) Vanna does not have a good self defense argument because, even though she was in her own apartment, she voluntarily invited Pat to enter the apartment and he therefore became a co-occupant.

(c) Vanna had no obligation to retreat because she was in her own apartment when she shot Pat.

(d) Answers (a) and (b) are correct, but answer (c) is incorrect.

The following facts apply to Questions 15–6 and 15–7 below:

Kevin and Bailey, husband and wife, were engaged in a violent domestic dispute in their own living room, arguing bitterly, screaming, and throwing things at one another. Finally, Kevin ran into the kitchen and picked up a carving knife. He returned to the living room with the knife in his hand, brandished it in front of him, and said to Bailey: "So help me, Bailey, if you don't leave this house this very minute, I'll carve you up like a turkey!"

In response, Bailey ran to the front door, opened it and started to step outside. But then she paused. She turned back around and faced Kevin and snarled to him: "Wait a minute, buster! I'm not going anywhere. This is my house, too. F* * * you, a* * ** * **! And you know what? I'm not afraid of you either." After saying that, Bailey reached into her purse and pulled out a handgun and aimed it directly at Kevin's heart.

Kevin growled back: "You don't have the guts to shoot me, Bailey. You're a wimp. You always have been." And, after saying that, he came after her with the carving knife. But Kevin was wrong. Whether or not she was a wimp, Bailey did have the guts to shoot him. Bailey stood her ground and just before Kevin reached her with the knife, she calmly shot him six times in the chest.

Kevin died as a result of these gunshot wounds. Bailey was subsequently charged with first degree murder as a result of the shooting and killing of her husband, Kevin. Her defense counsel, Preston, has argued, however, that Bailey's actions were justified as she was acting in self defense in response to Kevin's threatened attack on her with a knife.

Question 15–6: Is Preston correct? Does Bailey have a good self defense argument in these circumstances? Which of the following is most accurate:

(a) Bailey does not have a good self defense argument because she did not have the right to use deadly force.

(b) Bailey does not have a good self defense argument because she was the aggressor in this situation.

(c) Bailey does not have a good self defense argument because it was not reasonable for her to believe that Kevin posed an immediate threat to her.

(d) None of the above.

Question 15–7: The jurisdiction in which this occurred has a "retreat requirement" similar to that found in the Model Penal Code as part of its self-defense law. Which of the following is most accurate:

(a) Even though she was in her own home, Bailey had an obligation to retreat if she could do so safely before shooting Pat.

(b) Bailey and Pat were co-habitants in their own home and, hence, neither of them had an obligation to retreat.

(c) Bailey had no obligation to retreat because she was in her own home when she shot Pat.

(d) None of the above.

DEFENSE OF OTHERS

The following facts apply to Questions 15–8 and 15–9 below:

When Brandy emerged from the supermarket with a shopping cart full of groceries, she saw her husband, Omar, who had been waiting for her in the family car, being threatened by a stranger (who turned out to be Jabari) who was holding a gun on him. She could see that Omar had his hands up in the air and he looked scared.

Brandy immediately reached into her purse and pulled out her hand gun. She then took one shot at Jabari, hitting him in his lower back and causing him to fall to the ground and drop the gun he was holding on Omar. Jabari survived the gunshot wound. But he was partially and permanently paralyzed as a result of the resultant injury to his spinal cord from the bullet.

The District Attorney in the jurisdiction where these events took place is trying to decide whether or not to charge Brandy with the crime of attempted murder in the shooting of Jabari. She has asked you, an Assistant District Attorney in her office, to advise her whether or not Brandy has a good defense to this charge.

Question 15–8: Which of the following is most accurate:

(a) Brandy does not have a good defense of others argument because she did not have the right to use deadly force.

(b) Brandy does not have a good defense of others argument because she was the aggressor in this situation.

(c) Brandy does not have a good defense of others argument because it was not reasonable for her to believe that Jabari posed an immediate threat to her or her husband.

(d) None of the above.

Question 15–9: The jurisdiction in which this occurred has a "retreat requirement" similar to that found in the Model Penal Code as part of its self-defense law. Which of the following is most accurate:

(a) Brandy had no obligation to retreat before shooting Jabari because Jabari was threatening Omar, not her.

(b) Brandy had an obligation to retreat before shooting Jabari but only if she and Omar could both do so safely.

(c) Brandy had an obligation to retreat instead of shooting Jabari because she could have retreated in complete safety.

(d) None of the above.

The following facts apply to Questions 15–10 and 15–11 below:

When Randi emerged from the supermarket with a shopping cart full of groceries, she saw her husband, Oran, who had been waiting for her in the family car, apparently being threatened by a stranger (who turned out to be Jerry) who was holding a gun on him. She could see that Oran had his hands up in the air and he looked scared.

Randi immediately reached into her purse and pulled out her hand gun. She then took one shot at Jerry, hitting him in his lower back and causing him to fall to the ground and drop the gun he was holding on Oran. Jerry survived the gunshot wound. But he was partially and permanently paralyzed as a result of the resultant injury to his spinal cord from the bullet.

As it turned out, however, what Randi thought she had seen was not what it appeared to be. Randi only had a side view of Jerry from where she was standing with her shopping cart. She thought (reasonably) that Oran was being held up at gunpoint. In fact, Jerry was a mime. His face was painted white (which Randi could not see from the side), and the gun he was holding on Oran was a toy gun. In fact, the word "BANG" was printed on each side of it (although Randi could not see that from where she was standing). Oran had his hands up simply to go along with Jerry-the-mime's gag hold up. What Randi saw as fear on Oran's face was actually Oran laughing.

The District Attorney in the jurisdiction where these events took place is trying to decide whether or not to charge Randi with the crime of attempted murder in the shooting of Jerry. She has asked you, an Assistant District Attorney in her office, to advise her whether or not Randi has a good defense to this charge.

Question 15–10: The jurisdiction in which this occurred has a defense of others statute that is similar to the Model Penal Code. Which of the following is most accurate:

(a) Randi has a good defense of others argument and had the right to use deadly force in these circumstances.

(b) Randi does not have a good defense of others argument because, as irritating as mimes can be, she was still not entitled to use deadly force.

(c) Randi does not have a good defense of others argument because it was not reasonable for her to believe that Jerry posed an immediate threat to her or her husband.

(d) Answers (b) and (c) are correct, but answer (a) is incorrect.

Question 15–11: The jurisdiction in which this occurred has a "retreat requirement" similar to that found in the Model Penal Code as part of its defense-of-others law. Which of the following is most accurate:

(a) Randi had no obligation to retreat before shooting Jerry because Jerry appeared to be threatening Oran, not her.

(b) Randi had an obligation to retreat before shooting Jerry because it was unreasonable to believe that Jerry's toy gun was a real gun and posed a threat of deadly force.

(c) Randi had an obligation to retreat instead of shooting Jerry because she could have retreated in complete safety.

(d) None of the above.

DEFENSE OF PROPERTY

Question 15–12: Lenny was walking on the sidewalk in an urban, residential block when he saw a girl's red bicycle lying on the ground in front of someone's home. Although he didn't own the bicycle or know to whom it belonged, Lenny nonetheless grabbed it and quickly started to ride it away.

Cherie lived in the house from which the bicycle was being taken. It was her eleven year-old daughter's bike. When Cherie saw Lenny taking it and starting to pedal away, she immediately started running after him, screaming at him at the top of her lungs for him to stop. Lenny couldn't ride very fast as he is a grown man and the bicycle was child-sized. As a result, Cherie easily caught up with him and grabbed him by the shoulders and dragged him off the bike. As a result of being dragged in that fashion by Cherie, Lenny's foot got caught in the rear wheel and he broke his ankle as he fell awkwardly to the street.

Lenny has filed a private criminal complaint against Cherie for assault. If Cherie is actually prosecuted for that criminal offense, does she have a good defense? Which of the following is most accurate:

(a) Cherie has a good defense of property defense in these circumstances.

(b) Cherie does not have a good defense of property defense in these circumstances because that defense does not permit the actor to physically assault someone.

(c) Cherie does not have a good defense of property defense in these circumstances because the bicycle in question was her daughter's, not Cherie's.

(d) Answers (b) and (c) are correct, but answer (a) is incorrect.

DEFENSE OF HABITATION

Question 15–13: Norman was sound asleep in the upstairs bedroom of his home late one evening when he heard what he thought were noises coming from downstairs. Norman got out of bed and walked quietly into the upstairs hallway. He couldn't hear anything more. "Who's there? Is anyone there?," Norman yelled down the staircase.

In apparent response to his yelling, he heard some loud but garbled voices and what then sounded like people running and crashing into things. Quickly grabbing his shotgun from the upstairs closet, Norman ran downstairs to the kitchen. When he got there, he saw the kitchen door was wide open with the window smashed and glass from the broken window was all over the floor. A number of the cabinet doors and kitchen drawers were open with their contents strewn around all over the kitchen.

Norman ran to the kitchen doorway. Looking outside, he saw two men running away from his home at the far end of the back yard. "Stop!," he screamed at them, "Stop or I'll shoot!" The two men did not stop, and Norman shot twice and hit them both. Both men, who subsequently admitted that they had been burglarizing Norman's house thinking that no one was at home, were seriously but non-fatally wounded by the shotgun blasts.

Norman has been charged with two counts of aggravated assault, one count for each of the two men he shot and wounded. His defense counsel, Lee, has argued that Norman had every right to shoot these two men as they were burglarizing his home. Is Lee correct? Which of the following is most accurate:

(a) Norman has a good defense of habitation defense in these circumstances.

(b) Norman does not have a good defense of habitation defense in these circumstances because that defense does not permit the actor to use deadly force.

(c) Norman does not have a good defense of habitation defense in these circumstances because that defense only applies when the actor's actions were necessary to terminate the unlawful intrusion into the home.

(d) Answers (b) and (c) are correct, but answer (a) is incorrect.

IMPERFECT DEFENSES

Question 15–14: [Note: this is the same question is Question 13–14.] Wyatt, a first-year law student, moved into a new studio apartment near his Law School just in time for school to start. The apartment and the Law School were both located in a downtown, urban area with high crime rates. Wyatt was from a rural area in another state and was more than a little apprehensive about walking in his new neighborhood at night. As much as he could, he tried not to go out in the evenings.

One evening during his third week of school, however, Wyatt had to stay late at the law school for a meeting of his first-year section. Knowing that he was going to have to return home late that evening and, still apprehensive even after having lived in the neighborhood for nearly a month, Wyatt put his handgun in his backpack and took it to school with him. He was not licensed to carry this gun in the state in which he now resided.

Walking home from school late that evening, Wyatt kept looking around anxiously and walking as fast as he could. After a couple of minutes, he could hear footsteps behind him, which made him walk even faster. As he picked up his pace, the footsteps behind him came quicker. Wyatt broke into a run. The quickening footsteps behind him indicated that the person following him was running as well.

Wyatt wheeled around, reaching inside his backpack for his gun at the very same moment. As he wheeled around, Wyatt could see that a young boy (who turned out to be Levi) was chasing after him, carrying what looked to be a large, brightly multi-colored, plastic "weapon" in his hands. That "weapon" was actually a massive squirt gun, commonly called a "super soaker." But Wyatt did not know what the "weapon" actually was. He had never seen a super soaker or a squirt gun of that size. Terrified, Wyatt fired three shots at Levi's chest, just after Wyatt pulled the trigger on his super soaker and doused Wyatt with water. Levi subsequently died from the bullet wounds.

Wyatt has been charged with murder. Wyatt's defense counsel, Katherine, referred to him by his Criminal Law professor, has argued that since Wyatt thought that Levi was going to shoot him, the most serious homicide offense of which he could be found guilty is voluntary manslaughter. The jurisdiction in which this occurred permits the use of so-called "imperfect defenses." Which of the following is most accurate:

(a) If the fact-finder accepts the facts set out above, Wyatt has a good defense of imperfect self defense.

(b) If the fact-finder accepts the facts set out above, Wyatt's act of killing Levi would be mitigated to voluntary manslaughter.

(c) If the fact-finder accepts the facts set out above, Wyatt cannot likely be convicted of a homicide offense more serious than voluntary manslaughter.

(d) All of the above are true.

NECESSITY

Question 15–15: Ike and Eden were cross-country skiing in a remote, wilderness area when an unexpected blizzard hit. The snowfall became so heavy that they became completely disoriented and lost. While Ike had a mobile phone with him, there was no reception during the storm and—although he tried—Ike failed to reach anyone to ask for help. In truth, even if Ike had reached someone, given the severity of the storm and their remote location, it was doubtful that anyone could have reached them quickly enough to offer them any real assistance.

Ike and Eden feared with good reason that they might get lost and be seriously injured or die in the snowstorm, either through exposure or just by falling and hurting themselves. Luckily for them, however, at the height of the storm, they stumbled upon an unoccupied cabin in the woods. They broke the lock on the cabin door and stayed inside for a day and a half, until the storm subsided. At that point, the owner of the cabin showed up and called for assistance for them.

The owner of the cabin also called the police and asked them to arrest Ike and Eden. He was not sympathetic to the dilemma that caused them to break into his cabin as he had already had to repair the cabin a dozen times after hikers had broken into it. The cabin owner was just plain tired of the break-ins and he wanted to teach someone a lesson. So he filed a criminal complaint for breaking and entering and criminal trespass against both Ike and Eden.

If Ike and Eden are actually prosecuted for one or both of these criminal offenses, do they have a good defense? Which of the following is most accurate:

(a) Ike and Eden do not have a good defense of necessity to these charges because they had other non-criminal alternatives open to them to escape from harm.

(b) Ike and Eden do not have a good defense of necessity to these charges because the dangers they faced were the result of a natural event not an imminent threat from another person.

(c) Ike and Eden have a good defense of necessity to these charges.

(d) Answers (a) and (b) are true, and answer (c) is false.

Question 15–16: Mike and Ellen were cross-country skiing in a remote, wilderness area when an unexpected blizzard hit. The snowfall became so heavy that they became completely disoriented and lost. While Mike had a mobile phone with him, there was no reception during the storm and—although he tried—Mike failed to reach anyone to ask for help. In truth, even if Mike had reached someone, given the severity of the storm and their remote location, it was doubtful that anyone could have reached them quickly enough to offer them any real assistance.

Mike and Ellen feared with good reason that they might get lost and be seriously injured or die in the snowstorm, either through exposure or just by falling and hurting themselves. Luckily for them, however, at the height of the storm, they stumbled upon a cabin in the woods. Mike knocked on the cabin door and the owner, Zeb, opened the door just a crack while he kept the door secured with a security chain.

"Let us in. Please, please, mister, let us in!," Ellen cried out, "we're freezing out here. We're lost. We'll die out here! Let us in!" Zeb responded coldly: "Get the hell out of here! There's only room for one person in here. And that's me!" And then Zeb slammed the door shut.

Mike and Ellen huddled on the front porch of the cabin as long as they could. But after a couple of hours, they were frozen and nearly covered with drifting snow and they both began hammering on the cabin door with their fists, screaming at Zeb to let them in. At first, Zeb did not respond at all, but then he screamed back at them through the closed and locked door: "Get the f* * * outta here! I got a rifle. If I hear anything more out of you two, I'll open the door and shoot you both. Clear out!"

Eventually, Mike and Ellen decided they had no choice. If they stayed huddled outside any longer, they were likely to die. They talked about it and they decided that there was two of them and only one person inside the cabin. If they had to kill Zeb to get inside, then, as Mike said: "So be it. It's better that two people survive than that just one person survive. I'm going in."

Mike then pulled out the pistol he carried in his backpack, and shot off the cabin door lock. As he and Ellen rushed inside, they saw Zeb, who had apparently been asleep, stumble toward his rifle. Mike shot and killed him.

Mike has now been charged with first degree murder in the shooting death of Zeb. His defense counsel, Allyson, has argued that Mike was justified in shooting and killing Zeb because—just as Mike had reasoned before entering the cabin—the commission of that crime was justified because it resulted in a net increase in the amount of lives saved from the storm: two rather than one. Is this a good defense to this charge? Which of the following is most accurate:

(a) Mike does not have a good defense of necessity to this charge because he did not face an imminent threat of serious harm to himself if he did not reach a place of shelter quickly.

(b) Mike does not have a good defense of necessity to this charge because he killed another person.

(c) Mike has a good defense of necessity to this charge.

(d) None of the above.

CHAPTER 16
EXCUSES

DURESS

Question 16–1: Stewart had sexual intercourse with Allie forcibly and without her consent. Stewart was forced against his will to commit this sexual act by Logan, Allie's bitter and psychotic ex-boyfriend.

Logan held a loaded gun on Stewart, and was present during the entire event. He told Stewart that he would shoot him if Stewart did not rape Allie immediately. After the sexual act was completed, Logan shot and killed himself.

Stewart has been charged with the crime of the rape of Allie. Does Stewart have a tenable defense to this charge? Which of the following is most accurate:

(a) Stewart has a good duress defense to this charge.

(b) Stewart does not have a good duress defense to this charge because the threat made to him was one that a reasonable person would have and should have resisted.

(c) Stewart does not have a good duress defense to this charge because actions undertaken in response to a threat never justify an act of forcible rape.

(d) Answers (b) and (c) are true, and answer (a) is false.

Question 16–2: Stuart brutally beat Ellie to death with a lead pipe, hitting her violently in the head more than two dozen times. Stuart was forced to commit this criminal act by Loomis, Ellie's bitter and psychotic ex-boyfriend.

Loomis held a loaded gun on Stuart, and was present during the entire event. He told Stuart that he would shoot him if Stuart did not beat

Ellie with the lead pipe immediately until she stopped moving. He would not let Stuart stop beating her until that moment. After the assault was completed and Ellie lay unmoving on the floor, Loomis shot and killed himself.

Stuart has been charged with the crime of murder in the death of Ellie. Does Stuart have a tenable defense to this charge? Which of the following is most accurate:

(a) Stuart has a good duress defense to this charge.

(b) Stuart does not have a good duress defense to this charge because the threat made to him was one that a reasonable person would have and should have resisted.

(c) Stuart does not have a good duress defense to this charge because actions undertaken in response to a threat never justify an act of homicide.

(d) Answers (b) and (c) are true, and answer (a) is false.

INSANITY & OTHER PSYCHOLOGICAL DEFENSES

The following facts apply to Questions 16–3 and 16–4 below:

Livonia, who lived alone and had a long history of mental illness, honestly believed that aliens from outer space were watching her every move and beaming harmful rays into her body. As a result of these irrational fears, Livonia rarely ventured outside of her home and she kept all of the doors closed and the window blinds shut all day and night long.

One day, peeking through the drawn blinds of her front window, Livonia saw the two young children who lived across the street from her set up a lemonade stand in their front yard facing her home. Livonia believed that the space aliens had taken over the two children's bodies and that the lemonade stand was really a cover for the aliens' cameras and laser beams which were aimed at her house.

As a result of her panic about this development, Livonia rushed upstairs to retrieve her late father's old .22 caliber rifle from the attic. She then loaded it with five old bullets that she found lying next to the rifle. Then she cracked open her front door and shot five times at the two children who were running the lemonade stand across the street. Fortunately for everyone, Livonia was not a good shot. She missed hitting either of the children—or anyone else—with any of her five shots.

Livonia has been arrested and charged with two counts of attempted murder, one for each of the children she shot at with the rifle. Livonia's defense counsel, Charles, plans to use an insanity defense on her behalf in defense of these charges.

Question 16–3: This jurisdiction uses the *M'Naghten* test to determine whether an accused defendant was insane at the time of the alleged criminal act. What are Livonia's chances of being found not guilty by reason of insanity in these circumstances? Which of the following is most accurate:

(a) Livonia has a good insanity defense to these charges.

(b) Livonia does not have a good insanity defense to these charges because she knew the nature and quality of her act.

(c) Livonia does not have a good insanity defense to these charges because she clearly knew that what she was doing was wrong.

(d) Answers (b) and (c) are true, and answer (a) is false.

Question 16–4: This jurisdiction uses the ALI Model Penal Code test to determine whether an accused defendant was insane at the time of the alleged criminal act. What are Livonia's chances of being found not guilty by reason of insanity in these circumstances? Which of the following is most accurate:

(a) If it can be established that Livonia lacked substantial capacity either to appreciate the wrongfulness of her conduct or to conform her conduct to the requirements of the law, she would have a good insanity defense to these charges.

(b) If it can be established that Livonia knew the nature and quality of her act, she would have a good insanity defense to these charges.

(c) If it can be established that Livonia acted in response to an irresistible impulse, she would have a good insanity defense to these charges.

(d) All of the above.

The following facts apply to Questions 16–5 and 16–6 below:

Daniel killed his wife, Iris, by striking her repeatedly in the head with a hammer. He confessed to the police that he did this because he believed that she was possessed by the Devil. Although Daniel claimed that he loved Iris very much, he nonetheless told the authorities that he believed that only by killing Iris could he free her soul from the clutches of evil.

At trial for the murder of Iris, Daniel's defense counsel, trying to establish an insanity defense, put a psychiatrist on the stand who testified that Daniel was in a psychotic state when he killed Iris and that "he was acting on the basis of delusional ideas with homicidal impulses. These impulses were related to a suppressed post-traumatic stress disorder resulting from Daniel's having been sexually abused as a preschool child. This precipitated a psychotic rage and led to him killing Iris with a hammer. A rational person would not have assumed that his wife was possessed by the Devil. Daniel was basically in an intense psychotic state, acting without thought. This was not a rational person, it was a psychotic rage. There was little thought given to his criminal actions."

In rebuttal, the prosecution presented testimony by a forensic psychiatrist who opined that "Daniel was psychosis-free when he killed Iris, but there are two other possible explanations for his behavior: paranoia and schizophrenia. I am confident that Daniel knew exactly what he was doing when he beat her to death. In my opinion, he would not have been able to do what he did to Iris if he had been psychotic."

Question 16–5: This jurisdiction uses the *M'Naghten* test to determine whether an accused defendant was insane at the time of the alleged criminal act. Given the competing expert testimony set out above, what are Daniel's chances of being found not guilty of murder by reason of insanity? Which of the following is most accurate:

(a) Daniel has a good insanity defense to murder.

(b) Daniel does not have a good insanity defense to murder because he knew the nature and quality of his act.

(c) If a jury finds that Daniel was aware that killing his wife (even if she was possessed by the Devil) was wrong, then he would not have a good insanity defense to murder.

(d) Answers (b) and (c) are true, and answer (a) is false.

Question 16–6: This jurisdiction uses the ALI Model Penal Code test to determine whether an accused defendant was insane at the time of the alleged criminal act. Given this competing expert testimony, what are Daniel's chances of being found not guilty of murder by reason of insanity in these circumstances? Which of the following is most accurate:

(a) If it can be established that Daniel knew the nature and quality of his act, he would have a good insanity defense to these charges.

(b) If it can be established that Daniel lacked substantial capacity either to appreciate the wrongfulness of his conduct or to conform his conduct to the requirements of the law, he would have a good insanity defense to these charges.

(c) If it can be established that Daniel acted in response to an irresistible impulse, he would have a good insanity defense to these charges.

(d) None of the above.

ENTRAPMENT

The following facts apply to Questions 16–7 and 16–8 below:

Bart asked Jamie if she could get him some marijuana. "Just a little bit for the weekend. An ounce would be great," he told her. Jamie responded that while she used marijuana "from time to time," she had no idea where to get any as she hadn't had the cash so she hadn't used any in two or three years.

"Look," Bart persisted, "I've got a deal for you. I've got a hot date this weekend. We're going to a concert in the park. I really, really need some marijuana and, you know, I'm new to town so I don't know where to get any or who to talk to. You've lived here a long time. So, look, if you can find some for me—just an ounce, just an ounce, that's all I need—I'll buy you an ounce for yourself, too. Okay? Isn't that a good deal?" Jamie said that she would try and find some marijuana for him, but she didn't know if she would succeed.

After checking with some friends, Jamie finally came up with a friend of a friend who said that she could get Jamie two ounces of "some awesome weed" for $450. Jamie then checked with Bart, who agreed on the price, and gave her the $450 in cash. Jamie then got back to the friend of a friend, arranged a meeting to give her the money, and received in return two ounces of (very low quality) marijuana.

Jamie kept one of the ounces of marijuana. And when she delivered the other ounce of marijuana to Bart, she was promptly arrested. As it turned out, Bart was an undercover agent, working for the Narcotics Division of the local Police Department.

Jamie has been charged with the crime of sale of marijuana. She plans to use entrapment as her sole defense at trial.

Question 16–7: This jurisdiction uses a subjective entrapment test. What chance of success does she have in using that defense in these circumstances? Which of the following is most accurate:

(a) Jamie does not have a good entrapment defense because she had acquired and used marijuana in the past and, hence, was predisposed to commit this crime.

(b) Jamie does not have a good entrapment defense because Bart's conduct was not sufficiently outrageous.

(c) Jamie has a good entrapment defense.

(d) Answers (a) and (b) are correct, and answer (c) is incorrect.

Question 16–8: This jurisdiction uses an objective entrapment test. What chance of success does she have in using that defense in these circumstances? Which of the following is most accurate:

(a) Jamie does not have a good entrapment defense because she had acquired and used marijuana in the past and, hence, was predisposed to commit this crime.

(b) Jamie does not have a tenable entrapment defense because that defense does not apply when an accused provides marijuana to an undercover agent.

(c) If the jury finds that Bart's conduct was sufficiently outrageous, Jamie has a good entrapment defense.

(d) None of the above.

The following facts apply to Questions 16–9 and 16–10 below:

Douglas, using the name "bigboy99" on an on-line website, chatted on and off for a period of four weeks with a thirteen year-old girl, who was using the on-line name of "blueyes2." After much discussion about the fact that blueyes2 was a virgin and wanted to have some sexual experience, Douglas persuaded her to meet and have sexual intercourse with him. He told her that he was twenty-one years old and single, when in fact he was thirty-seven years old and married. Douglas also assured blueyes2—in response to her oft-stated concern—that he would use a condom and that she would not get pregnant.

When Douglas arrived at the mall where he was to meet blueyes2, he discovered that he had been chatting not with a thirteen year-old girl, but rather with a forty-seven year old, 234–pound male detective, Clanton. Douglas was immediately arrested. The search of his person after his arrest revealed that he was carrying two condoms in his pants pocket. Douglas was subsequently charged with the crimes of unlawful contact or communication with a minor, corruption of minors, attempt to commit unlawful contact or communication with a minor, attempt to commit indecent assault, attempt to commit involuntary deviate sexual intercourse, attempt to commit statutory sexual assault, and attempt to commit corruption of minors.

Douglas plans to use an entrapment defense as one of his defenses at trial.

Question 16–9: This jurisdiction uses a subjective entrapment test. What chance of success does Douglas have in using an entrapment defense in these circumstances? Which of the following is most accurate:

(a) Douglas does not have a good entrapment defense because Clanton's conduct was not sufficiently outrageous.

(b) Douglas does not have a good entrapment defense because he was predisposed to have sexual intercourse with a minor.

(c) Douglas has a good entrapment defense.

(d) None of the above.

Question 16–10: This jurisdiction uses an objective entrapment test. What chance of success does Douglas have in using an entrapment defense in these circumstances? Which of the following is most accurate:

(a) Douglas does not have a good entrapment defense because he was predisposed to have sexual intercourse with a minor.

(b) Douglas does not have a good entrapment defense because Clanton's conduct was not sufficiently outrageous.

(c) Douglas has a good entrapment defense because Clanton's behavior in pretending to be a thirteen year old girl looking for sex was outrageous.

(d) Answers (a) and (b) are correct, and answer (c) is incorrect.

CHAPTER 17
MULTIPLE CHOICE MIXED-TOPICS EXAM #1

The following facts apply to Questions 17–1 through 17–11 below:

In the early morning hours of October 13, 2003, Christian and two sisters drove to the Savannah at City View apartments. Christian and the sisters went inside Megan's apartment on the second floor. Christian let the sisters leave with his car while he stayed in the apartment.

When the sisters did not come back right away, Christian became very upset. He raised his voice and used curse words at Megan who managed to calm him down by giving him some of her antidepressant drug, Prozac. Christian then called his friend, Eric, to come over and help him find his car. When Megan told him that the sisters had returned, Christian walked to the balcony and saw Christopher, Buddy, and Michael walking from the parking lot with the two women. Christian and Christopher started arguing about what the three men were doing with the sisters, but eventually everyone went inside the apartment.

Inside, someone pushed Christian down on the couch and when he stood up, Christopher hit him in the face. Eric then arrived and took Christian out of the apartment, followed by Christopher, Buddy, and Michael who began to taunt and threaten him.

As Christian and Eric walked toward the parking lot, Christian took a gun from Eric and walked back to the others who were standing at the bottom of the stairs. Witnesses testified that Christian came from around a corner and pointed his gun at Christopher's head. When Christopher realized Christian was pointing a gun at him, he attempted to slap his hand away, but the gun discharged and resulted in his being shot. After Christopher fell down, Christian kicked him several times and then fled the scene.

Christian controverted the eye-witness testimony. He testified that he held the gun up to scare everyone and that Christopher ran toward him with his "gun" pointed at Christian and hit Christian's gun and then it discharged. He further testified that he kicked Christopher because he thought he was still coming after him. Christian testified that he did not point the gun at Christopher's head as other witnesses had testified and that the gun discharged even though he did not have his finger over the trigger. Christopher died from the gunshot wound.

Question 17–1: You are an Assistant District Attorney in the jurisdiction where the events described above took place. The District Attorney has asked you what chances of success you have of convicting both Christian and Eric on conspiracy to commit murder charges. Which of the following is true:

(a) On these facts, there is not enough evidence for a judge or jury to reasonably conclude that both Christian and Eric conspired to commit murder.

(b) On these facts, there is enough evidence for a judge or jury to reasonably conclude that both Christian and Eric conspired to commit murder.

(c) On these facts, there is enough evidence for a judge or jury to reasonably conclude that Christian conspired to commit murder, but not that Eric conspired to commit murder.

(d) On these facts, there is enough evidence for a judge or jury to reasonably conclude that Eric conspired to commit murder, but not that Christian conspired to commit murder.

Question 17–2: You are an Assistant District Attorney in the jurisdiction where the events described above took place. The District Attorney has asked you what chances of success you have of convicting Christian on homicide charges. Which of the following is most accurate:

(a) Christian is not likely to be found guilty of homicide if the eyewitness' account is believed and the shot resulted from Christopher's slap of the gun, because Christian's act of shooting was not voluntary.

(b) Christian is not likely to be found guilty of first degree murder because Christian's acts were not the cause of Christopher's death.

(c) On these facts, in a prosecution of Christian for homicide, both the actus reus and causation elements have been satisfied.

(d) Both answers (a) and (b) are correct, and answer (c) is incorrect.

Question 17–3: You are an Assistant District Attorney in the jurisdiction where the events described above took place. The District Attorney has asked you what chances of success you have of convicting Christian on first-degree murder charges. Which of the following is most accurate:

(a) If the fact-finder concludes that the shot that was fired was due to Christopher's act of slapping the pistol, causing it to accidently discharge, then Christian did not commit first-degree murder.

(b) If the fact-finder concludes that the shot that was fired was not an accidental discharge, then Christian clearly satisfied the malice element of first-degree murder.

(c) A fact-finder could reasonably conclude, on these facts, that Christian satisfied the premeditation element of first-degree murder.

(d) All of the above.

(e) Answers (a) and (b) are true, but answers (c) and (d) are not true.

Question 17–4: You are an Assistant District Attorney in the jurisdiction where the events described above took place. The District Attorney has asked you what chances of success you have of convicting Christian on a first degree (premeditated) murder charge. Which of the following is most accurate:

(a) Assuming that Christian's act of shooting Christopher was voluntary, he nonetheless is not likely to be found guilty of first degree murder because he lacked malice.

(b) Christian is not likely to be found guilty of first degree murder because a reasonable jury could not conclude that he premeditated and deliberated this killing act.

(c) On these facts, in a prosecution of Christian for first degree murder, the mens rea element has likely been satisfied.

(d) None of the above.

Question 17–5: You are an Assistant District Attorney in the jurisdiction where the events described above took place. The District Attorney has asked you what chances of success you have of convicting Christian on homicide charges other than first-degree murder. Which of the following is true:

(a) A fact-finder could reasonably conclude, on these facts, that Christian was guilty of felony murder.

(b) A fact-finder could reasonably conclude, on these facts, that Christian was guilty of involuntary manslaughter.

(c) A fact-finder could reasonably conclude, on these facts, that Christian was guilty of voluntary manslaughter.

(d) All of the above.

Question 17–6: You are an Assistant District Attorney in the jurisdiction where the events described above took place. The District Attorney has asked you what chances of success you have of convicting Christian on a felony murder charge. Which of the following is true:

(a) Christian is likely to be found guilty of felony murder.

(b) Christian is not likely to be found guilty of felony murder because he did not commit a felony.

(c) Christian is not likely to be found guilty of felony murder because he did not commit an appropriate triggering felony.

(d) Christian is not likely to be found guilty of felony murder because he lacked malice.

Question 17–7: You are an Assistant District Attorney in the jurisdiction where the events described above took place. The District Attorney has asked you what chances of success you have of convicting Eric as an accomplice on homicide charges. Which of the following is most accurate:

(a) On these facts, there is not enough evidence for a judge or jury to reasonably conclude that Eric committed homicide as an accomplice due to the absence of mens rea.

(b) On these facts, there is not enough evidence for a judge or jury to reasonably conclude that Eric committed homicide as an accomplice due to the absence of a sufficient act of assistance.

(c) Both (a) and (b) are true.

(d) On these facts, there is enough evidence for a judge or jury to reasonably conclude that Eric committed homicide as an accomplice.

Question 17–8: You are an Assistant District Attorney in the jurisdiction where the events described above took place. The District Attorney has asked you what possible defenses Christian might have to potential charges which might be filed against him. Which of the following is true:

(a) A fact-finder could reasonably conclude, on these facts, that Christian was not guilty of any homicide offense due to his voluntary intoxication.

(b) A fact-finder could reasonably conclude, on these facts, that Christian was not guilty of any homicide offense due to self defense.

(c) A fact-finder could reasonably conclude, on these facts, that Christian was not guilty of any homicide offense due to an imperfect self defense.

(d) All of the above.

(e) None of the above.

Question 17–9: You are an Assistant District Attorney in the jurisdiction where the events described above took place. The District Attorney has asked you what chances of success Christian may have in using a provocation defense mitigating a murder charge to voluntary manslaughter. Which of the following is most accurate:

(a) Christian is likely to be able to establish provocation sufficient to mitigate to voluntary manslaughter.

(b) Christian is not likely to be able to establish provocation sufficient to mitigate to voluntary manslaughter because his response to Christopher's actions toward him was not sudden.

(c) Christian is not likely to be able to establish provocation sufficient to mitigate to voluntary manslaughter because Christopher's actions were not sufficiently serious to justify such a response.

(d) Answers (b) and (c) are correct, and answer (a) is incorrect.

Question 17–10: You are an Assistant District Attorney in the jurisdiction where the events described above took place. The District Attorney has asked you what chances of success Christian may have in using an intoxication or drugged condition defense if he is charged with a homicide offense. Which of the following is most accurate:

(a) Christian is likely to be able to successfully defend against a murder charge, but not a manslaughter charge, on grounds of intoxication or drugged condition.

(b) Christian is likely to be able to successfully defend against a manslaughter charge, but not a murder charge, on grounds of intoxication or drugged condition.

(c) Christian is likely to be able to successfully defend against a first degree murder charge, but not a second degree murder charge, on grounds of intoxication or drugged condition.

(d) None of the above.

Question 17–11: You are an Assistant District Attorney in the jurisdiction where the events described above took place. The District Attorney has asked you what chances of success Christian may have in a self defense or imperfect self defense defense if he is charged with a homicide offense. Which of the following is most accurate:

(a) Christian is likely to be able to successfully defend against a homicide charge on grounds of self defense.

(b) Christian is likely to be able to successfully defend against a homicide charge on grounds of imperfect self defense.

(c) Christian is not likely to be able to successfully defend against a homicide charge on grounds of self defense or imperfect self defense.

(d) Christian is not likely to be able to successfully defend against a homicide charge on grounds of self defense, but is likely to be able to mitigate a murder charge to voluntary manslaughter on grounds of an imperfect self defense.

The following facts apply to Questions 17–12 through 17–16 below:

On the evening of October 2, 1998, Andrew and Jason met at a Joplin restaurant. After eating dinner and drinking beer, they decided to go to a downtown nightclub. Andrew and Jason got into Andrew's 1996 Ford F–150 pickup. En route, they stopped at a convenience store. Andrew remained in the vehicle while Jason entered the store and purchased a 40–ounce bottle of beer and a can of chewing tobacco. While in line, Jason stood behind Tammy.

Tammy was the girlfriend of Gary, who was also parked outside the store, sitting in his car, smoking marijuana. When Jason exited the store, Tammy pointed him out to Gary. (Tammy later testified that she was upset and told Gary—falsely—that Jason made "a pass" at her.) Jason and Andrew then left the store in the pickup. Gary and Tammy were in Gary's car, driving close behind.

When Andrew stopped at a stoplight, Gary pulled alongside in the right lane. Gary began to "exchange words" with Jason, accusing him of "messing with my woman." Gary got out of his car, reached through the passenger window of the pickup, and stabbed Jason in the neck, nearly severing his carotid artery and completely severing his jugular vein. Gary immediately returned to his car and fled the jurisdiction.

The stab wound—4.5 to 6 inches deep—bled profusely. Bystanders attempted to slow the bleeding with clothing and towels. Paramedics arrived to find Jason unresponsive, from massive blood loss. Blood drained into Jason's airway, depriving him of oxygen. Jason died three months later. The cause of death was said to be from an infection in the area of the stab wound. The infection was a staph infection he acquired while hospitalized.

Question 17–12: You are an Assistant District Attorney. The District Attorney has asked you for your opinion whether Gary was the cause of Jason's death for purposes of charging him with a homicide offense. Which of the following is most accurate:

(a) Gary was not the "but for" cause of Jason's death; the staph infection was the "but for" cause.

(b) It was reasonably foreseeable that Jason would die as a result of Gary's actions, and his death was not too remote a consequence of Gary's actions to impose criminal culpability.

(c) The hospital's negligent medical treatment, resulting in Jason's death from a staph infection, "broke the causal chain" with respect to Gary's prior actions.

(d) All of the above.

Question 17–13: You are an Assistant District Attorney. The District Attorney has asked you for your opinion whether, aside from any consideration of the causation issue, Gary can be successfully prosecuted for murder on these facts. Which of the following is most accurate:

(a) Gary is guilty of first-degree murder.

(b) Gary is guilty of felony murder.

(c) Gary is guilty of murder.

(d) All of the above.

(e) Gary is not guilty of murder.

Question 17–14: You are an Assistant District Attorney. The District Attorney has asked you for your opinion whether, aside from any consideration of the causation issue, Gary can be successfully prosecuted for manslaughter on these facts. Which of the following is most accurate:

(a) A fact-finder could reasonably conclude, on these facts, that Gary was guilty of involuntary manslaughter.

(b) A fact-finder could reasonably conclude, on these facts, that Gary was not guilty of involuntary manslaughter.

(c) A fact-finder could reasonably conclude, on these facts, that Gary was guilty of voluntary manslaughter.

(d) Answers (a) and (c) are correct, but answer (b) is incorrect.

Question 17–15: You are an Assistant District Attorney. The District Attorney has asked you for your opinion whether Gary could successfully defend himself against homicide charges on these facts by claiming that he was so high when he killed Jason that he did not possess the requisite mens rea for the crime. Which of the following is true:

(a) This would be a good defense for Gary against any homicide charge.

(b) This would not be a good defense for Gary against any homicide charge.

(c) This would be a good defense for Gary against a charge of first-degree murder, but not against a charge of voluntary manslaughter.

(d) This would be a good defense for Gary against a charge of first-degree murder, but not against a charge of involuntary manslaughter.

Question 17–16: You are an Assistant District Attorney. The District Attorney has asked you for your opinion whether, aside from any consideration of the causation issue, Tammy can be successfully prosecuted as Gary's accomplice for a homicide offense arising out of these facts. Which of the following is most accurate:

(a) Tammy could be found guilty of homicide as Gary's accomplice.

(b) It is unlikely that Tammy could be found guilty of homicide as Gary's accomplice because she lacked the requisite mens rea.

(c) It is unlikely that Tammy could be found guilty of homicide as Gary's accomplice because she lacked the requisite actus reus.

(d) Both (b) and (c) are correct, and (a) is incorrect.

Question 17–17: Teisha surreptitiously put a few drops of arsenic in her boyfriend, Bob Lee's, coffee every morning for months. After weeks of declining health, including diarrhea, vomiting, blood in his urine, cramping muscles, hair loss, stomach pain, and convulsions, Bob Lee subsequently died of arsenic poisoning. Teisha was then charged with first degree murder. In the jurisdiction where this took place, first degree murder has a mens rea element of "purposeful" conduct, i.e. to be guilty of first degree murder, the prosecution must prove, *inter alia*, that the accused had the "conscious object to cause" the resulting death of the victim.

Teisha contends that she is not guilty of first degree murder because she mistakenly thought that the substance she was putting into Bob Lee's coffee was fish oil, and she was actually doing that with the intention of improving his health, not killing him. Assuming that Teisha's contention is true, which of the following is most accurate:

(a) Teisha is not guilty of first degree murder because she did not consciously intend to kill Bob Lee if her mistaken belief that the substance she was putting into his coffee was not poisonous was reasonable.

(b) Teisha is not guilty of first degree murder because involuntary manslaughter is the more appropriate homicide charge where the accused acted criminally negligently not purposefully.

(c) Teisha is guilty of first degree murder because she should have realized that she was poisoning Bob Lee as she watched his health decline over a period of weeks.

(d) None of the above.

The following facts apply to Questions 17–18 and 17–19 below:

As part of her new landscaping, Rita had a wood-burning fire pit installed at the back of her property, close to the wooden fence that separates her lot from a neighbor. On a chilly evening in early October, she left the fire unattended and went into the house to answer the telephone. While she was inside, a strong wind came up and suddenly sparks from the fire pit blew onto the wooden fence. The fence caught fire, and the fire quickly spread to Rita's neighbor's house, which nearly burned to the ground before the fire department got the blaze under control. Rita has been charged with arson, which requires, in this jurisdiction, a showing of intent or purpose to commit the offense.

Question 17–18: Which of the following best describes what the prosecutor must prove to convict Rita of this offense?

(a) Rita should have known that leaving the fire unattended could result in this damage.

(b) Rita knew that leaving the fire unattended could result in this damage, but she did it anyway.

(c) A reasonable person would have known not to leave the fire unattended.

(d) When she left the fire unattended, Rita consciously meant to burn her neighbor's house down.

Question 17–19: At a bench trial, the trial judge ruled that Rita was not aware of the risk that criminal conduct would result from her act of leaving the fire unattended. Indeed, the judge concluded, Rita did not even think about that risk but, he added, she should have been aware that a risk that the fire would spread to an adjoining property existed. From this analysis, what mens rea did the judge conclude that Rita showed?

(a) Rita acted intentionally or purposefully.

(b) Rita acted knowingly.

(c) Rita acted recklessly.

(d) Rita acted criminally negligently.

Question 17–20: Sarah was looking out her bedroom window late one night when she saw a person dressed in dark clothing climbing over her back garden wall and starting to head toward her back kitchen door. He or she had some sort of dark object in his hand. Sarah immediately grabbed one of her semi-automatic rifles and ran downstairs to the kitchen, without turning on any lights. When she saw through the kitchen door window that the apparent intruder was about two feet from the door, she fired off three shots in rapid succession right through the door.

The shots killed Paul, the individual standing outside the door, immediately. It was never determined why Paul was out there, i.e. whether he was really intending to commit a crime or not. The object in his hand was a travel mug, which was half full of hot coffee.

Sarah has been charged with second degree murder. She argues that she had every right to shoot Paul as she reasonably believed he was about to commit a crime in her home. Which of the following is most accurate:

(a) Sarah has a good defense of habitation defense in these circumstances.

(b) Sarah does not have a good defense of habitation defense in these circumstances because that defense only permits the actor to use unlawful not deadly force.

(c) Sarah does not have a good defense of habitation defense in these circumstances because that defense only applies when the actor's actions were necessary to prevent or terminate an unlawful intrusion into the home.

(d) None of the above.

Question 17–21: Alicia asked her friend, Yasir, to help her steal an expensive, black leather bomber jacket that she had seen and coveted at Bloomingdale's, a retail store. Yasir feigned agreement, demanding that Alicia have sexual intercourse with him in exchange for his help. She agreed, and she did have sex with Yasir.

But Yasir never truly planned to help Alicia steal the jacket. Instead, he reported Alicia's planned theft to the police, and when he and Alicia emerged from Bloomingdale's with Alicia in possession of the leather jacket she had stolen while Yasir pretended to be on the lookout for store security, Alicia was promptly arrested.

Alicia has now been charged with conspiring to commit retail theft with Yasir. Which of the following is most accurate:

(a) In a unilateral conspiracy jurisdiction, Alicia is guilty of the crime of conspiracy to commit retail theft.

(b) In a bilateral conspiracy jurisdiction, Alicia is guilty of the crime of conspiracy to commit retail theft.

(c) Alicia would be found guilty of the crime of conspiracy to commit retail theft in a unilateral or a bilateral conspiracy jurisdiction.

(d) Alicia would not be found guilty of the crime of conspiracy to commit retail theft in a unilateral or a bilateral conspiracy jurisdiction.

Question 17–22: While Mike was sitting at a table, reading a book in the Public Library, his ex-girlfriend, April, quietly snuck up behind him. When she was only eight inches behind him, she then screamed out at the top of her lungs: "This man broke my heart! He could care less about anyone! He's a sleazebag and despicable and I hate him!"

Mike was so startled and shocked that he involuntarily threw his book up into the air and slid off his chair to the floor. Then he got up and ran toward the exit, with April following right after him, yelling more of the same sort of thing at the top of her lungs, until she was seized by the security guard at the library's front door.

April has been charged in state court with battery on Mike. All of these events took place in a jurisdiction which continues to use the common law definition of battery in its Crimes Code. Which of the following is most accurate:

(a) April is guilty of battery.

(b) April is not guilty of battery because she did not touch Mike.

(c) April is not guilty of battery because she did not injure Mike.

(d) Answers (b) and (c) are correct, and answer (a) is incorrect.

Question 17–23: Felicia asked Rhoda if she could borrow one of Rhoda's favorite dresses to wear to her cousin's wedding in Baltimore. Rhoda was, frankly, reluctant to lend it to Felicia because she really loved that dress, but—out of friendship—she agreed. "But, hey," she told Felicia, "really, really be careful. I love that dress. Don't stain it or snag it or anything. And, you know, get it right back to me. I mean I really love that dress." Felicia agreed to be careful.

As luck would have it, however, the dress was badly stained at the wedding (chocolate sauce on the bodice), and Felicia took it straight to the cleaners when she got back in town. But the cleaners could not get the stains out. Felicia, afraid to show Rhoda her ruined dress, she just hung it in her own closet and told her instead that the cleaners lost the dress. She also immediately and tearfully offered to pay Rhoda whatever the dress had cost so that Rhoda could buy a new one.

But Rhoda was incensed at Felicia's carelessness. Instead of buying a new dress with money from Felicia, she instead filed a criminal complaint against her.

On these facts, is Felicia guilty of a common law or traditional theft crime? Which of the following is true:

(a) Felicia is not guilty of any common law or traditional theft crime.

(b) Felicia is guilty of false pretenses, but is not guilty of embezzlement.

(c) Felicia is guilty of larceny and false pretenses, but is not guilty of larceny by trick or embezzlement.

(d) Felicia is guilty of larceny, but is not guilty of larceny by trick.

Question 17–24: Hannah and Alfie, her date, left a fancy restaurant late one evening after being together for a long, romantic dinner. Hannah came out the restaurant door about 30 yards behind Alfie, because she had stopped for a minute to talk to the restaurant owner and compliment him on the meal and the service. As Hannah emerged, she could see that Alfie, 30 yards ahead, had his hands up in the air and appeared to be being threatened by someone (who turned out to be Dylan) who was holding a pistol. Hannah immediately reached into her purse and pulled out her pistol and shot Dylan, wounding her.

Hannah has been charged with aggravated assault on Dylan. Even though Dylan was in fact attempting to hold up Alfie when Hannah shot her, the prosecution has taken the position that Hannah had no right to shoot Dylan since Hannah could have safely retreated from this situation without harm to herself. The jurisdiction in which this episode occurred has a "retreat requirement" that is identical to that found in the Model Penal Code as part of its self-defense law. Which of the following is most accurate:

(a) Hannah had an obligation to retreat instead of shooting Dylan because she could have retreated in complete safety.

(b) Hannah had no obligation to retreat before shooting Dylan because Dylan was threatening Alfie, not her.

(c) Hannah had an obligation to retreat before shooting Dylan but only if she and Alfie could both do so safely.

(d) None of the above.

Question 17–25: Chris shot and killed, Geri, the person who delivered his morning newspaper to his front porch every day. Chris was a recluse who rarely left his home, and voices in his head told him that Geri was really Satan, disguised as a newspaper delivery person. In order to save the world from Satan's clutches, Chris waited at the front door for Geri to arrive with the morning paper and he simply shot her through the head with a single bullet as she walked up the front path to his home.

Chris has been charged with the premeditated murder of Geri. His defense counsel has indicated that he will assert an insanity defense. The jurisdiction where this occurred uses the *M'Naghten* test to determine whether an accused defendant was insane at the time of an alleged criminal act. Which of the following is most accurate:

(a) Chris does not have a good insanity defense to murder because he knew the nature and quality of his act.

(b) If a jury finds that Chris was aware that killing Geri (even if she was, in fact, Satan in disguise) was wrong, then he would not have a good insanity defense to murder.

(c) Chris has a good insanity defense to murder.

(d) Answers (a) and (b) are true, and answer (c) is false.

CHAPTER 18
MULTIPLE CHOICE MIXED-TOPICS EXAM #2

The following facts apply to Questions 18–1 through 18–4 below:

Kenyatta testified that he met with Quentin (a/k/a "Heat") to discuss the sale of one and one-quarter kilograms of cocaine that he (Kenyatta) had in his possession. Quentin told Kenyatta that he knew someone who would buy the cocaine. Kenyatta responded that he didn't want the buyer to know that he was selling drugs, and that Quentin would have to "serve" him. That evening, Kenyatta drove a Lexus sports utility vehicle (SUV) to the home of Quentin's girlfriend. Quentin then joined him in the SUV, and they set out to locate the buyer.

Following Quentin's directions, Kenyatta drove to the Concordia Apartments on Westwood Drive. Quentin exited the vehicle, carrying the cocaine in a plastic garbage bag. Quentin walked a short distance and met with a man Kenyatta later identified as Damaris. Damaris and Quentin walked toward one of the apartment buildings and disappeared from view, while Kenyatta waited in the SUV.

When Quentin failed to return after nearly half an hour, Kenyatta placed a call to his cellular telephone. He asked Quentin why the transaction was taking so long. Quentin told Kenyatta that the buyer wanted to negotiate some changes in the original agreement. Kenyatta then exited the SUV and Damaris approached him and told him that he would take him to Quentin.

Kenyatta and Damaris walked along the outside of one of the nearby apartment buildings. At this time, Kenyatta did not see Quentin. But Kenyatta observed that Damaris flinched nervously each time they passed a doorway. Immediately after they had passed the fourth doorway, Quentin burst out of it from where he was hiding and yelled "I just can't do it. Run, Kenyatta! Get the f* * * outta here!" Then Quentin ran off.

Alarmed, Kenyatta turned to Damaris and said, "wait a minute. What's going on? I'm going to waste you right now, you're screwing with me." Kenyatta then shoved Damaris against the apartment building wall. But Damaris pulled a gun out of the waistband of his pants, pointed it at Kenyatta, and said, "Give it up, man. Give me all of your cash." Kenyatta attempted to grab for the gun, but Damaris fired at him first. A bullet went through Kenyatta's shoulder and hit his face, and he fell to the ground. Damaris fled the scene on foot.

A nearby resident called the police. Kenyatta told an officer at the scene that Heat had set him up, and that Heat's real first name was Quentin. Kenyatta was transported to the hospital, where his injuries were treated.

Question 18–1: You are an Assistant Public Defender, defending Quentin and Damaris who have both been charged with conspiracy to rob Kenyatta. Which of the following is true:

(a) Quentin has a tenable abandonment defense to the charge of conspiracy to rob Kenyatta.

(b) Quentin does not have a tenable abandonment defense to the charge of conspiracy to rob Kenyatta.

(c) Quentin has a tenable abandonment defense to the charge of conspiracy to rob Kenyatta in a unilateral jurisdiction, but not in a bilateral jurisdiction.

(d) Quentin has a tenable abandonment defense to the charge of conspiracy to rob Kenyatta in a bilateral jurisdiction, but not in a unilateral jurisdiction.

Question 18–2: You are an Assistant Public Defender, defending Quentin and Damaris who have both been charged with conspiracy to rob Kenyatta. Which of the following is true:

(a) If Quentin's abandonment defense fails, Quentin and Damaris are both guilty of conspiracy to rob Kenyatta.

(b) If Quentin's abandonment defense fails, Quentin and Damaris are both guilty of conspiracy to rob Kenyatta in a bilateral conspiracy jurisdiction, but not in a unilateral conspiracy jurisdiction.

(c) If Quentin's abandonment defense succeeds, Damaris could not be found guilty of conspiracy to rob Kenyatta whether or not this is a unilateral or bilateral conspiracy jurisdiction.

(d) None of the above.

Question 18–3: You are an Assistant Public Defender, defending Damaris who has been charged with the attempted murder of Kenyatta. Which of the following is most accurate:

(a) Damaris is not likely to be found guilty of attempted murder as he can raise a good defense of self defense because Kenyatta was the initial aggressor.

(b) Damaris is not likely to be found guilty of attempted murder as he can raise a good defense of self defense because he only wounded Kenyatta.

(c) Damaris will likely be found guilty of attempted murder.

(d) Both answers (a) and (b) are correct, and answer (c) is incorrect.

Question 18–4: You are an Assistant Public Defender, defending Quentin who has been charged as Damaris' accomplice with the attempted murder of Kenyatta. Which of the following is most accurate:

(a) If Quentin and Damaris are not found guilty of conspiring together to rob Kenyatta, Quentin is not likely to be found guilty of attempted murder as he can raise a good defense of abandonment.

(b) Whether or not Quentin and Damaris are found guilty of conspiring together to rob Kenyatta, Quentin is not likely to be found guilty of attempted murder as he can raise a good defense of self defense because Damaris only wounded Kenyatta.

(c) If Quentin and Damaris are found guilty of conspiring together to rob Kenyatta, Quentin may be found guilty of attempted murder since it was reasonably foreseeable that a shooting might occur in the course of the robbery.

(d) Both answers (a) and (c) are correct, and answer (b) is incorrect.

The following facts apply to Questions 18–5 through 18–9 below:

Elizabeth was walking in County Park one evening when she noticed that she was being followed by a stranger, Mark, who was dressed only in a dirty black raincoat. Elizabeth began to walk faster, tripping into tree branches as she picked up her pace. In fact, Mark was a local resident who intended Elizabeth no harm. He was simply out for an evening's walk in the park after having taken a shower at home.

While walking, Mark saw something drop from Elizabeth's purse onto the ground and he began to run after her to tell her. When Elizabeth heard Mark start running behind her, however, she became nervous as to his intentions, and began to run away from him. As it had rained earlier in the day, the ground was slippery and Elizabeth slipped to the ground while running. Mark, running up behind her, slipped as well and fell on top of her. As he fell, his raincoat opened, revealing that he was naked underneath.

Finding a strange, nearly-naked man on top of her, Elizabeth began screaming: "Help! Help!" Hearing that, Mark jumped off of her and looked around to see what and where the emergency was. When he turned his back to Elizabeth, she struck him over the head with a large tree branch she picked up off of the ground.

Dazed and bleeding from a scalp laceration, Mark staggered further into the park where he came across Kerry, who was skating along on roller blades. Because his vision was blurred from his injuries, Mark thought that Kerry was actually Elizabeth and he screamed at her: "Why did you hit me! I was just trying to help you! I'll teach you a lesson you'll never forget!"

Mark then grabbed a large rock from the ground and threw it at Kerry's head. The rock struck Kerry right between the eyes, knocking her unconscious and sending her careening into John, another roller blader, who in turn rolled right over Robert, who was laying on the ground, fast asleep. Robert suffered major cranial injuries from the roller blade injuries (John rolled right over his head) and shortly thereafter, he died.

Question 18–5: You are an Assistant Public Defender in the jurisdiction where all of these events occurred. Mark has been charged with the crime of assault of Elizabeth. The Chief Public Defender has asked you to defend Mark against this charge. Which of the following is most accurate:

(a) Mark is guilty of the assault of Elizabeth as Elizabeth was honestly and reasonably in fear of being touched against her will.

(b) Mark is not guilty of the assault of Elizabeth because he did not act intentionally.

(c) Mark is not guilty of the assault of Elizabeth because his act of touching Elizabeth was involuntary.

(d) Both answers (b) and (c) are correct, and answer (a) is incorrect.

Question 18–6: You are an Assistant Public Defender in the jurisdiction where all of these events occurred. Mark has been charged with the crime of attempted rape of Elizabeth. The Chief Public Defender has asked you to defend Mark against this charge. Which of the following is most accurate:

(a) Mark is guilty of the attempted rape of Elizabeth as Elizabeth was honestly and reasonably in fear of being sexually assaulted.

(b) Mark is not guilty of the attempted rape of Elizabeth because he did not intend to have sexual contact with Elizabeth.

(c) Mark is not guilty of the attempted rape of Elizabeth because he did not actually have sexual contact with Elizabeth, including penetration.

(d) None of the above.

Question 18–7: You are an Assistant Public Defender in the jurisdiction where all of these events occurred. Mark has been charged with the crime of attempted murder of Kerry. The Chief Public Defender has asked you to defend Mark against this charge. Which of the following is most accurate:

(a) Mark is guilty of the attempted murder of Kerry.

(b) Mark is not guilty of the attempted murder of Kerry because he did not intend to kill her.

(c) Mark is not guilty of the attempted murder of Kerry because he did not commit an actual killing act.

(d) Answers (b) and (c) are correct, and answer (a) is incorrect.

Question 18–8: You are an Assistant Public Defender in the jurisdiction where all of these events occurred. Mark has been charged with the crime of involuntary manslaughter of Robert. The Chief Public Defender has asked you to defend Mark against this charge. Which of the following is most accurate:

(a) If the mens rea element for involuntary manslaughter in this jurisdiction is criminal negligence, the prosecution can clearly establish that element.

(b) If the mens rea element for involuntary manslaughter in this jurisdiction is recklessness, the prosecution can clearly establish that element.

(c) Whether the mens rea element for involuntary manslaughter in this jurisdiction is criminal negligence or recklessness, the prosecution can clearly establish that element.

(d) None of the above.

Question 18–9: You are an Assistant Public Defender in the jurisdiction where all of these events occurred. Mark has been charged with the crime of involuntary manslaughter of Robert. The Chief Public Defender has asked you to defend Mark against this charge. Which of the following is most accurate:

(a) Mark was clearly the "but for" cause of Robert's death.

(b) A reasonable jury could conclude that Robert's death in these circumstances was too remote or accidental in relation to Mark's acts to find causation to exist.

(c) Mark can make a good lack-of-causation defense to defend against these charges.

(d) All of the above.

The following facts apply to Questions 18–10 through 18–15 below:

Zeke, Mindy, and Lola became fast "friends" with one another on a social networking site on line. None of the three of them had ever met in person. But they chatted with one another incessantly on line.

Zeke claimed in his posts that he was a twenty year-old college student living on campus. In fact, he was twenty-six years old, unemployed, and living with his parents. Mindy claimed in her posts that she was a nineteen year-old college student living at home with her parents. Mindy was, in fact, living with her parents, but she was actually a fifteen year-old high school student. Lola claimed in her posts that she was a fifteen year old high school student living with her parents. In fact, almost none of this was true. Lola was actually a male rather than a female. His name was Ralph, not Lola. He was forty-two, not fifteen. And he was a police officer, working undercover to catch sexual predators, not a high school student. It was true, however, that he lived with one of his parents, his widowed mother.

Zeke and Mindy's on-line friendship blossomed to the point that they decided to meet one another in person at a local coffee shop. They discovered when they met that they really liked one another quite a lot, although neither one of them ever revealed to the other one his or her true age or circumstances. They both stuck to the false stories that they told each other in their posts. It was easy for each of them to believe the age the other one was claiming to be. Mindy was very physically mature and looked like she might be nineteen. And Zeke was youthful in appearance and looked like he might be only twenty.

After their first meeting, Zeke and Mindy met repeatedly and their friendship blossomed into a romantic and sexual relationship. They met a number of times at the apartment of a friend of Zeke's and each time they met, they engaged in sexual intercourse.

Zeke and Mindy also talked about their relationship on line, not only between themselves, but with their on-line friend, Lola. Lola posted many times how jealous she was that her two friends were sexually involved with one another, and how she felt left out. She insisted repeatedly that Zeke and Mindy include her in their sexual relationship. But Zeke and Mindy resisted that invitation because (they thought) she was only fifteen years old and—as she had told them in a number of her posts—a virgin. "Hey, chill, Lola. Just wait a year," Zeke suggested, "then we can party. We got time." But Lola was persistent in her requests to both of them that they all get together "for a threesome."

Eventually, her persistence paid off. Zeke and Mindy finally agreed to meet Lola at the apartment where the two of them had been meeting so that they could all engage in sexual relations together. But when Zeke and Mindy showed up at the apartment, ready to party (Zeke brought a dozen condoms with him), fifteen year-old Lola—who was really forty-two year-old Ralph—was waiting for them, and Ralph/Lola arrested them both.

Question 18–10: Zeke has been charged with a number of counts of statutory rape as a result of his sexual relationship with Mindy. The age of consent in this jurisdiction is sixteen years old. Which of the following is true:

(a) Zeke is not guilty of statutory rape because he honestly and reasonably believed that Mindy was 19.

(b) Zeke is not guilty of statutory rape because all of the acts of sexual intercourse were consensual.

(c) In the absence of an affirmative defense, Zeke is guilty of statutory rape.

(d) Zeke is not guilty of statutory rape because the difference between his age and Mindy's age is too small to find him culpable.

Question 18–11: Zeke has been charged with the attempted statutory rape of a fifteen year old girl, Lola. The age of consent in this jurisdiction is sixteen years old. This jurisdiction also uses the Model Penal Code test for the actus reus element of attempt. Without considering the possible defense of impossibility (*see* Question 18–13), which of the following is most accurate:

(a) Zeke is likely to be found guilty of attempted statutory rape.

(b) Zeke is not guilty of attempted statutory rape because there is no evidence that he actually intended to have sexual intercourse with a fifteen year old.

(c) Zeke is not guilty of attempted statutory rape because he did not take a substantial step toward commission of the crime of statutory rape.

(d) Answers (b) and (c) are both correct, and answer (a) is incorrect.

Question 18–12: Mindy has been charged with the attempted statutory rape of a fifteen year old girl, Lola. The age of consent in this jurisdiction is sixteen years old. This jurisdiction also uses the Model Penal Code test for the actus reus element of attempt. And the statutory rape statute in this jurisdiction does *not* excuse actors who are close in age to the victim.

Without considering the possible defense of impossibility (*see* Question 18–13), which of the following is true:

(a) Mindy is likely to be found guilty of attempted statutory rape.

(b) Mindy is not guilty of attempted statutory rape because she and the supposed victim were both females.

(c) Mindy is not guilty of attempted statutory rape because she did not take a substantial step toward commission of the crime of statutory rape.

(d) Mindy is not guilty of attempted statutory rape because she did not intend to have sexual intercourse with Lola or to assist Zeke in having sex with Lola.

Question 18–13: Zeke has been charged with the attempted statutory rape of a fifteen year old girl, Lola. He plans to defend against these charges using the defense of impossibility. This jurisdiction follows the Model Penal Code approach to the defense of impossibility. Which of the following is most accurate:

(a) This is not a good defense in these circumstances because this is a case involving factual impossibility rather than legal impossibility.

(b) This is not a good defense because Zeke intended to have sex with a fifteen year-old.

(c) This is a good defense because Zeke did not commit a crime since Lola. the supposed fifteen year-old girl, did not exist.

(d) Answers (a) and (b) are correct, but answer (c) is incorrect.

Question 18–14: Zeke and Mindy have been charged with the attempted statutory rape of a fifteen year old girl, Lola. They plan to defend against these charges using the defense of entrapment. This jurisdiction uses a subjective entrapment test. What chance of success do they have in using that defense in these circumstances? Which of the following is most accurate:

(a) Zeke and Mindy do not have a good entrapment defense because they simply responded to Lola's/Ralph's offer to commit this crime.

(b) Zeke and Mindy do not have a good entrapment defense because Ralph's conduct was not sufficiently outrageous.

(c) Zeke and Mindy have a good entrapment defense.

(d) Answers (a) and (b) are correct, and answer (c) is incorrect.

Question 18–15: Zeke and Mindy have been charged with the attempted statutory rape of a fifteen year old girl, Lola. They plan to defend against these charges using the defense of entrapment. This jurisdiction uses an objective entrapment test. What chance of success do they have in using that defense in these circumstances? Which of the following is most accurate:

(a) Zeke and Mindy do not have a good entrapment defense because they simply responded to Lola's/Ralph's offer to commit this crime.

(b) Zeke and Mindy do not have a tenable entrapment defense because that defense does not apply when an accused is responding to an on-line solicitation.

(c) If the jury finds that Zeke's and Mindy's conduct was sufficiently outrageous, they have a good entrapment defense.

(d) Answers (a) and (c) are correct, but answer (b) is incorrect.

Question 18–16: Olander stopped Yasmin as she was walking down the street late one night and, holding a knife on her, demanded that she give him her purse. Yasmin complied immediately, and Olander ran away with it. Unfortunately for him, a police officer observed all of the foregoing and Olander was immediately arrested.

Olander has now been charged with armed robbery and battery. All of these events took place in a jurisdiction which continues to use the common law definition of battery in its Crimes Code. Which of the following is most accurate:

(a) Olander is guilty of battery.

(b) Olander is not guilty of battery because he did not injure Yasmin.

(c) Olander is not guilty of battery because he did not touch Yasmin.

(d) Answers (b) and (c) are correct, and answer (a) is incorrect.

Question 18–17: The Johnsons, husband and wife, are charged with providing alcohol to minors in violation of a criminal statute. The Johnsons purchased beer for—and were present at—a party given by their son, and many of the guests were under the legal drinking age of 21. The statute does not include a required mental state, but courts in their jurisdiction have ruled that the legislative intent was to hold those who provide minors with alcohol strictly liable. Which of the following is most accurate:

(a) The Johnsons did not violate the statute if they can show that they did not know any of the party guests were under the legal drinking age.

(b) The Johnsons could not violate the statute because the language of the statute does not include a required mental state.

(c) The Johnsons violated the statute because they should have known that many of their son's guests were below the legal drinking age, but they served them alcohol anyway.

(d) None of the above.

Question 18–18: In most jurisdictions, voluntary intoxication or drugged condition can be a defense to some criminal charges under certain, limited circumstances. Which of the following is most accurate with respect to the nature of those circumstances:

(a) Intoxication or being in a drugged condition is a defense to any crime if but only if the accused did not intend to commit the criminal act.

(b) Intoxication or being in a drugged condition is a defense to a general intent crime, but it is not a defense to a crime that requires proof of specific intent.

(c) Intoxication or being in a drugged condition is a defense to strict liability crimes.

(d) Intoxication or being in a drugged condition may be shown by trace amounts of drugs or alcohol in the individual's bloodstream.

(e) Answers (b) and (d) are correct, but answers (a) and (c) are incorrect.

Question 18–19: Lucinda asked her boyfriend, Eldon, to help her to kill her parents. "They are such pains, man," she told him, "they are always on my case about something. I bet they have lots of insurance or something. We could just run away and do whatever we wanted." Eldon, nodded and responded: "Yeah. Whatever. You do whatever I want, baby, and I'll do whatever you want." "It's a deal," said Lucinda. But, that was as far as it went. Neither Lucinda nor Eldon brought up the subject again.

Is Lucinda guilty of the crime of soliciting Eldon to murder her parents? Which of the following is most accurate:

(a) Yes, Lucinda is guilty of the crime of soliciting Eldon to murder her parents.

(b) No, Lucinda is not guilty of the crime of soliciting Eldon to murder her parents because there is not enough evidence that she was serious.

(c) No, Lucinda is not guilty of the crime of soliciting Eldon to murder her parents because neither of them took a step toward actually committing this crime.

(d) Answers (b) and (c) are correct, and answer (a) is incorrect.

Question 18–20: Denzel kidnaped Allison's four-year old daughter, Cindy, and told Allison that he would harm her if Allison did not provide him with 25 grams of crack cocaine by 4:00 p.m. that afternoon. Terrified for her daughter's safety, Allison immediately ran to the bank and withdrew her savings and then found a drug dealer who would sell her the cocaine. Driving to Denzel's home to give him the cocaine, Allison was stopped by the police for speeding, and a subsequent search of her purse unearthed the crack cocaine.

Allison has been charged with the crime of the possession of narcotics. Which of the following is most accurate:

(a) Allison does not have a good duress defense to this charge because the threat made to her was one that a reasonable person would have and should have resisted.

(b) Allison does not have a good duress defense to this charge because she did not reasonably believed that Denzel would subject Cindy to death or serious injury imminently if she did not obtain the narcotics.

(c) Allison has a good duress defense to this charge.

(d) Answers (a) and (b) are correct, and answer (c) is incorrect.

Question 18–21: Gizem walked into a coffee shop, and seeing Patricia sitting there with a cup of coffee, immediately marched over and shoved Patricia to the floor. "Where in the hell do you get off sleeping with MY boyfriend," she thundered. Patricia jumped right up off the floor, her lip swollen and bleeding. She then grabbed into her purse and pulled out a pocket knife, and stabbed Gizem in the cheek with it, cutting her cheek wide open with a gaping wound.

Patricia has been charged with aggravated assault as a result of her stabbing of Gizem. She argues in her defense that she was justified in stabbing Gizem because she was acting in self defense in response to being physically accosted by Gizem.

Which of the following is most accurate:

(a) Patricia has a good self defense argument.

(b) Patricia does not have a good self defense argument because she was the aggressor in this situation.

(c) Patricia does not have a good self defense argument because Gizem did not threaten her with deadly force.

(d) None of the above.

Question 18–22: The Legislature in the state in which Rudolfo lives, recently amended its Crimes Code, criminalizing the knowing possession of "exotic animals." "Exotic animals" are defined as "rare or unusual animal pets," specifically including, *inter alia*, "lions, tigers, and bears." Prior to this amendment, possession of exotic animals was not a crime in this jurisdiction.

Rudolfo keeps a 300–pound, pet bear in his backyard. He says, "hey, man, that bear—Herman—is just like one of the family." In fact, every adult member of Rudolfo's family is over 300 pounds and hairy. Nonetheless, family or not, Rudolfo has been arrested and charged with possession of an exotic animal under the new statute. Rudolfo claims that he did not know about the new law and honestly believed that it was not against the law to possess a bear in this jurisdiction. Is that a good defense for him? Which of the following is most accurate:

(a) Yes, because the new statute criminalizes only "knowing" conduct.

(b) Yes, but only if his belief that possessing a bear was lawful is found by a jury to be a reasonable one.

(c) No, it would not be a good defense.

(d) Answers (a) and (b) are correct, and answer (c) is incorrect.

Question 18–23: Anne had a severe epileptic seizure while she was driving her car in a residential neighborhood. She had never had a seizure before. As a result of the seizure, Anne lost control of the car and it careened off the road and hit a pedestrian, seriously injuring him.

Which of the following is most accurate:

(a) Anne committed a criminal, assaultive act if but only if the crime with which she is charged is a strict liability offense.

(b) Anne did not commit a criminal act because her actions were involuntary since she was not in control of her actions at the time she injured the pedestrian.

(c) Both (a) and (b) are correct.

(d) Neither (a) nor (b) is correct.

Question 18–24: Gary heard a commotion outside of his home, and went to the front door to look outside and find out what was going on. When he did, he saw that Morris and Janine were across the street, loading his wicker rocking chair, that had been sitting on his front porch, into the back of a pick-up truck. "Hey, what the f* * * do you f* * ***s think you are doing! Bring that f* * *ing rocker right back here this f* * *ing minute!," Gary yelled at them.

Hearing that, Janine made an obscene gesture toward Gary, and both Morris and Janine got into the truck and Morris started the engine. Gary then grabbed his hunting rifle from the hall closet and, running outside, shot at the departing pick up truck three times. One of the bullets hit Janine in the head. She survived, but suffered brain damage and is also now blind in one eye.

Gary has been charged with attempted murder of Janine. His defense counsel argues that he shot at Morris and Janine in lawful defense of his stolen property. Which of the following is most accurate:

(a) Gary has a good defense of property defense in these circumstances.

(b) Gary does not have a good defense of property defense in these circumstances because it was not necessary to use force to keep Morris and Janine from leaving with his property.

(c) Gary does not have a good defense of property defense in these circumstances because he was not entitled to use deadly force to keep Morris and Janine from leaving with his property.

(d) Answers (b) and (c) are correct, but answer (a) is incorrect.

Question 18–25: Dolfus, a high school student, was fooling around with his newly-purchased laser pointer, leaning out a window of his family's apartment, and aiming it at pedestrians walking past on the street below, watching the red laser dot appear on their bodies. Unfortunately, one of the pedestrians that Dolfus targeted with his laser pointer was walking right in front of Johnny. When Johnny saw the red dot appear on the back of the head of the pedestrian in front of him, he assumed that the dot was made by a laser sight on a rifle. Johnny did not know for sure, but he had heard that laser sight on rifles produced just such a red dot, and he had never ever heard of laser pointers. He did not even know that laser pointers even existed.

As a result, Johnny, who was licensed to and was in fact carrying a firearm, dropped to the ground, looked around for the person he thought was about to shoot at the pedestrian, spotted Dolfus in the window across the street holding his laser pointer, and Johnny shot and killed him.

Johnny has been charged with the murder of Dolfus. The jurisdiction in which these events occurred permits the use of "imperfect defenses" to mitigate murder to voluntary manslaughter. Which of the following is most accurate:

(a) If the fact-finder accepts the facts as set out above, Johnny may have a good mitigating defense of imperfect defense of others.

(b) If the fact-finder accepts the facts as set out above, Johnny is guilty of voluntary manslaughter.

(c) If the fact-finder accepts the facts as set out above, Johnny cannot be convicted of first-degree murder.

(d) All of the above are true.

CHAPTER 19
MULTIPLE CHOICE EXAM #3

The following facts apply to Questions 19–1 through 19–6 below:

The Spittsburgh, Spennsylvania (a state in the United States) Police Department received an anonymous call reporting that a young man in a black and gold jacket was leaning against the wall of the Spitt Law School Building, smoking marijuana. Immediately, a SWAT Team rushed to the site. When they arrived, they saw two young men, Barack and Mitt, and a young woman, Hillary, leaning against the wall. Barack was wearing a black and gold jacket and was smoking something that looked like a cigarette. The police officers rushed toward him, grabbed the cigarette, and Barack yelled: "Don't be taking my weed, man!" (A subsequent test of the contents of the "cigarette" revealed, however, that it was a blend of tobacco, oregano, and garlic powder.) After the officers grabbed his cigarette, Barack immediately ran away. Mitt and Hillary also ran away, but in a different direction.

After running for two blocks, Barack dashed into the street and smacked right into John, who was riding a bicycle, knocking John to the ground. John's bike careened into a pedestrian, Ron, who had just been released from a mental institution that morning. Ron, believing the bike was actually a poisoned spear that had just been thrown at him by John, reached into his backpack and removed a semi-automatic weapon and sprayed the area with gunfire. Barack was wounded, and John was killed by the gunfire.

Meanwhile, Mitt and Hillary were still running away in a different direction. As they were running, they saw Fred sitting on a motor scooter, blocking their path. Not wanting to slow down, Mitt and Hillary both hurled themselves at the scooter and toppled it over. Fred fell off the scooter and broke his nose.

Fred's scooter then careened into a pedestrian, Johnna, causing her purse to fall off of her shoulder and the contents to spill out on the street. Mitt and Hillary saw that jewelry spilled from the purse and they looked at each other, then they each grabbed some of the jewelry and began to run off once again.

Unfortunately for Mitt and Hillary, they ran right into a police officer who arrested them both. In a subsequent pat-down search of Hillary, the officer found that she was carrying strange-looking, hand-rolled cigarettes in her pockets. "Hey, don't be taking our tobacco-oregano-garlic powder smokes, man!," both Mitt and Hillary cried out. (A subsequent test of the contents of the cigarettes revealed, however, that they contained marijuana. Only marijuana. No tobacco. No oregano. No garlic.)

Question 19–1: You are an Assistant Public Defender in the county where these events took place. The Chief Public Defender has asked you to defend against conspiracy to commit theft charges against Mitt and Hillary for taking Johnna's jewelry. Which of the following is true:

(a) Mitt and Hillary are not guilty of the crime of conspiracy to commit theft because no conspiratorial agreement is present.

(b) Mitt and Hillary are not guilty of the crime of conspiracy to commit theft because no conspiratorial intent is present.

(c) Mitt and Hillary are not guilty of the crime of conspiracy to commit theft because no overt act has been committed.

(d) None of the above.

Question 19–2: You are an Assistant Public Defender in the county where these events took place. The Chief Public Defender has asked you to defend against second degree murder charges brought against Ron for the death of John. Which of the following is true:

(a) Ron is not likely to be convicted of guilty of murder because he has a good imperfect self-defense defense, entitling him to a voluntary manslaughter verdict.

(b) Ron is not likely to be convicted of guilty of murder because Barack, not John, was the primary cause of John's death.

(c) Ron is not likely to be convicted of guilty of murder because he was provoked at the time that he acted and has a mitigating defense, entitling him to a voluntary manslaughter verdict.

(d) None of the above.

Question 19–3: You are an Assistant Public Defender in the county where these events took place. The Chief Public Defender has asked you to defend against second degree murder charges brought against Barack for the death of John. Which of the following is most accurate:

(a) Barack is not likely to be convicted of guilty of murder because he did not commit a killing act.

(b) Barack is not likely to be convicted of guilty of murder because John, not Barack was the primary cause of John's death.

(c) Barack is not likely to be convicted of guilty of murder because he lacked malice.

(d) Barack is not likely to be convicted of guilty of murder because he was not acting as Ron's accomplice.

(e) All of the above.

Question 19–4: You are an Assistant Public Defender in the county where these events took place. The Chief Public Defender has asked you to defend against attempted possession of marijuana charges brought against Barack. Which of the following is true:

(a) Barack is not likely to be convicted of attempted possession of marijuana because the substance he possessed was, in fact, not marijuana.

(b) Barack is not likely to be convicted of attempted possession of marijuana because there is not enough evidence that he actually intended to possess marijuana.

(c) Barack is likely to be convicted of attempted possession of marijuana because he took a substantial step toward the attempted possession of marijuana.

(d) Barack is likely to be convicted of attempted possession of marijuana because he clearly intended to possess marijuana.

Question 19–5: You are an Assistant Public Defender in the county where these events took place. The Chief Public Defender has asked you to defend against assault charges against Mitt and Hillary for breaking Fred's nose. Which of the following is true:

(a) Mitt and Hillary are not guilty of assault because they did not intend that Fred break his nose.

(b) Mitt and Hillary are not guilty of assault, although they may be guilty of the separate criminal offense of battery.

(c) Mitt and Hillary are guilty of assault on Fred.

(d) None of the above.

Question 19–6: You are an Assistant Public Defender in the county where these events took place. The Chief Public Defender has asked you to defend against possession of marijuana charges against Mitt and Hillary. Which of the following is true:

(a) If they did not know that the substance was marijuana, Mitt and Hillary are not guilty of possession of marijuana.

(b) Mitt cannot be found guilty of possession of marijuana as the marijuana was not on his person.

(c) Both answer (a) and (b) is correct.

(d) Neither answer (a) nor (b) is correct.

The following facts apply to Questions 19–7 through 19–13 below:

Tyrone and his girlfriend, Faye, went to a club to celebrate Jeffrey's birthday, where they both drank heavily. Tyrone got into a fight outside of the club, and one of his punches landed on Faye's face. Faye told Tyrone that she did not want him to live in her apartment any longer, and that he would have to leave. She left the club with Jeffrey and headed home. Tyrone was already there when Faye and Jeffrey arrived. Faye began to put Tyrone's possessions on the front porch, and she asked him to return her key, which he did.

Tyrone was very upset at being thrown out of Faye's apartment. After awhile, Jeffrey was able to calm Tyrone down; but Tyrone and Faye continued to argue with one another. Soon thereafter, Marco drove up to wish Jeffrey a happy birthday. Marco told Tyrone to "chill out" and Tyrone responded that Marco should "stay out of it." An argument ensued and Tyrone told Marco to go get his guns, adding that he (Tyrone) had his. Faye went into a back bedroom, yelling, "Kill each other for all I care. Go ahead! Good riddance!"

Marco went to his vehicle and retrieved two handguns. He approached the porch with his arms crossed and a gun in each hand. Tyrone took a gun out of the waistband of his pants and started shooting. He wounded Marco and he fatally shot Jeffrey. Shortly thereafter, Tyrone was arrested and placed in the back of a patrol car. As he was being driven to the police station, Tyrone spontaneously said: "I did not mean to kill Jeff. Jeff got in the way. Jeff is my best friend."

Question 19–7: You are a public defender in the jurisdiction where the facts set out above took place. Tyrone has been charged with the attempted murder of Marco. Which of the following is most accurate:

(a) In the absence of a good affirmative defense, Tyrone is guilty of the attempted murder of Marco.

(b) Tyrone is not guilty of the attempted murder of Marco because he did not intend to kill him.

(c) Tyrone is not guilty of the attempted murder of Marco because he did not commit an actual killing act.

(d) None of the above.

Question 19–8: You are a public defender in the jurisdiction where the facts set out above took place. Tyrone has been charged with the first degree murder of Jeffrey. Which of the following is most accurate:

(a) Tyrone is not likely to be found guilty of first degree murder because he lacked malice.

(b) Tyrone is not likely to be found guilty of first degree murder because a reasonable jury is not likely to conclude that he premeditated and deliberated this killing act.

(c) On these facts, in a prosecution of Tyrone for first degree murder, the mens rea element has likely been satisfied.

(d) None of the above.

Question 19–9: You are a public defender in the jurisdiction where the facts set out above took place. Tyrone has been charged with the first degree murder of Jeffrey. Which of the following is most accurate:

(a) Tyrone was not the "but for" cause of Jeffrey's death as Jeffrey's death was entirely accidental.

(b) It was reasonably foreseeable that Jeffrey would die as a result of Tyrone's actions, and his death was not too remote a consequence of Tyrone's actions to impose criminal culpability.

(c) Tyrone was not the proximate cause of Jeffrey's death because Jeffrey's act of getting in the way while Tyrone was firing at Marco "broke the causal chain."

(d) None of the above.

Question 19–10: You are a public defender in the jurisdiction where the facts set out above took place. Tyrone has been charged with the first degree murder of Jeffrey. The Chief Public Defender has asked you what chances of success Tyrone may have in using a provocation defense mitigating the murder charge to voluntary manslaughter. Which of the following is most accurate:

(a) Tyrone is likely to be able to establish provocation sufficient to mitigate the murder charge to voluntary manslaughter.

(b) Tyrone is not likely to be able to establish provocation sufficient to mitigate the murder charge to voluntary manslaughter because his action was not sudden.

(c) Tyrone is not likely to be able to establish provocation sufficient to mitigate the murder charge to voluntary manslaughter because Jeffrey did not provoke Tyrone.

(d) Tyrone is not likely to be able to establish provocation sufficient to mitigate the murder charge to voluntary manslaughter because the alleged provocative acts were mere words.

(e) Answers (b), (c), and (d) are correct, and answer (a) is incorrect.

Question 19–11: You are a public defender in the jurisdiction where the facts set out above took place. Tyrone has been charged with the first degree murder of Jeffrey. The Chief Public Defender has asked you what chances of success Tyrone may have in using an intoxication or drugged condition defense to that charge. Which of the following is most accurate:

(a) Tyrone is likely to be able to successfully defend against a first degree murder charge on grounds of intoxication or drugged condition.

(b) Tyrone is not likely to be able to successfully defend against a first degree murder charge on grounds of intoxication or drugged condition because intoxication or drugged condition cannot be a defense to first degree murder, a specific intent offense.

(c) Tyrone is not likely to be able to successfully defend against a first degree murder charge on grounds of intoxication or drugged condition because the evidence makes it appear that he was not sufficiently intoxicated to be able to prove this defense.

(d) Answers (b) and (c) are correct, and answer (a) is incorrect.

Question 19–12: You are a public defender in the jurisdiction where the facts set out above took place. Tyrone has been charged with the first degree murder of Jeffrey. The Chief Public Defender has asked you what chances of success Tyrone may have in using a self defense defense to that charge. Which of the following is most accurate:

(a) Tyrone is likely to be able to successfully defend against a first degree murder charge on grounds of self defense if but only if this is not a jurisdiction requiring retreat before using deadly force and if Marco is viewed as the aggressor.

(b) Tyrone is not likely to be able to successfully defend against a first degree murder charge on grounds of self defense in a jurisdiction requiring retreat before using deadly force since he cannot use the "castle exception" to the retreat doctrine because he was not acting in his own home.

(c) If Tyrone was the aggressor and could have retreated safely, Tyrone is not likely to be able to successfully defend against a first degree murder charge on grounds of self defense in a jurisdiction requiring retreat before using deadly force.

(d) All of the above.

Question 19–13: You are a public defender in the jurisdiction where the facts set out above took place. Faye has been charged as Tyrone's accomplice with the attempted murder of Marco and the murder of Jeffrey. Which of the following is true:

(a) Faye could be found guilty of attempted murder of Marco as Tyrone's accomplice, but could not be found guilty as an accomplice in the murder of Jeffrey.

(b) Faye could be found guilty of the murder of Jeffrey as Tyrone's accomplice, but could not be found guilty as an accomplice in the attempted murder of Marco.

(c) It is unlikely that Faye could be found guilty of either crime as Gary's accomplice because she lacked the requisite mens rea.

(d) Faye could be found guilty of the murder of Jeffrey as Tyrone's accomplice and as an accomplice in the attempted murder of Marco.

Question 19–14: Donetta knew that her partner, Monica, was deathly afraid of cats. She told her brother, Les, about Monica's fear. That was not a good idea. Late one evening, when Les was sleeping over at the women's apartment on the living room couch, he snuck out and returned with two feral cats which he then shoved inside Donetta's and Monica's bedroom, and then he wedged the bedroom door so that it would not open easily.

Waiting outside with a twisted, anticipatory smile on his face, Les was soon rewarded by hearing Monica scream hysterically as the cats jumped on the bed while she and Donetta were sound asleep. Then, when Monica tried to flee, she discovered that she couldn't open the bedroom door, and she became even more hysterical until, Les, finally relenting, unstuck the door and opened it.

Neither Monica nor Donetta was physically harmed by Les' actions. But, unsurprisingly, that was the last time he was permitted in the women's apartment. And, more seriously, even though Donetta counseled against it, Monica filed a criminal complaint against Les, and he was subsequently charged with criminal assault on Monica as a result of these actions. Les' defense counsel contends that this was just a silly, sophomoric prank that harmed no one and that, as a result, Les did not commit a criminal act. Which of the following is most accurate:

(a) Assuming that Monica's fear of these cats was deemed reasonable, Les criminally assaulted Monica.

(b) Les did not criminally assault Monica because Les' actions were not intended to actually harm her.

(c) Les did not criminally assault Monica because Les' actions did not actually harm Monica.

(d) Answers (b) and (c) are correct, and answer (a) is incorrect.

Question 19–15: Santonio was employed as a school crossing guard. His job was to assist elementary school children in crossing a very busy intersection on their way to and from school. One morning, however, Santonio left his post in order to run into some nearby bushes to urinate. But, before he returned, seven-year old Rosa showed up at the intersection and, looking for but not seeing the crossing guard, she tried to cross the busy street by herself. Unsuccessfully. She was struck by a car and killed.

Santonio has been charged with involuntary manslaughter in the death of Rosa. His defense counsel claims that he is not guilty of these charges, *inter alia*, because he committed no criminal act. Rather, Santonio simply failed to act, an omission. Which of the following is most accurate:

(a) Santonio's failure to act satisfies the actus reus element of involuntary manslaughter in these circumstances.

(b) Santonio's failure to act satisfies the actus reus element of involuntary manslaughter in these circumstances, but only if he had a direct familial relationship with Rosa.

(c) Santonio's failure to act does not satisfy the actus reus element of involuntary manslaughter in these circumstances.

(d) None of the above.

Question 19–16: Olivier and his wife, Olivia, own a small "mom-and-pop" fudge business. They produce and sell sixteen types of fudge and three fudge sauces which they sell to various candy shops in their area for over-the-counter resale to customers. Their business in incorporated and Oliver is the CEO. Olivia is the Chief Operating Officer, i.e. she actually makes the fudge and fudge sauces. Unfortunately, one of their low-acid fudge sauces was the source of seven individuals' food poisoning.

It is a crime in the jurisdiction where Olivier and Olivia live to distribute such tainted food products. The District Attorney in this jurisdiction has asked you, an Assistant District Attorney, whether it is possible to prosecute Olivier as CEO for this crime, or whether any criminal prosecution would have to be limited to a prosecution only of their small corporation. Which of the following is most accurate:

(a) Olivier may not be personally prosecuted for distributing tainted food products, because he was acting in his corporate capacity.

(b) Olivier may be personally prosecuted for distributing tainted food products if but only if he had the power to prevent the distribution of the tainted fudge sauce from occurring.

(c) Olivier may not be personally prosecuted for distributing tainted food products because the acts of the corporation are not attributable to him unless he knew about and ratified them.

(d) Answers (a) and (c) are correct, and answer (b) is incorrect.

The following facts apply to Questions 19–17 and 19–18 below:

It is a misdemeanor in this state for the driver of a "passenger car" to talk on a mobile telephone while his or her car is in motion. Elvira was seen by a police officer talking on her telephone while driving on the interstate, and was immediately stopped and arrested for this offense.

Question 19–17: Elvira had just moved to this state. In the state that she moved from, there is no comparable criminal statute. If Elvira can convince a jury that she honestly believed that it was not against the law to talk on a mobile phone while driving, would that be a good defense for her? Which of the following is most accurate:

(a) Yes, if the statute is a strict liability statute.

(b) Yes, if her belief was a reasonable one.

(c) Yes, but only if the statute includes a mens rea element of purposeful, intentional, or knowing behavior.

(d) None of the above.

Question 19–18: If Elvira can convince a jury that she honestly and reasonably believed that she was not in violation of this statute because she was driving in an SUV with a truck base and she believed that was not a "passenger car" subject to coverage under this statute, would that be a good defense?

(a) Yes, if the statute is strict liability.

(b) Yes, if the statute contains a mens rea element of purposeful conduct.

(c) No, it would not be a good defense.

Question 19–19: Brian has been charged with criminal assault for punching Vincent and causing injuries that required Vincent to be hospitalized. Before this encounter, Brian drank one beer, and his attorney is considering an intoxication defense. Assuming this occurred in a majority jurisdiction which recognizes an intoxication defense, which of the following is most accurate:

(a) This defense is not likely to be successful because assault is a general intent crime.

(b) This defense is likely to be successful because the beer will show up in Brian's blood alcohol level and establish that he was intoxicated when he committed the assault.

(c) The defense is likely to be successful because assault is a general intent crime.

(d) The defense is likely to be successful because assault is a specific intent crime.

(e) Answers (b) and (d) are correct, but answers (a) and (c) are incorrect.

Question 19–20: Kenosha kidnaped her neighbor's two-month old infant, Iris, in the mistaken, deluded, and irrational belief that the child was really her daughter. She honestly believed that her neighbor was a witch and had magically stolen Iris from Kenosha when Iris was only a fetus in Kenosha's womb.

Kenosha has been charged with kidnaping. Her defense is that she was insane at the time of the alleged criminal act. This jurisdiction uses the *M'Naghten* test to determine whether an accused defendant is not guilty by reason of insanity? Which of the following is most accurate:

(a) It is possible for Kenosha to make out a good insanity defense even if the prosecution establishes that she was aware of the nature and quality of her act.

(b) It is possible for Kenosha to make out a good insanity defense even if the prosecution establishes that she knew that kidnaping is wrong and a criminal offense.

(c) If a jury finds that Kenosha was aware that she was kidnaping Iris and that that act was a crime, then she would not have a good insanity defense.

(d) All of the above.

Question 19–21: Necia, a college student, was walking back to her apartment after a late night in the college library studying, Arn, Elliot, and Russ jumped out of an alley right in front of her. Arn pointed a gun at her, but said nothing. Necia screamed, and started to run away, but Elliot and Russ each grabbed one of her arms and held her there. Then Elliot grabbed her purse and Russ grabbed her backpack, and all three of her assailants quickly ran off into the night. The whole episode lasted for no more than 15 seconds.

On these facts alone, which of the following is true:

(a) Arn, Elliot, and Russ are not guilty of the crime of conspiracy to commit robbery because they could not have known in advance that Necia would be where she was, so there was no evidence that they had previously agreed to commit this crime together.

(b) Arn, Elliot, and Russ are not guilty of the crime of conspiracy to commit robbery because there was no evidence that each of them intended to commit the crime of robbery.

(c) Arn, Elliot, and Russ are guilty of the crime of conspiracy to commit robbery.

(d) None of the above.

Question 19–22: Dolan offered Ellen $100 to have sex with him, and Ellen flatly refused. But, she added, "hey, you know, I'd do you for like $200. Cash up front." Dolan said, "Okay, it's a deal." But Ellen quickly responded: "Hey, I was joking, man. I'm not doing nothing with you." Hearing that, Dolan grabbed Ellen, dragged her behind some bushes as she struggled to get away, ripped her jeans and underwear off, and got on top of her and had sexual intercourse. Ellen did not resist him during this entire episode. She just laid there underneath him. But when he had finished, she quickly grabbed her clothes and ran away, yelling back at him "You're an asshole, Dolan!"

Ellen went straight to a police station and reported the incident. Dolan was arrested, and he was subsequently charged with rape. Which of the following is true:

(a) Dolan is likely to be found guilty of raping Ellen.

(b) Dolan is not likely to be found guilty of raping Ellen because Ellen did not resist him when they had intercourse.

(c) Dolan is not likely to be found guilty of raping Ellen because he did not force her to have sex with him.

(d) Dolan is not likely to be found guilty of raping Ellen because Ellen consented to have intercourse with him and they were simply negotiating over the price.

Question 19–23: Tia did nothing when Eduardo, her boyfriend, violently and repeatedly punched her daughter, Rosa. While Tia did not participate in the beating in any way, she also neither said nor did anything to stop Eduardo from punching Rosa. Eduardo hit Rosa, a 2 ½ year-old toddler, because he said that he was tired of her always wetting her pants instead of using the toilet. As a result of Eduardo's violence toward Rosa, she suffered a skull fracture and she subsequently died.

Tia has been charged with involuntary manslaughter in the death of Rosa. She contends, however, that she is not guilty because she did not commit a criminal act related to Rosa's death. Eduardo is the person who killed Rosa, not Tia. Or, at least, that is Tia's argument. Which of the following is most accurate:

(a) Tia's failure to act does not satisfy the actus reus element of involuntary manslaughter.

(b) Tia's failure to act satisfies the actus reus element of involuntary manslaughter.

(c) Tia's failure to act satisfies the actus reus element of involuntary manslaughter, but only if a statute exists created a duty for people to act to assist others who are in need of emergency assistance.

(d) None of the above.

Question 19–24: Paulie was driving home in a horrible thunderstorm late one night, when his car skidded on the we pavement and careened into an intersection through a red light, injuring two pedestrians and killing another who were crossing the street with a WALK signal. When the accident occurred, Paulie was driving at the speed limit. But the tires on his car were more than six years old, and they did not have the type of skid-resistant features often found today on newer tires. One expert on traffic accidents opined that had Paulie's car been fitted out with newer tires with better skid-resistant features, this accident—and the pedestrian's death—would probably not have occurred.

Paulie has been charged with involuntary manslaughter in the death of the pedestrian. Which of the following is true:

(a) Paulie is likely to be convicted of involuntary manslaughter because he negligently failed to equip his car with skid-resistant tires.

(b) Paulie is not likely to be convicted of involuntary manslaughter because the pedestrian who was killed assumed the risk that he might die or be seriously injured when he crossed into the intersection in the middle of a thunderstorm.

(c) Whether Paulie will be convicted of involuntary manslaughter on these facts turns on whether he acted maliciously in taking a substantial and unjustifiable risk that death or serious bodily injury might occur as a result of his driving with old tires in a thunderstorm.

(d) Whether Paulie will be convicted of involuntary manslaughter on these facts turns on the issue whether he should have been aware of a substantial and unjustifiable risk that death or serious bodily injury might result from driving on old tires in a thunderstorm.

Question 19–25: "Man, I am really, really broke." That's what Alton said to his roommate, Ed, late one night, while the two of them were just hanging out in their basement apartment, watching TV. "Man, I have got to find some way to come up with some cash. Like I really got to. Things are getting bad," he added. "Look," he continued, "that old lady in the house down the street—you know, that nasty house with the cracked, green front door? She's got cash stashed away, I know it. Would you come with me and just—you know—like just watch out for cops and stuff while I go inside and look around? That's all. That's it. No big deal. Huh? So? Would you do that for me? Man, I'll make it worth your while if I find something good in there. I promise."

Ed responded: "Sure. Sure. Whatever." But he didn't mean it. He was just trying to keep Alton quiet, to humor him, so he could keep watching TV in peace.

Alton never brought up the subject again.

Is Alton guilty of the crime of soliciting Ed to assist him in committing a burglary? Which of the following is most accurate:

(a) No, Alton is not guilty of the crime of soliciting Ed to assist him in committing a burglary because there is not enough evidence that he really meant it when he proposed the plan.

(b) No, Alton is not guilty of the crime of soliciting Ed to assist him in committing a burglary because there is not enough evidence that he was serious about this solicitation.

(c) Yes, Alton is guilty of the crime of soliciting Ed to assist him in committing a burglary.

(d) Answers (a) and (b) are correct, and answer (c) is incorrect.

ANSWERS

SPECIFIC SUBJECT MATTER MULTIPLE CHOICE ANSWERS

CHAPTER 1
JUSTIFICATIONS FOR CRIMINAL PUNISHMENT

Answer 1–1: The correct answer is (d).

The primary rationales for the imposition of criminal punishment are: general deterrence; specific deterrence; incapacitation; rehabilitation; retribution; and the expression of community values. These rationales are not, of course, like mathematical formulae, automatically producing a predictable and invariable end result. Rather, in this setting, they are simply useful guides for channeling the exercise of judicial discretion in sentencing. They, hopefully, help judges (and lawyers who are arguing to judges) make fair and rational sentencing decisions, and avoid arbitrariness in sentences. It is, accordingly, neither certain nor even likely that any two judges using these same justifications in an identical factual situation would sentence Linda in exactly the same way. But use of these justifications would help educate and focus the analysis of both of these judges in desirable ways. Hence, answer (d) is correct, and answers (a), (b), and (c) are incorrect since they treat some or all of these rationales for the imposition of criminal punishment as requirements rather than useful guides for the judge.

[For additional discussion of this subject, see John M. Burkoff, Acing Criminal Law, Chapt. 1(B) (West)]

Answer 1–2: The correct answer is (c).

Considering the rationale of general deterrence, the question is what sort of sentence would serve best to deter *others* (not Linda herself) from engaging in criminal conduct like this? One could argue that people who commit criminal acts to feed their children—if Linda is telling the ruth about her reason for acting—cannot be easily deterred. But that argument applies the general deterrence notion too narrowly. A severe sentence for armed robbery might well serve to deter some non-parents-of-hungry-children from engaging in such unlawful conduct. Hence, answer (a) is incorrect as the focus of general deterrence is on deterring others not the accused herself.

Of course, even if a very severe criminal sentence might conceivably have a general deterrent effect, that does not mean necessarily that it is the best or most appropriate sentence to impose. Sentencing judges need to weigh the nature of the particular crime and of the offender herself against the social value presumably gained in (maybe) deterring others. The crimes here are serious ones: two counts of armed robbery. The victims could conceivably have been seriously hurt or even killed. And the victims were elderly and perhaps defenseless. But, the offender's circumstances are sad and troubling, too: her unemployment; her history of narcotics use; her hungry children.

Indeed, specific deterrence might well dictate a heavier rather than a lighter sentence here. Pursuant to this aim of criminal punishment, the sentencing judge has to make a judgment about what sort of punishment would most effectively (and fairly) ensure that Linda (not others) would not rob again. Hence, answer (b) is incorrect as the focus of specific deterrence is on deterring the accused herself, not other people.

As to incapacitation, a sentence including incarceration would certainly keep Linda off the streets for whatever period of time she was behind bars. Hence, answer (c) is correct, and ipso facto answer (d) is incorrect. (Of course, such a sentence would likely be a terrible burden for Linda's innocent children.)

[For additional discussion of this subject, see John M. Burkoff, ACING CRIMINAL LAW, Chapt. 1(B) (West)]

Answer 1–3: The correct answer is (b).

Rehabilitation? Would it work here? Did Linda's crimes stem from a "bad mind." Or might it have been due instead to her desperation and the need to feed her children? What are the odds that Linda could be "trained"—in a prison setting—to be a better person? Based on experience, the odds may not be high. Indeed, maybe more to the point, would a long stretch in prison really "cure" her ... or might it instead make her life, her prospects, her desperation, and her odds of recidivism upon release worse rather than better? In any event, answer (a) is incorrect because a judge, even considering rehabilitative goals, is not mandated to incarcerate an accused. As a result, answer (d) is incorrect since answer (a) is incorrect.

With respect to retribution, there is no question but that Linda committed serious crimes. She robbed two elderly victims, threatening them with a knife. Certainly the concepts of just desserts and vengeance would justify serious criminal punishment in this setting. Hence, answer (b) is correct.

The expression of community values justification for criminal punishment cuts two ways. Certainly we want to reaffirm our strong abhorrence of this sort of antisocial behavior. On the other hand, we might also want to demonstrate our empathy (if not our forgiveness) given the unfortunate life circumstances that may have caused Linda to act by moderating the severity of her sentence. That is an educative lesson, too, of course. Hence, answer (c) is incorrect.

So, parenthetically, what is the result here? Well, it depends on the judge. One might anticipate, on balance, that the nature of the crimes (knife point, elderly victims) which support sending a deterrent message will be balanced against the circumstances of the offense (the defendant's concern about her children's welfare, if deemed credible by the judge) which make prospects for rehabilitation speculative in coming up with an appropriate sentence. The likelihood then is a sentence including some incarceration, but nowhere near the maximum.

[For additional discussion of this subject, see John M. Burkoff, ACING CRIMINAL LAW, Chapt. 1(B) (West)]

Answer 1–4: The correct answer is (d).

As to general deterrence, the legislator would want to assess whether the criminalization of a veterinarian's failure to report animal abuse would actually work to deter veterinarians generally from failing to so report such episodes. The answer to that question might well depend, at least in part, on the *need* for such general deterrence, e.g. is there really an existing problem with non-reporting that needs to be deterred? If so, there is still the issue of balancing this need for action against the proposed *severity* of the criminal penalties to be enacted. If general deterrence is the principal aim of this proposed legislation, a $5 fine would not be very deterrent, while a possible incarceration of up to thirty days in jail might have a dramatic deterrent effect.

Of course, even if strict and certain criminal penalties might have a discernable general deterrent effect on veterinarians, that does not mean necessarily that it is good public policy to enact criminal laws like these. That is a totally different question. The use of the death penalty to punish people who jaywalk might work as an effective general deterrent, but it's simply not good public policy as a matter of proportionate culpability.

Furthermore, the efficacy of any proposed general deterrence of veterinarians would presumably depend as well on the *certainty* (or lack thereof) that they would actually be arrested for this new offense ... and prosecuted and convicted. Hence, answer (a) is correct. Moreover, this legislator might also want to consider whether the enactment of such a crime might have a counterproductive effect, namely by generally deterring some people who have abused their animals (or think that a veterinarian might wrongfully believe that they had) from seeking medical treatment for them.

Making the failure of veterinarians to report animal abuse a crime would certainly seem likely to accomplish the end of specific deterrence. Punishment for this conduct would seem quite likely to keep the specific veterinarian punished from committing that particular criminal act again. As to incapacitation, incarceration as a justification for criminalizing the failure of veterinarians to report animal abuse would certainly work (inmates would not be treating animals and, hence, not in a position to fail to report abuse), although it does raise the question whether or not jail time is an appropriate sanction for such conduct as a matter of sensible public policy as a proportionate response to the conduct criminalized. Nonetheless, answer (b) is correct.

Rehabilitation as a justification for such a criminal statute raises an interesting question. Can we "cure" veterinarians from their failure to report animal abuse ? Wholly aside from the question whether or not we want to do that, is this the kind of conduct that is a proper subject for training and reeducation? Likely not.

With respect to retribution, just how antisocial is this behavior anyway? If, in fact, the problem of non-reporting is not a common one and if, further, such a criminal law might end up deterring some people from seeking care for their abused animals from veterinarians for fear of their own potential culpability, the notions of just desserts and vengeance would not seem to justify criminal punishment in this particular setting. Hence, answer (c) is correct.

Finally albeit parenthetically, even though it is not part of this question, of all the traditional justifications for punishment, the expression of community values may come the closest to supporting this proposed criminal statute. The question is whether the legislator considering proposing this legislation really believes that this sort of conduct—the non-reporting of animal abuse—demands criminal punishment in order to educate veterinarians about how wrong such non-reporting really is. In any event, answer (d) is the most accurate answer to this question as answers (a), (b), and (c) are all correct.

[For additional discussion of this subject, see John M. Burkoff, ACING CRIMINAL LAW, Chapt. 1(B) (West)]

CHAPTER 2
ACTUS REUS

VOLUNTARY ACT

Answer 2–1: The correct answer is (a).

A criminal act must be committed voluntarily. If an accused person shows that his or her actions were "involuntary," no crime has been made out. An act is voluntary if it is a product of a person's free will, manifested by a corresponding, external body movement. Conversely, an act is involuntary if it is *not* a product of a person's free will, manifested by a corresponding, external body movement. If Sergio can establish that his act of falling onto and injuring Ilsa was strictly a result of his sleepwalking rather than the product of his conscious free will, this act was involuntary and no crime was committed. Hence answer (a) is correct, and ipso facto answer (d) is incorrect.

Whether or not the criminal offense was a strict liability offense does not change this answer. The act (actus reus) element is different from the criminal intent (mens rea) element. An accused has not committed a voluntary criminal act if he or she has acted involuntarily whatever the requisite criminal intent element required, i.e. the fact that the mens rea element is satisfied has no bearing on the question whether the actus reus element has been satisfied. Hence, answer (b) is incorrect, and ipso facto answer (c) is also incorrect.

[For additional discussion of this subject, see John M. Burkoff, Acing Criminal Law, Chapt. 2(A) (West)]

Answer 2–2: The correct answer is (a).

If Sergio was aware that he suffered from this sleep disorder and that sleepwalking and other bodily movements could occur as a result and he was in a position to do something about that, e.g. through taking appropriate medication, but did not, a voluntary act may be established. That voluntary act, however, would not be Sergio's actions at the time that he tripped and fell on Ilsa. Rather, it would be at the moment when he knew that he could act to prevent his sleepwalking symptoms, but choose not to do so. Hence, answer (a) is correct, and ipso facto answers (b) and (d) are incorrect.

Moreover, actions and behavior which are the result of a person's *voluntary* intoxication or drugged condition are not subject to an involuntary-act defense for the same reason discussed above, namely that the earlier act of becoming intoxicated or drugged was a voluntary act. Hence, answer (c) is also incorrect.

Parenthetically, if Sergio's actions resulting in Ilsa's injuries had been the result of Sergio's *involuntary* intoxication or drugged condition, the involuntary-act defense would still apply. This eventuality might have occurred in this problem if, for example, Sergio's injurious actions were entirely the result of an unforseen drug interaction with the alcohol he had ingested that he did not or reasonably could not have foreseen.

[For additional discussion of this subject, see John M. Burkoff, Acing Criminal Law, Chapt. 2(A) (West)]

Answer 2–3: The correct answer is (a).

A criminal act must be committed voluntarily. If an accused person shows that his or her actions were "involuntary," no crime has been made out. An act is voluntary if it is a product of a person's free will, manifested by a corresponding, external body movement. Conversely, an act is involuntary if it is *not* a product of a person's free will, manifested by a corresponding, external body movement. The death of the small child which was caused by a collision with Maria's car after she lost control of it was clearly not an act that was a product of Maria's conscious free will. As a result, her loss of control of the car was involuntary and, as a result, no crime was committed. Hence, answer (a) is correct, answer (c) is incorrect, and ipso facto answer (d) is incorrect.

Notably, however, this result may be different if it could be established (contrary to the facts set out in the problem) that Maria *knew* that she had a relevant history of such seizures. In that case, a voluntary act might well be established, occurring when she drove her car knowing that there was a significant chance that she might have a seizure and lose control of the vehicle. However, where a person did not know or have reason to know that she might have a seizure, he or she has not acted voluntarily. Hence, answer (b) is incorrect.

[For additional discussion of this subject, see John M. Burkoff, Acing Criminal Law, Chapt. 2(A) (West)]

POSSESSION

Answer 2–4: The correct answer is (d).

On these facts, Estelle is not guilty of the crime of possession of narcotics. To establish commission of a possessory offense, the prosecution must prove that the accused was aware of his or her possession of a contraband item to a degree sufficient to be able to exercise control over it, and that he or she acted knowingly and voluntarily in possessing it. In this case, Estelle was unaware of her possession of the crack cocaine which Thomas had left hidden in his backpack in the trunk of her car. Moreover, she did not act knowingly and voluntarily in possessing it. Hence, answers (a), (b), and (c) are incorrect, and answer (d) is correct.

[For additional discussion of this subject, see John M. Burkoff, Acing Criminal Law, Chapt. 2(B) (West)]

Answer 2–5: The correct answer is (b).

On these facts, Estelle is guilty of the crime of possession of narcotics. It does not matter the cocaine was not hers or that she did not intend to use any of it. The fact that there was cocaine in her car does not establish her culpability in and of itself. Hence, answer (a) is incorrect, and ipso facto answer (c) is also incorrect.

To establish commission of a possessory offense, the prosecution must prove that the accused was aware of his or her possession of a contraband item to a degree sufficient to be able to exercise control over it, and that he or she acted knowingly and voluntarily in possessing it. In this case, Estelle was aware of her possession of cocaine in the trunk of her car and she could easily have divested herself of control over it by removing either the entire backpack or simply the cocaine itself. Hence, answer (b) is correct, and ipso facto answer (d) is incorrect.

[For additional discussion of this subject, see John M. Burkoff, Acing Criminal Law, Chapt. 2(B) (West)]

Answer 2–6: The correct answer is (b).

Doc and Andrea are each guilty of the crime of possession of marijuana.

It does not matter that the marijuana plant may have belonged to only one of them, and not the other. To establish commission of a possessory offense, the prosecution must simply prove that the accused was aware of his or her possession of a contraband item to a degree sufficient to be able to exercise control over it, and that he or she acted knowingly and voluntarily in possessing it. In this case, given the fact that the marijuana plant was sitting out in the open on the kitchen table, both Doc and Andrea would have been aware of its existence to a degree sufficient to be able to exercise control over it. Hence, answer (a) is incorrect, and answer (b) is correct.

Moreover, items may be possessed by more than one person, i.e. "jointly," as here, when it is found in a place where more than one person was aware of its existence and exercised control over it. Hence, answer (d) is incorrect.

Similarly, a person can be found guilty of possession of contraband even when it is not found on his or her person or immediate vicinity. Contraband is possessed constructively when it is found in a place where the accused is shown to have been aware of its existence and to have exercised control over it. Hence, answer (c) is incorrect.

[For additional discussion of this subject, see John M. Burkoff, Acing Criminal Law, Chapt. 2(B) (West)]

Answer 2–7: The correct answer is (c).

Doc and Andrea are still each guilty of the crime of possession of marijuana.

It does not matter that the marijuana plant may have belonged to another person. To establish commission of a possessory offense, the prosecution must simply prove that the accused was aware of his or her possession of a contraband item to a degree sufficient to be able to exercise control over it, and that he or she acted knowingly and voluntarily in possessing it. In this case, given the fact that the marijuana plant was sitting out in the open on the kitchen table, both Doc and Andrea would have been aware of its existence to a degree sufficient to be able to exercise control over it. Hence, answer (a) is incorrect, and ipso facto answer (d) is also incorrect.

Moreover, items may be possessed by more than one person, i.e. "jointly," as here, when it is found in a place where more than one person was aware of its existence and exercised control over it. Hence, answer (b) is incorrect.

Similarly, a person can be found guilty of possession of contraband even when it is not found on his or her person or immediate vicinity. Contraband is possessed constructively when it is found in a place where the accused is shown to have been aware of its existence and to have exercised control over it. Hence, answer (c) is correct.

[For additional discussion of this subject, see John M. Burkoff, Acing Criminal Law, Chapt. 2(B) (West)]

OMISSIONS

Answer 2–8: The correct answer is (b).

Deidre cannot be prosecuted successfully as an accomplice in Olivia's child abuse for failing to report to the authorities her belief that these two children were being abused.

Deidre committed no criminal act, rather she failed to act, a classic omission. Omissions are not ordinarily held to be culpable at criminal law. Although what she did may or may not be morally objectionable—and note that Deidre possessed no firm evidence of the child abuse, only unconfirmed suspicions—it is not punished by the criminal law in the absence of a specific statute requiring such reporting, or some other legal duty to act. Hence, answer (b) is correct, and answers (a), (c), and (d) are incorrect.

[For additional discussion of this subject, see John M. Burkoff, Acing Criminal Law, Chapt. 2(D) (West)]

Answer 2–9: The correct answer is (b).

Bill is not likely to be able to defend himself successfully with this omissions argument.

It is true that omissions—mere failures to act—are not ordinarily held to be culpable at criminal law. But the exception to that general rule is that an omission is treated as a criminal act when the person failing to act had a legal duty to do so. A classic legal duty of this sort is where a contractual obligation exists.

In this case, Bill was employed as a lifeguard and, hence, had the contractual duty to look out for—and come to the aid of—drowning swimmers. As a result, Bill's negligent failure to perform this contractual duty resulting in the death of little Cindy does expose him to criminal responsibility for his inaction. Hence, answer (b) is correct, and answers (a), (c), and (d) are incorrect.

[For additional discussion of this subject, see John M. Burkoff, Acing Criminal Law, Chapt. 2(D) (West)]

CHAPTER 3
MENS REA

DISTINGUISHING MENS REA ELEMENTS

Answer 3–1: The correct answer is (b).

Sandy is not guilty of first degree murder because he did not act purposefully.

For the prosecution to prove that he committed this act purposefully, it would have to prove that Sandy had the "conscious object to cause" Tim's death. (This definition of purposeful conduct is, by the way, similar to that set forth in the Model Penal Code.) But, although he was aware that his brakes were bad, there is no evidence that Sandy had the conscious object to crash his truck into another car and to kill someone inside it. Accordingly, he is not guilty of first degree murder because he did not act purposefully. Hence, answer (b) is correct, and answer (a) is incorrect.

Whether or not Sandy had the money to repair his brakes adds nothing to the analysis set out above. Since there is no evidence that Sandy had the conscious object to crash his truck into another car and to kill someone inside it, he did not act purposefully. Hence, answer (c) is incorrect.

Of course, Sandy might well be guilty of a different homicide crime, involuntary manslaughter perhaps, with a mens rea of recklessness. But that is not the crime with which he has been charged. Hence, answer (d) is incorrect.

[For additional discussion of this subject, see John M. Burkoff, Acing Criminal Law, Chapt. 3(A) (West)]

Answer 3–2: The correct answer is (b).

Diana is not guilty of recklessly endangering another person.

For the prosecution to prove that Diana committed this act recklessly, it would have to prove, at minimum, that she consciously disregarded a substantial and unjustifiable risk that her actions might place another person in danger of death or serious bodily injury. But there is no evidence in this problem that she actually disregarded such a risk as there was no bomb in fact, so there was no actual danger. Hence, answer (b) is correct, and answer (a) is incorrect.

Because recklessness is the applicable mens rea for this criminal offense, Diana's conscious intention to harm anyone is not the relevant test. Hence, answer (c) is incorrect, and ipso facto answer (d) is also incorrect.

Of course, parenthetically, Diana might well be guilty of a different crime with different elements arising out of this same conduct, terroristic threats perhaps. But that is not the crime with which she was charged.

[For additional discussion of this subject, see John M. Burkoff, ACING CRIMINAL LAW, Chapt. 3(A) (West)]

Answer 3–3: The correct answer is (c).

Larry is probably not guilty of second degree murder.

(Parenthetically, there is also an issue in this problem of whether Larry actually "acted" or whether, instead, he failed to act, i.e. whether or not this was an omission deemed to be culpable in the criminal law. *See* Chapter 2. Assuming Larry owed a legal duty to Dan and Candy as occupants of his house, however, his failure to warn them of any danger they faced would be deemed culpable in the criminal law as a proper *actus reus*.)

For the prosecution to prove that Larry acted recklessly, it would have to prove that he consciously disregarded a substantial and unjustifiable risk that he was placing other people in danger of death or serious bodily injury. The key inquiry here is the "consciously" element, i.e. did Larry *actually* realize and disregard the risk that the furnace put Dan and Candy in danger of death or serious bodily injury?

Larry knew that his furnace was old and that it had a problem in producing enough heat to warm his home sufficiently. But there is no evidence in this problem that he *knew* that the furnace was or could be leaking carbon monoxide and thus posed a serious danger to his friends' lives. As a result, it is not likely (although it is still possible) that he would be convicted of second degree murder on these facts. Hence, answer (c) is correct, and answer (a) is incorrect.

Answer (b) is incorrect because it states that Larry is not guilty using a standard higher than recklessness—purposeful or intentional conduct.

An accused could have failed to act purposefully and still acted recklessly. Hence, answer (b) is incorrect, and answer (d) ipso facto is incorrect as well.

[For additional discussion of this subject, see John M. Burkoff, ACING CRIMINAL LAW, Chapt. 3(A) (West)]

Answer 3–4: The correct answer is (a).

Larry may be found guilty of involuntary manslaughter.

(Parenthetically, as in Question 3–3, there is an initial issue in this problem of whether Larry actually "acted" or whether, instead, he failed to act, i.e. whether this was an omission not deemed to be culpable in the criminal law. *See* Chapter 2. Assuming Larry owed a legal duty to Dan and Candy as occupants of his house, however, his failure to warn them of any danger they faced would be deemed culpable in the criminal law.)

For the prosecution to prove that Larry acted criminally negligently, it would have to prove that he *should have been* aware that there was a substantial and unjustifiable risk that he was placing Dan and Candy in danger of death or serious bodily injury by letting them live in his house with a defective furnace. Unlike the mens rea of recklessness which includes a subjective element—the accused must have "*consciously*" disregarded a "substantial and unjustifiable" risk—criminal negligence is strictly an objective concept, i.e. to be negligent, the accused merely *should have* been aware of such a risk.

Larry knew that his furnace was old and that it had a problem in producing enough heat to warm his home sufficiently. The question is: should he have realized as a result of this knowledge that it might leak carbon monoxide and thus pose a serious danger to his friends' lives. A jury could certainly decide this factual question either way, but there is certainly a strong chance—if not a probability—that it would conclude that Larry should have realized this risk existed. If the jury does so conclude, Larry would be convicted of the crime of involuntary manslaughter. Hence, answer (a) is correct, and answers (d) and ipso facto (e) are incorrect.

Answer (b) is incorrect because it states that Larry is not guilty using a standard higher than negligence—purposeful or intentional conduct. An accused could have failed to act purposefully and still have acted negligently. Hence, answer (b) is incorrect.

Answer (c) is incorrect because it states that Larry is not guilty using a standard higher than negligence—recklessness. An accused could have failed to act recklessly and still have acted negligently. Hence, answer (c) is incorrect.

[For additional discussion of this subject, see John M. Burkoff, Acing Criminal Law, Chapt. 3(A) (West)]

STRICT LIABILITY

Answer 3–5: The correct answer is (a).

Tony's contention that he thought Lizzie was over sixteen years of age is not a good defense to this charge of statutory rape and there are no other defenses apparent in the facts of this problem.

Tony is trying to argue that he did not possess the mens rea required to establish the crime of statutory rape as he mistakenly believed that Lizzie was over sixteen years of age. But there is no express mens rea element in this offense. It is, moreover, common for the crime of statutory rape to be defined as a strict liability offense as it is here.

In the absence of another statute creating a reasonable mistake of fact defense to this crime or a court decision finding such a defense to exist implicitly (a minority position), Tony cannot defend against these charges by trying to establish that he was acting pursuant to a mistaken belief that Lizzie was over sixteen. Hence, answer (a) is correct, and answers (b), (c), and (d) are all incorrect.

[For additional discussion of this subject, see John M. Burkoff, Acing Criminal Law, Chapt. 3(B) (West)]

Answer 3–6: The correct answer is (d).

A criminal prosecution of Stewart on these three charges is likely to be successful.

Most regulatory criminal offenses like this one, regulating potentially harmful or injurious items—so called "public welfare" offenses—are strict liability. It is perfectly lawful and quite common for legislatures to enact regulatory criminal statutes that do not contain mens rea elements.

As a result, it is not a good defense to these charges that Stewart did not know that the cribs contained lead-based paint, or that he did not generally have a blameworthy intent. It only matters that Stewart did in fact violate the criminal law by offering or providing the cribs for use by his guests. Hence, answer (d) is correct, and answers (a), (b), and (c) are incorrect.

[For additional discussion of this subject, see John M. Burkoff, Acing Criminal Law, Chapt. 3(B) (West)]

Answer 3–7: The correct answer is (c).

Strict liability offenses do not require proof of any mens rea at all. It makes no difference that the manufacturer here neither knew of its criminal actions (excessive release of gas) nor intended to violate the criminal law. Hence, answer (a) is incorrect, and ipso facto answer (d) is incorrect.

It also makes no difference that the manufacturer was not aware that this criminal offense even existed. In determining that this statute is a strict liability offense, the courts have presumably reasoned that people should be on notice that public welfare regulation of this sort exists. And, in any event, strict liability offenses do not require any mens rea at all, so ignorance of the existence of the statute is not a defense. Hence, answer (b) is incorrect.

Accordingly, given the existence of this strict liability criminal offense, the manufacturer has no possible mens rea defense in these circumstances. Hence, answer (c) is correct.

[For additional discussion of this subject, see John M. Burkoff, Acing Criminal Law, Chapt. 3(B) (West)]

INTOXICATION & DRUGGED CONDITION

Answer 3–8: The correct answer is (c).

Intoxication or drugged condition is not a good defense to the crime of rape.

In a majority of jurisdictions, the fact that an accused was intoxicated or drugged at the time he or she committed a criminal act is considered to be a valid defense, but only if the crime has a specific intent mens rea element and the intoxication or drugged condition is so extreme as to negative that element. However, in this jurisdiction (as in most U.S. jurisdictions), the rape statute does not contain a mens rea element at all. Where a rape statute is deemed to be strict liability, there can be no intoxication or drugged condition defense.

Even if the courts in this jurisdiction were to find that the rape statute contained—implicitly—a mens rea element, it would be a general rather than a specific intent mens rea. The distinction between general and specific intent crimes varies by jurisdiction. Typically, a crime is considered general intent when the mens rea requires only the intent to do the act that causes the harm. In contrast, a crime is deemed to be specific intent when the required mens rea requires proof of an additional intent beyond committing the act that causes the harm. In this case, if a mens rea was found to exist implicitly, it would be the intention to have sexual intercourse with another person by means of forcible compulsion: a general intent crime.

As a result, either because this statute is strict liability (most likely) or because it contains a general intent element (less likely), Kenneth will not be able to defend against this charge successfully be relying upon the fact that he was intoxicated when it occurred. Hence, answer (c) is correct, and answers (a) and (d) are incorrect.

Answer (b) is also incorrect as it mixes up the separate defenses of involuntary act and intoxication or drugged condition. In order to make an unconsciousness—involuntary act—defense, the accused must establish that the act in question was involuntary as it was not a product of his or her free will, manifested by a corresponding, external body movement. *Voluntary* intoxication does reflect an act of free will by the accused.

[For additional discussion of this subject, see John M. Burkoff, Acing Criminal Law, Chapt. 3(C) (West)]

Answer 3–9: The correct answer is (a).

An intoxication or drugged condition defense is likely to be a good defense for Keisha to these first degree murder charges.

(Parenthetically, it is also likely that she has another viable defense to these charges that does not involve her intoxicated and drugged state, namely that she did not possess the mens rea—intentional conduct—for a conviction for premeditated first degree murder. *See* Chapter 13.)

In a majority of jurisdictions, the fact that an accused was intoxicated or drugged at the time he or she committed a criminal act is considered to be a valid defense, but only if the crime has a specific intent mens rea element and the intoxication or drugged condition is so extreme as to negative that element.

Is first degree murder a specific intent crime? The answer is "yes." First degree murder is considered a specific intent crime because the actor's intention goes beyond the assaultive conduct being committed and includes the further intention that that conduct result in the death of the victim.

But was Keisha sufficiently intoxicated and/or drugged that she really could not possess the appropriate mens rea for this crime? Again, the answer is probably "yes." Certainly the odds are high that a jury will find extreme intoxication and/or drugged condition in this case due to the fact that Keisha had been both smoking crack and drinking heavily before she got into her car. Hence, answer (a) is correct, and answers (b), (c), and ipso facto (d) are incorrect.

[For additional discussion of this subject, see John M. Burkoff, Acing Criminal Law, Chapt. 3(C) (West)]

Answer 3–10: The correct answer is (b).

Intoxication or drugged condition is not a good defense to involuntary manslaughter charges.

In a majority of jurisdictions, the fact that an accused was intoxicated or drugged at the time he or she committed a criminal act is considered to be a valid defense, but only if the crime has a specific intent mens rea element and the intoxication or drugged condition is so extreme as to negative that element.

Is involuntary manslaughter a specific intent crime? The answer is "no." Involuntary manslaughter is not a specific intent crime because the requisite mens rea (generally criminal negligence) requires only that the actor act with gross negligence, without requiring proof of a further criminal intention. Hence, answer (b) is correct, and answers (a) and (c) and ipso facto answer (d) are incorrect.

[For additional discussion of this subject, see John M. Burkoff, Acing Criminal Law, Chapt. 3(C) (West)]

Answer 3–11: The correct answer is (a).

This likely will be a good defense for Harley.

In a majority of jurisdictions, the fact that an accused was intoxicated or drugged at the time he or she committed a criminal act is considered to be a valid defense, but only if the crime has a specific intent mens rea element and the intoxication or drugged condition is so extreme as to negative that element.

The distinction between general and specific intent crimes varies by jurisdiction. Typically, a crime is deemed to be general intent when the mens rea requires only the intent to do the act that causes the harm. In contrast, a crime is deemed to be specific intent when the required mens rea requires proof of some additional intent beyond committing the act that causes the harm.

Is this arson statute a specific intent crime? In a basic respect, it appears to be a classic specific intent crime. The statute criminalizes a person's act of "starting a fire or causing an explosion," but—significantly—with an additional intent beyond the mere commission of that act, namely "with the purpose of destroying a building or occupied structure of another."

If this statute is deemed to be one of specific intent in fact, then there is one further issue to be resolved: was Harley sufficiently intoxicated that he really could not possess the appropriate mens rea for this crime? The answer to this question is likely to be in the affirmative as it appears very unlikely that Harley would not satisfy this element of the defense after drinking an entire fifth of whiskey. In fact, it is pretty incredible that he was actually conscious when the burning took place. Hence, answer (a) is correct, and answers (c) and (d) are incorrect.

Answer (b) is also incorrect as it mixes up the separate defenses of involuntary act and intoxication or drugged condition. In order to make an unconsciousness—involuntary act—defense, the accused must establish that the act in question was involuntary as it was not a product of his or her free will, manifested by a corresponding, external body movement. *Voluntary* intoxication does reflect an act of free will by the accused.

[For additional discussion of this subject, see John M. Burkoff, ACING CRIMINAL LAW, Chapt. 3(C) (West)]

CHAPTER 4
MISTAKE

MISTAKE OF FACT

Answer 4–1: The correct answer is (b).

Donald may well have a good mistake of fact defense to this first degree murder charge.

A mistake of fact defense is one way of trying to negative the mens rea element of a criminal offense. First degree murder in this jurisdiction requires proof of the mens rea of purposeful conduct. Donald is arguing that he did not in fact act purposefully because it was not his conscious desire to commit this criminal act (shooting Edward) or to obtain this criminal result (killing Edward). Model Penal Code § 2.04(1)(a) provides, in relevant part, that "[i]gnorance or mistake as to a matter of fact ... is a defense if ... the ignorance or mistake negatives the purpose ... required to establish a material element of the offense."

In jurisdictions using an approach identical or similar to the Model Penal Code, if the jury believes Donald's story about his mistaken belief, the required mens rea—purposefulness—simply did not exist and he should not be found guilty of first degree murder.

In some other jurisdictions, however, an accused trying to make a mistake of fact defense must establish not only that he or she honestly believed in the mistaken circumstance that negative the mens rea required for the offense charged (a subjective test), but he or she must also establish that such a mistaken belief was reasonable as well (an objective test). Even in a jurisdiction that takes this approach, Donald would have a strong likelihood of convincing a jury that his subjective belief that the gun was unloaded was also an objectively reasonable belief. Donald watched his friend unload the gun—or so he thought. And his friend—the gun's owner—told Donald that the gun was then unloaded. Assuming that a jury would find that it was reasonable for Donald to rely on this observation and report from his friend, his mistaken belief that the gun was unloaded would be deemed honest and reasonable and he would have a good defense to this charge of first degree murder. Hence, answer (b) is correct, and answer (a) is incorrect.

But, if so charged, Donald could be found guilty of a different homicide offense, e.g. a homicide offense with a requisite mens rea of recklessness or criminal negligence, in these same circumstances. Hence, answer (c) is incorrect, and ipso facto answer (d) is incorrect as well.

[For additional discussion of this subject, see John M. Burkoff, ACING CRIMINAL LAW, Chapt. 4(A) (West)]

Answer 4–2: The correct answer is (a).

As discussed in the answer to Question 4–1, *see above*, Donald could be found guilty of a homicide offense with a requisite mens rea of recklessness or criminal negligence in these circumstances. Even though he did not actually intend to shoot and kill Edward, a reasonable person should be aware of the risk of death that is inherent in playing a joke on someone with an operable handgun. In such instances, gross negligence is certainly clear. Hence, answer (a) is correct, and answers (b), (c), and (d) are all in correct.

[For additional discussion of this subject, see John M. Burkoff, ACING CRIMINAL LAW, Chapt. 4(A) (West)]

Answer 4–3: The correct answer is (a).

This is not a good defense for Cyril.

A mistake of fact defense is one way of trying to negative the mens rea element of a criminal offense. The Model Penal Code § 2.04(1)(a) provides, for example, in relevant part, that "[i]gnorance or mistake as to a matter of fact ... is a defense if ... the ignorance or mistake negatives the purpose ... required to establish a material element of the offense." The mens rea of attempted murder is the intent to commit the crime of first degree murder.

The mistake that Cyril is relying upon is not a mistake as to that intention. He did in fact intend to kill someone, namely Abe. He concedes as much. The fact that the person he intended to kill was not the person he did try to kill is irrelevant to any element of the crime charged. As a result, this is not a good defense in these circumstances and Cyril will be convicted of the crime of attempted murder. Hence, answer (a) is correct, and answers (b), (c), and (d) are incorrect.

[For additional discussion of this subject, see John M. Burkoff, ACING CRIMINAL LAW, Chapt. 4(A) (West)]

Answer 4–4: The correct answer is (c).

Frank cannot successfully defend against this rape charge by proving that he honestly and reasonably believed that Maya was consenting to the act of sexual intercourse.

Frank is trying to defend himself by establishing that he mistakenly believed that Maya was consenting. However, the crime of rape is usually a strict liability offense and mistake of fact is a mens rea defense. Strict liability crimes have no mens rea. Accordingly, absent some separate statute (or court decision) establishing a mistake of fact affirmative defense, this contention provides no tenable defense for Frank. Hence, answer (c) is correct, and answer (b) and ipso facto answer (d) are incorrect.

Moreover, even if mistake of fact was a potentially good defense and even if Frank truly believed Maya was consenting, Frank could not establish that his belief in Maya's consent was reasonable given the fact that she gave him no affirmative indication of consent but rather expressed to him precisely the opposite. Hence, answer (a) is incorrect.

[For additional discussion of this subject, see John M. Burkoff, ACING CRIMINAL LAW, Chapt. 4(A) (West)]

MISTAKE OF LAW

Answer 4–5: The correct answer is (c).

This is not a good defense for Cheech. A mistaken belief that a criminal act is not criminal is not a good defense. Ignorance of the law is simply no defense. It does not matter whether the statute is or is not strict liability, or whether it includes any particular mens rea element. Hence, answer (c) is correct, and answers (a), (b), and (d) are incorrect.

[For additional discussion of this subject, see John M. Burkoff, ACING CRIMINAL LAW, Chapt. 4(B) (West)]

Answer 4–6: The correct answer is (d).

Cheech might have a good defense if he can convince a jury that he honestly and reasonably believed that the marijuana plants growing in his garden were actually oregano. This is a mistake of fact defense.

Whether this is a good defense or not for Cheech depends on the mens rea element of the possession of narcotics statute under which he has been charged. If the offense is strict liability, for example, he has no defense as mistake of fact is a mens rea defense and a strict liability crime has no mens rea element. Hence, answers (a) and (b) are incorrect.

If the offense does have a mens rea and if Cheech can convince a jury that his mistaken belief was honest and reasonable, that is a good defense. As Model Penal Code § 2.04(1)(a) provides, for example, in relevant part, "[i]gnorance or mistake as to a matter of fact ... is a defense if ... the ignorance or mistake negatives the purpose ... required to establish a material element of the offense." Hence, answer (d) is correct, and answer (c) is incorrect.

[For additional discussion of this subject, see John M. Burkoff, ACING CRIMINAL LAW, Chapt. 4(A) (West)]

Answer 4–7: The correct answer is (c).

It is a good defense for Sylvie under the terms of this criminal statute.

Ordinarily, the arresting officer was correct. A mistaken belief that a criminal act is not criminal is not a good defense. Ignorance of the law is no defense.

But where a criminal statute provides that a person's knowledge that his or her conduct is unlawful is an element of the crime—as here, with the statutory requirement that the owner "know[] that this conduct is unlawful"—mistake of law is a defense because it negatives expressly that prescribed element. Hence, answer (c) is correct, and answer (a) is incorrect. Because the statute does not expressly require that the actor's lack of knowledge about the leash law be reasonable, reasonableness does not have to be established by the accused. Hence, answer (b) is incorrect.

Finally, it does not matter whether the statute contains any particular mens rea element. The lack-of-knowledge element is still a statutory element that the prosecution is obligated to prove beyond a doubt in order to convict Sylvie under this statute. Hence, answer(d) is incorrect.

[For additional discussion of this subject, see John M. Burkoff, ACING CRIMINAL LAW, Chapt. 4(B) (West)]

CHAPTER 5
CAUSATION

Answer 5–1: The correct answer is (a).

Neither Celia nor Lewis has a good causation defense to homicide charges based upon these facts.

Proof of causation is an element of all homicide offenses. To establish causation, the prosecution must establish both that: (1) that the accused's conduct actually caused the criminal result; and (2) that the accused's conduct was a legally sufficient cause of the criminal result.

More than one person can be the actual (or "but for") cause of the same criminal result, even if they act independently. Celia, who shot Barry, is certainly a but for cause of her death. But for the shooting, he wouldn't have been in the ambulance where he died when he did. And the but for test is also satisfied by Lewis' actions. But for his reckless driving, Barry would not have died when he did.

In addition, both Celia's and Lewis' actions were a proximate cause of Barry's death in that the relationship between each of their conduct and his death was legally sufficient as closely enough related to justify their criminal culpability. It is certainly reasonably foreseeable that shooting someone in the chest might lead to their death, and that driving down a one-way street in the wrong direction might lead to the death of a passenger.

Moreover, in Model Penal Code terms, Celia's conduct in mortally wounding Barry was not "too remote or accidental" from Barry's resulting death to justify the imposition of criminal sanctions. And Lewis' conduct in recklessly driving down a one-way street was also not too remote or accidental from Barry's resulting death to justify the imposition of criminal sanctions.

Accordingly, neither Celia nor Lewis is likely to be able to defend successfully against homicide charges on the ground that the causation element was not satisfied. Hence, answer (a) is correct, and answers (b), (c), and (d) are incorrect.

[For additional discussion of this subject, see John M. Burkoff, Acing Criminal Law, Chapt. 5 (West)]

Answer 5–2: The correct answer is (d).

Lack of causation is not likely to be a good defense for Eileen to the charge of involuntary manslaughter in the death of Jay, unless this jurisdiction uses the common law "year and a day rule."

Proof of causation is an element of all homicide offenses. To establish causation, the prosecution must establish both that: (1) that the accused's conduct actually caused the criminal result; and (2) that the accused's conduct was a legally sufficient cause of the criminal result.

Actual—so-called "but for"—causation is easily established on these facts. But for Eileen's illegal conduct (running a red light), Jay would not have been injured.

Similarly, Eileen's action was a proximate cause of Jay's death. There is no question but that the relationship between her conduct and his death was legally sufficient to justify her criminal culpability. It is certainly reasonably foreseeable that running a red traffic light might result in serious injury to a pedestrian. Moreover, in Model Penal Code terms, Eileen's conduct in running over Jay was clearly not "too remote or accidental" from Jay's resulting death to justify the imposition of criminal sanctions.

Nonetheless, at common law, a "year and a day rule" applied. If a death resulted from an actor's conduct, but did not occur within a year and a day from that conduct, no culpability attached for the criminal result. In this case, Jay died a year and two days after Eileen's triggering conduct. Accordingly, if this jurisdiction is one of the small minority of jurisdictions that still follow this common law rule, Eileen does have a good causation defense to the charge of involuntary manslaughter. If this jurisdiction follows the majority—which have repealed the year and a day rule—Eileen does not have a good causation defense to this charge. Hence, answer (d) is correct, and answers (a), (b), and (c) are all incorrect.

[For additional discussion of this subject, see John M. Burkoff, Acing Criminal Law, Chapt. 5 (West)]

Answer 5–3: The correct answer is (c).

This intervening-cause argument is probably not a good defense for George.

Proof of causation is an element of all homicide offenses. To establish causation, the prosecution must establish both that: (1) the accused's conduct actually caused the criminal result; and (2) the accused's conduct was a legally sufficient cause of the criminal result.

Actual—"but for"—causation is easily established on these facts. But for George's shooting of Rudolfo, Rudolfo would not have been in the hospital where the hospital employee's failure to secure him properly to the gurney most immediately led to his death.

However, defense counsel for George is arguing, in essence, that George was not the proximate cause of Rudolfo's death, nor was it reasonably foreseeable that Rudolfo would die in this bizarre fashion. Or, in Model Penal Code terminology, defense counsel's argument is that the way in which Rudolfo died—falling from a gurney and breaking his neck as a result of a hospital employee's negligence—was too remote or accidental to hold George culpable at criminal law.

However, in many jurisdictions, mere negligent medical treatment leading to the death of a victim who was hospitalized as the result of a prior criminal assault has been held not to break the causal chain with respect to the perpetrator of the assault. He or she is still guilty of homicide, assuming that the other elements of the particular homicide offense charged are met. Gross negligence, on the other hand, has been deemed a sufficiently remote or intervening eventuality to serve to break the causal chain. In essence, ordinary negligence is reasonably foreseeable, but gross negligence is not. The latter breaks the causal chain; the former does not.

Rudolfo's death was most immediately caused by the hospital employee's actions in failing to properly secure his body to the gurney. If the jury finds this failure to have been merely negligent—as is most likely—then it would not be an intervening event that would break the causal chain, and would not, accordingly, provide George with a good defense. If, however, the jury finds instead that this failure was instead one of *gross* negligence, that would be an intervening event that would break the causal chain and that would give George a good causation defense. Since the facts give indicate that the hospital employee's actions were merely negligent, the correct answer here is answer (c). For the same reasons, answers (a) and (b) and, ipso facto, answer (d) are all incorrect.

[For additional discussion of this subject, see John M. Burkoff, Acing Criminal Law, Chapt. 5 (West)]

Answer 5–4: The correct answer is (c).

This is not a good defense for Keith.

Proof of causation is an element of all homicide offenses. To establish causation, the prosecution must establish both that: (1) that the accused's conduct actually caused the criminal result; and (2) that the accused's conduct was a legally sufficient cause of the criminal result.

Actual—"but for"—causation is easily established on these facts. But for Keith's shooting of Andy, he would not have been in the hospital where the doctors' act of terminating his life support at Andy's wife's request led to his immediate death.

However, Keith argues, in essence, that he was not the proximate cause of Andy's death, nor was it reasonably foreseeable that Andy would die in this fashion after he was shot. Or, in Model Penal Code terminology, Keith's argument is that the way in which Andy actually died—through the termination of life support—was too remote from his triggering actions to hold Keith culpable at criminal law.

As to legal causation, in many jurisdictions, death is defined as brain death. Andy was in fact brain dead when his life support was terminated. This was established by the absence of brain waves. Accordingly, in those states, Andy was dead for purposes of the criminal law before his doctors discontinued the use of the artificial ventilator to keep his heart beating and Keith was the direct—and only—cause of his death.

However, assuming these facts took place in a jurisdiction where a person with a beating heart is still considered to be alive (despite brain death), the doctors' actions here would not be a sufficient intervening cause to break the causal chain between Keith's shooting and Andy's death. It is reasonably foreseeable that a shooting victim's family might choose to end his life in this fashion after he no longer has any brain function.

In many jurisdictions, mere negligent medical treatment leading to the death of a victim who was hospitalized as the result of a prior criminal assault has been held not to break the causal chain with respect to the perpetrator of the assault. He or she is still guilty of homicide, assuming that the other elements of the particular homicide offense charged are met. Gross negligence, on the other hand, has been deemed a sufficiently remote or intervening eventuality to serve to break the causal chain. In essence, ordinary negligence is reasonably foreseeable, but gross negligence is not. The latter breaks the causal chain; the former does not.

Accordingly, in this case, even if the doctors here acted negligently in soliciting or effecting this discontinuation of life support, it is not likely that their actions at this stage were the sort of gross negligence that might break the causal chain.

Accordingly, assuming that all of the other elements of first degree murder are met, Keith is guilty of first degree murder and does not have a tenable causation defense. Hence, the correct answer (c), and answers (a) and (b) and, ipso facto, answer (d) are all incorrect.

[For additional discussion of this subject, see John M. Burkoff, ACING CRIMINAL LAW, Chapt. 5 (West)]

Answer 5–5: The correct answer is (c).

This is not likely to be a good defense for Bianca to the charges of involuntary manslaughter.

Proof of causation is an element of all homicide offenses. To establish causation, the prosecution must establish both that: (1) the accused's conduct actually caused the criminal result; and (2) the accused's conduct was a legally sufficient cause of the criminal result.

Actual—"but for"—causation is easily established on these facts. But for Bianca's act of flicking her still-burning cigarette overboard, the ferry boat would not have burned up and Bernard and Penny would still be alive.

However, defense counsel for Bianca is arguing, in essence, that she was not the proximate cause of their deaths, nor was it reasonably foreseeable that the wind would catch her cigarette and blow it back onto the boat, causing the conflagration that led to their deaths. Or, in Model Penal Code terminology, defense counsel's argument is that the wind blowing the cigarette back onto the ship and into a bucket of flammable liquid was simply too remote or accidental an occurrence to hold Bianca culpable at criminal law. In essence, counsel contends that the strong wind served as an intervening cause that broke the causal chain between Bianca's actions and the deaths of Bernard and Penny.

But this is not likely to be a good defense. Bianca was at the rail up on deck where she could feel the strong force of the wind as the ferry boat moved though the water. Accordingly, a jury is likely to find that it was reasonably foreseeable that a still-burning cigarette might be blown back onto the boat. The mere fact that the wind was causally independent of Bianca's action does not alone make it an intervening factor that breaks the causal chain. Hence, answers (a) and (b), and ipso facto answer (d), are all incorrect.

As a result, assuming that all of the other elements of involuntary manslaughter are met, Bianca is guilty of both counts and does not have a tenable causation defense. Hence, answer (c) is correct.

[For additional discussion of this subject, see John M. Burkoff, ACING CRIMINAL LAW, Chapt. 5 (West)]

CHAPTER 6
ACCOMPLICE LIABILITY

Answer 6–1: The correct answer is (d).

On these facts, Ellie and Miranda have not done anything wrong.

The common law distinctions between parties to a crime—principals in the first degree, principals in the second degree, accessories before the fact, and accessories after the fact—have been abrogated by statute in the great majority of jurisdictions. With one exception—accessories after the fact—the categories of principal and accessory are said to have "merged."

Accordingly, if the prosecution can establish that Ellie and Miranda were complicit in the crime of arson endangering property, they can be convicted of that crime. But to be convicted as accessories here, it must be proved that each of them actually intended to assist another person in committing this particular crime and intended, further, that that person actually commit that crime.

Although this mens rea is often established circumstantially, mere presence at the scene of a crime is never enough to establish this mens rea. In fact, on these facts, mere presence is all that the prosecution can establish. Hence, the appropriate mens rea is lacking and Ellie and Miranda are not guilty of being accessories to the crime of arson endangering property. Hence, answer (b) is correct, and answer (a) is incorrect.

Moreover, to be convicted as an accessory, an accused must also have actively assisted another person in the commission of a crime. And—just as with proof of mens rea—mere physical presence at the scene of a crime is not enough to establish that such a criminal act occurred. Once again, on these facts, mere presence is all that the prosecution can apparently establish. Accordingly, the appropriate actus reus is also lacking and Ellie and Miranda are not guilty of being accessories to the crime of arson endangering property on this independent ground as well. Hence, answer (c) is correct, and the most accurate answer is answer (d) since both (b) and (c) are correct.

[For additional discussion of this subject, see John M. Burkoff, Acing Criminal Law, Chapt. 6(A) (West)]

Answer 6–2: The correct answer is (d).

Ernesto is not guilty as an accomplice on these facts.

A person can be found guilty of a crime simply because he or she aided someone else in the commission of that crime. However, to establish such complicity, the accused must have actively assisted another person in the commission of that crime. The extent of the accused's assistance is irrelevant.

However, unwittingly assisting an undercover agent who is trying to find a criminal to sell him narcotics is not enough of an act in and of itself to establish the requisite active assistance. That is exactly what occurred in this case. Ernesto simply responded to Darius' questions about where he could probably obtain cocaine. There is no evidence that Ernesto had any relationship with the actual drug seller, DeJuan. As a result, on these facts, the actus reus of accomplice liability has not been established. Hence, answer (c) is correct, and answer (a) is incorrect.

Moreover, to be convicted as an accomplice, the accused must also be shown to have had the intention to assist another person in committing a crime and the intention that that person actually commit that crime. This mens rea is often established circumstantially. However, on these facts, there is no indication—even circumstantial—that Ernesto had the intention to assist DeJuan in the sale of narcotics. Nor is there record evidence establishing Ernesto's intention that DeJuan actually commit that crime. Accordingly, the mens rea of accomplice liability has not been established either. Hence, answer (b) is correct as well.

Hence, Ernesto is not guilty as an accomplice on these facts. Hence, the most accurate answer is answer (d) since both (b) and (c) are correct.

[For additional discussion of this subject, see John M. Burkoff, Acing Criminal Law, Chapt. 6(A) (West)]

Answer 6–3: The correct answer is (b).

This is not a good defense.

The common law distinctions between parties to a crime—principals in the first degree, principals in the second degree, accessories before the fact, and accessories after the fact—have been abrogated by statute in the great majority of jurisdictions. With one exception—accessories after the fact—the categories of principal and accessory are said to have "merged."

If this jurisdiction follows the majority rule, Kailee may be convicted of shoplifting simply by proving the elements of accomplice liability with respect to that crime. In essence, an accomplice is treated as if she actually committed—as a principal—the crime that she assisted. Hence, answers (a) and (c), and ipso facto answer (d) as well, are all incorrect.

Significantly, as a result of this merger, the culpability of an accessory no longer turns on whether a principal has been convicted previously of the same crime. An accomplice to a crime can be convicted of that crime simply by proving that she was an accomplice, regardless of what has happened—if anything—to the principal. As Model Penal Code § 2.06 (7) provides, "[a]n accomplice may be convicted on proof of the commission of the offense and of his complicity therein, though the person claimed to have committed the offense has not been prosecuted or convicted or has been convicted of a different offense or degree of offense or has an immunity to prosecution or conviction or has been acquitted."

Hence, the fact that Diem was previously acquitted of shoplifting on the same facts is irrelevant in most jurisdictions. Kailee may still be tried and convicted—as an accomplice—for the same crime. Hence, answer (b) is correct.

Parenthetically, if this jurisdiction is one of the handful of minority jurisdictions that continue to follow the common law, an accomplice cannot be convicted unless or until the principal was convicted of the crime in question. In this case, since Diem was previously acquitted, Kailee could not be tried or convicted of this crime at this point.

[For additional discussion of this subject, see John M. Burkoff, Acing Criminal Law, Chapt. 6(A) (West)]

Answer 6–3: The correct answer is (a).

Kailee was complicit in the crime of shoplifting.

A person can be found guilty of a crime simply because he or she aided someone else in the commission of that crime. However, to establish such complicity, the accused must have actively assisted another person in the commission of that crime. The extent of the accused's assistance is irrelevant.

Acting as a "lookout" while someone else is committing a crime is certainly enough of an act in and of itself to establish the requisite active assistance. That is exactly what occurred in this case. As a result, on these facts, the actus reus of accomplice liability has been established. Hence, answer (c) is incorrect, and ipso facto answer (d) is incorrect as well.

Moreover, to be convicted as an accomplice, the accused must also be shown to have had the intention to assist another person in committing a crime and the intention that that person actually commit that crime. This mens rea is often established circumstantially. On these facts, the fact that Kailee acted as a lookout while Diem stole the scarf makes clear, albeit circumstantially, that she had the intention to assist Diem in committing that crime. Accordingly, the mens rea of accomplice liability has also been established. Hence, answer (b) is incorrect as well.

Accordingly, Kailee is guilty of aiding and abetting Diem's act of shoplifting on these facts. Hence, answer (a) is correct.

Answer 6–5: The correct answer is (d).

Vinny is not an accomplice in these burglaries.

The common law distinctions between parties to a crime—principals in the first degree, principals in the second degree, accessories before the fact, and accessories after the fact—have been abrogated by statute in the great majority of jurisdictions. With one exception—accessories after the fact—the categories of principal and accessory are said to have "merged."

In this scenario, Vinny is an accessory after the fact. His intent to assist and his actual assistance to the individuals who actually committed the burglaries was offered only after the crimes were completed. Accordingly, he was not complicit in these burglaries. Hence, answer (a) is incorrect, and answers (b) and (c) are each correct. Because answers (b) and (c) are each correct, answer (d) is the most accurate answer.

(Parenthetically, an accessory after the fact can be convicted of a separate crime. But that crime must relate to criminal activity that was committed after another crime was committed. Vinny, for example, is likely guilty of the crime of receiving stolen property. As a principal. Not as an accomplice.)

[For additional discussion of this subject, see John M. Burkoff, ACING CRIMINAL LAW, Chapt. 6(A) (West)]

Answer 6–6: The correct answer is (c).

Claire was an accomplice in Eddie's sale of marijuana.

For Claire to be convicted as an accomplice to Eddie's criminal actions, the prosecution must prove that she intended to assist him in committing a crime and that she intended that Eddie actually commit that crime. Assuming the facts as described in the problem are accurate, this will not be difficult. Claire took the job as a lookout, knowing what Eddie was doing and being paid to assist him in doing it. Hence, answer (a) is incorrect, and ipso facto answer (d) is incorrect as well.

Although mere presence at the scene of a crime is never enough to establish the mens rea of complicity, Claire was not merely present. Instead, she was employed to be present to serve as a lookout for Eddie.

With respect to an appropriate accomplice actus reus, Claire can be found guilty if she is found to have aided Eddie in the commission of the crime charged, sale of marijuana. Her assistance must be active assistance in order to suffice to establish this element of the crime. In this case, her assistance was active. She was employed to—and actually did—serve as a lookout.

The fact that she was a bad lookout and did not do her job well is irrelevant. The extent of an accused person's assistance to a principal—Eddie in this case—is irrelevant. The key is that she offered active assistance and that is clear on these facts in Claire's case. Hence, answer (b) is incorrect, and answer (c) is correct.

[For additional discussion of this subject, see John M. Burkoff, ACING CRIMINAL LAW, Chapt. 6(A) (West)]

Answer 6–7: The correct answer is (c).

David is guilty as charged as an accomplice to the bank robbery.

Before withdrawing from the robbery planning, David met all of the elements of accomplice liability, as an accessory before the fact. An accessory before the fact is a person who aids or encourages principals before a crime occurs, but he is not present at the crime scene. With respect to the appropriate mens rea, the prosecution would have to prove that David intended to assist the others in committing the bank robbery and that he intended that the crime actually be committed. Prior to his withdrawal, that intention was absolutely clear. Hence, answer (a) is incorrect, and ipso facto answer (d) is incorrect.

With respect to the actus reus element, to be convicted as an accomplice, an accused must have actively assisted another person or persons in the commission of a crime. David clearly met that element as well as he scouted the scene of the crime and prepared his drawing for the others to use to plan how to accomplish the robbery most effectively. Hence, answer (b) is incorrect.

The common law distinctions between parties to a crime—principals in the first degree, principals in the second degree, accessories before the fact, and accessories after the fact—have been abrogated by statute in the great majority of jurisdictions. With one exception—accessories after the fact—the categories of principal and accessory are said to have "merged." As a result, since David was an accessory before the fact in this scenario, he can be convicted just as if he was a principal for the crime of bank robbery. Hence, answer (c) is correct.

[For additional discussion of this subject, see John M. Burkoff, ACING CRIMINAL LAW, Chapt. 6(A) (West)]

Answer 6–8: The correct answer is (d).

David does not have a good withdrawal defense to the complicity charge, but not for the reasons set out in these answers.

David's counsel argues that he was no longer a party to the bank robbery when it occurred, i.e. that he withdrew and/or renounced his participation in the offense. The majority rule, however, is that an accomplice may not successfully withdraw or renounce his or her criminal intention *after* a criminal act has already taken place. In this instance, David's act of complicity had already occurred.

However, in a minority of jurisdictions, withdrawal is a good defense, but it only applies where it has taken place before the criminal act itself *and where the actor has kept the crime from occurring*. Model Penal Code § 2.06 (6), for example, recognizes this defense where the actor "(i) wholly deprives [the assistance] of effectiveness in the commission of the offense; or (ii) gives timely warning to the law enforcement authorities or otherwise makes proper effort to prevent the commission of the offense."

Since David kept silent instead of alerting the police and/or preventing the commission of the bank robbery altogether, he does not have a good withdrawal or renunciation defense even in a minority jurisdiction where such a defense is possible. Hence, answers (a), (b), and (c) are all incorrect, and ipso facto answer (d) is correct.

[For additional discussion of this subject, see John M. Burkoff, Acing Criminal Law, Chapt. 6(A) (West)]

Answer 6–9: The correct answer is (d).

This is likely to be a good defense for Diane.

The common law distinctions between parties to a crime—principals in the first degree, principals in the second degree, accessories before the fact, and accessories after the fact—have been abrogated by statute in the great majority of jurisdictions. With one exception—accessories after the fact—the categories of principal and accessory are said to have "merged." As a result, Diane would have been guilty of the crime of assault on Bruce if she was Megan's accomplice in that assault.

But Diane had the intention to aid—and did aid—Megan in the commission of a different crime, stealing from parking meters. The majority rule is that an accomplice can be convicted only for those crimes that he or she actually intended to assist with, or could reasonably have foreseen would have resulted from his or her assistance.

In this instance, Diane did not actually intend to assist—or actually and actively assist—Megan with her assault on Bruce. Moreover, it is highly unlikely that a jury would find that Diane could reasonably have foreseen that Megan would have committed this assault. There is no indication from the facts set out in this problem that assaulting people who spotted either one of them in their criminal activity was a part of the criminal plan. Hence, answer (c) is incorrect, and answers (a) and (b) are each correct. Because answers (b) and (c) are each correct, answer (d) is the most accurate answer.

[For additional discussion of this subject, see John M. Burkoff, ACING CRIMINAL LAW, Chapt. 6(A) (West)]

Answer 6–10: The correct answer is (b).

Diane met all of the elements of accomplice liability, at the very least, as an accessory before the fact. An accessory before the fact is a person who aids or encourages principals before a crime occurs, but he is not present at the crime scene. With respect to the appropriate mens rea, the prosecution would have to prove that Diane intended to assist Megan in committing the theft and that she intended that the crime actually be committed. Diane's intention to assist Megan was absolutely clear. Hence, answer (a) is incorrect, and ipso facto answer (d) is incorrect as well.

With respect to the actus reus element, to be convicted as an accomplice, an accused must have actively assisted another person or persons in the commission of a crime. Diane clearly met that element as well as she stuffed the parking meters so that the coins would collect and be easy for Megan to remove. The fact that she was not present at the scene when the actual theft occurred is irrelevant. Hence, answer (c) is incorrect.

The common law distinctions between parties to a crime—principals in the first degree, principals in the second degree, accessories before the fact, and accessories after the fact—have been abrogated by statute in the great majority of jurisdictions. With one exception—accessories after the fact—the categories of principal and accessory are said to have "merged." As a result, since Diane was, at minimum, an accessory before the fact in this scenario, and she can be convicted just as if she was a principal for the theft from the parking meters. It makes no difference to this analysis and to Diane's culpability that Megan, the principal, was not charged with this offense. Hence, answer (b) is correct.

[For additional discussion of this subject, see John M. Burkoff, ACING CRIMINAL LAW, Chapt. 6(A) (West)]

CHAPTER 7
VICARIOUS LIABILITY

Answer 7–1: The correct answer is (a).

Arguing that only Cherie was culpable is not likely to be a good defense for Manny.

An accused person may be convicted of a crime vicariously—on the basis of another person's criminal conduct—where the accused is held to be responsible by law. This is true even though the accused was not directly involved in any criminal activity himself or herself.

Model Penal Code § 2.06 (1) provides, for example, that a "person is guilty of an offense if it is committed by his own conduct or by the conduct of another person for which he is legally accountable, or both." And Model Penal Code § 2.06 (2)(b) provides further that a "person is legally accountable for the conduct of another person" when that first person "is made accountable for the conduct of such other person by the Code or by the law defining the offense."

In most jurisdictions, statutes have been enacted that provide that a liquor licensee—like Manny—is vicariously responsible for the actions of his or her employees who have served alcohol to minors. Accordingly, since the jurisdiction in which these facts took place is just such a majority jurisdiction, Manny has been made vicariously responsible for the actions of Cherie pursuant to the criminal law and it is not a good defense for him to claim that he was not there or that he did not know about, ratify, nor assist Cherie's criminal actions in furnishing alcohol to minors. Hence, answer (a) is correct, and answers (b), (c), and (d) are all incorrect.

[For additional discussion of this subject, see John M. Burkoff, ACING CRIMINAL LAW, Chapt. 6(B) (West)]

Answer 7–2: The correct answer is (b).

It may be possible to prosecute Jimmy as well as Stick–T–It Enterprises, depending on exactly what Jimmy's role was with respect to the distribution of the tainted peanut products, i.e. whether or not he had the power to prevent this activity.

Corporations may be held criminally responsible—just like individuals can be—for their criminal actions. But a corporate officer is not usually held vicariously responsible for the corporation's criminal acts unless that officer was directly involved in the criminal activity. As Model Penal Code § 2.07 (6)(a) provides, for example, "[a] person is legally accountable for any conduct he performs or causes to be performed in the name of the corporation or an unincorporated association or in its behalf to the same extent as if it were performed in his own name or behalf."

Accordingly, in this case, in order to prosecute Jimmy for distributing tainted food products, if this jurisdiction follows the majority—and the Model Penal Code—approach, the prosecutor would need to establish that Jimmy was directly responsible for such distribution, either personally or through acts that he caused other people in the corporation to perform, whether or not he actually knew about or ratified those acts. Hence, answer (c) is incorrect, and ipso facto answer (d) is incorrect as well.

Moreover, if Jimmy is prosecuted for this offense, he may possess a "powerlessness" defense. The Supreme Court has ruled that, although corporate officials may be subject to criminal responsibility for their corporation's criminal offenses, they possess a "powerlessness defense" where they can show that they did not possess the actual power and control to keep the criminal activity in question from taking place. *U.S. v. Park*, 421 U.S. 658 (1975). If Jimmy can establish his powerlessness over the distribution of the tainted peanut products, he cannot be found guilty of this criminal offense. Hence, answer (b) is correct, and answer (a) is incorrect.

[For additional discussion of this subject, see John M. Burkoff, ACING CRIMINAL LAW, Chapt. 6(B) (West)]

Answer 7–3: The correct answer is (c).

Criminal charges cannot be filed against Wayne based on Gary's conduct in these circumstances.

Corporate officers and supervisors cannot usually be held vicariously responsible for the criminal acts of their subordinates unless they were directly involved in the subordinate's activity whatever their supervisory relationship. Hence, answers (a) and (b) are incorrect, and ipso facto answer (d) is incorrect as well.

Accordingly, in this instance, in the absence of additional facts which might indicate, for example, that Wayne knew that Gary had previously imbibed alcohol at lunch or had driven recklessly and/or while intoxicated, there is no reason to believe that Wayne was directly involved in any way in Gary's criminal activity. If Wayne did know these sorts of things, he would in fact be directly involved in his subordinate's activity and he could be held responsible for the subordinate's criminal activity. Hence, answer (c) is correct.

[For additional discussion of this subject, see John M. Burkoff, ACING CRIMINAL LAW, Chapt. 6(B) (West)]

CHAPTER 8
ATTEMPT

ACTUS REUS

Answer 8–1: The correct answer is (c).

Robbie cannot be successfully prosecuted for attempted robbery of the convenience store.

A person cannot be convicted of an attempt offense entirely on the basis of his or her thinking about or decision to commit that crime. Proof of the actus reus element of attempt requires the prosecution to establish beyond a reasonable doubt that the accused went farther than simply engaging in "mere preparation" to commit a crime.

In this case, there is no evidence that Robbie did anything more than think about the crime, decide to do it, and to tell her roommate. That is not enough action on her part to establish the actus reus of an attempt crime. Hence, answer (c) is correct, and answer (a) is incorrect.

However, an attempt *could* have existed even if Robbie did not actually enter the store. In a majority of jurisdictions, the ALI Model Penal Code test applies to define the actus reus element of attempt. Under the MPC, the prosecution must prove that the accused took a "substantial step in a course of conduct planned to culminate in … commission of the crime." The "substantial step" test was not satisfied here, but not because Robbie did not enter the store. She could have done any number of things, e.g. buy a weapon to use in the robbery, which would have been a substantial step even if she never ventured anywhere near the store.

In a minority of jurisdictions, however, various forms of proximity tests are used instead of the MPC test in order to assess the existence of the actus reus of attempt. Such tests focus on the question how close the actor came to commission of the criminal act in question, as opposed to looking at how far he or she had gone (the ALI Model Penal Code—and majority—approach). But even in a jurisdiction using a test like this, Robbie would not have needed to actually enter the store to come close to committing a criminal attempt. Accordingly, she was not guilty of attempted robbery, as discussed above, but not because she had not entered the convenience store. Hence, answer (b) is incorrect, and ipso facto answer (d) is incorrect as well.

[For additional discussion of this subject, see John M. Burkoff, ACING CRIMINAL LAW, Chapt. 7(A) (West)]

Answer 8–2: The correct answer is (a).

Omar and Franklin can be successfully prosecuted for the crime of attempted arson of the building housing the dry cleaning shop.

The facts make it a given that they each had the requisite intent to commit the crime of arson. The pivotal question is, therefore, whether the actus reus element of attempt was satisfied on these facts.

In a majority of jurisdictions, the ALI Model Penal Code test applies, and the prosecution must prove that the accused took a "substantial step in a course of conduct planned to culminate in … commission of the crime." In this case, the "substantial step" test is easily satisfied. Omar and Franklin each purchased materials to be used to burn down the shop. That is a substantial step in and of itself. But, what is more, each of them also used those purchased materials in an effort to try to burn the building up. Clearly, actions of this sort are substantial steps on the parts of each of these actors.

In a minority of jurisdictions, however, various forms of proximity tests are used instead to assess the existence of the actus reus of attempt. Such tests focus on the question how close the actor came to commission of the criminal act in question, as opposed to looking at how far he or she had gone (the ALI Model Penal Code—and majority—approach). But even in a jurisdiction using a test like this, Omar and Franklin have also committed the act of attempt. They—each of them acting together—came extremely close to the ultimate commission of the crime of arson. Only the fortuitous intercession of the police kept the crime intended by the two of them from being committed in only a matter of minutes, if not seconds.

Accordingly, there is no question but that Omar and Franklin can be successfully prosecuted for the crime of attempted arson of the dry cleaning shop. Hence, answer (a) is correct, and answers (b), (c), and (d) are all incorrect.

[For additional discussion of this subject, see John M. Burkoff, ACING CRIMINAL LAW, Chapt. 7(A) (West)]

Answer 8–3: The correct answer is (a).

[Note: This question contains the same facts as Question 8–1 with the names changed slightly, except that Bobbie actually purchased a gun to use to commit the robbery. This change, in a majority jurisdiction, makes a big difference in the outcome.] In a majority of jurisdictions, Bobbie can be successfully prosecuted for attempted robbery of the convenience store.

The facts make it a given that Bobbie had the requisite intent to commit the crime of robbery. The pivotal question is, therefore, whether the actus reus element of attempt was satisfied on these facts.

In a majority of jurisdictions, the ALI Model Penal Code test applies, and the prosecution must prove that the accused took a "substantial step in a course of conduct planned to culminate in ... commission of the crime." In this case, the "substantial step" test is easily satisfied. Bobbie purchased a gun to be used to commit the robbery. That is a substantial step. Hence, answer (a) is correct, and answers (b), (c), and (d) are all incorrect.

[For additional discussion of this subject, see John M. Burkoff, Acing Criminal Law, Chapt. 7(A) (West)]

Answer 8–4: The correct answer is (c).

[Note: Just like Question 8–3, this question contains the same facts as Question 8–1 with the names changed slightly, except that Bobbie actually purchased a gun to use to commit the robbery. This change, in a minority jurisdiction, makes no difference in the outcome.] In a minority of jurisdictions, Bobbie *cannot* be successfully prosecuted for attempted robbery of the convenience store.

In a minority of jurisdictions, various forms of proximity tests are used instead of the Model Penal Code approach to assess the existence of the actus reus of attempt. Such tests, taken from the common law, focus on the question how close the actor came to commission of the criminal act in question, as opposed to looking at how far he or she had gone—the Model Penal Code—and majority—approach—by determining whether or not she had taken a substantial step. Hence, answer (b) is incorrect, and ipso facto answer (d) is incorrect as well.

In a jurisdiction using a minority approach to actus reus like this one, Bobbie has likely *not* done enough to commit the act of attempt. She did not come close enough to actually complete the crime of robbery to satisfy the proximity actus reus test. Hence, answer (a) is incorrect, and answer (c) is correct.

[For additional discussion of this subject, see John M. Burkoff, Acing Criminal Law, Chapt. 7(A) (West)]

MENS REA

Answer 8–5: The correct answer is (c).

On these facts standing alone, there is not likely to be enough evidence of the requisite mens rea to convict George of the crime of attempted rape.

There may well be sufficient evidence to satisfy the actus reus element of attempted rape on these facts. By forcibly dragging Susan into the alleyway, George certainly took a substantial step—the actus reus test in a majority of jurisdictions—toward committing the crime of rape. And in minority jurisdictions which use some form of proximity test (how close did the actor come to completing the crime?), Doria's conduct may well be viewed as coming close enough to the commission of the crime of rape to suffice to establish that element as well. Hence, answer (b) is incorrect, and ipso facto answer (d) is incorrect as well.

But it is unlikely, in any event, that the prosecution can establish the mens rea element of attempted rape on these facts alone. The mens rea of any attempt crime is the defendant's intent to commit the specific crime that was the alleged criminal objective of the attempt. In this case, on these facts, it is not clear that George's specific intent was to commit the crime of rape or any other sexual assault, as opposed to, for example, the commission of a simple assault and/or a robbery.

It is true that the intent to commit a specific crime can be established circumstantially. And it's also true that George ripped off part of Susan's blouse, a fact which could have a sexual overtone. But that act of ripping her blouse occurred as George grabbed at her as Susan broke away and subsequently escaped from him. It is not clear that he ripped her blouse in an attempt to engage in sexually assaultive conduct.

Nor is there any evidence in this problem, for example, that George said anything or did anything further which clearly established—beyond a reasonable doubt—his intention to sexually assault her. Forcing Susan to turn away from him in the alley *could* have been the precursor to a sexual assault from behind, but there are a host of other reasons he may have ordered her to do that. If sexual assault was George's intention, it simply was not clear at the point that Susan escaped from him.

Accordingly, although George clearly some committed some other criminal acts on these facts, it is not likely that the prosecution could establish the commission of the crime of attempted rape on the basis of these facts standing alone. Hence, answer (c) is correct, and answer (a) is incorrect.

[For additional discussion of this subject, see John M. Burkoff, ACING CRIMINAL LAW, Chapt. 7(B) (West)]

Answer 8–6: The correct answer is (a).

Dwight can be prosecuted successfully for the crime of attempted murder.

The actus reus element of attempted murder is easily satisfied. By shooting at a police officer, Dwight clearly took a substantial step—the actus reus test in a majority of jurisdictions—toward committing the crime of murder. And in minority jurisdictions which use some form of proximity test (how close did the actor come to completing the crime?), Dwight's act of shooting was clearly an action coming close enough to the commission of the crime of murder to suffice to establish that element as well. How much closer can you come without killing someone? Hence, answer (b) is incorrect.

Moreover, the prosecution should be able to easily establish the mens rea element of attempted murder on these facts. The mens rea of any attempt crime is the defendant's intent to commit the specific crime that was the alleged criminal objective of the attempt. In this case, on these facts, Dwight shot a firearm at a police officer. The intent to commit a specific crime can be established circumstantially. It appears clear that Dwight intended to shoot and kill that officer. The fact that he failed to do so is irrelevant to the attempt analysis. Hence, answer (c) is incorrect.

Accordingly, Dwight can be successfully prosecuted for attempted murder. Hence, answer (a) is correct, and answer (d) is ipso facto incorrect.

[For additional discussion of this subject, see John M. Burkoff, ACING CRIMINAL LAW, Chapt. 7(B) (West)]

Answer 8–7: The correct answer is (b).

Gloria cannot be prosecuted successfully for the crime of attempted murder on these facts as she did not intend to kill anyone.

The actus reus element of attempted murder is easily satisfied. By throwing the television set out of a tenth floor window with a sidewalk below, Gloria clearly took a substantial step—the actus reus test in a majority of jurisdictions—toward committing the crime of murder. And in minority jurisdictions which use some form of proximity test (how close did the actor come to completing the crime?), Gloria's act of propelling the set onto its downward flight was clearly an action coming close enough to the commission of the crime of murder to suffice to establish that element as well. It landed only one foot away from a pedestrian. How much closer can you come to murder without actually killing someone? Hence, answer (c) is incorrect, and ipso facto answer (d) is incorrect as well.

However, the prosecution cannot establish the mens rea element of attempted murder on these facts. The mens rea of any attempt crime is the defendant's intent to commit the specific crime that was the alleged criminal objective of the attempt. In this case, on these facts, Gloria did not intend to kill Yves. She simply intended to destroy the television set so that Mario could not use it to watch his precious soccer games. Because she did not specifically intend to commit the crime of murder, she cannot be prosecuted successfully for attempted murder when no killing actually occurred. Hence, the correct answer is (b), and answer (a) is incorrect.

[For additional discussion of this subject, see John M. Burkoff, ACING CRIMINAL LAW, Chapt. 7(B) (West)]

Answer 8–8: The correct answer is (d).

[Note: this question contains the same facts as Question 8–7 with the names changed slightly, except that Doria has been charged with attempted involuntary manslaughter rather than attempted murder.] Doria cannot be prosecuted successfully for the crime of attempted involuntary manslaughter because no such crime exists. It does not make sense to say that someone intended to act negligently. If that were the case, they would be acting intentionally.

Involuntary manslaughter is an unintentional, not an intentional, crime. The mens rea is either criminal negligence or recklessness, depending on the jurisdiction. But conviction of an attempt crime requires proof of the actual intent to commit a specific crime. As a result, most jurisdictions do not recognize the existence of attempt crimes where the mens rea for the offense attempted is recklessness or negligence.

Since Doria has been charged with commission of a crime that does not exist, she cannot be successfully prosecuted for its commission. Hence, answer (a) is incorrect.

Answer (b) is also incorrect because, even if the crime of attempted involuntary manslaughter existed, Doria may well have—indeed, likely—acted recklessly or negligently in shoving the large television set out the window. And answer (c) is incorrect because, even if the crime of attempted involuntary manslaughter existed, Doria clearly took a substantial step toward killing Yves by throwing the television set out of a tenth floor window with a sidewalk below. Indeed, even in a minority jurisdiction which uses some form of proximity test (how close did the actor come to completing the crime?), Doria's act of propelling the set onto its downward flight was clearly an action coming close enough to the commission of the crime of murder to suffice to establish that element as well. It landed only one foot away from a pedestrian. How much closer can you come to murder without actually killing someone? Hence, the correct answer to this question is answer (d), None of the Above.

[For additional discussion of this subject, see John M. Burkoff, ACING CRIMINAL LAW, Chapt. 7(B) (West)]

ABANDONMENT

Answer 8–9: The correct answer is (a).

Defense counsel will not be successful in making an abandonment defense on Darius' behalf in these circumstances.

Abandonment is a good defense to attempt crimes—and other so-called inchoate offenses, like conspiracy and solicitation—in a majority of jurisdictions. But Darius was not charged with the crime of *attempted* purse snatching. He was charged instead with the completed (choate) criminal offense of purse snatching, a specific type of robbery. Significantly, unlike the case with inchoate offenses in many jurisdictions, there is no abandonment defense to a criminal act which has already been completed. Hence, answer (b) is incorrect, and ipso facto answer (d) is incorrect as well.

Moreover, unless the statute provided otherwise, it is no defense to theft of a purse that the purse's owner did not notice that it had been stolen. Hence, answer (c) is incorrect.

Therefore, although Darius' defense counsel can and probably should raise at the time of sentencing the fact that Darius returned the purse of his own volition, thus trying to persuade the judge to reduce his sentence, abandonment is simply not a good defense to this criminal offense. Hence, answer (a) is the correct answer to this question.

[For additional discussion of this subject, see John M. Burkoff, ACING CRIMINAL LAW, Chapt. 7(D) (West)]

Answer 8–10: The correct answer is (a).

Defense counsel will not be successful in making this defense on Barby and Harvey's behalf on these facts.

Abandonment is a good defense to attempt crimes—and other so-called inchoate offenses, like conspiracy and solicitation—in a majority of jurisdictions. But in order to establish this defense, the accused must show that their abandonment was both voluntary and complete.

An apparent abandonment by an accused is not voluntary, however, if it is motivated, in whole or in part, by circumstances that were not present or apparent at the beginning of the course of conduct that increase the probability of detection or apprehension or make it more difficult to accomplish.

In this case, of course, Barby and Harvey's abandonment was not voluntary at all. They only put the groceries that they otherwise intended to shoplift back on a shelf after they noticed security personnel checking bags and purses. Checks of that sort obviously increased the probability of their detection or apprehension, and make it more difficult for them to accomplish the criminal objective of shoplifting.

Accordingly, defense counsel would not be successful in making an abandonment defense on Barby and Harvey's behalf as their change in plan, leading to desistance, was in fact not voluntary. Hence, answer (b) is incorrect, and ipso facto answer (d) is incorrect as well.

Answer (c) is, moreover, incorrect because Barby and Harvey are being charged with an attempt crime, not a choate offense. Accordingly, the fact they never actually took the groceries in question out of the store is simply irrelevant to the commission of an *attempted* retail theft offense, assuming—as is the case here—that they either took a substantial step toward accomplishing this criminal end (majority rule) or came close to committing it (minority rule).

Since there is no viable defense to these charges, Barby and Harvey will be convicted of retail theft. Hence, answer (a) is correct.

[For additional discussion of this subject, see John M. Burkoff, ACING CRIMINAL LAW, Chapt. 7(D) (West)]

IMPOSSIBILITY

Answer 8–11: The correct answer is (b).

Today, in the great majority of jurisdictions, following the Model Penal Code approach, impossibility is simply not a good defense to an attempt crime. That is to say that it is not a good defense to a charge that an accused person attempted to commit a particular crime where—because of circumstances unknown to that person—he or she could not have actually committed that crime in these circumstances.

More specifically, in this case, it is *not* a good defense to the crime of *attempted* sale of cocaine that the substance in question was not actually cocaine where the accused actually intended to sell cocaine. (It would, however, be a good defense to a charge of *sale*—not attempted sale—of cocaine as one of the elements of that crime would be that the substance in question was actually cocaine.) Hence, answer (b) is correct. And answer (c) is incorrect as it was not Bruce's intention to possess or sell quinine; rather it was his intention to possess and sell cocaine.

Nonetheless, in a small minority of jurisdictions, the old English rule is still followed which distinguishes between "factual impossibility" which was not considered a valid defense to an attempt crime, and "legal impossibility" which was considered a valid defense:

Factual impossibility was said to exist when the actual facts, unknown to the accused, made the commission of the crime he or she intended impossible. Legal impossibility was said to exist when the accused engaged in actions which did not satisfy the elements of the attempt crime charged due to the factual circumstances.

The problem with this distinction is that the very same actions can be categorized as factual or legal impossibility depending entirely on just how the factual circumstances are viewed. If Bruce intended to sell cocaine (as is the case here) but failed simply because the substance in question was—unknown to him—not cocaine, that could be viewed as factual impossibility, and this is no defense to an attempt charge. But the same facts can also be deemed to be legal impossibility as Bruce engaged in actions where it was impossible to sell cocaine (because he didn't really have any cocaine, although he thought that he did).

In any event, since most jurisdictions today reject any application at all of the impossibility defense in attempt cases—factual or legal—it is not a good defense for Bruce that he is faced with the charge of attempted sale of cocaine, when he actually sold quinine. Hence, answer (a) is incorrect, and ipso facto answer (d) is incorrect as well.

[For additional discussion of this subject, see John M. Burkoff, Acing Criminal Law, Chapt. 7(E) (West)]

Answer 8–12: The correct answer is (c).

Since Bryce knew that he was selling quinine to the undercover officer, but simply pretended that he was selling her cocaine instead, he could not be convicted of the crime of attempted sale of cocaine because he lacked the necessary mens rea needed to establish that attempt, i.e. the intent to commit the specific crime of sale of cocaine. Hence, answer (c) is correct, and answers (a), (b), and (d) are all incorrect.

[For additional discussion of this subject, see John M. Burkoff, Acing Criminal Law, Chapts. 7(B) & 7(E) (West)]

Answer 8–13: The correct answer is (b).

Today, in the great majority of jurisdictions, following the Model Penal Code approach, impossibility is not a good defense to an attempt crime. That is to say that it is not a good defense to a charge that an accused person attempted to commit a particular crime where—because of circumstances unknown to that person—he or she could not have actually committed that crime in these circumstances.

More specifically, in this case, it is not a good defense to the crime of *attempted* jury tampering that the person approached and offered money to acquit her brother was not actually a juror where the accused actually intended to bribe a juror. (It would, however, be a good defense to a charge of jury tampering itself as one of the elements of that crime would be that the person sought to be bribed was in fact a juror.) Hence, answer (b) is correct. And answer (c) is incorrect as it was not Mary Lou's intention to bribe a non-juror; rather it was her intention to bribe an actual juror.

Nonetheless, in a small minority of jurisdictions, the old English rule is still followed which distinguishes between "factual impossibility" which was not considered a valid defense to an attempt crime, and "legal impossibility" which was considered a valid defense:

Factual impossibility was said to exist when the actual facts, unknown to the accused, made the commission of the crime he or she intended impossible. Legal impossibility was said to exist when the accused engaged in actions which did not satisfy the elements of the attempt crime charged due to the factual circumstances.

The problem with this distinction is that the very same actions can be categorized as factual or legal impossibility depending entirely on just how the factual circumstances are viewed. If Mary Lou actually intended to bribe a juror (as is the case here) but she failed simply because the person in question was—unknown to her—not a juror, that could be viewed as factual impossibility, and this is no defense to an attempt charge. But the same facts can also be deemed to be legal impossibility as Mary Lou engaged in actions where it was impossible to bribe a juror (because the person approached wasn't really a juror, although Mary Lou thought that she was).

In any event, since most jurisdictions today reject any application at all of the impossibility defense in attempt cases, it is not a good defense for Mary Lou that she faced with the charge of attempted jury tampering, when she actually tried to bribe a person who wasn't on a jury. Hence, answer (a) is incorrect, and ipso facto answer (d) is incorrect as well.

[For additional discussion of this subject, see John M. Burkoff, ACING CRIMINAL LAW, Chapt. 7(E) (West)]

CHAPTER 9
CONSPIRACY

UNILATERAL-BILATERAL

Answer 9–1: The correct answer is (b).

Whether or not Hamilton is actually guilty of the crime of conspiracy to distribute marijuana depends entirely upon the approach taken to conspiracy law in the jurisdiction where he is prosecuted.

The actus reus of conspiracy is an agreement between one or more persons to commit a criminal act or to use criminal means to commit a lawful act. In this problem, Sonia was not actually agreeing to commit a criminal act with Hamilton. She was instead feigning agreement, and she subsequently participated in Hamilton's criminal plan only as a police informant in order to assist in his arrest and incarceration.

But because there was no *actual* agreement between Sonia and Hamilton to commit a criminal act, no conspiracy would or could exist if the jurisdiction in which this prosecution takes place is a "bilateral" conspiracy jurisdiction. In a "bilateral" jurisdiction, at least two people must actually *agree* on a criminal plan in order for a conspiracy to exist. And, once again, Sonia was not actually agreeing. Hence, answers (a) and (c) are both incorrect.

However, a majority of jurisdictions that criminalize criminal conspiracies today follow the Model Penal Code approach to conspiracy law and permit conviction of a criminal defendant for a "unilateral" conspiracy. In a unilateral conspiracy jurisdiction, the act of a single person who believes—rightly or wrongly—that he or she is agreeing with another person to commit a crime is sufficient to establish a conspiracy. There does not need to be, as in a unilateral jurisdiction, a "meeting of the minds" in order to have an agreement sufficient to support a conspiracy conviction. In a unilateral jurisdiction, a defendant *can* be convicted lawfully of criminal conspiracy even if his or her supposed co-conspirator did not actually agree to commit a criminal act. Hence, answer (d) is incorrect.

Accordingly, since Sonia was not actually agreeing to commit the criminal act of distribution of marijuana with Hamilton, Hamilton was not guilty of conspiracy to commit that criminal act in a (minority) bilateral jurisdiction. But because Sonia's feigned agreement would be entirely irrelevant in a (majority) unilateral jurisdiction, Hamilton would be guilty of conspiracy if prosecuted there. Hence, answer (b) is correct.

[For additional discussion of this subject, see John M. Burkoff, Acing Criminal Law, Chapt. 8(A) (West)]

Answer 9–2: The correct answer is (d).

Whether Jon and Elizabeth—either one or both of them—are guilty of the criminal offense of conspiracy to commit incest depends entirely upon the approach taken to conspiracy law in the jurisdiction where they are prosecuted.

The actus reus of conspiracy is an agreement between one or more persons to commit a criminal act or to use criminal means to commit a lawful act. In this problem, Jon and Elizabeth clearly agreed with one another to have sexual intercourse even though they were parent and child, and this sexual activity was prohibited by the criminal law in this jurisdiction as the crime of incest.

However, Jon and Elizabeth were nonetheless not guilty of a criminal conspiracy if this sexual activity took place in a "bilateral" conspiracy jurisdiction. In a "bilateral" conspiracy jurisdiction, at least two people must agree on a criminal plan in order for a conspiracy to exist. But, there is a significant exception to this rule called "Wharton's Rule." Under Wharton's Rule, two people may not be convicted of a conspiracy where each of them has agreed to commit a crime that necessarily requires the participation of both of them. Incest is just such a crime. The crime of incest would not have existed without the participation of both of them. Hence, answers (a) and (c) are incorrect.

But a majority of jurisdictions that criminalize criminal conspiracies today follow the Model Penal Code approach to conspiracy law and permit conviction of a criminal defendant for a "unilateral" conspiracy. In a unilateral conspiracy jurisdiction, the act of a single person who believes—rightly or wrongly—that he or she is agreeing with another person to commit a crime is sufficient to establish a conspiracy. In a unilateral jurisdiction where the focus of the conspiracy offense is upon the actions of each individual and the participation of an agreeing party is irrelevant, Wharton's Rule does not apply. Hence, answer (b) is incorrect.

Accordingly, if this prosecution takes place in a (minority) bilateral conspiracy jurisdiction, neither Jon nor Elizabeth are guilty of conspiracy to commit incest due to the application of Wharton's Rule. If this prosecution takes place instead in a (majority) unilateral conspiracy jurisdiction, Jon and Elizabeth—either one or both of them—are guilty of conspiracy to commit incest. Hence, answer (d) is correct.

[For additional discussion of this subject, see John M. Burkoff, ACING CRIMINAL LAW, Chapt. 8(A) (West)]

AGREEMENT

Answer 9–3: The correct answer is (d).

Moe, Larry, and Curly were not guilty of six separate conspiracies.

The actus reus of conspiracy is an agreement between one or more persons to commit a criminal act or to use criminal means to commit a lawful act. The actus reus of conspiracy is *not* the criminal act or acts that were planned to be committed as a product of the concerted activity. Accordingly, the number of separate conspiracies committed by accused persons is determined by looking to the number of separate conspiratorial agreements, not the number of criminal planned.

In this problem, Moe, Larry, and Curly made only one conspiratorial agreement, although it was an agreement to commit multiple criminal acts of robbery, six in total. Hence, answers (a) and (b) are incorrect because they assume six separate conspiracies.

Because all three of the accused were guilty of only one criminal conspiracy based on that one agreement, answer (d) is correct, and answers (c) and (e) are incorrect.

[For additional discussion of this subject, see John M. Burkoff, ACING CRIMINAL LAW, Chapt. 8(C) (West)]

Answer 9–4: The correct answer is (a).

In a jurisdiction that has a criminal conspiracy offense in its crime code, Don and Ron are guilt of conspiracy to commit bank robbery.

Robbery is a more serious offense than theft, and focuses on the use or threat of violence or force when a theft of property is committed.

Whether it is a unilateral or a bilateral conspiracy jurisdiction, the actus reus of conspiracy is an agreement between one or more persons to commit a criminal act or to use criminal means to commit a lawful act. Such agreement can be—and often is—established circumstantially. This is just such a case. Don's and Ron's actions in robbing the bank appeared choreographed. One watched the premises and patrons while the other one acquired the cash. Accordingly, there is clear, albeit circumstantial, evidence that Don and Ron had agreed to engage in this criminal activity.

To establish the mens rea of conspiracy, the prosecutor must prove the alleged conspirators' intent to agree with each other to commit the crime, and the intent to commit the crime itself. In this problem, the crime was actually committed so the latter mens rea element is clear. And, just as with proof of the actus reus, Don's and Ron's intent to agree with each other to rob the bank is clearly established circumstantially. Hence, answer (c) is incorrect.

Accordingly Don and Ron are each guilty of the criminal offense of conspiracy to commit bank robbery. Hence, answer (a) is correct, and answers (b) and (d) are incorrect.

[For additional discussion of this subject, see John M. Burkoff, Acing Criminal Law, Chapt. 8(C) (West)]

MENS REA

Answer 9–5: The correct answer is (c).

On these facts, Ginger is not guilty of the crime of conspiracy to distribute narcotics.

The actus reus of conspiracy is an agreement between one or more persons to commit a criminal act or to use criminal means to commit a lawful act. While Ginger did not agree to help with the cutting, bagging, or distribution of the cocaine, she *did* agree with Fred to stay away from their apartment while these criminal acts took places, an act—the act of staying away—which could potentially be viewed as *active* complicity. Hence, neither answer (b) nor (d) is correct.

However, whether or not the actus reus of conspiracy could be established in Ginger's case on these facts, the mens rea of conspiracy cannot be proved. To establish the mens rea of conspiracy, the prosecutor must prove the an alleged conspirators' intent to agree with another person to commit the crime, and the intent to commit the crime itself. In this problem, there is no evidence of record that Ginger intended to agree with Fred to commit the crime of distribution of cocaine, nor is there any evidence that Ginger actually intended to commit that crime itself.

The mens rea of conspiracy is not established simply by proof of the fact that Ginger knew that Fred intended to commit the crime of distribution of narcotics. Mere knowledge of someone else's intended criminal conduct is not enough to establish a conspiracy. Accordingly,

Ginger is not guilty of the crime of conspiracy to distribute narcotics due to the absence of conspiratorial intent. Hence, answer (c) is correct, and answer (a) is incorrect.

[For additional discussion of this subject, see John M. Burkoff, ACING CRIMINAL LAW, Chapt. 8(B) (West)]

Answer 9–6: The correct answer is (d).

Neither Abdul nor Mariyah is guilty of the crime of conspiracy to commit reckless driving.

The actus reus of conspiracy is an agreement between one or more persons to commit a criminal act or to use criminal means to commit a lawful act. Such agreement can be—and often is—established circumstantially. It could be argued that this is such a case, that Abdul and Mariyah implicitly agreed to cooperate with one another in Abdul's reckless driving. Abdul played the music so loud that he could not hear the approach of emergency vehicles. And Mariyah urged him, even if teasingly, to continue this arguably criminal course of conduct.

But, even if the actus reus of conspiracy could be established, the requisite mens rea is lacking, whether this is a unilateral or bilateral conspiracy jurisdiction. To establish the mens rea of conspiracy, the prosecutor must prove that an alleged conspirators' intent to agree with another person to commit the crime, and the intent to commit the crime itself. In this problem, the crime that Abdul and Mariyah allegedly conspired to commit, reckless driving, has a mens rea—obviously—of recklessness. But—logically—one cannot intend to be reckless as recklessness is unintentional conduct. As a result, in most jurisdictions at least, a person cannot be found guilty of conspiring to commit a crime that involves a mens rea of recklessness (or negligence).

Accordingly, while Abdul might well be guilty of the substantive criminal offense of reckless driving, and while Mariyah might be guilty as his accomplice in that criminal offense, neither of them can be convicted of the crime of conspiracy to commit reckless driving. Hence, answer (d) is correct, and answers (a), (b) and (c) are incorrect.

[For additional discussion of this subject, see John M. Burkoff, ACING CRIMINAL LAW, Chapt. 8(B) (West)]

OVERT ACT

Answer 9–7: The correct answer is (a).

Xavier, Yarone and Zeb all engaged in a conspiracy to rob the clothing store.

The actus reus of conspiracy is an agreement between one or more persons to commit a criminal act or to use criminal means to commit a lawful act. The agreement to rob the clothing store is acknowledged in the facts of this problem.

Moreover, to establish the mens rea of conspiracy, the prosecutor must prove that alleged conspirators' intended to agree with one another to commit the crime, and that they intended to commit the crime itself. The intent to agree appears clear on these facts. And the intention to commit the crime appears clear as well.

The remaining question then is whether or not the co-conspirators in this problem committed an overt act. In a majority of jurisdictions, the existence of a criminal conspiracy requires proof of the commission by at least one of the co-conspirators of an "overt act" tending to demonstrate the seriousness of the conspirators' purpose. An overt act need not be significant. Far less is required than is necessary, for example, to establish the existence of a substantial step for purposes of making out an attempt offense. In this case, Zeb's act of surveillance of the intended robbery target is more than adequate to establish an overt act on behalf of all three co-conspirators. Accordingly, even in a majority jurisdiction requiring commission of an overt act, Zeb's surveillance suffices, and Xavier, Yarone and Zeb did engage in a conspiracy to rob the clothing store. Hence, answer (a) is correct, and answers (b) and (c) are both incorrect.

[For additional discussion of this subject, see John M. Burkoff, Acing Criminal Law, Chapt. 8(D) (West)]

Answer 9–8: [Note: this question contains the same facts as Question 9–7 with the names changed slightly, except that no one surveilled the robbery target. This change makes a big difference in the outcome.] The correct answer, *i.e. the one statement that is false*, is (a).

Whether Javier, Barone and Deb have engaged in a conspiracy to rob the clothing store depends entirely upon the elements of conspiracy law in the jurisdiction where these acts took place.

The actus reus of conspiracy is an agreement between one or more persons to commit a criminal act or to use criminal means to commit a lawful act. The agreement to rob the clothing store is acknowledged in the facts of this problem.

Moreover, to establish the mens rea of conspiracy, the prosecutor must prove that alleged conspirators' intended to agree with one another to commit the crime, and that they intended to commit the crime itself. The intent to agree appears clear on these facts. And the intention to commit the crime appears clear as well.

The remaining question then is whether the crime of conspiracy in the jurisdiction where these actions took place contains an overt act element. In a majority of jurisdictions, the existence of a criminal conspiracy requires proof of the commission by at least one of the co-conspirators of an "overt act" tending to demonstrate the seriousness of the conspirators' purpose. An overt act need not be significant. Far less is required than is necessary, for example, to establish the existence of a substantial step for purposes of making out an attempt offense. In this case, however, none of the would-be conspirators did anything at all after agreeing to commit the robbery. As a result, the overt act requirement was not satisfied. Hence, answer (a) is correct (because it is false and the question asks you to find the answer that is false) and answer (b) is incorrect because it is true.

Accordingly, in a majority jurisdiction requiring commission of an overt act, Javier, Barone and Deb did not engage in a conspiracy to rob the clothing store as none of them committed an overt act. In a minority jurisdiction, however, where no overt act element exists as part of the criminal conspiracy offense, Javier, Barone and Deb did engage in a conspiracy to rob the clothing store. Hence, answer (c) is incorrect because it is true (and the question asks you to find the answer that is false).

[For additional discussion of this subject, see John M. Burkoff, ACING CRIMINAL LAW, Chapt. 8(D) (West)]

RENUNCIATION & WITHDRAWAL

Answer 9–9: The correct answer is (d). Manny and Doug are guilty of conspiracy to commit theft and to pass bad checks, but Charlie is probably not guilty.

The actus reus of conspiracy is an agreement between one or more persons to commit a criminal act or to use criminal means to commit a lawful act. The agreement to steal Frances' checks and forge her signature and cash them is acknowledged in the facts of this problem.

The mens rea of conspiracy is proof that the alleged conspirators' intended to agree with one another to commit the crime, and that they intended to commit the crime itself. The intent to agree appears clear on these facts. And the intention to commit the crime appears clear as well.

In a majority of jurisdictions, the existence of a criminal conspiracy also requires proof of the commission by at least one of the co-conspirators of an "overt act" tending to demonstrate the seriousness of the conspirators' purpose. An overt act need not be significant. Far less is required than is necessary, for example, to establish the existence of a substantial step for purposes of making out an attempt offense. In this case, Charlie's act of practicing Frances' signature for purposes of forging it on her stolen checks is more than adequate to establish an overt act.

For these reasons, Manny and Doug are clearly conspirators. Hence, answers (b) and (c) are incorrect.

The remaining question with respect to Charlie is whether this jurisdiction follows the majority approach and allows a conspirator to renounce his or her conspiratorial intent and withdraw from the conspiracy. Where such withdrawal is a defense, it must be voluntary and complete, and the withdrawing conspirator generally must at least cooperate with law enforcement authorities to prevent commission of the crime by the remaining conspirators. In this case, although Charlie tried to withdraw but then told Doug that he would not withdraw—under duress—his actual renunciation and withdrawal was made clear by his voluntary confession to the police.

Accordingly, while Manny and Doug have no defense to a charge of conspiracy to commit theft and to pass bad checks, Charlie is probably not guilty of that offense in a jurisdiction that recognizes a renunciation defense. Hence, answer (d) is correct, and answer (a) is incorrect.

[For additional discussion of this subject, see John M. Burkoff, ACING CRIMINAL LAW, Chapt. 8(E) (West)]

Answer 9–10: [Note: this question contains the same facts as Question 9–8 with the names changed slightly, except that one of the participants revealed the robbery plan to an undercover agent. This change makes a big difference in the outcome in some jurisdictions.] The correct answer is (b). Assuming that the statute of limitations has run, Bouvier, Darren and Zeke are not guilty of engaging in a conspiracy to rob the clothing store.

The actus reus of conspiracy is an agreement between one or more persons to commit a criminal act or to use criminal means to commit a lawful act. The agreement to rob the clothing store is acknowledged in the facts of this problem.

Moreover, to establish the mens rea of conspiracy, the prosecutor must prove that alleged conspirators' intended to agree with one another to commit the crime, and that they intended to commit the crime itself. The intent to agree appears clear on these facts. And the intention to commit the crime appears clear as well.

In a majority of jurisdictions, the existence of a criminal conspiracy also requires proof of the commission by at least one of the co-conspirators of an "overt act" tending to demonstrate the seriousness of the conspirators' purpose. An overt act need not be significant. Far less is required than is necessary, for example, to establish the existence of a substantial step for purposes of making out an attempt offense. In this case, however, none of the would-be conspirators did anything at all after agreeing to commit the robbery, hence, the overt act requirement was not satisfied. Accordingly, in a majority jurisdiction requiring commission of an overt act, Bouvier, Darren and Zeke did not engage in a conspiracy to rob the clothing store as none of them committed an overt act. Hence, answer (b) is correct, and answer (a) is incorrect.

In a minority jurisdiction, where no overt act element exists as part of the criminal conspiracy offense, Bouvier, Darren and Zeke did engage in a conspiracy to rob the clothing store. However, abandonment of a conspiracy is presumed if none of the conspirators commits an overt act in furtherance of the conspiratorial objective prior to the running of the statute of limitations. Assuming then that the statute of limitations for conspiracy is less than ten years in this jurisdiction, Bouvier, Darren and Zeke cannot be convicted of this crime at this point in time. Hence, answer (c) is incorrect.

[For additional discussion of this subject, see John M. Burkoff, ACING CRIMINAL LAW, Chapt. 8(E) (West)]

UNKNOWN CO-CONSPIRATORS

Answer 9–11: The correct answer is (d).

Leah's argument will fail. The conspiracy charge need not be dismissed on this ground.

A co-conspirator does not need to know precisely who his or her co-conspirators are in order for a conspiracy to exist with them included. As long as the accused knew that another person or persons were involved in the criminal scheme, he or she was a co-conspirator with them even though he or she did not know their actual identity. Hence, answers (a) and (c) are incorrect. In this case, Nora knew Marcus and knew that Marcus was distributing the crack to someone else (who turned out to be Eddie). And Eddie knew Marcus and knew that Marcus was obtaining the crack cocaine from someone else (who turned out to be Nora).

Accordingly, Nora, Marcus, and Eddie may all be properly charged together with commission of a single conspiracy: conspiracy to distribute narcotics. Hence, answer (d) is correct, and answer (b) is incorrect.

[For additional discussion of this subject, see John M. Burkoff, ACING CRIMINAL LAW, Chapt. 8(G) (West)]

CHAPTER 10
SOLICITATION

Answer 10–1: The correct answer is (d).

Lucas is not guilty of the crime of soliciting Charlie to murder Lucas' wife.

The mens rea of the crime of solicitation is the intent to promote or facilitate the commission of a specific crime to be undertaken by another person solicited to commit it. It is not clear from these facts whether or not Lucas truly possessed this intent.

But what is clear is that the requisite actus reus did not exist. The actus reus of solicitation is the act of commanding, encouraging, or requesting another person to commit a particular crime, murder in this case. But, significantly, a person's actions are not the crime of solicitation where they consists only of obviously hollow threats, joking, or bragging. In this problem, there is no evidence that Lucas was seriously soliciting Charlie to commit this crime. In fact, they both laughed after their supposed agreement for Charlie to murder Lucas' wife in exchange for a six-pack of beer.

Accordingly, on these facts, Lucas did not commit the crime of criminal solicitation. Hence, answer (c) is incorrect. Answers (a), (b), and (d) are all correct, and the most accurate answer is answer (d) since both (a) and (b) are correct.

[For additional discussion of this subject, see John M. Burkoff, Acing Criminal Law, Chapt. 9 (West)]

Answer 10–2: The correct answer is (c).

Lolita committed the crime of solicitation to commit prostitution.

The mens rea of solicitation is the intent to promote or facilitate the commission of a specific crime to be undertaken by another person solicited to commit it. It appears clear from these facts that Lolita intended to promote the commission of the crime of prostitution. (If this conduct took place in a jurisdiction where prostitution is not a crime, however, then solicitation to commit prostitution would not be a crime either.)

Moreover, the actus reus of solicitation also existed on these facts. The actus reus of solicitation is the act of commanding, encouraging, or requesting another person to commit a particular crime, prostitution in this case. Lolita clearly both requested and encouraged Clyde to assist her to engage in an act of prostitution. Hence, answer (b) is incorrect, and ipso facto answer (d) is incorrect as well.

Moreover and significantly, the crime of criminal solicitation exists whether or not the criminal act solicited actually took place or whether the person solicited took any steps to accomplish it. Hence, the fact that Clyde did not respond affirmatively to Lolita's acts of solicitation is irrelevant. Hence, answer (a) is incorrect.

Accordingly, on these facts, Lolita did commit the crime of criminal solicitation. Hence, answer (c) is correct.

[For additional discussion of this subject, see John M. Burkoff, ACING CRIMINAL LAW, Chapt. 9 (West)]

Answer 10–3: The correct answer is (c).

Gilda is guilty of the crime of soliciting Hermione to commit the crime of accomplice to bribery or jury tampering.

The mens rea of solicitation is the intent to promote or facilitate the commission of a specific crime to be undertaken by another person solicited to commit it. It appears clear from these facts that Gilda intended to promote the commission of the crime of bribery or jury tampering (depending upon just how these crimes are defined in that jurisdiction) by making the person she solicited an accomplice in that offense.

Moreover, the actus reus of solicitation also existed on these facts. The actus reus of solicitation is the act of commanding, encouraging, or requesting another person to commit a particular crime. Gilda clearly both requested and encouraged the supposed juror to assist her in bribing a juror. Hence, answer (b) is incorrect.

It is not a defense to a charge of criminal solicitation that the person being solicited could not commit the crime for which he or she was solicited. Moreover, the crime of criminal solicitation exists whether or not the criminal act solicited actually took place or whether the person solicited took any steps to accomplish it. Hence, the fact that Hermione was not a juror at all and did not assist and could not have assisted Gilda in the commission of this offense by accepting money is irrelevant. Hence, answer (a) is incorrect.

Accordingly, on these facts, Gilda did commit the crime of criminal solicitation. Hence, answer (c) is correct, and ipso facto answer (d) is incorrect.

[For additional discussion of this subject, see John M. Burkoff, ACING CRIMINAL LAW, Chapt. 9 (West)]

Answer 10–4: The correct answer is (a).

Some jurisdictions permit a person who is charged with a solicitation offense to use a renunciation defense, proving that he or she completely and voluntarily renounced his or her criminal intent and prevented the commission of the crime. But such a renunciation is not complete if the person engaging in it merely abandons the solicitation of one person while continuing to try to solicit others to accomplish his or her criminal objective. That appears to be exactly what happened on these facts when Gilda abandoned Hermione, who was not a juror, in search of the real juror who she still hoped to induce to accept money to vote to acquit her husband. Hence, answer (b) is incorrect, and ipso facto answer (d) is incorrect as well.

Moreover, an apparent abandonment by an accused is not voluntary if it is motivated, in whole or in part, by circumstances that were not present or apparent at the beginning of the course of conduct that increase the probability of detection or apprehension or make it more difficult to accomplish.

In this case, of course, Gilda's abandonment was not voluntary at all. She only abandoned her plan when she discovered that she was soliciting the wrong person and that fact clearly made it more difficult for her to accomplish her criminal objective. Hence, answer (c) is incorrect.

Since there is no viable renunciation defense to such a charge, Gilda will be convicted of soliciting Hermione to commit a criminal offense. Hence, answer (a) is correct.

CHAPTER 11
ASSAULT

Answer 11–1: The correct answer is (a).

Defense counsel is not correct. Ellen did in fact commit an assault on Chloe.

At common law and in a minority of jurisdictions today, a person commits a criminal assault when he or she intentionally places another person in actual and reasonable fear of an imminent battery. A battery at common law and in a minority of jurisdictions today is committed when a person intentionally touches another person against the other person's will, thereby injuring him or her. In a majority of jurisdictions today, the separate common law offense of battery has merged into the criminal offense of assault. Accordingly, in those majority jurisdictions, an assault is committed when a person either intentionally places another person in actual and reasonable fear of an imminent battery or intentionally commits a battery.

In either event, whether the facts set out in this problem occurred in a minority or majority jurisdiction, Ellen has committed a criminal assault. She intentionally placed Chloe in actual and reasonable fear of an imminent battery when she burst into her bedroom in the middle of the night, screaming and brandishing a pistol.

Chloe's actual fear was a given, and certainly such actual fear on her part would be reasonable in these bizarre circumstances, particularly when a person is awakened so precipitously out of a deep sleep by someone with a gun. The fact that the pistol that Ellen brandished was unloaded is irrelevant, as is the fact that Chloe was—other than being frightened—otherwise unharmed. Hence, answers (b) and (c) are incorrect, and ipso facto answer (d) is incorrect as well.

Accordingly, on these facts, Ellen has committed a criminal assault on Chloe. Hence, answer (a) is correct.

[For additional discussion of this subject, see John M. Burkoff, ACING CRIMINAL LAW, Chapt. 11 (West)]

Answer 11–2: The correct answer is (d).

Henry is not guilty of the crime of assault.

At common law and in a minority of jurisdictions today, a person commits a criminal assault when he or she intentionally places another person in actual and reasonable fear of an imminent battery. A battery at common law and in a minority of jurisdictions today is committed when a person intentionally touches another person against the other person's will, thereby injuring him or her. In a majority of jurisdictions today, the separate common law offense of battery has merged into the criminal offense of assault. Accordingly, in those majority jurisdictions, an assault is committed when a person either intentionally places another person in actual and reasonable fear of an imminent battery or intentionally commits a battery.

In either event, whether the facts set out in this problem occurred in a minority or majority jurisdiction, Henry has not committed a criminal assault. He did not intentionally place Marielle in actual and reasonable fear of an imminent battery when he burst into her room yelling about chocolates. Hence, answer (a) is incorrect, and answer (b) is correct.

While Marielle was obviously scared, there is no evidence that she was actually afraid that Henry was about to commit a battery on her, i.e. intentionally touching her against her will, thereby injuring her. Henry scared her, but her fear was occasioned by his unexpected entry and tone of voice, not by a fear that he would hurt her.

Moreover, even if Marielle did actually fear that Henry was about to commit a battery on her, such fear was not reasonable. Again, Henry's behavior would not have reasonably given any occupant of the room reason to fear that he would hurt them, as opposed to simply giving them candy. He was brandishing a box of chocolates, not a weapon of any sort. Additionally, Marielle's fear may well have been a product of her confused condition and isolation and her reaction, accordingly, was not one that would be reasonably expected by a negligent intruder like Henry. Hence, answer (c) is correct.

Accordingly, on these facts, Henry did not commit a criminal assault on Marielle. Because answers (b) and (c) are both correct, answer (d) is the most accurate answer.

[For additional discussion of this subject, see John M. Burkoff, ACING CRIMINAL LAW, Chapt. 11 (West)]

Answer 11–3: The correct answer is (d).

Dennis is not guilty of the crime of battery.

At common law, a battery was committed when a person intentionally touched another person against the other person's will, thereby injuring him or her. The common law definition of battery continues to apply in this jurisdiction. Dennis did not commit a battery on Brenda for two reasons.

First, he did not touch her. Hence, answer (a) is correct, and answer (b) is incorrect.

Second, he did not injure her. Hence, answer (c) is correct.

As a result, on these facts, Dennis is not guilty of the crime of battery. Because answers (a) and (c) are both correct, answer (d) is the most accurate answer.

[For additional discussion of this subject, see John M. Burkoff, ACING CRIMINAL LAW, Chapt. 11 (West)]

Answer 11–4: The correct answer is (b).

Sierra is not likely to be convicted of assault.

At common law and in a minority of jurisdictions today, a person commits a criminal assault when he or she intentionally places another person in actual and reasonable fear of an imminent battery. A battery at common law and in a minority of jurisdictions today is committed when a person intentionally touches another person against the other person's will, thereby injuring him or her. In a majority of jurisdictions today, the separate common law offense of battery has merged into the criminal offense of assault. Accordingly, in those majority jurisdictions, an assault is committed when a person either intentionally places another person in actual and reasonable fear of an imminent battery or intentionally commits a battery.

In either event, whether the facts set out in this problem occurred in a minority or a majority jurisdiction, Sierra is not likely to be convicted of the commission of a criminal assault. She did not intentionally place John in actual and reasonable fear of an imminent battery when she thundered out of his office, muttering her threats to him.

In the first place, her threatened actions were not imminent in the slightest. Sierra was a law student and she talked about what she would do to John *when she was an attorney*, which might well be a number of years in the future (particularly if she keeps getting C-range grades in law school).

Second, Sierra did not place John in actual or reasonable fear of a battery. A battery is committed when a person intentionally touches another person against his or her will, causing injury. But Sierra's threats were much more lawyerly than they were physical in nature, i.e. she appeared to be intimating some sort of future legal or other non-physical types of action against John. While John may well have been shaken by Sierra's threatening actions and behavior, there is no indication that he actually feared that she would commit a battery upon him. Hence, answer (b) is correct, and answer (a) is incorrect.

Moreover, even if John did actually believed that Sierra threatened to commit a battery upon him, there is every chance that such a belief on his part would not be deemed by a judge or jury to be reasonable under these circumstances. Indeed, in some jurisdictions, a reasonable fear of a battery cannot be established as a matter of law solely by a person's verbal threats toward another person. Hence, answer (c) is incorrect, and ipso facto answer (d) is incorrect as well.

Accordingly, Sierra is not likely to be convicted of assault on the basis of these facts.

[For additional discussion of this subject, see John M. Burkoff, Acing Criminal Law, Chapt. 11 (West)]

CHAPTER 12
SEX CRIMES

USE OF FORCE OR ABSENCE OF CONSENT

Answer 12–1: The correct answer is (b).

Calvin is not likely to be convicted of the rape of Crystal on the basis of these facts.

In some American jurisdictions today, the crime of rape is defined as sexual intercourse with another person where the accused has used or threatened the use of force on the victim to accomplish the sex act. In other jurisdictions, a person commits rape when he or she has sexual intercourse with another person without that other person's consent. At common law, *both* of these elements—the use or threat of force *and* the absence of the victim's consent—were elements of the crime of rape. Whichever form of rape statute is used in this jurisdiction, Calvin is not likely to be convicted of rape.

If this jurisdiction has a rape statute with a use-of-force element, it is not likely to be deemed to be satisfied on these facts by a judge or jury. Although in many jurisdictions, this element includes the use of psychological pressure by the accused as well as the use or threat of physical force, to support a rape conviction, such a threat must be one of death or serious physical harm to the victim or another person. In this case, the pressure Calvin applied to Crystal was merely a financial inducement and, perhaps, the implicit threat of negative employment consequences if she did not have sexual relations with him. Such a threat is not likely to satisfy the use-of-force element.

Moreover, in a jurisdiction where the rape statute does not have a use-of-force element but does have an absence-of-consent by the victim element instead, Calvin is not likely to be convicted of rape either. Consent to sexual activity is effective if it is freely and voluntarily given by a competent person. Consent is not freely and voluntarily given when it is the product of the accused person's use of force, deception or duress, or where the victim is impaired mentally. Crystal was not mentally impaired, and she was not forced or tricked into having sexual relations with Calvin. Duress involves an unlawful and imminent threat of death or serious bodily harm to the person being coerced or a third party. As discussed above, such a threat did not exist in this situation either. Hence, answer (b) is correct, and answer (c) is incorrect.

Of course, Crystal may well have felt some significant level of psychological compulsion in this situation. She had no sexual interest in Calvin prior to his suggested financial inducement to her, and she may have believed—perhaps accurately—that her failure to have sexual intercourse with him would lead to negative employment consequences. Nonetheless, it seems likely (but not certain by any means) that a judge or jury would find that Crystal's agreement to have sexual intercourse with Calvin was freely and voluntarily given in these circumstances. Hence, answer (a) is incorrect, and ipso facto answer (d) is incorrect as well.

Accordingly, although Calvin may well have acted illegally in his conduct with Crystal, he is not likely to be convicted of the rape of Crystal on the basis of these facts.

[For additional discussion of this subject, see John M. Burkoff, ACING CRIMINAL LAW, Chapt. 11(A & B) (West)]

Answer 12–2: The correct answer is (c).

Lloyd is likely to be convicted of the rape of Mandy.

In some American jurisdictions today, the crime of rape is defined as sexual intercourse with another person where the accused has used or threatened the use of force on the victim to accomplish the sex act. In other jurisdictions, a person commits rape when he or she has sexual intercourse with another person without that other person's consent. At common law, *both* of these elements—the use or threat of force *and* the absence of the victim's consent—were elements of the crime of rape. Whichever form of rape statute is used in this jurisdiction, Lloyd is likely to be convicted of rape.

If this jurisdiction has a rape statute with a use-of-force element, it is likely to be deemed satisfied on these facts by a judge or jury since Lloyd ripped off Mandy's clothes, pushed her on his bed, and kept her from leaving by laying on top of her. As soon as he rolled off of her, she left immediately. Furthermore, the fact that Mandy did not resist him physically is irrelevant. Under the common law, a victim needed to resist to the utmost before a rape prosecution could succeed but this requirement has been eliminated in the United States. Hence, answers (a) and (b) are both incorrect.

Moreover, in a jurisdiction where the rape statute does not have a use-of-force element but does have an absence-of-consent by the victim element instead, Lloyd will clearly be convicted of rape. Consent to sexual activity is effective only if it is freely and voluntarily given by a competent person. In this case, Mandy repeatedly said "No" to Lloyd's overtures. The fact that she said nothing the final time he asked is irrelevant. The absence of consent does not have to be verbal. It can be—and often is—inferred from a person's actions. Mandy never indicated to Lloyd that she freely and voluntarily consented to have sexual intercourse with him. In fact, everything she said and did made clear exactly the opposite. Hence, answer (d) is incorrect.

Accordingly, Lloyd is likely to be convicted of the rape of Mandy. Hence, answer (c) is correct.

[For additional discussion of this subject, see John M. Burkoff, ACING CRIMINAL LAW, Chapt. 11(A & B) (West)]

Answer 12–3: The correct answer is (d).

Conan raped Margie.

In some American jurisdictions today, the crime of rape is defined as sexual intercourse with another person where the accused has used or threatened the use of force on the victim to accomplish the sex act. In other jurisdictions, a person commits rape when he or she has sexual intercourse with another person without that other person's consent. At common law, *both* of these elements—the use or threat of force *and* the absence of the victim's consent—were elements of the crime of rape. Whichever form of rape statute is used in this jurisdiction, Conan Committed the crime of rape.

If this jurisdiction has a rape statute with a use-of-force element, Conan satisfied that element since he pushed her onto the couch to have sex with her against her will, and kept her from leaving by laying on top of her. The fact that Margie did not resist Conan at this point is irrelevant. Under the common law, a victim needed to resist to the utmost before a rape prosecution could succeed but this requirement has been eliminated in the United States. Hence, answers (b) and (c) are incorrect.

Moreover, in a jurisdiction where the rape statute does not have a use-of-force element but does have an absence-of-consent by the victim element instead, Conan also committed an act of rape. Consent to sexual activity is effective only if it is freely and voluntarily given by a competent person. In this case, Margie told Conan "No" quite clearly and forcefully before he had intercourse with her. The fact that she had told him "yes" previously is irrelevant. A valid consent to sexual activity may be withdrawn at any point before sexual intercourse has actually begun. Sexual intercourse had not begun before Margie said "No." Hence, answer (a) is incorrect.

Accordingly, on these facts, Conan committed the crime of rape of Margie. Hence, answer (d) is correct.

[For additional discussion of this subject, see John M. Burkoff, ACING CRIMINAL LAW, Chapt. 11(A & B) (West)]

Answer 12–4: The correct answer is (c).

On these facts, Rodney is likely to be convicted of the rape of Desiree.

In this jurisdiction, an act of sexual intercourse without a victim's consent constitutes the crime of rape. Consent to sexual activity is only effective if it is freely and voluntarily given by a competent person. In this case, Desiree never consented at all.

In a minority of jurisdictions, an accused rapist can defend against a rape charge by proving that he or she honestly and reasonably believed that the victim consented to the act of sexual intercourse. In a majority of jurisdictions, this is no defense at all.

But even if this jurisdiction permits such a defense and even if Rodney truly believed that Desiree had consented by agreeing to go on a road trip with him, it seems very unlikely that a judge or jury would believe that it was reasonable to infer consent to sexual intercourse from the mere fact that two people were traveling together. Hence, answer (a) is incorrect, and ipso facto answer (d) is incorrect as well. Furthermore, answer (b) is incorrect as there is no evidence that Desiree had consented to have sexual intercourse with Rodney prior to his act of penetrating her.

Accordingly, on these facts, Rodney is likely to be convicted of the rape of Desiree. Hence, answer (c) is correct.

[For additional discussion of this subject, see John M. Burkoff, ACING CRIMINAL LAW, Chapt. 11(A & B) (West)]

SPOUSAL RAPE

Answer 12–5: The correct answer is (a).

At common law, a husband could not be convicted of raping his wife. Hence, since the common law rules still apply in this jurisdiction, answer (a) is correct, and answers (b), (c) and (d) are all incorrect.

[For additional discussion of this subject, see John M. Burkoff, ACING CRIMINAL LAW, Chapt. 11(D) (West)]

Answer 12–6: The correct answer is (b).

Today, in most jurisdictions, the common law rule that a husband could not be convicted of raping his wife has either been eliminated or a separate criminal offense has been enacted criminalizing spousal rape as a separate criminal offense. Since these events took place in a jurisdiction where the spousal rape exemption has been eliminated, Arnold is guilty of rape. The fact that Helen was his wife is irrelevant. Hence, answer (a) is incorrect, and answer (d) is ipso facto incorrect as well. Answer (c) is also incorrect as there is no impediment to criminalizing spousal rape the same as the rape of any other victim. Hence, answer (c) is also incorrect.

In some American jurisdictions today, the crime of rape is defined as sexual intercourse with another person where the accused has used or threatened the use of force on the victim to accomplish the sex act. In other jurisdictions, a person commits rape when he or she has sexual intercourse with another person without that other person's consent. At common law, *both* of these elements—the use or threat of force *and* the absence of the victim's consent—were elements of the crime of rape. Since the fact that the victim was his spouse is totally irrelevant under this rape statute, whichever form of rape statute is used in this jurisdiction, Arnold clearly committed the crime of rape.

If this jurisdiction has a rape statute with a use-of-force element, Arnold satisfied that element since the facts make clear that he had sex with Helen forcibly and against her will.

Moreover, in a jurisdiction where the rape statute does not have a use-of-force element but does have an absence-of-consent by the victim element instead, Arnold also committed an act of rape. Consent to sexual activity is effective only if it is freely and voluntarily given by a competent person. Helen did not consent to engage in sexual activity with Arnold.

Accordingly, Arnold is guilty of raping Helen. Hence, answer (b) is correct.

[For additional discussion of this subject, see John M. Burkoff, Acing Criminal Law, Chapt. 11(D) (West)]

Answer 12–7: The correct answer is (e).

Since these events took place in a jurisdiction where the spousal rape exemption continues as to the rape offense, but a separate spousal rape criminal offense has been enacted, Arnold is not guilty of rape. Hence, answer (d) is correct. Arnold would, however, be guilty, if he was charged properly, of the spousal rape offense itself.

A separate spousal rape statute applies exclusively to an accused person's criminal sexual activity with a spouse. Hence, answer (a) is incorrect. Not only is sexual activity with a spouse not exempted, it is one of the elements of the offense.

At common law, a "fresh complaint" element required the spousal victim to report the sexual offense by her spouse promptly to the police.

Since that element exists in this particular jurisdiction, it was clearly satisfied when Helen immediately called the police after Arnold finished sexually assaulting her. Hence, answer (b) is incorrect.

In some American jurisdictions today, the crime of rape is defined as sexual intercourse with another person where the accused has used or threatened the use of force on the victim to accomplish the sex act. In other jurisdictions, a person commits rape when he or she has sexual intercourse with another person without that other person's consent. At common law, *both* of these elements—the use or threat of force *and* the absence of the victim's consent—were elements of the crime of rape. Since the spousal rape statute in this jurisdiction incorporates all of the elements of the rape statute except for the latter's limitation to non-spousal victims, whichever form of rape statute as described above is used in this jurisdiction, Arnold clearly committed the crime of rape.

If this jurisdiction has a rape statute with a use-of-force element, Arnold satisfied that element since the facts make clear that he had sex with Helen forcibly and against her will. And in a jurisdiction where the rape statute does not have a use-of-force element but does have an absence-of-consent by the victim element instead, Arnold also committed an act of rape. Consent to sexual activity is effective only if it is freely and voluntarily given by a competent person. Helen did not consent to engage in sexual activity with Arnold. Hence, answer (c) is correct.

Finally, since answers (c) and (d) are correct, and answers (a) and (b) are incorrect, answer (e) is the most accurate answer.

[For additional discussion of this subject, see John M. Burkoff, Acing Criminal Law, Chapt. 11(D) (West)]

STATUTORY RAPE

Answer 12–8: The correct answer is (c).

It is very likely that Mike will be convicted of statutory rape for having had sexual intercourse with Alicia, a fifteen-year old girl.

Statutory rape is sexual intercourse with a minor who is below a specified age. Statutory rape is committed whether or not the minor who engaged in the act consented or not. Accordingly, since the specified age of consent in this jurisdiction is 16 years old, Mike is guilty of statutory rape despite the fact that the sexual act was initiated by Alicia and despite the fact that she engaged in the act freely and voluntarily. Hence, Answers (a) and (b) are incorrect, and ipso facto answer (d) is incorrect as well.

Parenthetically, in some jurisdictions, conviction of statutory rape also requires proof of a specified age gap between the accused and his or her victim. If this jurisdiction has such a provision in its statutory rape offense, the crime of statutory rape was not committed in this case if that gap is seven years or greater, the difference between Mike's and Alicia's ages. Typically, the statutory gap is only four years or so, hence, this is unlikely to be a good defense for Mike.

Accordingly, it is likely that Mike will be convicted of statutory rape on these facts. Hence, answer (c) is correct.

[For additional discussion of this subject, see John M. Burkoff, Acing Criminal Law, Chapt. 11(F) (West)]

Answer 12–9: The correct answer is (c).

It is likely that Spike will be convicted of the statutory rape of Edward.

At common law, the rape and statutory rape offenses applied only to the acts of male defendants upon female victims. Modern sexual assault statutes are, however, gender neutral. Hence the fact that both the accused and the victim in this case are male is irrelevant to the analysis. In addition, anal intercourse is expressly included in the statutory definition of sexual intercourse in this jurisdiction.

Statutory rape is sexual intercourse with a minor who is below a specified age. Statutory rape is committed whether or not the minor who engaged in the act consented or not. Accordingly, since the specified age of consent in this jurisdiction is 16 years old and Edward was 15 years old, Spike is guilty of statutory rape despite the fact that the sexual act was initiated by Edward and despite the fact that he engaged in the act freely and voluntarily. Hence, answer (a) is incorrect.

In some jurisdictions, parenthetically, conviction of statutory rape also requires proof of a specified age gap between the accused and his or her victim. If this jurisdiction has such a provision in its statutory rape offense, the crime of statutory rape was not committed in this case if that gap is seven years or greater, the difference between Spike's and Edward's ages. Typically, the statutory gap is only four years or so, hence, this is unlikely to be a good defense for Spike.

Finally, in a minority of jurisdictions, an accused can defend against a statutory rape charge when the victim is within a specified age range by proving that he honestly and reasonably believed that his or her sex partner consented to the act of sexual intercourse. In a majority of jurisdictions, this is no defense at all.

But even if this jurisdiction permits such a defense and even if Edward was within that age range and even if Spike truly believed that

Edward was 16 years old as his driver's license (falsely) stated, it seems very unlikely that a judge or jury would believe that this belief was reasonable. The reason that Spike looked at Edward's license was because he thought that Edward might be under 16 years of age. Given the fact that possession of fake driver's licenses is relatively common in this country, it was likely unreasonable for Spike to have relied upon Edward's as proof that he was old enough to have sex with him.

Accordingly, the likelihood that Spike will be convicted of statutory rape on these facts—while not a certainty—is nonetheless high. Hence, answer (c) is correct, and ipso facto answer (d) is incorrect.

[For additional discussion of this subject, see John M. Burkoff, ACING CRIMINAL LAW, Chapt. 11(F) (West)]

CHAPTER 13
HOMICIDE

FIRST DEGREE MURDER

Answer 13–1: The correct answer is (d).

Sid is not guilty of first degree murder in the death of Amir.

To support a conviction for murder, the prosecution must establish that the person accused of the crime, acting with malice, committed a killing act that caused the death of another person. "Malice" refers to a particularly heinous ill will on the part of a killer. It is not clear whether or not Sid's failure to adequately secure the lighting fixture would be viewed as malicious.

But, in addition to malice, in any event, to support a conviction for first degree murder, the prosecution must also establish that the accused had the specific intent to kill his or her victim, engaging in premeditation and deliberation about the killing act. In other words, a conviction for such premeditated murder requires proof of the accused person's actual, prior thought and reflection about the particular killing act in question.

In this case, there is no evidence on this record that Sid premeditated and deliberated about killing Amir, that he engaged in any prior thought and reflection about killing Amir at all. While Sid may well have acted maliciously, and while his act of failing to properly secure the light fixture may have been a substantial cause of Amir's death, there is no evidence that he specifically intended that result to occur. Hence, on these facts, while Sid may have acted recklessly or criminally negligently, the element of premeditation and deliberation cannot be satisfied.

Accordingly, the likelihood of a successful prosecution of Sid for first degree murder in the death of Amir is slim. Hence, the correct answer is (d), and answers (a), (b), and (c) are incorrect.

[For additional discussion of this subject, see John M. Burkoff, ACING CRIMINAL LAW, Chapt. 12(A)(1) (West)]

Answer 13–2: The correct answer is (e).

Lacey could be found guilty of first degree murder in the killing of Marcos.

To support a conviction for murder, the prosecution must establish that the person accused of the crime, acting with malice, committed a killing act that caused the death of another person. Malice is easy to establish here. "Malice" refers to a particularly heinous ill will on the part of a killer. Malice is often presumed where a person has killed another person by using a deadly weapon, e.g. a gun or a knife, on a vital part of the victim's body. That is, of course, exactly what happened here. Hence, answers (a) and (d) are incorrect.

In addition, to support a conviction for first degree murder, the prosecution must also establish that the accused had the specific intent to kill his or her victim, engaging in premeditation and deliberation about the killing act. In other words, a conviction for such premeditated murder requires proof of the accused person's actual, prior thought and reflection about the particular killing act in question.

In this case, Lacey stomped out into the backyard, still angry and fuming about Marcos' arguments and behavior. She had time—five minutes—to think about all of this before she returned to the kitchen. While five minutes is not a lot of time, in many jurisdictions, "no time is too short" for a person to premeditate and deliberate a killing. But an adequate amount of time is a necessary but not a sufficient requirement for a finding of premeditation and deliberation. There must also be sufficient evidence that the accused actually premeditated and deliberated the killing.

It is certainly possible that a judge or jury would conclude that that is exactly what Lacey did in the backyard, namely, in her extreme anger, premeditate and deliberate about killing Marcos. Indeed, when Lacey returned to the kitchen, she was still very angry at Marcos, she was screaming at him, and she headed straight toward the knife rack where she subsequently grabbed a knife and quickly stabbed him. Hence, answers (b) and (d) are incorrect.

Lacey's defense counsel will likely argue that Lacey did not actually decide to grab the knife and stab Marcos until the moment that he called her "irrational" at the very end of this episode. An "impulse killing" is, by definition, one that is not premeditated and deliberated.

Defense counsel will likely argue that Lacey acted impulsively in response to this insult and that she did not premeditate and deliberate about killing Marcos. Whether or not a judge or jury will believe this argument is impossible to predict with any certainty, but the fact that

Lacey was headed directly toward the knife rack when she returned to the kitchen makes defense counsel's likely account of her behavior somewhat less plausible. Hence, answers (c) and (d) are incorrect.

Accordingly, depending upon the factual conclusions found by the judge or jury hearing this case, Lacey could be found guilty of first degree murder in the killing of Marcos. Hence, answer (e) is correct.

[For additional discussion of this subject, see John M. Burkoff, ACING CRIMINAL LAW, Chapt. 12(A)(1) (West)]

Answer 13–3: The correct answer is (b).

Amos is not guilty of first degree murder in the shooting death of Tommy.

To support a conviction for murder, the prosecution must establish that the person accused of the crime, acting with malice, committed a killing act that caused the death of another person. "Malice" refers to a particularly heinous ill will on the part of a killer. Malice is often presumed where a person has killed another person by using a deadly weapon, e.g. a gun or a knife, on a vital part of the victim's body. Malice is present here since Amos used a gunshot to the head to kill Tommy. Hence, answers (a) and (c) are incorrect.

But, in addition to malice, to support a conviction for first degree murder, the prosecution must also establish that the accused had the specific intent to kill his or her victim, engaging in premeditation and deliberation about the killing act. In other words, a conviction for such premeditated murder requires proof of the accused person's actual, prior thought and reflection about the particular killing act in question.

In this case, there is no evidence on this record that Amos premeditated and deliberated—that he engaged in any prior thought and reflection—about killing Tommy or, for that matter, about killing anyone. While Amos may well have acted maliciously and recklessly, and while his act of shooting into the air was a substantial cause of Tommy's death, there is no evidence that he specifically intended that result to occur. Hence, on these facts, the element of premeditation and deliberation cannot be satisfied. Hence, answer (b) is correct.

Accordingly, while he could very likely be convicted of a different homicide offense, Amos is not guilty of first degree murder in the shooting death of Tommy. Hence, answer (d) is incorrect.

[For additional discussion of this subject, see John M. Burkoff, ACING CRIMINAL LAW, Chapt. 12(A)(1) (West)]

Answer 13–4: The correct answer is (d).

Alexander is likely to be found guilty of first degree murder with respect to the killing of Anthony.

To support a conviction for murder, the prosecution must establish that the person accused of the crime, acting with malice, committed a killing act that caused the death of another person. Malice is easy to establish here. "Malice" refers to a particularly heinous ill will on the part of a killer. Malice is often presumed where a person has killed another person by using a deadly weapon, e.g. a gun or a knife, on a vital part of the victim's body. That is, of course, exactly what happened here. Alexander shot and killed Anthony. Hence, answers (a) and (c) are incorrect.

In addition, to support a conviction for first degree murder, the prosecution must also establish that the accused had the specific intent to kill his or her victim, engaging in premeditation and deliberation about the killing act. In other words, a conviction for such premeditated murder requires proof of the accused person's actual, prior thought and reflection about the particular killing act in question.

In this case, Alexander's action of seeing Anthony rise and shooting him was almost instantaneous. However, in many jurisdictions, "no time is too short" for a person to premeditate and deliberate a killing. But an adequate amount of time is a necessary but not a sufficient requirement for a finding of premeditation and deliberation. There must also be sufficient evidence that the accused actually premeditated and deliberated the killing.

In this case, Chris and Alexander arrived at the bank with Alexander armed with an automatic pistol. Alexander brandished that pistol while ordering everyone in the bank to get down and stay down. Clearly, his threat implied that anyone who didn't obey this command risked being shot, which is, of course, exactly what happened. And just as clearly, this threat at gunpoint was the subject of prior thought and discussion between Chris and Anthony as part of the bank robbery plan. As a result, it appears likely that a judge or jury would find that Alexander had both adequate time to premeditate and deliberate this killing, and that there is substantial evidence that that is precisely what he did. Hence, answer (b) is incorrect.

Accordingly, Alexander is likely to be found guilty of first degree murder with respect to the killing of Anthony. Hence, answer (d) is correct.

[For additional discussion of this subject, see John M. Burkoff, ACING CRIMINAL LAW, Chapt. 12(A)(1) (West)]

SECOND DEGREE MURDER

Answer 13–5: The correct answer is (a).

Glenna can be convicted of murder on these facts.

To support a conviction for murder, the prosecution must establish that the person accused of the crime, acting with malice, committed a killing act that caused the death of another person. "Malice" refers to a particularly heinous ill will on the part of a killer.

Malice may be established expressly or implied from the circumstances. In many jurisdictions, it can be implied from the accused's act of gross recklessness or actions undertaken with extreme indifference to the value of human life. Malice is often presumed where a person has killed another person by using a deadly weapon, e.g. a gun or a knife, on a vital part of the victim's body. Although this presumption may not apply in this case as Lidia used the gun on her own body and of her own accord, it also may apply as Lidia pulled the trigger at Glenna's persistent urging.

In any event, a judge or jury could easily conclude that Glenna's act of convincing Lidia to play Russian roulette with a gun—even a supposedly unloaded gun—was impliedly malicious. It was malicious, first, because Glenna could be viewed as reckless in consciously disregarding a substantial and unjustifiable risk that death or serious bodily injury might occur as a result of this "game." Moreover, proposing to play a game of Russian roulette—even with a supposedly unloaded gun—would appear to clearly be an act undertaken with extreme indifference to the value of human life. Playing with guns is never without risk, as this problem demonstrates.

Accordingly, although a judge or jury might find Glenna guilty of another, lesser form of homicide, e.g. involuntary manslaughter, there is no question but that she could be convicted of murder on these facts. Hence, answer (a) is correct. Conversely, for the same reasons, Glenna is not likely to be found not guilty of murder on these facts for any reason, hence, answers (b), (c), and (d) are incorrect. Moreover, there is no assumption of the risk defense in criminal law.

[For additional discussion of this subject, see John M. Burkoff, Acing Criminal Law, Chapt. 12(A)(2) (West)]

Answer 13–6: The correct answer is (c).

It is not likely that Bernie will be convicted of the murder of Joshua.

To support a conviction for murder, the prosecution must establish that the person accused of the crime, acting with malice, committed a killing act that caused the death of another person. "Malice" refers to a particularly heinous ill will on the part of a killer.

Malice may be established expressly or implied from the circumstances. In many jurisdictions, it can be implied from the accused's act of gross recklessness or actions undertaken with extreme indifference to the value of human life. In this case, although Bernie was clearly speeding, it is not likely that a judge or jury will find that malice existed.

Express malice is not present. Speeding is a bad thing to do, but it is hardly evil or heinous conduct. As to implied malice, it is not likely that a judge or jury would find that Bernie acted with gross recklessness or with extreme indifference to the value of human life. Arguably, Bernie was not reckless because he did not *consciously* disregard a substantial and unjustifiable risk that death or serious bodily injury might occur as a result of his driving fifteen miles over the speed limit in good weather. Similarly, for the same reason, such conduct is not likely to be viewed as extreme indifference to the value of human life.

Accordingly, while he might well be convicted of a lesser homicide offense, e.g. involuntary manslaughter (*see* Question 13–16, below), if he was so charged, Bernie is not likely to be convicted of the murder of Joshua. Hence, answer (c) is correct, and answer (a) is incorrect. Moreover, there is no assumption of the risk defense in criminal law. Hence, answers (b) and (d) are also incorrect.

[For additional discussion of this subject, see John M. Burkoff, Acing Criminal Law, Chapt. 12(A)(2) (West)]

Answer 13–7: [Note: this question contains the same facts as Question 13–1 with the names changed slightly, but a different homicide offense charged. This change might make a big difference in the outcome.] The correct answer is (a).

It is definitely possible that Cy can be convicted of second degree murder in the death of Amos on these facts.

To support a conviction for murder, the prosecution must establish that the person accused of the crime, acting with malice, committed a killing act that caused the death of another person. "Malice" refers to a particularly heinous ill will on the part of a killer.

Malice may be established expressly or implied from the circumstances. In many jurisdictions, it can be implied from the accused's act of gross recklessness or actions undertaken with extreme indifference to the value of human life. In this case, it is possible that a judge or jury will find that malice existed impliedly.

Express malice is not present. Cy's indifference to the precarious condition of the lighting fixture was clearly problematic, but it was hardly evil or heinous conduct. His conduct would more likely be viewed as laziness or stupidity than depraved behavior. However, as to implied malice, it is quite possible that a judge or jury would find that Cy acted with gross recklessness or with extreme indifference to the value of human life when he let the lighting fixture stay as it was overnight. Arguably, Cy was reckless because he *consciously* disregarded a substantial and unjustifiable risk that death or serious bodily injury might occur as a result of his indifference. We know that he knew about the problem because Amos asked him about it and he indicated his knowledge of the fixture's precarious condition. Similarly, for the same reason, such conduct might well be viewed as extreme indifference to the value of human life. Hence, answers (b), (c), and (d) are incorrect.

Accordingly, there is a significant possibility that Cy could be successfully prosecuted for second degree murder in the death of Amos. Hence, answer (a) is correct.

[For additional discussion of this subject, see John M. Burkoff, Acing Criminal Law, Chapt. 12(A)(2) (West)]

Answer 13–8: The correct answer is (d).

It is very likely that Althea can be successfully prosecuted for murder in the death of Paige.

To support a conviction for murder, the prosecution must establish that the person accused of the crime, acting with malice, committed a killing act that caused the death of another person. "Malice" refers to a particularly heinous ill will on the part of a killer.

Malice may be established expressly or implied from the circumstances. In many jurisdictions, it can be implied from the accused's act of gross recklessness or actions undertaken with extreme indifference to the value of human life.

A judge or jury could easily conclude that Althea's act of jumping from a building over a crowded sidewalk below was either expressly or impliedly malicious. It could be viewed as expressly malicious because Althea knew full well that there were people who could be severely injured or killed who walking or standing just below her. But she jumped anyway, without any regard at all for the likely consequences of her action on anyone else but herself.

Moreover, Althea's actions are even more likely to be viewed as impliedly malicious. She was certainly—at the very least—reckless in consciously disregarding a substantial and unjustifiable risk that death or serious bodily injury might occur as a result of her leap from height of four stories onto a sidewalk crowded with passers by. Similarly, her act of jumping in this fashion in these circumstances would appear to clearly be an act which was undertaken with extreme indifference to the value of human life. Althea did not care about anything or anyone else when she jumped. She was only concerned about and committed to killing herself. Hence, answers (a), (b), and (c) are incorrect.

Accordingly, although a judge or jury might find Althea guilty of another, lesser form of homicide, e.g. involuntary manslaughter, it is very likely that she could and would be convicted of murder on these facts. Hence, answer (d) is correct.

[For additional discussion of this subject, see John M. Burkoff, ACING CRIMINAL LAW, Chapt. 12(A)(2) (West)]

FELONY MURDER

Answer 13–9: The correct answer is (b).

The chances of a successful prosecution of Lamar for felony murder in these circumstances are poor.

In a majority of jurisdictions, a death occurring when an accused person is committing or attempting to commit a felony is deemed to be the crime of felony murder. Assuming that this is just such a jurisdiction, Lamar can be charged with that offense.

Aggravated assault, a serious crime, would be a felony. Hence, answers (a) and (c) are incorrect. But, significantly, the felony murder doctrine does not apply to a death that occurs in the course of the commission or attempted commission of just any felony. In most jurisdictions, it applies only to a specified list of serious felonies. In other jurisdictions, it applies to a death occurring during the commission of any felony deemed to be inherently dangerous to human life.

However, in either event, the felony murder doctrine is applicable *only* where the triggering felonious act is collateral to the acts leading to the victim's death, e.g. a victim's death that occurs during a kidnaping. In this case, the triggering felony—the aggravated assault on Ray with the broken beer bottle—was not collateral to the acts leading to the victim's death. It was the act that led to the victim's death.

Accordingly, although a judge or jury might find Lamar guilty of a different form of homicide, e.g. second degree murder, he is not likely to be successfully prosecuted for the crime of felony murder in these circumstances. Accordingly, answer (b) is correct, and answers (d) is incorrect.

[For additional discussion of this subject, see John M. Burkoff, ACING CRIMINAL LAW, Chapt. 12(A)(3) (West)]

Answer 13–10: The correct answer is (d).

Jayden is likely to be found guilty of felony murder in the death of Aiden.

In a majority of jurisdictions, a death occurring when an accused person is committing, attempting to commit, or fleeing after committing a felony is deemed to be the crime of felony murder. Assuming that this is just such a jurisdiction, Jayden can certainly be charged with that offense.

But the felony murder doctrine does not apply to a death that occurs in the course of the commission or attempted commission of just any felony. In most jurisdictions, it applies only to a specified list of serious felonies. In other jurisdictions, it applies to a death occurring during the commission of any felony deemed to be inherently dangerous to human life. However, in either event, the felony murder doctrine would apply to deaths that occur during the course of a kidnaping, a crime that invariably appears in the lists of triggering crimes and which is also a felony deemed to be inherently dangerous to human life. Hence, answers (b) and (e) are incorrect.

In addition, the felony murder requirement applies only to a victim's death that occurs during the commission of the triggering felony. Most jurisdictions apply a res gestae requirement for this purpose, necessitating a showing of temporal and physical proximity between the death and the felony. The victim's death must be causally related to the felony. In these circumstances, the res gestae requirement would appear clearly to be satisfied. Aiden's death occurred during the course of the kidnaping as he had not yet been released or returned to his parents. The kidnaping crime had not been completed at the time of Aiden's death. Hence, answers (a) and (e) are incorrect.

Moreover, his death occurred while the kidnaper was transporting him, satisfying both the "but for" and legal causation tests which need to be satisfied in order to establish criminal causation. Aiden's death was directly related to the actions of his kidnapers. The fact that it is possible that Addison might also be responsible for Aiden's death—criminally or other wise—does not diminish Jayden's culpability. Hence, answers (c) and (e) are incorrect.

Accordingly, Jayden is likely to be guilty of felony murder in the death of Aiden. Hence, answer (d) is correct.

[For additional discussion of this subject, see John M. Burkoff, ACING CRIMINAL LAW, Chapt. 12(A)(3) (West)]

Answer 13–11: The correct answer is (a).

Jack and Owen are not likely to be successfully prosecuted for felony murder in the death of Anna in these circumstances.

In a majority of jurisdictions, a death occurring when an accused person is committing, attempting to commit, or fleeing after committing a felony like robbery is deemed to be the crime of felony murder. Assuming that this is just such a jurisdiction, Jack and Owen can certainly be charged with that offense.

But the felony murder doctrine does not apply to a death that occurs in the course of the commission or attempted commission of just any felony. In most jurisdictions, it applies only to a specified list of serious felonies. In other jurisdictions, it applies to a death occurring during the commission of any felony deemed to be inherently dangerous to human life. However, in either event, the felony murder doctrine would apply to deaths that occur during the course of an armed robbery, a crime that invariably appears in the lists of triggering crimes and which is also a felony deemed to be inherently dangerous to human life. Hence, answers (b) and (d) are incorrect.

The significant question at issue in this problem is whether or not Anna's death occurred while Jack and Owen were still escaping after the commission of the armed robbery. Certainly they had not yet been apprehended at the point the vehicle was spotted and the chase began.

There is mixed law about the test to be used to determine when such an escape—flight after the commission of a felony—has ended. Many courts use the test of assessing whether or not the felons in question had reached a point of "safe haven." At that point, the felony murder doctrine no longer applies. In this case, two days after the robbery had occurred, it is clear that Jack and Owen had, in fact, reached a place of safe haven after their commission of the robbery. Indeed, Owen remained in that place as he was not even in the car when the relevant events occurred leading to Anna's death.

Accordingly, although Jack may certainly be guilty of a different homicide offense, e.g. second degree murder, neither he nor Owen is likely to be prosecuted successfully for felony murder in the death of Anna. Hence, answer (a) is correct, and since answer (b) is incorrect (see above), answer (c) is also incorrect.

[For additional discussion of this subject, see John M. Burkoff, Acing Criminal Law, Chapt. 12(A)(3) (West)]

VOLUNTARY MANSLAUGHTER

Answer 13–12: The correct answer is (d).

Defense counsel is quite likely to succeed with a voluntary manslaughter defense in the murder prosecution of Doris.

Voluntary manslaughter is an intentional killing that has been mitigated from murder, usually because the accused was found to have been reasonably provoked by the victim. This provocation defense requires the accused to prove that he or she acted on the basis of a sudden, intense passion resulting from a provocation by the victim which was so serious that it would create such a passion in a reasonable person.

In this case, it is highly likely that a judge or jury might view Doris' actions after seeing her husband engaged in sexual relations with other people as having created a sudden and intense passion in her. Hence, answers (a) and (c) are incorrect. Moreover, it has traditionally been the case that viewing one's spouse committing adulterous acts is precisely the sort of triggering event that would create a passion in a reasonable person sufficient to mitigate murder to voluntary manslaughter. Hence, answers (b) and (c) are incorrect.

A passion of this sort will be seen as having dissipated as a matter of law when the killing act occurred after a reasonable cooling-off period has passed. In this case, there was insufficient time for Doris to have cooled off. She saw her husband and his furry friends engaged in sexual activity. She immediately ran and got her gun. And she quickly returned and shot him, her passion unabated.

Accordingly, defense counsel is quite likely to succeed with a voluntary manslaughter defense in the murder prosecution of Doris for the killing of her husband, Fred, in these circumstances. Hence, answer (d) is correct.

[For additional discussion of this subject, see John M. Burkoff, ACING CRIMINAL LAW, Chapt. 12(B)(1) (West)]

Answer 13–13: [Note: this question contains the same facts as Question 13–9 with the names changed slightly, but a different homicide offense charged and a specific defense put forward. This change could make a big difference in the outcome.] The correct answer is (b).

Defense counsel is unlikely to succeed with a voluntary manslaughter defense in the murder prosecution of Lashawn.

Voluntary manslaughter is an intentional killing that has been mitigated from murder, usually because the accused was found to have been reasonably provoked by the victim. This provocation defense requires the accused to prove that he or she acted on the basis of a sudden, intense passion resulting from a provocation by the victim which was so serious that it would create such a passion in a reasonable person.

In this case, it is certainly possible that a judge or jury might view Lashawn's actions after Raheem's muttered comments to him as having created a sudden and intense passion in him. Hence, answers (a) and (c) are incorrect. But it is unlikely that a judge or jury would conclude that this arguably provocative act—the muttered comments—were so serious that they would create such a passion in a reasonable person.

Traditionally, the rule was that a person's provocative words alone were never enough to establish an adequate and sufficient provocation defense, mitigating murder to manslaughter. That traditional rule has, however, been abrogated in many jurisdictions. Nonetheless, in this case, it hardly seems likely that a reasonable person would have considered Raheem's muttered comments as sufficiently serious as to justify a killing act in response to them. *(Author's Note: Please, no cards, letters or e-mails from rabid Dallas Cowboy fans.)* Hence, answer (b) is correct.

Accordingly, defense counsel is unlikely to succeed with a voluntary manslaughter defense in the murder prosecution of Lashawn in these circumstances. Hence, answer (d) is incorrect.

[For additional discussion of this subject, see John M. Burkoff, Acing Criminal Law, Chapt. 12(B)(1) (West)]

Answer 13–14: The correct answer is (d).

Attorney Katherine is likely correct in her assessment.

The traditional provocation defense—mitigating murder to voluntary manslaughter—will not work for Wyatt in these circumstances. Voluntary manslaughter is an intentional killing that has been mitigated from murder, usually because the accused was found to have been reasonably provoked by the victim. This provocation defense requires the accused to prove that he or she acted on the basis of a sudden, intense passion resulting from a provocation by the victim which was so serious that it would create such a passion in a reasonable person.

In this case, it is certainly possible that a judge or jury might view Wyatt's actions after Levi scared him with his super soaker as having created a sudden and intense passion in him. He thought he was being attacked by some sort of weapon. Hence, answer (a) is true. But it is unlikely that a judge or jury would conclude that this arguably provocative act on Levi's part—creating a threat that Wyatt would be harmed in some fashion by someone wielding a multi-colored plastic object—was so serious that it would create an adequate passion in a reasonable person sufficient to mitigate to voluntary manslaughter. Hence, answer (b) is also true.

However, there is another way for Wyatt to mitigate murder to voluntary manslaughter. In most jurisdictions, this can be accomplished where defense counsel can establish the existence of an "imperfect defense." An imperfect defense is a protective defense—like self defense—where the accused honestly believes that he or she needs to kill for self-protection or to protect others, but that belief is unreasonable. That is—arguably—exactly what occurred in this case.

A killing is justified when the person committing the killing act acts in self defense. The use of deadly force in self defense—such as the use of a gun—is justified when a person (not an aggressor) uses it for self-protection when attacked by another person who he or she reasonably believes is threatening him or her with the imminent use of deadly force, and deadly force is necessary to repel that attack. This traditional self defense defense does not work for Wyatt in and of itself because—as discussed above—Wyatt's belief in the deadly nature of the threat posed to him by Levi and his super soaker was unreasonable.

But the facts do nonetheless make clear that, although this belief may have been unreasonable, Wyatt nonetheless did honestly believe that he needed to respond to Levi's "attack" with deadly force because he perceived (albeit unreasonably) that the attack on him was of a deadly nature. Assuming that the judge or jury concludes that Wyatt did in fact possess this belief, he would then be entitled to mitigate a charge of murder to voluntary manslaughter by use of this imperfect defense. Hence, answer (c) is true.

Accordingly, again, assuming the judge or jury so concludes, Katherine is correct in arguing that since Wyatt honestly thought that Levi was going to shoot him, the most serious homicide offense of which he could be found guilty is voluntary manslaughter. Hence, answer (d) is the *most accurate* answer as the claims made in answers (a), (b), and (c) are all true.

[For additional discussion of this subject, see John M. Burkoff, ACING CRIMINAL LAW, Chapts. 12(B)(1) & 14(D) (West)]

INVOLUNTARY MANSLAUGHTER

Answer 13–15: The correct answer is (a).

Colin is quite likely to be convicted of involuntary manslaughter due to his role in the sale of his defective power saw to Garrett, the use of which resulted in Garrett's death.

Involuntary manslaughter is an unintentional killing committed without malice. The mens rea showing required for involuntary manslaughter is commonly gross negligence. Gross negligence is an objective element which is satisfied when the accused *should have* been aware of a substantial and unjustifiable risk that death or serious bodily injury might occur as a result of his actions. Unlike a recklessness element, to establish gross negligence, the prosecution does not have to establish that the accused was actually aware of this risk and "consciously" disregarded it.

In this case, it is certainly possible that a judge or jury would conclude on these facts that Colin should have been aware of a substantial and unjustifiable risk that death or serious bodily injury might occur as a result of anyone's use of this defective power saw. Indeed, Colin himself stopped using the saw due to his own nervousness about its dangerous kickback, the fact that it violently kicked upward and sometimes made his hand slip from the handle and the cutting chain jerk toward his arm and chest.

Although Colin was not injured by his own use of this powers saw, it seems extremely likely that a judge or jury would find that a reasonable person should have been concerned that serious injury might result from anyone's use of this saw and that, as a result, he should not have offered it for sale to Garrett. Or, at the very least, he should have warned him about this problem. Hence, answer (c) is incorrect. Moreover, there is no assumption of the risk defense in criminal law. Hence, answer (b) is incorrect.

Accordingly, it is quite likely that Colin will be convicted of involuntary manslaughter in these circumstances. Hence, answer (a) is correct, and answer (d) is incorrect.

[For additional discussion of this subject, see John M. Burkoff, Acing Criminal Law, Chapt. 12(B)(2) (West)]

Answer 13–16: [Note: this question contains the same facts as Question 13–6 with the names changed slightly, but a different homicide offense charged. This change makes a big difference in the outcome.] The correct answer is (a).

It is possible that Bonnie will be convicted of involuntary manslaughter in the death of Josiah, but also possible that she might not be convicted.

Involuntary manslaughter is an unintentional killing committed without malice. The mens rea showing required for involuntary manslaughter is commonly gross negligence. Gross negligence is an objective element which is satisfied when the accused *should have* been aware of a substantial and unjustifiable risk that death or serious bodily injury might occur as a result of his actions. Unlike a recklessness element, to establish gross negligence, the prosecution does not have to establish that the accused was actually aware of this risk and "consciously" disregarded it. Nor is there a malice element as part of involuntary manslaughter. Hence, answer (c) is incorrect.

In this case, it is certainly possible that a judge or jury would conclude on these facts that Bonnie should have been aware of a substantial and unjustifiable risk that death or serious bodily injury might occur as a result of her speeding in this residential neighborhood. On the other hand, it is also possible that a judge or jury might conclude the opposite, that Bonnie should not have been so aware given her clear line of sight, the good weather conditions, and the fact that Josiah dashed out in front of her unseen until he was actually in front of her car. Accordingly, while it is quite possible that Bonnie will be convicted of involuntary manslaughter in the death of Josiah, it is also possible that she will be acquitted of this charge. Hence, answer (a) is correct, and answer (d) is incorrect.

However, in either event, there is no assumption of the risk defense in criminal law. Hence, answer (b) is incorrect.

[For additional discussion of this subject, see John M. Burkoff, Acing Criminal Law, Chapt. 12(B)(2) (West)]

Answer 13–17: [Note: this question contains the same facts as Questions 13–1 and 13–7 with the names changed slightly and the gender of the victim changed, but a different homicide offense charged. This change makes a big difference in the outcome.] The answer is (c).

Ty will very likely be convicted of involuntary manslaughter in the death of Amy.

Involuntary manslaughter is an unintentional killing committed without malice. The mens rea showing required for involuntary manslaughter is commonly gross negligence. Gross negligence is an objective element which is satisfied when the accused *should have* been aware of a substantial and unjustifiable risk that death or serious bodily injury might occur as a result of his actions. Unlike a recklessness element, to establish gross negligence, the prosecution does not have to establish that the accused was actually aware of this risk and "consciously" disregarded it or that he or she acted maliciously. Hence, answers (a) and (b) are incorrect.

In this case, it is very likely that a judge or jury would conclude on these facts that Ty should have been aware of a substantial and unjustifiable risk that death or serious bodily injury might occur as a result of the large and heavy lighting fixture being so poorly secured high above the ground. Whatever Ty may have been thinking about the consequences of his inaction, a reasonable person surely should have realized the potential risk to life this poorly-secured fixture posed to anyone who might have been standing (or climbing, as it turned out) below it.

Accordingly, it is very likely that Ty can be successfully prosecuted for involuntary manslaughter in the death of Amy. Hence answer (c) is correct, and answer (d) is incorrect.

[For additional discussion of this subject, see John M. Burkoff, ACING CRIMINAL LAW, Chapt. 12(B)(2) (West)]

CHAPTER 14
THEFT

TRADITIONAL CRIMES

Answer 14–1: The correct answer is (b).

Miles is not guilty of a common law or traditional theft crime in these circumstances.

Miles was not guilty of common law larceny because he was in actual possession of the television set and he did not have the intent to convert it or to deprive Kate of it on a permanent basis, both necessary elements of the common law larceny offense. Hence, answers (a) and (d) are incorrect.

For much the same reason, Miles was not guilty of embezzlement because he did not fraudulently convert Kate's property—her television set—while he was in possession of it, a necessary element of embezzlement. It just sat there in his dwelling.

Nor was Miles guilty of common law larceny by trick because he did not gain possession of the television from Kate by means of any fraud or false pretenses, a necessary element of that offense. At the time that he borrowed the television set from her, he honestly intended to return it as they had agreed, first thing Monday morning. The subsequent call to Miles from his father that his mother was in the hospital prompted his failure to return it, something that he had not—and could not have—anticipated.

Finally, Miles was not guilty of the crime of false pretenses. He did not engage in false pretenses because he did not knowingly misrepresent any material facts to Kate in order to and with the result of defrauding her into giving him her television set, necessary elements of that particular offense. Hence, answer (c) is incorrect.

Accordingly, Miles is not guilty of a common law or traditional theft crime in these circumstances. Hence, answer (b) is correct.

[For additional discussion of this subject, see John M. Burkoff, Acing Criminal Law, Chapt. 13(A) (West)]

Answer 14–2: The correct answer is (b).

Heinrich did not commit the common law offense of larceny in these circumstances.

The elements of common law larceny are the wrongful taking and carrying away of personal property in the possession of another with the intent to convert it or to permanently deprive its possessor of the property.

The important point here is that the common law larceny crime applies only to personal property. It does not apply to the theft of services. Hence, answer (c) is incorrect. (Modern crimes codes, unlike the common law larceny offense, do specifically criminalize theft of services.) In this case, Heinrich was guilty of theft of services not personal property as he retained Laura and Michelle to perform their cleaning services in his basement and then—wrongfully, but not larcenously—he refused to pay them.

Accordingly, Heinrich did not commit the common law offense of larceny in these circumstances. Hence, answer (b) is correct, and answer (a) is incorrect.

[For additional discussion of this subject, see John M. Burkoff, Acing Criminal Law, Chapt. 13(A) (West)]

Answer 14–3: The correct answer is (d).

Inga committed the common law crime of larceny in these circumstances.

The elements of common law larceny are the wrongful taking and carrying away of personal property in the possession of another with the intent to convert it or to permanently deprive its possessor of the property. In this hypothetical, Inga did in fact did take Dee Dee's CDs with the intent to permanently deprive Dee Dee of (some of) them. CDs are personal property. Hence, answer (b) is incorrect.

Moreover, Dee Dee's temporary loan of the CDs to Inga was a bailment, the delivery of an asset by its owner to another person for his or her temporary care or usage. At common law, a bailee who took all of the goods with which he or she was entrusted was deemed not guilty of larceny as he or she only had "custody" not "possession" of the goods. But, significantly in this case, if the bailee only took *some* of the goods rather than all of them, this was called "breaking bulk" and the bailee lost possession of those goods. As a result, a person breaking bulk was guilty of common law larceny.

That is exactly what happened in these circumstances. Inga received the three bulky storage albums of CDs as a bailment. She then converted twelve of them by giving them to her friend Connie to keep thus depriving Dee Dee of them permanently. Hence, Inga engaged in the act of breaking bulk. Hence, answer (a) is incorrect.

Accordingly, Inga was guilty of the common law crime of larceny in these circumstances, without regard to whether she is or is not guilty of any other common law theft offense as well. Hence, answer (c) is incorrect, and answer (d) is correct.

[For additional discussion of this subject, see John M. Burkoff, ACING CRIMINAL LAW, Chapt. 13(A) (West)]

Answer 14–4: The correct answer is (c).

Colette was guilty of the crime of common law larceny for taking and keeping the scarf, but not for taking and keeping the two five dollar bills.

At common law, lost property that clearly belonged to someone else was treated as if its owner was still in possession of it. A person who found lost property and took it, intending to keep it rather than to try to return it to its owner, was therefore guilty of larceny. That is exactly what happened with the Hermes scarf. It clearly belonged to someone else and Colette found it and took it with the clear intent of keeping it.

The wadded-up currency that Colette found and kept is a different matter. In that case, there was no reason to believe that the five dollar bills belonged to someone else. As a result, Colette's act of picking them up and keeping them was not common law larceny.

Accordingly, Colette was guilty of the crime of common law larceny for taking and keeping the vintage Hermes scarf, but she not guilty of that offense for taking and keeping the two five dollar bills from the ground. Hence, answer (c) is correct, and answers (a), (b), and (d) are all incorrect.

[For additional discussion of this subject, see John M. Burkoff, ACING CRIMINAL LAW, Chapt. 13(A) (West)]

MERGER OF THEFT CRIMES

Answer 14–5: The correct answer is (a).

Whether or not the trial judge should dismiss the theft charge against Jimmy depends entirely upon the prevailing law of theft in the jurisdiction in which this case is being tried.

At common law and in some jurisdictions still today, if a prosecutor charges a person with one type of theft crime and the evidence at trial shows that he or she has committed an entirely different type of theft crime, the accused is not guilty and the charge should be dismissed.

But a majority of jurisdictions—like this one—have adopted the Model Penal Code's approach of consolidating the most common types of theft crimes at common law into a single, inclusive theft offense. In these jurisdictions, if the prosecution prosecutes a person for one type of included theft offense but the evidence at trial establishes the commission instead of a different type of included theft offense, the accused is still guilty of theft under a consolidated statute. Two of the most common types of included theft offense are the two at issue in the present circumstances: theft by unlawful taking and receiving stolen property.

Accordingly, since this jurisdiction follows the majority—consolidated-theft-offense—approach, the theft charge against Jimmy should not be dismissed simply because the prosecution proved the commission of one included type of theft offense rather than another. Hence, answer (a) is correct, and answers (b) and (c) and ipso facto answer (d) are all incorrect.

[For additional discussion of this subject, see John M. Burkoff, ACING CRIMINAL LAW, Chapt. 13(B) (West)]

CHAPTER 15
JUSTIFICATION DEFENSES

SELF DEFENSE

Answer 15–1: The correct answer is (d).

Haley is not correct. Wade does not have a good self defense argument in these circumstances.

Striking another person with a hard object—like a stadium horn—is assaultive conduct and is a criminal offense. At common law and in a minority of jurisdictions today, it would be a battery, committed when a person intentionally touches another person against the other person's will, thereby injuring him or her. In a majority of jurisdictions today, the separate common law offense of battery has merged into the criminal offense of assault. Accordingly, in those majority jurisdictions, an assault is committed when a person either intentionally places another person in actual and reasonable fear of an imminent battery or intentionally commits a battery, as here.

A person is sometimes justified, however, in using unlawful force against another person when he or she is acting in self defense. But the use of force in self defense is only justified where the person using it was not an aggressor and where he or she used it to protect himself or herself while reasonably believing that he or she was threatened with the imminent use of unlawful force by another person and that the use of responsive force was necessary to repel that threat or attack.

In these circumstances, Wade did not satisfy the required elements necessary to make out a good defense of self defense. First, Wade himself was the initial aggressor. He threw his seat cushion at Gabe, narrowly missing hitting him in the head. Hence, Wade—not Gabe—was the initial aggressor. Hence, answer (b) is correct, and answer (a) is incorrect.

Second, Wade could not have reasonably believed that it was necessary to strike Gabe in order to repel his threatened attack on Wade, rushing toward him with his fists balled up like he was about to slug him. At the moment that Wade struck him with the horn, Gabe was being restrained by his friends. He was in no position to pose an imminent threat of assault on Wade. Hence, it was not necessary for Wade to use force against him to repel the threat of an attack at that point. Hence, answer (c) is correct.

Accordingly, Wade does not have a good self defense argument with respect to his assault on Gabe. Hence, answer (d) is the most accurate answer because answers (b) and (c) are both correct.

[For additional discussion of this subject, see John M. Burkoff, ACING CRIMINAL LAW, Chapt. 14(A) (West)]

Answer 15–2: The correct answer is (d).

Zachary is not correct. Amanda does not have a good self defense argument in these circumstances.

Striking another person with a hard object—like a baseball bat—is assaultive conduct and is a criminal offense. At common law and in a minority of jurisdictions today, it would be a battery, committed when a person intentionally touches another person against the other person's will, thereby injuring him or her. In a majority of jurisdictions today, the separate common law offense of battery has merged into the criminal offense of assault. Accordingly, in those majority jurisdictions, an assault is committed when a person either intentionally places another person in actual and reasonable fear of an imminent battery or intentionally commits a battery, as here.

A person is sometimes justified, however, in using unlawful force against another person when he or she is acting in self defense. But the use of force in self defense is only justified where the person using it was not an aggressor and where he or she used it to protect himself or herself while reasonably believing that he or she was threatened with the imminent use of unlawful force by another person and that the use of responsive force was necessary to repel that threat or attack.

In these circumstances, Amanda did not satisfy the required elements necessary to make out a good defense of self defense. First, Amanda himself was the initial aggressor. While Sara was making threats against her, it was Amanda—not Sara—who actually resorted to assaultive violence. Hence, answer (b) is correct, and answer (a) is incorrect.

Second, the threat to Amanda posed by Sara was not an imminent threat. Sara's threat was to do something in the future, not right away. Sara might well have changed her mind. Or she might not have really intended to actually harm Amanda. If Amanda honestly believed that the threat from Sara was real, as she apparently did, she should have gone to the appropriate law enforcement authorities for help rather than acting as a vigilante. Hence, answer (c) is also correct.

Parenthetically, there is another reason Amanda does not have a good self-defense defense, namely because it was not necessary to use unlawful force against Sara at that time to repel the threat to her that Sara may or may not have actually posed sometime in the future.

Accordingly, Amanda does not have a good self defense argument with respect to her assault on Sara. Hence, answer (d) is the most accurate answer because answers (b) and (c) are both correct.

[For additional discussion of this subject, see John M. Burkoff, ACING CRIMINAL LAW, Chapt. 14(A) (West)]

Answer 15–3: The correct answer is (c).

Ursula is not correct. Marcel does not have a good self defense argument in these circumstances.

To support a conviction for second degree murder, the prosecution must establish that the person accused of the crime, acting with malice, committed a killing act that caused the death of another person. "Malice" refers to a particularly heinous ill will on the part of a killer.

Malice may be established expressly or implied from the circumstances. In many jurisdictions, it can be implied from the accused's act of gross recklessness or actions undertaken with extreme indifference to the value of human life. Malice is often presumed where a person has killed another person by using a deadly weapon, e.g. a gun or a knife, on a vital part of the victim's body. In this case, accordingly, malice would be presumed from Marcel's repeated stabbing of Carl in the chest.

As a result, although a judge or jury might find Marcel guilty of another, lesser form of homicide, e.g. involuntary manslaughter, there is no question but that he could be convicted of second degree murder on these facts in the absence of a complete or mitigating defense.

Self defense is a complete defense. A person is sometimes justified in using unlawful force against another person when he or she is acting in self defense. But the use of force in self defense is only justified where the person using it was not an aggressor and where he or she used it to protect himself or herself while reasonably believing that he or she was threatened with the imminent use of unlawful force by another person and that the use of responsive force was necessary to repel that threat or attack. All of these elements are satisfied in this case. Marcel was not the initial aggressor and he used force to protect himself from Carl's use of force upon him which Marcel could reasonably have believed was necessary at that moment to repel Carl's attack on him. Since Marcel was not the aggressor, answer (b) is incorrect, and ipso facto answer (d) is incorrect as well.

However, meeting these self defense elements only entitled Marcel to use unlawful force against Carl, not deadly force. Deadly force is force which creates a substantial risk of causing death or serious bodily harm. The use of a firearm or knife are classic examples of deadly force.

In order to use deadly force in self defense, a person must be responding to the use of deadly force against himself or herself. The use of deadly force is not justified in response to the use of unlawful, but not deadly, force. That is exactly what occurred here. Carl used unlawful force when he accosted Marcel by grabbing his arm in his robbery attempt. As a result, Marcel was entitled to use unlawful force against Carl in response to Carl's attack. But he was not entitled to use deadly force—such as the use of a knife—against Carl because Carl had not used or threatened the use of deadly force against him. Hence, answer (a) is incorrect.

Accordingly, Marcel does not have a good self defense argument in these circumstances due to the fact that he responded to Carl's assaultive force with deadly force. Hence, answer (c) is correct.

[For additional discussion of this subject, see John M. Burkoff, Acing Criminal Law, Chapt. 14(A) (West)]

Answer 15–4: The correct answer is (d).

Gina is correct. Vanna does have a good self defense argument in these circumstances.

To support a conviction for second degree murder, the prosecution must establish that the person accused of the crime, acting with malice, committed a killing act that caused the death of another person. "Malice" refers to a particularly heinous ill will on the part of a killer.

Malice may be established expressly or implied from the circumstances. In many jurisdictions, it can be implied from the accused's act of gross recklessness or actions undertaken with extreme indifference to the value of human life. Malice is often presumed where a person has killed another person by using a deadly weapon, e.g. a gun or a knife, on a vital part of the victim's body. In this case, accordingly, malice would be presumed from Vanna's use of a pistol to shoot Pat in the face.

As a result, although a judge or jury might find Vanna guilty of another, lesser form of homicide, e.g. voluntary manslaughter, there is no question but that she could be convicted of second degree murder on these facts in the absence of a complete or mitigating defense.

Self defense is a complete defense. A person is sometimes justified in using unlawful force against another person when he or she is acting in self defense. But the use of force in self defense is only justified where the person using it was not an aggressor and where he or she used it to protect himself or herself while reasonably believing that he or she was threatened with the imminent use of unlawful force by another person and that the use of responsive force was necessary to repel that threat or attack. All of these elements are satisfied in this case.

Vanna used force to protect herself from Pat's threatened attack on her with a knife. She could reasonably have believed that it was necessary to respond forcefully at that moment to keep Pat from stabbing her in the face. He made it clear to her that that was his intention and he was only a second or two away from accomplishing that goal when she acted. Hence, answer (c) is incorrect, and ipso facto answer (d) is incorrect as well.

It is true that Vanna was the initial aggressor toward Pat. But this fact does not negative an effective self defense defense in these circumstances. Pat was entitled to respond to Vanna's use of non-deadly force against him—her slapping and kicking—with his own use of non-deadly defensive force. But he was not entitled to respond to Vanna's use of non-deadly force against him with deadly force. Hence, answer (b) is incorrect.

Deadly force is force which creates a substantial risk of causing death or serious bodily harm. The use of a knife is a classic example of deadly force. Slapping and kicking are not. A person responds unlawfully—excessively—when he or she uses a level of force beyond that which he or she is lawfully entitled to use. When an initial aggressor who has used non-deadly force is faced with deadly force in response, he or she regains the right to respond defensively to that excessive forcible response. As a result, when Pat came after Vanna using deadly force—the outstretched knife with which he threatened to cut up her face—Vanna had the right to respond to this attack with deadly force. Which she did, firing her pistol at him in response. Hence, answer (a) is also incorrect.

Accordingly, since answers (a), (b), (c), and (d) are all incorrect, answer (e) (None of the above) is correct.

[For additional discussion of this subject, see John M. Burkoff, Acing Criminal Law, Chapt. 14(A) (West)]

Answer 15–5: The correct answer is (c).

In some jurisdictions, like this one, a person who is faced with the use of deadly force against him or her has the obligation to "retreat" if he or she can do so safely, rather than respond with the use of deadly force. See Model Penal Code § 3.04(2)(b).

But even though this jurisdiction uses the retreat doctrine, there is an exception to that rule when the person using defensive deadly force is acting in his or her own home. In that case, such a person does not have an obligation to retreat. That is exactly what occurred here. Vanna was in her own home when she shot Pat, who was attacking her with a knife. As a result, even if the retreat doctrine ordinarily applies in this jurisdiction, it would not apply to Vanna, who was acting in her own apartment, responding to the attack of someone who did not reside there. Hence, answer (a) is incorrect, and ipso facto answer (d) is incorrect as well.

The fact that she invited Pat to enter does not change this rule as it does not make him, ipso facto, a co-occupant. She invited him in; she didn't invite him in to stay or live there. Hence, answer (b) is incorrect.

Accordingly, Vanna does have a good self defense argument in these circumstances due to the fact that she responded with deadly force in her own apartment to Pat's threatened attack on her with deadly force. Hence, answer (c) is correct.

[For additional discussion of this subject, see John M. Burkoff, Acing Criminal Law, Chapt. 14(A) (West)]

Answer 15–6: The correct answer is (d).

To support a conviction for murder, the prosecution must establish that the person accused of the crime, acting with malice, committed a killing act that caused the death of another person. "Malice" refers to a particularly heinous ill will on the part of a killer.

Malice may be established expressly or implied from the circumstances. In many jurisdictions, it can be implied from the accused's act of gross recklessness or actions undertaken with extreme indifference to the value of human life. Malice is often presumed where a person has killed another person by using a deadly weapon, e.g. a gun or a knife, on a vital part of the victim's body. In this case, accordingly, malice would be presumed from Bailey's use of a pistol to shoot Kevin in the chest.

In addition to malice, to support a conviction for first degree murder, the prosecution must also establish that the accused had the specific intent to kill his or her victim, engaging in premeditation and deliberation about the killing act. In other words, a conviction for such premeditated murder requires proof of the accused person's actual, prior thought and reflection about the particular killing act in question.

In this case, Bailey aimed the pistol at Kevin's heart and made it clear that she would shoot him if he came after her with the carving knife. She certainly had some time to think about what she was going to do before she shot him. While it may not have been a lot of time, in many jurisdictions, "no time is too short" for a person to premeditate and deliberate a killing.

As a result, although a judge or jury might find Bailey guilty of another, lesser form of homicide, e.g. second degree murder or voluntary manslaughter, there is no question but that she could be convicted of first degree murder on these facts in the absence of a complete or mitigating defense.

Self defense is a complete defense. A person is sometimes justified in using unlawful force against another person when he or she is acting in self defense. But the use of force in self defense is only justified where the person using it was not an aggressor and where he or she used it to protect himself or herself while reasonably believing that he or she was threatened with the imminent use of unlawful force by another person and that the use of responsive force was necessary to repel that threat or attack. All of these elements are satisfied in this case. There is no indication on these facts that Bailey was the initial aggressor in this situation. Hence, answer (b) is incorrect.

Moreover, Bailey used force to protect herself from Kevin's threatened use of force upon her. Given their proximity, Bailey could reasonably have believed that the use of such force was reasonably necessary at that moment to repel Kevin's attack on her. Hence, answer (c) is incorrect.

However, meeting these self defense elements only entitled Bailey to use unlawful force against Kevin, not deadly force. Deadly force is force which creates a substantial risk of causing death or serious bodily harm. The use of a firearm or knife are classic examples of deadly force. Since Kevin threatened Bailey with deadly force—use of a carving knife—she did have the right to respond to that attack with deadly force—use of a pistol. Hence, answer (a) is incorrect.

Accordingly, since answers (a), (b), and (c) are all incorrect, answer (d) (None of the above) is correct.

Answer 15–7: The correct answer is (a).

In some jurisdictions, like this one, a person who is faced with the use of deadly force against him or her has the obligation to "retreat" if he or she can do so safely, rather than respond with the use of deadly force. *See* Model Penal Code § 3.04(2)(b)(ii).

But even though this jurisdiction uses the retreat doctrine, there is an exception to that rule when the person using defensive deadly force is acting in his or her own home. In that case, such a person does not have an obligation to retreat (this is often called the "castle doctrine"). *See* Model Penal Code § 3.04(2)(b)(ii)(A). That is exactly what occurred here. Bailey was in her own home (castle) when she shot Kevin, who was attacking her with a knife.

However, in most jurisdictions that apply the retreat doctrine, there is an exception to the castle doctrine. The no-retreat-in-the-home rule does not typically apply in those situations where the person seeking to use force in his or her home intends to use it against a co-habitant. That is also exactly what occurred here. Both Bailey and Kevin lived in the home where these events took place; they were co-habitants. Because they were co-habitants, Bailey did have a retreat obligation. Hence, answer (a) is correct, and answer (d) is ipso facto incorrect. Answers (b) and (c) are also both incorrect because neither of those answers recognize that the retreat obligation does apply to co-habitants.

[For additional discussion of this subject, see John M. Burkoff, ACING CRIMINAL LAW, Chapt. 14(A) (West)]

DEFENSE OF OTHERS

Answer 15–8: The correct answer is (d).

Brandy does have a good defense of others defense to an attempted murder charge.

A person is entitled to use force not only to defend himself or herself, but to defend third parties who are being threatened by others as well. Today, some jurisdictions apply an "alter ego" rule in this situation, permitting a person to use the same level of force against someone attacking another person that the person being attacked would be permitted to use. At common law, this approach was used but the defense was limited to the defense only of close relatives, including spouses.

Other jurisdictions—a majority—extend the availability of this defense of others defense to situations where the person using defensive force honestly and reasonably believes that it is justified and necessary under the circumstances, whether or not that assessment is actually correct.

Under any one of these tests, Brandy could successfully make out a defense of others defense. Omar, the person she was trying to defend, was her husband. That satisfies the restrictive limitation of the common law test.

If Brandy had been "in Omar's shoes" under the alter ego test, she would have had the right to use deadly force against Jabari. A person is sometimes justified in using unlawful force against another person when he or she is acting in self defense. The use of force in self defense is justified where the person using it was not an aggressor and where he or she used it to protect himself or herself while reasonably believing that he or she was threatened with the imminent use of unlawful force by another person and that the use of responsive force was necessary to repel that threat or attack.

All of these elements are satisfied in this case. There is no indication at all on these facts that Omar was the initial aggressor in this situation. Hence, answer (b) is incorrect.

Moreover, Omar was entitled to use force to protect himself from Jabari's threatened use of force upon him since Omar could reasonably have believed it was necessary at that moment to repel Jabari's attack on him. Jabari was holding a gun on him. In addition, Omar—and hence Brandy, standing in his shoes—was entitled to use deadly force against Jabari in this situation. Deadly force is force which creates a substantial risk of causing death or serious bodily harm. The use of a firearm or knife are classic examples of deadly force.

Since Jabari was threatening Omar with a gun—deadly force—he—and hence Brandy, standing in his shoes—clearly had the right to respond to that attack with deadly force. Hence, answer (a) is incorrect.

Additionally, in a majority jurisdiction where defense of others is extended to situations where the person using force honestly believes that it is justified and necessary under the circumstances (whether or not that is a correct assessment), Brandy could reasonably believe from what she saw when she came out of the supermarket—a stranger holding a gun on her husband who was standing there clearly scared and with his hands up in the air—that the use of force was justified and necessary under the circumstances to terminate the deadly threat that Jabari posed to her husband. Hence, answer (c) is incorrect.

Accordingly, since answers (a), (b), and (c) are all incorrect, answer (d) (None of the above) is correct.

[For additional discussion of this subject, see John M. Burkoff, Acing Criminal Law, Chapt. 14(B) (West)]

Answer 15–9: The correct answer is (b).

Brandy had the right to use a defense of others defense as discussed in the Answer to Question 15–8, set out above.

Moreover, in jurisdictions where the retreat doctrine exists as a limitation on the right to use deadly force in a defensive manner, it does not apply to the defense of others defense unless *both* the person using the force *and* the person who is being defended can retreat in complete safety. *See* Model Penal Code § 3.05(2). Hence, answer (b) is correct, and answer (d) is ipso facto incorrect.

Just as the obligation to retreat exists in self-defense situations when the accused is being threatened, the obligations exists even when third parties are being threatened. Hence, answer (a) is incorrect.

In this factual scenario, Brandy could certainly have retreated in complete safety. Jabari had not even seen her as she wheeled her cart out of the supermarket. But, significantly, Omar could not retreat from Jabari in complete safety. He was being held at gunpoint in a parking lot. He could not have run away faster than a bullet could catch him. Brandy had no obligation to retreat instead of shooting Jabari simply because she could have retreated in complete safety, when Omar could not. Hence, answer (c) is incorrect.

Accordingly, Brandy does have a good defense of others defense to an attempted murder charge in these circumstances despite the retreat requirement.

[For additional discussion of this subject, see John M. Burkoff, Acing Criminal Law, Chapt. 14(B) (West)]

Answer 15–10: The correct answer is (a). *[Note: this question contains the same facts as Question 15–8 and 15–9 with the names changed slightly, but with an explanation of what was really going on in the interactions between the parties. This factual addition could make a big difference in the outcome in some jurisdictions.]*

Randi has a good defense to an attempted murder charge.

A person is entitled to use force not only to defend himself or herself, but to defend third parties who are being threatened by others as well. Today, some jurisdictions apply an "alter ego" rule in this situation, permitting a person to use the same level of force against someone attacking another person that the person being attacked would be permitted to use. At common law, this approach was used but the defense was limited to the defense only of close relatives, including spouses.

Other jurisdictions—a majority—follow the Model Penal Code approach and extend the availability of this defense of others defense to situations where the person using defensive force honestly believes that it is justified and necessary under the circumstances, whether or not that assessment is actually correct. *See* Model Penal Code § 3.05(1).

If Randi had been "in Oran's shoes" under the alter ego test (whether or not it was limited by the common law restriction applying only to close relatives), she would not have had the right to use deadly force against Jerry. A person is sometimes justified in using unlawful force against another person when he or she is acting in self defense. The use of force in self defense is justified where the person using it was not an aggressor and where he or she used it to protect himself or herself while reasonably believing that he or she was threatened with the imminent use of unlawful force by another person and that the use of responsive force was necessary to repel that threat or attack.

These elements are not satisfied in this case. While there is no indication that Oran was an aggressor in this situation, Jerry was not using force against him—the gun was a prop and Jerry knew that it was being pointed at him as a joke—so he was not entitled to use force in response. Since Jerry was not threatening Oran with deadly force, he—and hence Randi, standing in his shoes—clearly did not have the right to respond to that joking "attack" with deadly force.

But, in this jurisdiction, however, where defense of others is extended to situations where the person using force honestly believes that it is justified and necessary under the circumstances (whether or not that is a correct assessment), Randi could reasonably have believed from what she saw when she came out of the supermarket—a stranger holding a gun on her husband who was standing there apparently scared and with his hands up in the air—that the use of deadly force was justified and necessary under the circumstances to terminate the deadly threat that Jabari posed to her husband. Hence, answer (c) is incorrect, and ipso facto answer (d) is incorrect as well.

Deadly force is force which creates a substantial risk of causing death or serious bodily harm. The use of a firearm or knife are classic examples of deadly force. Since Jerry reasonably appeared to be threatening Oran with a gun—deadly force—Brandy had the right to respond to that apparent deadly attack with deadly force. Hence, answer (b) is incorrect.

Accordingly, Randi does have a good defense of others defense to an attempted murder charge in these circumstances in this (majority rule) jurisdiction. But she would not have had a good defense of others defense to an attempted murder charge in these circumstances in a jurisdiction using the alter ego approach to defense of others. Hence, answer (a) is correct.

[For additional discussion of this subject, see John M. Burkoff, ACING CRIMINAL LAW, Chapt. 14(B) (West)]

Answer 15–11: The correct answer is (d). *[Note: this question contains the same facts as Question 15–8 and 15–9 with the names changed slightly, but with an explanation of what was really going on in the interactions between the parties. This factual addition could make a big difference in the outcome in some jurisdictions.]*

Randi had the right to use a defense of others defense as discussed in the Answer to Question 15–10, set out above.

Moreover, in jurisdictions where the retreat doctrine exists as a limitation on the right to use deadly force in a defensive manner, it does not apply to the defense of others defense unless *both* the person using the force *and* the person who is being defended can retreat in complete safety. *See* Model Penal Code § 3.05(2).

Just as the obligation to retreat exists in self-defense situations when the accused is being threatened, the obligations exists even when third parties are being threatened. Hence, answer (a) is incorrect.

In this factual scenario, Randi could certainly have retreated in complete safety. Jerry had not even seen her as she wheeled her cart out of the supermarket. But Randi could reasonably have believed that Oran could not retreat from Jerry in complete safety. He was being held at gunpoint in a parking lot. Or so she reasonably thought. She did not realize that Jerry was holding a real gun, a reasonable belief given the distance between her and Jerry. He could not have run away faster than a bullet could catch him. Randi had no obligation to retreat instead of shooting Jerry simply because she could have retreated in complete safety, when Oran could not have (or so she reasonably believed). Hence, answers (b) and (c) are incorrect.

Accordingly, Brandy does have a good defense of others defense to an attempted murder charge in these circumstances despite the retreat requirement. Because answers (a), (b), and (c) are all incorrect, answer (d) (None of the above) is the correct answer.

[For additional discussion of this subject, see John M. Burkoff, Acing Criminal Law, Chapt. 14(B) (West)]

DEFENSE OF PROPERTY

Answer 15–12: The correct answer is (a).

Cherie does have a good defense-of-property defense to an assault charge in these circumstances.

In most jurisdictions, the use of non-deadly force is held to be lawful when the person using it reasonably believes that it is necessary to use it to prevent or terminate an unlawful trespass or the unlawful carrying away of that person's property. Cherie was the owner of the bicycle, even though it was used by her daughter, so it was her property for these purposes. Hence, answer (c) is incorrect, and ipso facto answer (d) is incorrect as well.

That is exactly what occurred in these circumstances. Lenny was engaged in the act of unlawfully taking Cherie's property—her daughter's bicycle—and Cherie acted using non-deadly force to terminate his unlawful carrying away of her property. Hence, answer (b) is incorrect.

Accordingly, Cherie does have a good defense of property defense to an assault charge in these circumstances. Hence, answer (a) is correct.

[For additional discussion of this subject, see John M. Burkoff, Acing Criminal Law, Chapt. 14(C) (West)]

DEFENSE OF HABITATION

Answer 15–13: The correct answer is (c).

Lee is not correct. Norman does not have a good defense-of-habitation defense to these aggravated assault charges.

Norman used deadly force in shooting the two would-be burglars. Deadly force is force which creates a substantial risk of causing death or serious bodily harm. The use of a firearm—like a shotgun—is a classic example of deadly force.

Most jurisdictions permit the use of deadly force by a homeowner to prevent or terminate an unlawful entry into his or her home when he or she reasonably believes that the intruder intends to commit a felony inside. A minority of jurisdictions go further, permitting a homeowner to use deadly force when an unlawful entry into the home has taken place and he or she reasonably believes that nothing less than the use of deadly force would be adequate to terminate that entry. Hence, answer (b) is incorrect, and ipso fact answer (d) is incorrect as well.

Whichever rule of law is used in this jurisdiction, Norman has not satisfied the requisite elements to make out a good defense of his habitation. The entry in question by the two men that Norman shot had already terminated. Norman could not have believed—reasonably or otherwise—that it was necessary to use deadly force to terminate the entry as the entry was already terminated. Hence, answer (c) is correct, and answer (a) is incorrect.

Parenthetically, Norman had no right to shoot these two men in self defense. Self defense—like defense of habitation—is also a complete defense to assault charges. But the use of force in self defense—deadly or non-deadly—is only justified, *inter alia*, where the person using it acted to protect himself or herself while reasonably believing that he or she was threatened with the imminent use of unlawful force by another person and that the use of responsive force was necessary to repel that threat or attack. In this case, Norman had no reason to believe that he needed to protect himself from imminent attack when he shot the two running men nor was it reasonable to believe, as previously noted, that it was necessary to use deadly force to repel a threat or attack.

Accordingly, Norman does not have a good defense to the aggravated assault charges in these circumstances.

[For additional discussion of this subject, see John M. Burkoff, Acing Criminal Law, Chapt. 14(C) (West)]

IMPERFECT DEFENSES

Answer 15–14: The correct answer is (d).

Katherine is correct in her assessment.

The traditional provocation defense—mitigating murder to voluntary manslaughter—does not work for Wyatt in these circumstances. Voluntary manslaughter is an intentional killing that has been mitigated from murder, usually because the accused was found to have been reasonably provoked by the victim. This provocation defense requires the accused to prove that he or she acted on the basis of a sudden, intense passion resulting from a provocation by the victim which was so serious that it would create such a passion in a reasonable person.

In this case, it is certainly possible that a judge or jury might view Wyatt's actions after Levi scared him with his super soaker as having created a sudden and intense passion in him. He thought he was being attacked by some sort of weapon. But it is unlikely that a judge or jury would conclude that this arguably provocative act on Levi's part—creating a threat that Wyatt would be harmed in some fashion by someone wielding a multi-colored plastic object—was so serious that it would create an adequate passion in a reasonable person sufficient to mitigate to voluntary manslaughter. (*See* Answer to Question 13–14.)

However, there is another way for Wyatt to mitigate murder to voluntary manslaughter. In most jurisdictions, like this one, this can be accomplished where defense counsel can establish the existence of an "imperfect defense." An imperfect defense is a protective defense—like self defense—where the accused honestly believes that he or she needs to kill for self-protection or to protect others, but that belief is unreasonable. That is—arguably—exactly what occurred in this case.

A killing is justified when the person committing the killing act acts in self defense. The use of deadly force in self defense—such as the use of a gun—is justified when a person (not an aggressor) uses it for self-protection when attacked by another person who he or she reasonably believes is threatening him or her with the imminent use of deadly force, and deadly force is necessary to repel that attack. This traditional self defense defense does not work for Wyatt in and of itself because—as discussed above—Wyatt's belief in the deadly nature of the threat posed to him by Levi and his super soaker was unreasonable.

But the facts do nonetheless make clear that, although this belief may have been unreasonable, Wyatt nonetheless did honestly believe that he needed to respond to Levi's "attack" with deadly force because he perceived (albeit unreasonably) that the attack on him was of a deadly nature. Assuming that the judge or jury concludes that Wyatt did in fact possess this belief, he would then be entitled to mitigate a charge of murder to voluntary manslaughter by use of this imperfect defense.

Accordingly, again, assuming the judge or jury so concludes, Katherine is correct in arguing that since Wyatt honestly thought that Levi was going to shoot him, the most serious homicide offense of which he could be found guilty is voluntary manslaughter. Hence, answers (a), (b), and (c) are all correct, and answer (d) is the most accurate answer.

[For additional discussion of this subject, see John M. Burkoff, Acing Criminal Law, Chapt. 14(D) (West)]

NECESSITY

Answer 15–15: The correct answer is (c).

If Ike and Eden are actually prosecuted for breaking and entering and/or criminal trespass, they do have a good necessity defense to those charges.

In a majority of jurisdictions, a person can defend against criminal charges when he or she has committed a criminal act which it is reasonably necessary to commit in order to prevent a greater harm that faces him or her as a result of a natural event. Answer (b) is incorrect as it presupposes use of a duress not a necessity defense. Answer (d) is ipso facto also incorrect.

To make a necessity defense successfully, the natural event must have presented the accused with an imminent threat of serious injury and he or she must have had no reasonable and lawful alternative other than to commit the less serious crime at issue in order to avoid that threat.

That is, in fact, exactly what occurred in these circumstances. Ike and Eden were caught in a serious blizzard—a natural event—in a remote area. They faced the imminent threat of serious, even fatal, harm to themselves if they did not reach a place of shelter quickly. They tried to reach others to seek and obtain assistance, but they failed. As a result, they had no real choice if they wanted to assure their survival but to break into the unoccupied cabin. Breaking and entering and/or trespass are certainly less serious than the very real risk posed to Ike's and Eden's survival. Hence, answer (a) is incorrect.

Accordingly, Ike and Eden do have a good necessity defense to criminal charges of breaking and entering and/or criminal trespass in these circumstances. Hence, answer (c) is correct.

[For additional discussion of this subject, see John M. Burkoff, ACING CRIMINAL LAW, Chapt. 14(F) (West)]

Answer 15–16: The correct answer is (b). *[Note: this question contains some similar facts to Question 15–15 with the names changed slightly, but with the significant factual difference that the isolated cabin was occupied and the cabin's owner was shot and killed when the actors entered. These factual changes make a dispositive difference in the outcome.]*

This is not a good defense for Mike.

In a majority of jurisdictions, a person can defend against criminal charges when he or she has committed a criminal act which it is reasonably necessary to commit in order to prevent a greater harm that faces him or her as a result of a natural event. To make this necessity defense successfully, however, the natural event must have presented the accused with an imminent threat of serious injury and he or she must have had no reasonable and lawful alternative other than to commit the less serious crime at issue in order to avoid that threat.

That is, in fact, exactly what occurred in these circumstances. Mike and Ellen were caught in a serious blizzard—a natural event—in a remote area. They faced the imminent threat of serious, even fatal, harm to themselves if they did not reach a place of shelter quickly. They tried to reach others to seek and obtain assistance, but they failed. They tried to get into the cabin lawfully to obtain shelter, but they were refused entry. As a result, they had no real choice if they wanted to assure their survival but to break into the unoccupied cabin, even though Zeb—lawfully, as it was his cabin—did not permit them to enter and threatened to shoot them if they tried to break in. Hence, answer (a) is incorrect.

However, all of that said, Mike did more than just break into the cabin unlawfully. He shot and killed Zeb and that is the crime for which he is being prosecuted. Even though the elements of a necessity defense might otherwise be satisfied, most jurisdictions do not permit an actor to use this defense to justify the killing of another person, even when it was necessary for the actor to do so to save his or her or other persons' lives.

Accordingly, because the crime he is trying to justify is a crime of homicide, Mike cannot make a viable necessity defense in these circumstances. Hence, answer (b) is correct, and answer (c) is incorrect. Since answer (b) is correct, answer (d) is also ipso facto incorrect.

[For additional discussion of this subject, see John M. Burkoff, ACING CRIMINAL LAW, Chapt. 14(F) (West)]

CHAPTER 16
EXCUSES

DURESS

Answer 16–1: The correct answer is (a).

Stewart does have a good duress defense to the rape charge.

Duress may be used as a defense to a criminal charge when an accused person has been coerced by another person's unlawful threats into committing a crime because he or she reasonably believed that the other person would subject him or her or a third party to death or serious injury imminently if he or she did not commit that crime.

That is exactly what occurred in these circumstances. Logan held a gun on Stewart and forced him to commit a crime, the rape of Allie, threatening Stewart that he would shoot him if Stewart did not commit the sex act immediately.

The unlawful threat that must be established in order to support a duress defense must be a threat that a reasonable person could not be expected to resist. In this case, a reasonable person should not be expected to resist a threat issued at gunpoint by an obviously disturbed psychopath. Hence, answer (b) is incorrect, and ipso facto answer (d) is incorrect as well.

Accordingly, Stewart has a tenable duress defense to the charge of the rape of Allie in these circumstances. Hence, answer (a) is correct, and answer (c) is incorrect.

[For additional discussion of this subject, see John M. Burkoff, Acing Criminal Law, Chapt. 15(A) (West)]

Answer 16–2: The correct answer is (c). *[Note: this question contains some similar facts to Question 16–1 with the names changed slightly, but with the significant factual difference that a murder rather than a rape occurred. This factual addition makes a dispositive difference in the outcome.]*

Stuart does not have a good defense to the murder charge.

To support a conviction for murder, the prosecution must establish that the person accused of the crime, acting with malice, committed a killing act that caused the death of another person. "Malice" refers to a particularly heinous ill will on the part of a killer.

Malice may be established expressly or implied from the circumstances. In many jurisdictions, it can be implied from the accused's act of gross recklessness or actions undertaken with extreme indifference to the value of human life. Malice is often presumed where a person has killed another person by using a deadly weapon, e.g. a gun or a knife, on a vital part of the victim's body. In this case, Stuart's act of repeatedly and violently beating Ellie in the head with a lead pipe clearly establishes the existence of malice as such actions patently demonstrate his extreme indifference to the value of human life.

As a result, Stuart could certainly be convicted of murder on these facts in the absence of proof of a complete or mitigating defense.

Duress is a complete defense. It may be used as a defense to a criminal charge when an accused person has been coerced by another person's unlawful threats into committing a crime because he or she reasonably believed that the other person would subject him or her or a third party to death or serious injury imminently if he or she did not commit that crime.

That is exactly what occurred in these circumstances. Loomis held a gun on Stuart and forced him to commit a crime, the killing of Ellie, threatening Stuart that he would shoot him if Stewart did not commit this assaultive conduct immediately.

The unlawful threat that must be established in order to support a duress defense must be a threat that a reasonable person could not be expected to resist. In this case, a reasonable person should not be expected to resist a threat issued at gunpoint by an obviously disturbed psychopath. Hence, answer (b) is incorrect, and ipso facto answer (d) is incorrect as well.

However, all of that said, Stuart did more than simply assault Ellie. He kept beating her with the lead pipe until he had killed her. Even though the elements of a duress defense might otherwise be satisfied, most jurisdictions do not permit an actor to use this defense to justify the killing of another person, even when it was necessary for the actor to do so to save his or her—or other persons'—lives.

Accordingly, because the crime he is trying to justify is a crime of homicide, Stuart cannot establish a viable duress defense in these circumstances. Hence, answer (c) is correct, and answer (a) is incorrect.

[For additional discussion of this subject, see John M. Burkoff, ACING CRIMINAL LAW, Chapt. 15(A) (West)]

INSANITY & OTHER PSYCHOLOGICAL DEFENSES

Answer 16–3: The correct answer is (b).

Livonia does not have a good insanity defense using the *M'Naghten* test.

Some jurisdictions do not permit a defense of insanity. If this had been one of those jurisdictions, insanity would obviously not have been a good defense to these charges for Livonia.

In those jurisdictions that do have an insanity defense, the most commonly used test is the two-pronged *M'Naghten* test, the test that is used in this jurisdiction. Assuming that this jurisdiction uses both prongs of that test (some jurisdictions do not) since the problem refers to the *M'Naghten* test rather than a part of it, Charles would have to establish that Livonia was suffering from such a mental disease or defect as not to know the nature and quality of the act she committed or, if she did know, that she did not know that what she was doing was wrong.

As to the "nature and quality of her act"—the so-called cognitive prong of *M'Naghten*—Livonia did not meet this test. Livonia clearly understood that she was aiming her rifle at the two children (although she thought they were space aliens) and that she was shooting at them. In a jurisdiction that uses the full *M'Naghten* test (or only this first *M'Naghten* prong) as its insanity test, Livonia's insanity defense would most certainly fail on this ground. Hence, answer (b) is correct, and answer (a) is incorrect.

With respect to the second prong of *M'Naghten*—the so-called "moral incapacity" test—a jury might reasonably decide this issue either way. Most likely, a jury would find that Livonia was aware that shooting another person (even if he or she was taken over by space aliens) was wrong, but that she thought that she was justified in shooting in these circumstances for reasons of self-protection (although she did not have a valid self defense claim either as she was not threatened with the use of deadly force against her). Or a jury might find that Livonia's mental disorder was so severe that she did not even realize that shooting at the children was wrong. If the jury reached this conclusion and this jurisdiction uses *M'Naghten*—or only the moral incapacity prong of *M'Naghten*—as its insanity test, Livonia's insanity defense might well succeed. In any event, because this prong of the *M'Naghten* test has not been "clearly" established, answer (c) is wrong, and ipso facto answer (d) is wrong as well.

Parenthetically, there is no indication in the facts of this problem suggesting that Livonia acted in response to an irresistible impulse. This would be relevant if this jurisdiction was one of the few that adopted that supplementary test to *M'Naghten*.

[For additional discussion of this subject, see John M. Burkoff, Acing Criminal Law, Chapt. 15(C) (West)]

Answer 16–4: The correct answer is (a).

Since this jurisdiction has adopted the ALI Model Penal Codes' insanity test instead of using *M'Naghten*, Livonia's defense counsel, Charles, would need to establish that at the time of this shooting, as a result of her mental disease or defect, Livonia lacked substantial capacity either to appreciate the wrongfulness of her conduct or to conform her conduct to the requirements of the law. Hence, answer (a) is correct.

In these circumstances, as with the moral incapacity prong of the *M'Naghten* test and for the same reasons, a jury might reasonably decide this issue either way. Certainly, a reasonable jury might well conclude, for example, that Livonia's mental disorder—the panic that resulted from her fear of space aliens—resulted in her inability to adhere to the dictates of the criminal law.

Answers (b) and (c) are both incorrect. Answer (b) reflects use of the first prong of the *M'Naghten* test, not the Model Penal Code test used in this jurisdiction. And answer (c) reflects use of the irresistible impulse test, not the Model Penal Code test used in this jurisdiction. Because answers (b) and (c) are incorrect, ipso facto answer (d) (All of the above) is incorrect.

[For additional discussion of this subject, see John M. Burkoff, Acing Criminal Law, Chapt. 15(C) (West)]

Answer 16–5: The correct answer is (d).

Some jurisdictions do not permit a defense of insanity. If this had been one of those jurisdictions, insanity would obviously not have been a good defense for Daniel.

In those jurisdictions that do have an insanity defense, the most commonly used test is the two-pronged *M'Naghten* test, the test that is used in this jurisdiction. Assuming that this jurisdiction uses both prongs of that test (some jurisdictions do not) since the problem refers to the *M'Naghten* test rather than a part of it, Daniel's defense counsel would have to establish that Daniel was suffering from such a mental disease or defect as not to know the nature and quality of the act he committed or, if he did know, that he did not know that what he was doing was wrong.

As to the "nature and quality of his act"—the so-called cognitive prong of *M'Naghten*—Daniel did not meet this test. He clearly understood that he was trying to kill his wife by striking her with a hammer. In a jurisdiction that uses the full *M'Naghten* test (or only this first *M'Naghten* prong) as its insanity test, Daniel's insanity defense would most certainly fail. Hence, answer (b) is correct, and answer (a) is incorrect.

With respect to the second prong of *M'Naghten*—the so-called "moral incapacity" test—a jury might reasonably decide this issue either way. Most likely, a jury would find that Daniel was aware that killing his wife (even if she was possessed by the Devil) was wrong, but that he thought that he was justified in killing her in these circumstances in order to save her eternal soul. If the jury reached this conclusion, Daniel's insanity defense under *M'Naghten* would not be successful as neither prong of the *M'Naghten* test would be satisfied. Hence, answer (c) is correct. Accordingly, answer (d) is the most accurate answer since answers (b) and (c) are both correct, and answer (a) is false.

It is worth adding that there certainly is a chance on these facts that a jury might conclude that Daniel's mental disorder was so severe that he did not realize that killing his wife was wrong. If the jury reached this conclusion and this jurisdiction uses *M'Naghten*—or only the moral incapacity prong of *M'Naghten*—as its insanity test, Daniel's insanity defense might well succeed. The jury could certainly rely upon the defense expert testimony in reaching this conclusion, that Daniel was "acting without thought," for example. But the jury is not obligated to credit the expert testimony—defense or prosecution—relating to an accused's mental state.

Parenthetically and additionally, there is no indication in the facts of this problem suggesting that Daniel acted in response to an irresistible impulse. This would be relevant if this jurisdiction was one of the few that adopted that supplementary test to *M'Naghten*.

[For additional discussion of this subject, see John M. Burkoff, Acing Criminal Law, Chapt. 15(C) (West)]

Answer 16–6: The correct answer is (b).

Since this jurisdiction has adopted the ALI Model Penal Codes' insanity test instead of using *M'Naghten*, Daniel's defense counsel would need to establish that at the time of this shooting, as a result of his mental disease or defect, Daniel lacked substantial capacity either to appreciate the wrongfulness of his conduct or to conform his conduct to the requirements of the law. Hence, answer (b) is correct, and answer (d) is ipso facto incorrect.

In these circumstances, as with the moral incapacity prong of the *M'Naghten* test and for the same reasons, a jury might reasonably decide this issue either way. Certainly, the expert testimony presented by each side would support a conclusion either way. A reasonable jury might well conclude, for example, that Daniel suffered from a mental disease or disorder and that that disease or disorder—manifested by his delusional belief that he was saving his wife's soul by killing her—resulted in his inability to appreciate the wrongfulness of his conduct. Or the jury might reasonably believe instead, following the prosecution's expert testimony, that "Daniel knew exactly what he was doing when he beat her to death," in which case, the Model Penal Code insanity test would not be satisfied.

Answers (a) and (c) are both incorrect. Answer (a) reflects use of the first prong of the *M'Naghten* test, not the Model Penal Code test used in this jurisdiction. And answer (c) reflects use of the irresistible impulse test, not the Model Penal Code test used in this jurisdiction.

[For additional discussion of this subject, see John M. Burkoff, Acing Criminal Law, Chapt. 15(C) (West)]

ENTRAPMENT

Answer 16–7: The correct answer is (a).

Jamie will not be able to successfully use an entrapment defense in this jurisdiction.

Proof of an accused person's entrapment by the government is a complete defense to criminal charges. But there are two entirely different types of entrapment tests being used in the United States today. The federal courts and some states use a "subjective" entrapment test, just as this jurisdiction does. This is a test which asks whether the accused was predisposed to commit the crime charged, i.e. it focuses on the accused person's subjective state of mind.

Many other states use instead an "objective" entrapment test. The objective test focuses on the government rather than on the accused. It asks whether the government agents involved in the transaction encouraged or assisted the accused in committing the crime charged in an outrageous fashion.

Under either test, a law enforcement agent's act of merely giving the accused the opportunity to commit a crime is not enough, in and of itself, to establish entrapment. Moreover, the government's use of an undercover agent is not enough, in and of itself, to establish entrapment.

Under the subjective entrapment approach, Bart's overtures to—and behavior with—Jamie were probably not enough to establish an entrapment defense. The fact that Jamie admitted that she had acquired and used marijuana in the past (even though she had not used it recently) would likely make it difficult for her to make out a successful defense. A jury may consider the accused person's character and reputation in deciding whether or not entrapment existed. It is quite likely, accordingly, that the jury would find that Jamie was predisposed to commit this crime and that Bart merely gave her the opportunity to commit this crime. As a result, an entrapment defense would not be likely succeed for Jamie in a subjective jurisdiction. Hence, answer (a) is correct, and answer (c) is incorrect. Because (a) is correct and (c) is incorrect, answer (d) is also ipso facto incorrect.

Moreover, answer (b) is incorrect because it is an application of the wrong entrapment test in this jurisdiction, an objective rather than a subjective test.

[For additional discussion of this subject, see John M. Burkoff, ACING CRIMINAL LAW, Chapt. 15(D) (West)]

Answer 16–8: The correct answer is (c).

Proof of an accused person's entrapment by the government is a complete defense to criminal charges. But there are two entirely different types of entrapment tests being used in the United States today. The federal courts and some states use a "subjective" entrapment test. This is a test which asks whether the accused was predisposed to commit the crime charged, i.e. it focuses on the accused person's subjective state of mind.

Many other states use instead an "objective" entrapment test, just as this jurisdiction does. The objective test focuses on the government rather than on the accused. It asks whether the government agents involved in the transaction encouraged or assisted the accused in committing the crime charged in an outrageous fashion. In objective jurisdictions, the defendant's predisposition is irrelevant. Hence, answer (a) is incorrect.

Under either test, a law enforcement agent's act of merely giving the accused the opportunity to commit a crime is not enough, in and of itself, to establish entrapment. Moreover, the government's use of an undercover agent is not enough, in and of itself, to establish entrapment. But that does not mean that an undercover agent's conduct cannot be enough to establish entrapment (in an objective jurisdiction). Hence, answer (b) is incorrect.

In an objective jurisdiction like this one, the question is: how outrageous was Bart's conduct here? Again, as in a subjective jurisdiction, merely providing Jamie with an opportunity to obtain marijuana for him by lying to her about why he wanted it is not enough to establish entrapment in an objective entrapment jurisdiction.

Perhaps the strongest, tenable argument that Jamie can make relating to Bart's behavior is that his entreaties to her caused someone who had stopped using marijuana to start committing that criminal offense once again, something that—arguably—the government should play no role in doing. Moreover, Jamie can also argue that Bart essentially "paid her in marijuana" since he paid for her ounce of marijuana in order to get his own ounce.

A reasonable jury might well find that Bart's conduct in this regard was or was not outrageous. As a result, depending on resolution of that factual question, an entrapment defense might or might not succeed for Jamie in an objective entrapment jurisdiction. If the jury finds that Bart's conduct was sufficiently outrageous, Jamie does have a good entrapment defense. Hence, answer (c) is correct, and ipso facto answer (d) is incorrect.

Accordingly, Jamie does have a chance of success in defending against the sale of marijuana charge with an entrapment defense, but only in a jurisdiction that uses an objective entrapment test.

[For additional discussion of this subject, see John M. Burkoff, Acing Criminal Law, Chapt. 15(D) (West)]

Answer 16–9: The correct answer is (b).

Douglas is not likely to be successful in defending against these charges with an entrapment defense.

Proof of an accused person's entrapment by the government is a complete defense to criminal charges. But there are two entirely different types of entrapment tests being used in the United States today. The federal courts and some states use a "subjective" entrapment test, just as this jurisdiction does. This is a test which asks whether the accused was predisposed to commit the crime charged, i.e. it focuses on the accused person's subjective state of mind.

Many other states use instead an "objective" entrapment test. The objective test focuses on the government rather than on the accused. It asks whether the government agents involved in the transaction encouraged or assisted the accused in committing the crime charged in an outrageous fashion.

Under either test, a law enforcement agent's act of merely giving the accused the opportunity to commit a crime is not enough, in and of itself, to establish entrapment. Moreover, the government's use of an undercover agent is not enough, in and of itself, to establish entrapment.

Under the subjective entrapment approach, Clanton's on-line overtures to Douglas were clearly not enough to establish an entrapment defense in these circumstances. Douglas was undoubtedly predisposed to engage in criminal conduct: sexual intercourse with a minor. That is, apparently, why he was chatting with (what he thought was) a thirteen year-old girl in the first place.

Moreover, it was Douglas who sought to persuade this apparent thirteen year-old to have sex with him, trying to make the prospect more attractive to her by lying about his age and marital status. It is extremely likely, accordingly, that a jury would find that Douglas was predisposed to commit these crimes, and that Clanton merely gave him the opportunity to commit them. As a result, an entrapment defense would not be likely succeed for Douglas in a subjective entrapment jurisdiction. Hence, answer (b) is correct, answer (c) is incorrect, and answer (d) is ipso facto incorrect.

Moreover, answer (a) is incorrect because it is an application of the wrong entrapment test in this jurisdiction, an objective rather than a subjective test.

[For additional discussion of this subject, see John M. Burkoff, ACING CRIMINAL LAW, Chapt. 15(D) (West)]

Answer 16–10: The correct answer is (b).

Proof of an accused person's entrapment by the government is a complete defense to criminal charges. But there are two entirely different types of entrapment tests being used in the United States today. The federal courts and some states use a "subjective" entrapment test. This is a test which asks whether the accused was predisposed to commit the crime charged, i.e. it focuses on the accused person's subjective state of mind.

Many other states use instead an "objective" entrapment test, just as this jurisdiction does. The objective test focuses on the government rather than on the accused. It asks whether the government agents involved in the transaction encouraged or assisted the accused in committing the crime charged in an outrageous fashion. In objective jurisdictions, the defendant's predisposition is irrelevant. Hence, answer (a) is incorrect, and ipso facto answer (d) is incorrect as well.

Under either test, a law enforcement agent's act of merely giving the accused the opportunity to commit a crime is not enough, in and of itself, to establish entrapment. Moreover, the government's use of an undercover agent is not enough, in and of itself, to establish entrapment.

In an objective jurisdiction like this one, the question is: how outrageous was Clanton's conduct here? Again, just as in a subjective jurisdiction, Clanton's actions in merely providing Douglas with an opportunity to commit these crimes by lying to him about his age and gender and interests on-line is not enough to establish entrapment in and of itself.

It seems highly unlikely that a reasonable jury would find that Clanton's conduct in playing along with Douglas' overtures was sufficiently outrageous to justify a claim of entrapment. He merely gave Douglas the opportunity to engage in criminal activity. As a result, an entrapment defense is not likely to succeed for him in an objective entrapment jurisdiction. Hence, answer (b) is correct, and answer (c) is incorrect.

Accordingly, Douglas is not likely in these circumstances to successfully defend against these charges with an entrapment defense in either an objective or subjective entrapment test jurisdiction.

[For additional discussion of this subject, see John M. Burkoff, ACING CRIMINAL LAW, Chapt. 15(D) (West)]

CHAPTER 17
MULTIPLE CHOICE EXAM #1

Answer 17–1: The correct answer is (b).

The District Attorney is considering charging Christian and Eric with conspiracy to commit murder. The actus reus of a conspiracy is an agreement between one or more persons to commit a criminal act or to use criminal means to commit a lawful act. Such agreement can be—and often is—established circumstantially. This might well be viewed by a judge or jury as just such a case. Christian and Eric participated in a transfer of the pistol used to shoot and kill Christopher. On the basis of that act alone, there is some circumstantial evidence that the two of them agreed to engage in a criminal plan to kill Christopher (and/or his two friends, Buddy, and Michael). Or, at least, so a judge or jury could reasonably conclude.

In addition, to establish the mens rea of conspiracy, the prosecutor must prove the alleged conspirators' intent to agree with each other to commit the crime, and the intent to commit the crime itself. In this problem, a finding by the judge or jury that Christian and Eric agreed to engage in a criminal plan to kill Christopher (and/or his two friends, Buddy, and Michael), satisfies as well the requisite intention on the part of both of them to commit that criminal offense. And, just as with proof of the actus reus, Christian and Eric's intent to agree with each other to commit this homicide offense would appear to be established circumstantially.

The remaining question is whether or not Christian and Eric committed an overt act. In a majority of jurisdictions, the existence of a criminal conspiracy requires proof of the commission by at least one of the co-conspirators of an "overt act" tending to demonstrate the seriousness of the conspirators' purpose. In this case, Eric's act of giving Christian the pistol used to shoot Christopher is more than adequate to establish the existence of an overt act. Accordingly, since there is sufficient evidence based upon which a reasonable judge or jury could conclude that both Christian and Eric committed the crime of conspiring to commit murder, answer (b) is correct, and answers (a), (c) and (d) are incorrect as they conclude that one or both of the accused could not be so convicted.

[Portions of this question were taken from Trujillo v. State, 227 S.W.3d 164 (Tex. App. Houston [1st Dist.] 2006). You might also consider looking at that decision to see how that court handled some of these issues.]

[For additional discussion of this subject, see John M. Burkoff, ACING CRIMINAL LAW, Chapt. 8 (West)]

Answer 17–2: The correct answer is (a).

To support a conviction for homicide, the prosecution must establish that the person accused of the crime, *inter alia*, committed a killing act that caused the death of another person.

As to the killing act, Christian clearly shot Christopher. But was that act voluntary or involuntary? An act is voluntary if it is a product of a person's free will, manifested by a corresponding, external body movement. An act is involuntary if it is *not* a product of a person's free will, manifested by a corresponding, external body movement. If the a judge or jury believes the eyewitness account that the shot that was fired was not the product of Christian's exercise of conscious free will but rather because Christopher slapped the pistol and it accidently discharged, then this act was involuntary and no crime was committed. Hence, answer (a) is correct, and answer (c) is ipso facto incorrect.

As to the requisite causation element necessary to convict someone for a homicide, to establish causation, the prosecution must prove both that: (1) that Christian's conduct actually caused the criminal result; and (2) that Christian's conduct was a legally sufficient cause of the criminal result.

Actual—so-called "but for"—causation is easily established on these facts. But for Christian's actions in approaching Christopher with his gun, Christopher would not have been shot and killed.

Similarly, Christian's action was a proximate cause of Christopher's death. There is no question but that the relationship between Christian's conduct and Christopher's subsequent death as a result of his gunshot wound was legally sufficient to justify his criminal culpability. It is certainly reasonably foreseeable that confronting another person with a loaded pistol—whether Christian fired it or the gun went off accidentally—might result in serious injury to or the death of that other person. Moreover, in Model Penal Code terms, Christian's conduct in shooting Christopher was clearly not "too remote or accidental" from Christopher's resulting death to justify the imposition of criminal sanctions. They were, instead, directly related to one another. Hence, answer (b) is incorrect, and answer (d) is ipso facto incorrect as well.

[Portions of this question were taken from Trujillo v. State, 227 S.W.3d 164 (Tex. App. Houston [1st Dist.] 2006). You might also consider looking at that decision to see how that court handled some of these issues.]

[For additional discussion of these subjects, see John M. Burkoff, ACING CRIMINAL LAW, Chapts. 2(A) & 5 (West)]

Answer 17–3: The correct answer is (d).

Murder:

To support a conviction for murder, the prosecution must establish that the person accused of the crime, acting with malice, committed a killing act that caused the death of another person.

As to the killing act, Christian clearly shot Christopher. But was that act voluntary or involuntary? An act is voluntary if it is a product of a person's free will, manifested by a corresponding, external body movement. An act is involuntary if it is *not* a product of a person's free will, manifested by a corresponding, external body movement. If the judge or jury believes that the shot that was fired was not the product of Christian's exercise of conscious free will but rather because Christopher slapped the pistol and it accidently discharged, then this act was involuntary and no crime was committed. Hence, answer (a) is correct.

Malice is easy to establish in these circumstances. "Malice" refers to a particularly heinous ill will on the part of a killer. Malice is often presumed where a person has killed another person by using a deadly weapon, e.g. a gun or a knife, on a vital part of the victim's body. That is, of course, exactly what happened here. Assuming that the fact-finder has not found that what occurred was an involuntary act, Christian shot Christopher with a gun, ipso facto, he acted maliciously. Hence, answer (b) is correct.

Parenthetically, as to the requisite causation element necessary to convict someone for a homicide, to establish causation, the prosecution must prove both that: (1) that Christian's conduct actually caused the criminal result; and (2) that Christian's conduct was a legally sufficient cause of the criminal result.

Actual—so-called "but for"—causation is easily established on these facts. But for Christian's actions in approaching Christopher with his gun, Christopher would not have been shot and killed.

Similarly, Christian's action was a proximate cause of Christopher's death. There is no question but that the relationship between Christian's conduct and Christopher's subsequent death as a result of his gunshot wound was legally sufficient to justify his criminal culpability. It is certainly reasonably foreseeable that confronting another person with a loaded pistol—whether Christian fired it or the gun went off accidentally—might result in serious injury to or the death of that other person. Moreover, in Model Penal Code terms, Christian's conduct in shooting Christopher was clearly not "too remote or accidental" from Christopher's resulting death to justify the imposition of criminal sanctions. They were, instead, directly related to one another.

First Degree Murder

To support a conviction for first degree (premeditated) murder instead of unpremeditated murder (often called second degree murder), the prosecution must also establish—in addition to the elements discussed above—that Christian had the specific intent to kill Christopher, premeditating and deliberating about the killing act. A conviction for such premeditated murder requires proof of the accused person's actual, prior thought and reflection about the particular killing act in question.

In many jurisdictions, "no time is too short" for a person to premeditate and deliberate a killing. In this case, there would seem to have been adequate time for premeditation under the rules in effect in any jurisdiction. After being struck by Christopher and taunted by Christopher and the others, Christian and Eric walked toward the parking lot together before Christian took a gun from Eric and then walked back to the others who were standing at the bottom of the stairs. As a result, Christian had enough time to think about just what he planned to do.

But an adequate amount of time is a necessary but not a sufficient requirement for a finding of premeditation and deliberation. There must also be sufficient evidence that the accused *actually* premeditated and deliberated the killing. Since Christopher acted only after arguing with, being struck in the face by, and being taunted and threatened by Christopher and his companions, it would appear that Christian had both plenty of time (under the law in any jurisdiction) and sufficient motive—anger, humiliation, fear, the desire for revenge—to decide to kill Christopher.

As a result, a judge or jury could certainly find that Christian had both adequate time to premeditate and deliberate this killing, and that there is substantial evidence that that is precisely what he did. Accordingly, answer (c) is correct. On the other hand, a judge or jury could find instead that Christian did not intend to kill Christopher at all, but simply intended to confront him when his gun went off by accident after Christopher tried to slap it away. If a judge or jury concluded that, Christian might still be guilty of murder, as discussed above, but not first degree murder.

Because answers (a), (b), and (c) are all correct, answer (d) (All of the above) is the most accurate answer. Similarly, because answers (a), (b), and (c) are all correct, answer (e) is incorrect.

[Portions of this question were taken from Trujillo v. State, 227 S.W.3d 164 (Tex. App. Houston [1st Dist.] 2006). You might also consider looking at that decision to see how that court handled some of these issues.]

[For additional discussion of these subjects, see John M. Burkoff, Acing Criminal Law, Chapts. 2(A), 5 & 12(A) (West)]

Answer 17–4: The correct answer is (c).

To support a conviction for murder, the prosecution must establish that the person accused of the crime, acting with malice, committed a killing act that caused the death of another person.

Malice is easy to establish in these circumstances. "Malice" refers to a particularly heinous ill will on the part of a killer. Malice is often presumed where a person has killed another person by using a deadly weapon, e.g. a gun or a knife, on a vital part of the victim's body. That is, of course, exactly what happened here. Assuming that the fact-finder has not found that what occurred was an involuntary act, Christian shot Christopher with a gun, ipso facto he acted maliciously. Hence, answer (a) (which expressly assumes the voluntariness of Christian's act) is incorrect.

Moreover, to support a conviction for first degree (premeditated) murder instead of unpremeditated murder (often called second degree murder), the prosecution must also establish that Christian had the specific intent to kill Christopher, premeditating and deliberating about the killing act. A conviction for such premeditated murder requires proof of the accused person's actual, prior thought and reflection about the particular killing act in question.

In many jurisdictions, "no time is too short" for a person to premeditate and deliberate a killing. In this case, there would seem to have been adequate time for premeditation under the rules in effect in any jurisdiction. After being struck by Christopher and taunted by Christopher and the others, Christian and Eric walked toward the parking lot together before Christian took a gun from Eric and then walked back to the others who were standing at the bottom of the stairs. As a result, Christian had enough time to think about just what he planned to do.

But an adequate amount of time is a necessary but not a sufficient requirement for a finding of premeditation and deliberation. There must also be sufficient evidence that the accused *actually* premeditated and deliberated the killing. Since Christopher acted only after arguing with, being struck in the face by, and being taunted and threatened by Christopher and his companions, it would appear that Christian had both plenty of time (under the law in any jurisdiction) and sufficient motive—anger, humiliation, fear, the desire for revenge—to decide to kill Christopher.

As a result, a reasonable judge or jury could certainly find that Christian had both adequate time to premeditate and deliberate this killing, and that there is substantial evidence that that is precisely what he did. Hence, answer (b) is incorrect. Of course, although this is not the likely result, a judge or jury could find instead that Christian did not intend to kill Christopher at all, but simply intended to confront him when his gun went off by accident after Christopher tried to slap it away. If a judge or jury concluded that, Christian might still be guilty of murder, but not first degree murder.

Accordingly, in these circumstances, in a prosecution of Christian for first degree murder, the mens rea element has likely been satisfied. Hence, answer (c) is correct, and answer (d) (None of the above) is therefore incorrect.

[Portions of this question were taken from Trujillo v. State, 227 S.W.3d 164 (Tex. App. Houston [1st Dist.] 2006). You might also consider looking at that decision to see how that court handled some of these issues.]

[For additional discussion of this subject, see John M. Burkoff, Acing Criminal Law, Chapt. 12(A) (West)]

Answer 17–5: The correct answer is (b).

Felony Murder

In a majority of jurisdictions, a death occurring when an accused person is committing or attempting to commit a felony is the crime of felony murder. But the felony murder doctrine does not apply to a death that occurs in the course of the commission or attempted commission of just any felony. In most jurisdictions, it applies only to a specified list of serious felonies. In other jurisdictions, it applies to a death occurring during the commission of any felony deemed to be inherently dangerous to human life.

However, in either event, the felony murder doctrine is inapplicable where the triggering felonious act is collateral to the very act leading to the victim's death. In this case, the triggering felony—the aggravated assault on Christopher—was collateral to the act leading to Christopher's death. This assault was the very act that led to Christopher's death.

Accordingly, a successful prosecution of Christian for felony murder is not likely to be successful. Hence, answer (a) is incorrect, and, as a result, answer (d) is also incorrect.

Involuntary Manslaughter

Involuntary manslaughter is an unintentional killing committed without malice. The mens rea showing required for involuntary manslaughter is commonly gross negligence. Gross negligence is an objective element which is satisfied when the accused *should have* been aware of a substantial and unjustifiable risk that death or serious bodily injury might occur as a result of his actions. Unlike a recklessness element, to establish gross negligence, the prosecution does not have to establish that the accused was actually aware of this risk and "consciously" disregarded it.

In this case, if a judge or jury does not find that Christian committed murder because he did not act intentionally or with malice, it is almost certain that that judge or jury would nonetheless conclude on these facts that he should have been aware of a substantial and unjustifiable risk that death or serious bodily injury might occur as a result of his act of accosting and threatening Christopher with a pistol.

Moreover, even if this jurisdiction requires a showing of recklessness to establish involuntary manslaughter, it is still likely that Christian would be found guilty of involuntary manslaughter. To prove that Christian acted recklessly, the prosecution would have to show that he consciously disregarded a substantial and unjustifiable risk that he was placing Christopher in danger of death or serious bodily injury. The key inquiry here is the "consciously" element, i.e. did Christian actually realize and disregard the risk that accosting and threatening Christopher with a pistol put him in danger of death or serious bodily injury? While a judge or jury might conclude that Christian is so stupid that he did not actually realize that, such a conclusion would appear counterintuitive and unlikely. Hence, answer (b) is correct.

Voluntary Manslaughter

Voluntary manslaughter is an intentional killing that has been mitigated from murder, usually because the accused was found to have been reasonably provoked by the victim. This provocation defense requires the accused to prove that he or she acted on the basis of a sudden, intense passion resulting from a provocation by the victim which was so serious that it would create such a passion in a reasonable person.

In this case, it appears that Christian was extremely upset and disturbed by Christopher and his friends' actions toward him, particularly their insulting comments and threats. While a judge or jury might likely conclude that his state of mind supported a finding of intense passion, it is nonetheless not likely that a judge or jury would find this impassioned state sufficient to entitle him to a provocation defense—mitigating murder to voluntary manslaughter—for at least two reasons.

First, Christian's action in shooting Christopher was not "sudden." Passion sufficient to mitigate murder to voluntary manslaughter is viewed as having dissipated as a matter of law where the killing act occurred after a reasonable cooling-off period has passed. In this case, a court could reasonably conclude that there was sufficient time for Christian to have cooled off after Christopher struck him and Christopher, Buddy, and Michael taunted and threatened him. As previously noted in the discussion of premeditation, after being taunted by Christopher and the others, Christian and Eric then walked toward the parking lot together before Christian took a gun from Eric and then walked back to the others who were standing at the bottom of the stairs. This clearly took some time.

Second, traditionally, the rule has been that a person's provocative words alone were never enough to establish an adequate and sufficient provocation defense, mitigating murder to manslaughter. Accordingly, Christopher and his friend's verbal taunts and threats would not have been an adequate provocation to support mitigation to voluntary manslaughter.

The rule that words alone are not enough to provoke has, however, been abrogated in many jurisdictions. Nonetheless, even in a jurisdiction that takes that position and considering the fact that Christopher had previously struck Christian in the face as well, it is quite likely that a judge or jury would conclude that this blow and these taunts and threats by the victim and his friends were not sufficiently serious that they would create an intense passion in a reasonable person.

Accordingly, for both of these reasons—the existence of an adequate cooling-off period and the fact that these events were likely not sufficiently serious that they would create an intense passion in a reasonable person—a mitigating provocation defense offered by Christian, trying to reduce a murder charge to voluntary manslaughter, would be unlikely to succeed. Hence, answer (c) is incorrect.

[Portions of this question were taken from Trujillo v. State, 227 S.W.3d 164 (Tex. App. Houston [1st Dist.] 2006). You might also consider looking at that decision to see how that court handled some of these issues.]

[For additional discussion of these subjects, see John M. Burkoff, Acing Criminal Law, Chapts. 12(A)(3), 12(B)(1) & 12(B)(2) (West)]

Answer 17–6: The correct answer is (c).

In a majority of jurisdictions, a death occurring when an accused person is committing or attempting to commit a felony is the crime of felony murder. Felony murder is generally viewed as one way to establish murder by imputing malice through transferred intent from the accused person's commission of a felonious act. Accordingly, a separate showing of malice (outside of mere commission of the felony) is unnecessary. Hence, answer (d), which assumes the necessity of a showing of malice, is incorrect.

The felony murder doctrine does not, however, apply to a death that occurs in the course of the commission or attempted commission of just *any* felony. In most jurisdictions, it applies only to a specified list of serious felonies. In other jurisdictions, it applies to a death occurring during the commission of any felony deemed to be inherently dangerous to human life.

However, in either event, the felony murder doctrine is inapplicable where the triggering felonious act is collateral to the very act leading to the victim's death. In this case, there was a triggering felony, namely the aggravated assault on Christopher. Hence, answer (b) is incorrect. But this felony—the aggravated assault—was collateral to the act leading to Christopher's death. Indeed, this assault was the very act that led to Christopher's death. Hence, answer (c) is correct as Christian is likely to be found not guilty because he did not commit an appropriate triggering felony sufficient to make out that offense.

Accordingly, a successful prosecution of Christian for felony murder is not likely to be successful. Hence, answer (a) is incorrect.

[Portions of this question were taken from Trujillo v. State, 227 S.W.3d 164 (Tex. App. Houston [1st Dist.] 2006). You might also consider looking at that decision to see how that court handled some of these issues.]

[For additional discussion of this subject, see John M. Burkoff, Acing Criminal Law, Chapt. 12(A)(3) (West)]

Answer 17–7: The correct answer is (d).

Eric committed no killing act and he cannot, as a result, be found guilty of a homicide offense *directly*. But the common law distinctions between parties to a crime—principals in the first degree, principals in the second degree, accessories before the fact, and accessories after the fact—have been abrogated by statute in the great majority of jurisdictions. With one exception—accessories after the fact—the categories of principal and accessory are said to have "merged." Accordingly, if the prosecution can establish only that Eric was complicit in a homicide crime relating to Christopher's death, then he can be convicted of that same homicide offense.

To be convicted as an accomplice here, the prosecution must prove the mens rea of complicity: that Eric intended to assist Christian in killing Christopher and that he intended that Christian actually kill Christopher.

Although this mens rea is often established circumstantially, mere presence at the scene of a crime is never enough to establish it. In this case, however, Eric was not only present at the scene, but he also supplied Christian with the very pistol that Christian then used to shoot and kill Christopher. Unfortunately, we do not know what, if anything, Christopher said to Eric or how Eric responded when the pistol was handed off. Nonetheless, given Eric's presence at all of the triggering events—the arguments, the taunting, and he threats—and given that Eric had a very good indication of Christian's agitated mental state from their ongoing conversations, there is every possibility that a judge or jury might conclude that Eric possessed the appropriate mens rea: the intent to assist Christian in killing Christopher and the intent that Christian actually kill Christopher. Hence, answer (a) is incorrect, and so, ipso facto, is answer (c).

Moreover, to be convicted as an accomplice, an accused must also have actively assisted another person in the commission of a crime. And—just as with proof of mens rea—mere physical presence at the scene of a crime is not enough to establish that such a criminal act occurred. Once again, however, Eric was not only present at the scene, but he also supplied Christian with the very pistol that Christian then used to shoot and kill Christopher. This act was clearly an act of active assistance. Accordingly, the appropriate actus reus for accomplice culpability in Christopher's killing is also present and Eric very likely could be found guilty of being an accomplice to a homicide offense. Hence, answer (d) is correct, and answer (b) is incorrect.

Parenthetically, if Christian and Eric are found to have conspired together to kill Christopher (and/or his two friends), Eric's complicity in the homicide offense may be established in another way, independent of an accomplice-liability analysis. In many jurisdictions, co-conspirators are held criminally responsible for the reasonably foreseeable actions of their co-conspirators undertaken in furtherance of the conspiracy. This rule is called the "*Pinkerton* Doctrine" after a well-known Supreme Court decision applying it to federal criminal law.

In this case, if Eric agreed with Christian to kill and then provided him with the murder weapon, certainly it would appear clear that the subsequent shooting and killing of Christopher with that very same pistol was reasonably foreseeable. Accordingly, on this ground independent of the law relating to accomplices, Eric would also be guilty of murder. Hence, once again, answer (d) is correct, and answer (b) is incorrect.

[Portions of this question were taken from Trujillo v. State, 227 S.W.3d 164 (Tex. App. Houston [1st Dist.] 2006). You might also consider looking at that decision to see how that court handled some of these issues.]

[For additional discussion of this subject, see John M. Burkoff, ACING CRIMINAL LAW, Chapt. 6(A) (West)]

Answer 17–8: The correct answer is (e).

Intoxication or Drugged Condition

Christian's defense counsel might argue that he should not be found guilty of any homicide offense relating to the death of Christopher because he used his friend's Prozac just before the killing occurred so that he has a good intoxication or drugged condition defense. Christian is not likely, however, to be successful in making such a defense.

In a majority of jurisdictions, the fact that an accused was intoxicated or drugged at the time he or she committed a criminal act is considered to be a valid defense, but only if the crime (1) has a specific intent mens rea element, and (2) the intoxication or drugged condition is so extreme as to negative that element.

First degree murder and—usually—voluntary manslaughter (which is mitigated murder) are considered specific intent crimes because the actor's intention went beyond the assaultive conduct being committed and included the further intention that that conduct result in the death of the victim. Murder which is not first degree and involuntary manslaughter are not specific intent crimes and, accordingly, there is no intoxication or drugged condition defense to those charges. Felony murder is a specific intent crime only if the triggering felony requires specific intent. Accordingly, even in a jurisdiction that possesses an intoxication or drugged condition defense, it does not apply to all of the homicide offenses with which Christian may be charged.

But even for those homicide offenses where intoxication or drugged condition may be a defense in some jurisdictions, e.g. first degree murder, it is not likely that a judge or jury would find that Christian was sufficiently drugged from merely using Prozac that he could not have possessed the appropriate mens rea required for these homicide offenses. Christian retained sufficient motor control to walk and to handle a gun. More significant, he was able to speak coherently to Eric and to all of the others on the scene. There is, accordingly, no indication from these facts that Christian was drugged so extremely from the Prozac that he could not possibly possess the intent to kill. Hence, answer (a) is incorrect.

Involuntary Intoxication

Christian's defense counsel might argue, additionally and parenthetically, that he should not be found guilty of any homicide offense relating to the death of Christopher because his actions were the result of an involuntary drugged condition.

An act is involuntary if it is *not* a product of a person's free will, manifested by a corresponding, external body movement. If the a judge or jury believes that reasonably unforeseen and unknown (to Christian) side effects from the Prozac that he ingested caused Christian to act as he did, then his actions were involuntary and, as a result, no crime was committed. Such a defense is, however, unlikely to be successful in the absence of compelling and convincing expert testimony establishing both that a single dose of Prozac can produce such an effect and that that is precisely what Christian experienced in this case.

Self Defense & Imperfect Self Defense

Christian may raise a self-defense defense. But it is highly unlikely to be successful. While a person is sometimes justified in using unlawful force against another person in self defense, the use of force in self defense is only justified where the person using it was not an aggressor and where he or she used it to protect himself or herself while reasonably believing that he or she was threatened with the imminent use of unlawful force by another person and that the use of responsive force was necessary to repel that threat or attack.

In these circumstances, Christian clearly did not satisfy the required elements necessary to make out a good defense of self defense. For one thing, he was the aggressor in this encounter. He walked back to the others who were standing at the bottom of the stairs, pointing a gun at them. Christian may argue that, in fact, Christopher was the aggressor as it was Christopher who first resorted to the use of force, striking him in the face. But, after striking Christian, Christopher withdrew completely from the fray and it was Christian who resumed it, becoming the aggressor by accosting and threatening Christopher and his friends with a pistol.

Furthermore, in order to use deadly force in self defense—as Christian did by firing the pistol in his hand—a person must be responding to the use of deadly force against himself or herself. The use of deadly force is not justified in response to the use of merely unlawful, but not deadly, force. That is exactly what occurred here. Christian used deadly force when he was only threatened (if that) by Christopher's earlier act of striking him with his hand and/or by Christopher's act of slapping at his gun, i.e. deadly force was never directed against Christian by Christopher. Hence, answer (b) is incorrect.

However, in most jurisdictions, Christian could nonetheless mitigate murder to voluntary manslaughter if he can establish the existence of an "imperfect defense." An imperfect defense is a protective defense—like self defense—where the accused honestly believes that he or she needs to kill for self-protection or to protect others, but that belief is unreasonable. There is no indication from these facts that Christian actually believed—unreasonably or not—that Christopher was about to use deadly force against him. As a result, an imperfect self-defense defense in these circumstances would not be likely to succeed. Hence, answer (c) is incorrect.

Since answers (a), (b), and (c) are all incorrect, answer (d) (all of the above) is also clearly incorrect, and answer (e) (none of the above) is correct.

[Portions of this question were taken from Trujillo v. State, 227 S.W.3d 164 (Tex. App. Houston [1st Dist.] 2006). You might also consider looking at that decision to see how that court handled some of these issues.]

[For additional discussion of these subjects, see John M. Burkoff, ACING CRIMINAL LAW, Chapts. 2(A), 12(B)(1)(b), 14(A) & 15(B) (West)]

Answer 17–9: The correct answer is (d).

Voluntary manslaughter is an intentional killing that has been mitigated from murder, usually because the accused was found to have been reasonably provoked by the victim. This provocation defense requires the accused to prove that he or she acted on the basis of a sudden, intense passion resulting from a provocation by the victim which was so serious that it would create such a passion in a reasonable person.

In this case, it appears that Christian was extremely upset and disturbed by Christopher and his friends' actions toward him, particularly their insulting comments and threats. While a judge or jury might likely conclude that his state of mind supported a finding of intense passion, it is nonetheless not likely that a judge or jury would find this impassioned state sufficient to entitle him to a provocation defense—mitigating murder to voluntary manslaughter—for at least two reasons.

First, Christian's action in shooting Christopher was not "sudden." Passion sufficient to mitigate murder to voluntary manslaughter is viewed as having dissipated as a matter of law where the killing act occurred after a reasonable cooling-off period has passed. In this case, a court could reasonably conclude that there was sufficient time for Christian to have cooled off after Christopher struck him and Christopher, Buddy, and Michael taunted and threatened him. After being taunted by Christopher and the others, Christian and Eric then walked toward the parking lot together before Christian took a gun from Eric and then walked back to the others who were standing at the bottom of the stairs. This clearly took some time. Hence, answer (b) is correct, and answer (a) is incorrect.

Second, traditionally, the rule has been that a person's provocative words alone were never enough to establish an adequate and sufficient provocation defense, mitigating murder to manslaughter. Accordingly, Christopher and his friend's verbal taunts and threats would not have been an adequate provocation to support mitigation to voluntary manslaughter.

The rule that words alone are not enough to provoke has, however, been abrogated in many jurisdictions. Nonetheless, even in a jurisdiction that takes that position and considering the fact that Christopher had previously struck Christian in the face as well, it is quite likely that a judge or jury would conclude that this blow and these taunts and threats by the victim and his friends were not sufficiently serious that they would create an intense passion in a reasonable person. Hence, answer (c) is correct.

Accordingly, for both of these reasons—the existence of an adequate cooling-off period and the fact that these events were likely not sufficiently serious that they would create an intense passion in a reasonable person—a mitigating provocation defense offered by Christian, trying to reduce a murder charge to voluntary manslaughter, would be unlikely to succeed. Because answers (b) and (c) are both correct and answer (a) is incorrect, answer (d) is the most accurate answer.

[Portions of this question were taken from Trujillo v. State, 227 S.W.3d 164 (Tex. App. Houston [1st Dist.] 2006). You might also consider looking at that decision to see how that court handled some of these issues.]

[For additional discussion of this subject, see John M. Burkoff, ACING CRIMINAL LAW, Chapt. 12(B)(1)(a) (West)]

Answer 17–10: The correct answer is (d).

Christian's defense counsel is likely to argue that he should not be found guilty of any homicide offense relating to the death of Christopher because he used his friend's Prozac just before the killing occurred so that he has a good intoxication or drugged condition defense. Christian is not likely, however, to be successful in making such a defense.

In a majority of jurisdictions, the fact that an accused was intoxicated or drugged at the time he or she committed a criminal act is considered to be a valid defense, but only if the crime (1) has a specific intent mens rea element, and (2) the intoxication or drugged condition is so extreme as to negative that element.

First degree murder and—usually—voluntary manslaughter (which is mitigated murder) are considered specific intent crimes because the actor's intention went beyond the assaultive conduct being committed and included the further intention that that conduct result in the death of the victim. Murder which is not first degree and involuntary manslaughter are not specific intent crimes and, accordingly, there is no intoxication or drugged condition defense to those charges. Felony murder is a specific intent crime only if the triggering felony requires specific intent. Accordingly, even in a jurisdiction that possesses an intoxication or drugged condition defense, it does not apply to all of the homicide offenses with which Christian may be charged.

But even for those homicide offenses where intoxication or drugged condition may be a defense in some jurisdictions, e.g. first degree murder, it is not likely that a judge or jury would find that Christian was sufficiently drugged from merely using Prozac that he could not have possessed the appropriate mens rea required for these homicide offenses. Christian retained sufficient motor control to walk and to handle a gun. More significant, he was able to speak coherently to Eric and to all of the others on the scene. There is, accordingly, no indication from these facts that Christian was drugged so extremely from the Prozac that he could not possibly possess the intent to kill. Hence, answers (a), (b), and (c) are all incorrect, and accordingly, answer (d) (None of the above) is correct.

[Portions of this question were taken from Trujillo v. State, 227 S.W.3d 164 (Tex. App. Houston [1st Dist.] 2006). You might also consider looking at that decision to see how that court handled some of these issues.]

[For additional discussion of this subject, see John M. Burkoff, ACING CRIMINAL LAW, Chapt. 15(B) (West)]

Answer 17–11: The correct answer is (c).

Christian may raise a self-defense defense. But it is highly unlikely to be successful. While a person is sometimes justified in using unlawful force against another person in self defense, the use of force in self defense is only justified where the person using it was not an aggressor and where he or she used it to protect himself or herself while reasonably believing that he or she was threatened with the imminent use of unlawful force by another person and that the use of responsive force was necessary to repel that threat or attack.

In these circumstances, Christian clearly did not satisfy the required elements necessary to make out a good defense of self defense. For one thing, he was the aggressor in this encounter. He walked back to the others who were standing at the bottom of the stairs, pointing a gun at them. Christian may argue that, in fact, Christopher was the aggressor as it was Christopher who first resorted to the use of force, striking him in the face. But, after striking Christian, Christopher withdrew completely from the fray and it was Christian who resumed it, becoming the aggressor by accosting and threatening Christopher and his friends with a pistol.

Furthermore, in order to use deadly force in self defense—as Christian did by firing the pistol in his hand—a person must be responding to the use of deadly force against himself or herself. The use of deadly force is not justified in response to the use of merely unlawful, but not deadly, force. That is exactly what occurred here. Christian used deadly force when he was only threatened (if that) by Christopher's earlier act of striking him with his hand and/or by Christopher's act of slapping at his gun, i.e. deadly force was never directed against Christian by Christopher. Hence, answer (a) is incorrect.

In most jurisdictions, Christian could nonetheless mitigate murder to voluntary manslaughter if he can establish the existence of an "imperfect defense." An imperfect defense is a protective defense—like self defense—where the accused honestly believes that he or she needs to kill for self-protection or to protect others, but that belief is unreasonable. There is no indication from these facts that Christian actually believed—unreasonably or not—that Christopher was about to use deadly force against him. As a result, an imperfect self-defense defense in these circumstances would not be likely to succeed. Hence, answers (b) and (d) are incorrect.

Since neither the defense of self defense nor an imperfect self defense is likely to work for Christian in these circumstances, the correct answer is answer (c).

[Portions of this question were taken from Trujillo v. State, 227 S.W.3d 164 (Tex. App. Houston [1st Dist.] 2006). You might also consider looking at that decision to see how that court handled some of these issues.]

[For additional discussion of these subjects, see John M. Burkoff, ACING CRIMINAL LAW, Chapts. 12(B)(1)(b) & 14(A) (West)]

Answer 17–12: The correct answer is (b).

As to the requisite causation element, to establish causation, the prosecution must prove both: (1) that Gary's conduct actually caused the criminal result; and (2) that Gary's conduct was a legally sufficient cause of the criminal result.

More than one person or event can be the actual ("but for") cause of the same criminal result, even if the people act or the events occur independently. Gary, who stabbed Jason, is certainly a but for cause of his death. But for the stabbing, Jason would not have been in the hospital where he died from an infection in the area of his stab wound. Hence, answers (a) and (d) are incorrect.

In addition, Gary's action in stabbing Jason was a proximate cause of Jason's death in that the relationship between Gary's conduct and the resulting death was legally sufficient as closely enough related to justify criminal culpability. It is certainly reasonably foreseeable that stabbing someone in the neck—nearly severing the victim's carotid artery and completely severing his jugular vein—might lead to the victim's death.

Moreover, in Model Penal Code terms, Gary's conduct in mortally wounding Jason was not "too remote or accidental" from Jason's resulting death to justify the imposition of criminal sanctions. Gary might argue that Jason did not end up dying from the stab wound, but rather he died from a staph infection that he acquired in the hospital and that that "intervening event" caused his death. He might argue further that it was the hospital's negligence in permitting Jason to pick up that infection which was the true and supervening cause of Jason's death. But this attempted defensive argument is not likely to be successful. Hence, answer (b) is correct.

In many jurisdictions, mere negligent medical treatment leading to the death of a victim who was hospitalized as the result of a prior criminal assault has been held not to break the causal chain with respect to the perpetrator of the assault. He or she is still guilty of homicide, assuming that the other elements of the particular homicide offense charged are met. Gross negligence, on the other hand, has been deemed a sufficiently remote or intervening eventuality to serve to break the causal chain.

In essence, ordinary negligence is reasonably foreseeable, but gross negligence is not. The latter breaks the causal chain; the former does not. There is no evidence on the facts in this problem that Jason picked up the staph infection which led to his death as a result of the gross negligence of hospital staff. Hence, answer (c) is incorrect.

[Portions of this question were taken from State v. Black, 50 S.W.3d 778 (Mo. 2001). You might also consider looking at that decision to see how that court handled some of these issues.]

[For additional discussion of this subject, see John M. Burkoff, Acing Criminal Law, Chapt. 5 (West)]

Answer 17–13: The correct answer is (c).

Murder:

To support a conviction for murder, the prosecution must establish that the person accused of the crime, acting with malice, committed a killing act that caused the death of another person. Clearly Gary committed a killing act here when he stabbed Jason in the neck with his knife.

Malice is also easy to establish in these circumstances. "Malice" refers to a particularly heinous ill will on the part of a killer. Malice is often presumed where a person has killed another person by using a deadly weapon, e.g. a gun or a knife, on a vital part of the victim's body. That is, of course, exactly what happened here. Again, Gary stabbed Jason with a knife. Hence, answer (c) is correct, and answer (e) is incorrect.

First Degree Murder

To support a conviction for first degree (premeditated) murder instead of unpremeditated murder (often called second degree murder), the prosecution must also establish—in addition to the elements discussed above—that Gary had the specific intent to kill Jason, premeditating and deliberating about the killing act. A conviction for such premeditated murder requires proof of the accused person's actual, prior thought and reflection about the particular killing act in question.

In many jurisdictions, "no time is too short" for a person to premeditate and deliberate a killing. In this case, Gary followed the car in which Jason was a passenger for some period of time before he got out of his car at a stoplight and accosted him and ultimately, stabbed him.

But an adequate amount of time is a necessary but not a sufficient requirement for a finding of premeditation and deliberation. There must also be sufficient evidence that the accused actually premeditated and deliberated the killing. Since Tammy told Gary (falsely) that Jason had made a pass at her even before Jason got into his vehicle and Gary then set off to follow him, it would appear that Gary had both plenty of time (under the law in any jurisdiction) and sufficient motive—jealousy—to decide to kill Jason.

As a result, a judge or jury could certainly find that Gary had both adequate time to premeditate and deliberate this killing, and that there is substantial evidence that that is precisely what he did. On the other hand, a judge or jury could find instead that Gary only intended to hurt Jason by stabbing him, not to kill him. If a judge or jury decided that, Gary would still be guilty of murder, but not first degree murder. Hence, answers (a) and (d) are incorrect.

Felony Murder

In a majority of jurisdictions, a death occurring when an accused person is committing or attempting to commit a felony is the crime of felony murder. But the felony murder doctrine does not apply to a death that occurs in the course of the commission or attempted commission of just any felony. In most jurisdictions, it applies only to a specified list of serious felonies. In other jurisdictions, it applies to a death occurring during the commission of any felony deemed to be inherently dangerous to human life.

However, in either event, the felony murder doctrine is inapplicable where the triggering felonious act is collateral to the very act leading to the victim's death. In this case, the triggering felony—the aggravated assault on Jason with a knife—was collateral to the act leading to Jason's death. This assault was the very act that led to Jason's death. Accordingly, a successful prosecution of Gary for felony murder is not likely to be successful. Hence, answer (b) is incorrect.

[Portions of this question were taken from State v. Black, 50 S.W.3d 778 (Mo. 2001). You might also consider looking at that decision to see how that court handled some of these issues.]

[For additional discussion of these subjects, see John M. Burkoff, Acing Criminal Law, Chapts. 12(A) (West)]

Answer 17–14: The correct answer is (a).

Involuntary Manslaughter

Involuntary manslaughter is an unintentional killing committed without malice. The mens rea showing required for involuntary manslaughter is commonly gross negligence. Gross negligence is an objective element which is satisfied when the accused *should have* been aware of a substantial and unjustifiable risk that death or serious bodily injury might occur as a result of his actions. Unlike a recklessness element, to establish gross negligence, the prosecution does not have to establish that the accused was actually aware of this risk and "consciously" disregarded it.

In this case, if a judge or jury does not find that Gary committed murder because he did not act intentionally or with malice, it is almost certain that that judge or jury would nonetheless conclude on these facts that he should have been aware of a substantial and unjustifiable risk that death or serious bodily injury might occur as a result of his act of stabbing Jason in the neck with a knife.

Moreover, even if this jurisdiction requires a showing of recklessness to establish involuntary manslaughter, it is likely that Gary would be found guilty of involuntary manslaughter. To prove that Gary acted recklessly, the prosecution would have to show that he consciously disregarded a substantial and unjustifiable risk that he was placing other people in danger of death or serious bodily injury. The key inquiry here is the "consciously" element, i.e. did Gary actually realize and disregard the risk that stabbing Jason in the neck with a knife put him in danger of death or serious bodily injury? While a judge or jury might conclude that Gary is so stupid that he did not actually realize that, such a conclusion would appear counterintuitive and unlikely. Hence, answer (a) is correct, and answer (b) is incorrect.

Voluntary Manslaughter

Voluntary manslaughter is an intentional killing that has been mitigated from murder, usually because the accused was found to have been reasonably provoked by the victim. This provocation defense requires the accused to prove that he or she acted on the basis of a sudden, intense passion resulting from a provocation by the victim which was so serious that it would create such a passion in a reasonable person.

In this case, it appears clear that Gary was intensely passionate as a result of his jealous belief that Jason had made "a pass" at his girlfriend. But his passion is not likely to be viewed by a judge or jury as sufficient to entitle him to a provocation defense mitigating murder to voluntary manslaughter for at least two reasons.

First, Gary's action in stabbing Jason was not "sudden." Passion sufficient to mitigate murder to voluntary manslaughter is viewed as having dissipated as a matter of law where the killing act occurred after a reasonable cooling-off period has passed. In this case, there was sufficient time for Gary to have cooled off. He heard about Jason's alleged pass at Tammy, but he did not act on that disturbing information immediately. He followed Jason's vehicle for some distance before he yelled at him and before he actually got out of his car and confronted him.

Second, traditionally, the rule has been that a person's provocative words alone were never enough to establish an adequate and sufficient provocation defense, mitigating murder to manslaughter. Accordingly, even if Jason had made a verbal "pass" at Tammy, that would not have been an adequate provocation to support mitigation to voluntary manslaughter.

The rule that words alone are not enough to provoke has, however, been abrogated in many jurisdictions. Nonetheless, even in a jurisdiction that takes that position, it was not in fact Jason's words that provoked Gary, it was Tammy's words to him, reporting falsely what Jason had allegedly said to her. As a result, even in a words-are-sufficient jurisdiction, the provocative act at issue here did not come from the victim himself. Since a provocation defense is only permitted when the victim engages in the provocative act at issue, adequate provocation to support this defense is lacking. Hence, answer (c) is incorrect, and, ipso facto, answer (d) is incorrect as well.

[Portions of this question were taken from State v. Black, 50 S.W.3d 778 (Mo. 2001). You might also consider looking at that decision to see how that court handled some of these issues.]

[For additional discussion of this subject, see John M. Burkoff, ACING CRIMINAL LAW, Chapt. 12(B) (West)]

Answer 17–15: The correct answer is (b).

Gary may claim that he is not guilty of any homicide offense relating to the death of Jason because he had been smoking marijuana just before the killing occurred so that he has a good intoxication or drugged condition defense. He is not likely, however, to be successful in making such a defense.

In a majority of jurisdictions, the fact that an accused was intoxicated or drugged at the time he or she committed a criminal act is considered to be a valid defense, but only if the crime (1) has a specific intent mens rea element, and (2) the intoxication or drugged condition is so extreme as to negative that element.

First degree murder and—usually—voluntary manslaughter (which is mitigated murder) are considered specific intent crimes because the actor's intention went beyond the assaultive conduct being committed and included the further intention that that conduct result in the death of the victim. Hence, answer (c) is incorrect because this defense—successful or not—would be the same for both first degree murder and voluntary manslaughter.

Murder which is not first degree and involuntary manslaughter are not specific intent crimes and, accordingly, there is no intoxication or drugged condition defense to those charges. (Parenthetically, felony murder is a specific intent crime only if the triggering felony requires specific intent.) Accordingly, even in a jurisdiction that possesses an intoxication or drugged condition defense, it would not apply to all of the homicide offenses with which Gary could be charged.

But even for those homicide offenses where intoxication or drugged condition may be a defense in some jurisdictions, e.g. first degree murder and voluntary manslaughter, it is not likely that a judge or jury would find that Gary was sufficiently drugged from merely smoking some marijuana in his car that he could not have possessed the appropriate mens rea required for these homicide offenses.

Gary retained sufficient motor control to drive his car, to walk, and to handle a knife. More significant, he was able to speak coherently to Jason, to "exchange words" with him prior to the stabbing, accusing him expressly of "messing with my woman." There is, accordingly, no indication from these facts that Gary was drugged so extremely from marijuana use that he could not possibly possess the intent to kill. Hence, answer (b) is correct, and answers (a) and (d) are incorrect.

[Portions of this question were taken from State v. Black, 50 S.W.3d 778 (Mo. 2001). You might also consider looking at that decision to see how that court handled some of these issues.]

[For additional discussion of this subject, see John M. Burkoff, Acing Criminal Law, Chapt. 15(B) (West)]

Answer 17–16: The correct answer is (d).

It is very unlikely that Tammy can be successfully prosecuted for homicide.

Tammy committed no killing act and she cannot, as a result, be found guilty of a homicide offense directly. But the common law distinctions between parties to a crime—principals in the first degree, principals in the second degree, accessories before the fact, and accessories after the fact—have been abrogated by statute in the great majority of jurisdictions. With one exception—accessories after the fact—the categories of principal and accessory are said to have "merged." Accordingly, if the prosecution can establish only that Tammy was complicit with Gary in a homicide crime relating to Jason, then she can be convicted of that same homicide offense.

To be convicted as an accomplice here, the prosecution must prove the mens rea of complicity: that Tammy intended to assist Gary in killing Jason and that she intended that Gary actually kill Jason.

Although this mens rea is often established circumstantially, mere presence at the scene of a crime is never enough to establish it. In this case, although Tammy clearly tried to make Gary jealous by falsely accusing Jason of making a pass at her, there is no evidence on these facts that she intended that Gary kill him, or that she intended to assist Gary in killing Jason. As a result, Tammy's mere presence at the scene is pretty much all that the prosecution can establish for sure here. Hence, the appropriate mens rea is lacking and Tammy should not be found guilty of being an accomplice to a homicide offense. Hence, answer (a) is incorrect, and answer (b) is correct.

Moreover, to be convicted as an accomplice, an accused must also have actively assisted another person in the commission of a crime. And—just as with proof of mens rea—mere physical presence at the scene of a crime is not enough to establish that such a criminal act occurred. Once again, on these facts, Tammy's mere presence is all that the prosecution can apparently establish. Hence, the appropriate actus reus is also lacking and Tammy is not guilty of being an accomplice to a homicide offense on this independent ground as well. Hence, answer (c) is correct, but answer (d) is the most accurate answer as it includes the accuracy of both answers (b) and (c).

[Portions of this question were taken from State v. Black, 50 S.W.3d 778 (Mo. 2001). You might also consider looking at that decision to see how that court handled some of these issues.]

[For additional discussion of this subject, see John M. Burkoff, Acing Criminal Law, Chapt. 6(A) (West)]

Answer 17–17: The correct answer is (a).

Teisha has a good mistake of fact defense to this first degree murder charge.

A mistake of fact defense is one way of trying to negative the mens rea element of a criminal offense. First degree murder in this jurisdiction requires proof of the mens rea of purposeful conduct. Teisha is arguing that she did not in fact act purposefully because it was not her conscious desire to commit this criminal act (poisoning Bob Lee) or to obtain this criminal result (killing Bob Lee). Model Penal Code § 2.04(1)(a) provides, in relevant part, that "[i]gnorance or mistake as to a matter of fact ... is a defense if ... the ignorance or mistake negatives the purpose ... required to establish a material element of the offense."

In jurisdictions using an approach identical or similar to the Model Penal Code, given the fact that we are to accept as true Teisha's mistaken belief, the required mens rea—purposefulness—simply did not exist and she should not be found guilty of first degree murder. Answer (c) is incorrect as it applies a negligence test (should have known) rather than a purposefulness mens rea test.

In some other jurisdictions, however, an accused trying to make a mistake of fact defense must establish not only that he or she honestly believed in the mistaken circumstance that negative the mens rea required for the offense charged (a subjective test), but he or she must also establish that such a mistaken belief was reasonable as well (an objective test). Since answer (a) assumes the reasonableness of her belief, it is correct, and answer (d) (None of the above) is ipso facto incorrect.

It may be true that, if so charged, Teisha could be and should be found guilty of a different homicide offense, e.g. a homicide offense with a requisite mens rea of recklessness or criminal negligence, in these same circumstances. But the fact that that is what the prosecution should have done perhaps, is simply irrelevant to the question whether a mistake of fact defense would work in these circumstances. Hence, answer (b) is incorrect.

[For additional discussion of this subject, see John M. Burkoff, Acing Criminal Law, Chapt. 4(A) (West)]

Answer 17–18: The correct answer is (d).

The arson statute contains a mens rea element of "intent or purpose" to commit the arson offense. Answers (a) and (c) are, accordingly, incorrect because these answers reflects proof of a negligence standard instead. Under the Model Penal Code, for example, "[a] person acts negligently with respect to a material element of an offense when he should be aware of a substantial and unjustifiable risk that the material element exists or will result from his conduct. The risk must be of such a nature and degree that the actor's failure to perceive it, considering the nature and purpose of his conduct and the circumstances known to him, involves a gross deviation from the standard of care that a reasonable person would observe in the actor's situation."

Answer (b) is also incorrect because this answer reflects proof of a recklessness standard. It does not reflect proof of intentional or purposeful conduct, but rather requires only that the prosecution establish that Rita consciously disregarded a substantial and unjustifiable risk that she was placing another in danger of death or serious bodily injury.

Answer (d) is correct because it reflects proof of Rita's conscious intention or purpose to commit the offense of arson, which is precisely the mens rea that is required by the statute.

[For additional discussion of this subject, see John M. Burkoff, Acing Criminal Law, Chapt. 3(A) (West)]

Answer 17–19: The correct answer is (d).

Purposeful or intentional conduct is the most difficult mens rea term to satisfy and the prosecution must prove the accused person's actual intention to commit the crime at issue to satisfy this requirement. The trial judge here expressly ruled that this was not proved. Hence, answer (a) is patently incorrect.

Proof that an actor acted knowingly requires establishing that a person is aware that it is practically certain that his or her conduct will cause the criminal activity in question. Unlike purposeful or intentional conduct, proving that an accused knowingly acted or caused a particular result does not require the prosecution to establish that the act or result was the actor's "conscious object." Nonetheless, the trial judge in this case ruled that Rita did not even think about the fact that the burning of property would or could result. Hence, answer (b) is incorrect.

Establishing recklessness requires proof that the actor consciously disregarded a substantial and unjustifiable risk and, once again, the trial judge ruled in this case that Rita was not aware of any such risk. Hence, answer (c) is incorrect.

A showing of criminal negligence requires proof that the accused *should have* been aware of a "substantial and unjustifiable risk," rather than having *actually* been aware of the risk in order to "consciously" disregard it, as is required to establish recklessness. That is precisely what the trial judge ruled in this case, i.e. that Rita should have been aware of this risk. Hence, the judge concluded that Rita acted with criminal negligence, and as a result, answer (d) is correct.

[For additional discussion of this subject, see John M. Burkoff, Acing Criminal Law, Chapt. 3(A) (West)]

Answer 17–20: The correct answer is (c).

Sarah does not have a good defense-of-habitation defense to these aggravated assault charges.

Sarah used deadly force when she shot Paul. Deadly force is force which creates a substantial risk of causing death or serious bodily harm. The use of a firearm—like a rifle, semi-automatic or not—is a classic example of deadly force.

Most jurisdictions permit the use of deadly force by a homeowner to prevent or terminate an unlawful entry into his or her home when he or she reasonably believes that the intruder intends to commit a felony inside. A minority of jurisdictions go further, permitting a homeowner to use deadly force when an unlawful entry into the home has taken place and he or she reasonably believes that nothing less than the use of deadly force would be adequate to terminate that entry. Hence, answer (b) is incorrect.

Whichever rule of law is used in this jurisdiction, Sarah has not satisfied the requisite elements to make out a good defense of her habitation. No unlawful entry had been made. Paul was still two feet from the door. Once it was clear that Paul was attempting to make an unlawful entry, Sarah would have been justified—under the law in most jurisdictions—in preventing his entry by using deadly force.

Moreover, in a minority jurisdiction, Sarah could not have believed—reasonably or otherwise—that it was necessary to use deadly force to terminate the entry as the entry had not occurred. Hence, answer (c) is correct, and answers (a) and (d) are incorrect.

Accordingly, Sarah does not have a good defense to the second degree murder charge in these circumstances.

[For additional discussion of this subject, see John M. Burkoff, Acing Criminal Law, Chapt. 14(C) (West)]

Answer 17–21: The correct answer is (a).

Whether or not Alicia is guilty of the crime of conspiracy to commit retail theft depends entirely upon the approach taken to conspiracy law in the jurisdiction where she is prosecuted.

The actus reus of conspiracy is an agreement between one or more persons to commit a criminal act or to use criminal means to commit a lawful act. In this problem, Yasir was not actually agreeing to commit a criminal act with Alicia. He was instead only feigning agreement, and he subsequently participated in Alicia's criminal plan only as a police informant, knowing that the police were aware of the plan.

But because there was no *actual* agreement between Alicia and Yasir to commit a criminal act, no conspiracy would or could exist if the jurisdiction in which this prosecution takes place is a "bilateral" conspiracy jurisdiction. In a "bilateral" jurisdiction, at least two people must *actually* agree on a criminal plan in order for a conspiracy to exist. And, once again, Yasir was not actually agreeing. Hence, answers (b) and (c) are both incorrect.

However, a majority of jurisdictions that criminalize criminal conspiracies today follow the Model Penal Code approach to conspiracy law and permit conviction of a criminal defendant for a "unilateral" conspiracy. In a unilateral conspiracy jurisdiction, the act of a single person who believes—rightly or wrongly—that he or she is agreeing with another person to commit a crime is sufficient to establish a conspiracy. There does not need to be, as in a unilateral jurisdiction, a "meeting of the minds" in order to have an agreement sufficient to support a conspiracy conviction. In a unilateral jurisdiction, a defendant *can* be convicted lawfully of criminal conspiracy even if his or her supposed co-conspirator did not actually agree to commit a criminal act. Hence, answer (d) is incorrect.

Accordingly, since Yasir was not actually agreeing to commit the criminal act of retail theft with Alicia, Alicia was not guilty of conspiracy to commit that criminal act in a (minority) bilateral jurisdiction. But because Yasir's feigned agreement would be entirely irrelevant in a (majority) unilateral jurisdiction, Alicia would be guilty of conspiracy if prosecuted there. Hence, answer (a) is correct.

[For additional discussion of this subject, see John M. Burkoff, ACING CRIMINAL LAW, Chapt. 8(A) (West)]

Answer 17–22: The correct answer is (d).

At common law, a battery was committed when a person intentionally touched another person against the other person's will, thereby injuring him or her. The common law definition of battery continues to apply in this jurisdiction. April did not commit a battery on Mike for two reasons.

First, she did not touch him. Hence, answer (b) is correct, and answer (a) is incorrect.

Second, she did not injure him (except for his pride). Hence, answer (c) is correct.

As a result, on these facts, April is not guilty of the crime of battery. Because answers (b) and (c) are both correct, answer (d) is the most accurate answer.

[For additional discussion of this subject, see John M. Burkoff, ACING CRIMINAL LAW, Chapt. 11 (West)]

Answer 17–23: The correct answer is (a).

Felicia is not guilty of a common law or traditional theft crime in these circumstances.

Felicia is not guilty of common law larceny because she was in actual possession of the dress and she did not have the intent to convert it or to deprive Rhoda of it on a permanent basis, both necessary elements of the common law offense of larceny. Hence, answers (c) and (d) are both incorrect.

Felicia is, furthermore, not guilty of embezzlement because she did not fraudulently convert Rhoda's property—the dress—while she was in possession of it, a necessary element of the offense of embezzlement. The dress still hangs there—forlornly, perhaps—in Felicia's closet.

Felicia is also not guilty of common law larceny by trick because she did not gain possession of the dress from Rhoda by means of any fraud or false pretenses, a necessary element of that offense. At the time that she borrowed the dress, Felicia honestly intended to return it to Rhoda—unstained and good as new—just as soon as she got back to town from the wedding.

Finally, Felicia is not guilty of the crime of false pretenses. She did not engage in false pretenses because she did not knowingly misrepresent any material fact to Rhoda in order to and with the result of defrauding her into lending Felicia the dress, necessary elements of that specific offense. Hence, answer (b) is incorrect.

Accordingly, Felicia is not guilty of a common law or traditional theft crime in these circumstances. Hence, answer (a) is correct, and Rhoda should just take the money offered and buy herself a new dress. Just saying.

[For additional discussion of this subject, see John M. Burkoff, ACING CRIMINAL LAW, Chapt. 13(A) (West)]

Answer 17–24: The correct answer is (c).

In jurisdictions where the retreat doctrine exists as a limitation on the right to use deadly force in a defensive manner, it does not apply to the defense of others defense unless *both* the person using the force *and* the person who is being defended can retreat in complete safety. *See* Model Penal Code § 3.05(2). Hence, answer (c) is correct, and answer (d) is ipso facto incorrect.

However, just as the obligation to retreat exists in self-defense situations when the accused is being threatened, the obligations exists even when third parties are being threatened. Hence, answer (b) is incorrect.

In this factual scenario, Hannah could apparently have retreated in complete safety. There is no indication that Dylan had even seen her as she left the restaurant 30 yards behind Alfie. But, significantly, Alfie could not have retreated from Dylan in complete safety. He was being threatened at gunpoint. He could not have run away faster than a bullet could have "caught" him. Hannah had no obligation to retreat instead of responding with deadly force to Dylan's threat of deadly force against Alfie because, although she could have retreated in complete safety, Alfie could not have. Hence, answer (a) is incorrect.

Accordingly, the prosecution's position that Hannah had no right to shoot Dylan since Hannah could have safely retreated from this situation without harm to herself is incorrect.

[For additional discussion of this subject, see John M. Burkoff, ACING CRIMINAL LAW, Chapt. 14(B) (West)]

Answer 17–25: The correct answer is (d).

Some jurisdictions do not permit a defense of insanity. If this had been one of those jurisdictions, insanity would obviously not have been a good defense for Chris.

In those jurisdictions that do have an insanity defense, the most commonly used test is the two-pronged *M'Naghten* test, the test that is used in this jurisdiction. Assuming that this jurisdiction uses both prongs of that test (some jurisdictions do not) since the problem refers to the *M'Naghten* test rather than a part of it, Chris's defense counsel would have to establish that he was suffering from such a mental disease or defect as not to know the nature and quality of the act he committed or, if he did know, that he did not know that what he was doing was wrong.

As to the "nature and quality of his act"—the so-called cognitive prong of *M'Naghten*—Chris did not meet this test. He clearly understood that he was trying to kill Geri (who he thought was Satan) by shooting her. In a jurisdiction that uses the full *M'Naghten* test (or only this first *M'Naghten* prong) as its insanity test, Chris's insanity defense would most certainly fail. Hence, answer (a) is correct, and answer (c) is incorrect.

With respect to the second prong of *M'Naghten*—the so-called "moral incapacity" test—a jury might reasonably decide this issue either way. Most likely, a jury would find that Chris was aware that killing Geri (even if she was actually Satan) was wrong, but that he thought that he was justified in killing her in these circumstances in order to save the world. If the jury reached this conclusion, Chris's insanity defense under *M'Naghten* would not be successful as *neither* prong of the *M'Naghten* test would be satisfied. Hence, answer (b) is correct. Accordingly, answer (d) is the most accurate answer since answers (a) and (b) are both correct, and answer (c) is incorrect.

Parenthetically, there is no indication in the facts of this problem suggesting that Chris acted in response to an irresistible impulse. This would be relevant if this jurisdiction was one of the few that adopted that supplementary test to *M'Naghten*.

[For additional discussion of this subject, see John M. Burkoff, Acing Criminal Law, Chapt. 15(C) (West)]

CHAPTER 18
MULTIPLE CHOICE EXAM #2

Answer 18–1: The correct answer is (b).

Quentin will likely seek to defend himself against the conspiracy count by claiming that he abandoned the conspiracy before the crime that was the object of the conspiracy—robbery—actually occurred. But this defense is not likely to be successful.

Most jurisdictions recognize that it is a valid defense to a conspiracy charge if the accused renounced his or her conspiratorial intent and voluntarily and completely withdrew from the conspiracy before the criminal objective was completed. However, in most jurisdictions, to be effective, such a renunciation must also include action on the part of the person seeking to abandon the conspiracy aimed at preventing the commission of the criminal objective by his or her co-conspirators.

As with his alleged abandonment of the attempted murder crime, a judge or jury might reasonably conclude that Quentin thought better of his and Damaris' original plan to rob Kenyatta and that he subsequently sought to avoid its completion by popping out of the doorway and yelling: "I just can't do it. Run, Kenyatta! Get the f* * * outta here!" But, significantly, Quentin did nothing else other than to yell at Kenyatta. He did nothing else aimed at keeping his remaining co-conspirator, Damaris, from going ahead and trying to accomplish the criminal objective—the robbery of Kenyatta—which was the object of their conspiratorial agreement.

Accordingly, an abandonment defense is not likely to succeed for Quentin with respect to this particular charge. Hence, answer (a) is incorrect, and answer (b) is correct.

Whether or not an abandonment defense is available does not depend at all on whether the jurisdiction in question uses a unilateral or bilateral conspiracy test. Hence, answers (c) and (d) are both incorrect.

[Portions of this question were taken from State v. Wiley, 880 So. 2d 854 (La. App. 5 Cir. 2004). You might also consider looking at that decision to see how that court handled some of these issues.]

[For additional discussion of this subject, see John M. Burkoff, ACING CRIMINAL LAW, Chapt. 8(E) (West)]

Answer 18–2: The correct answer is (a).

Conspiracy

Robbery is an aggravated form of theft that involves a taking of property from another person that is accomplished by the use of violence or a threat of violence. Damaris and Quentin have been charged with the crime of conspiracy to commit robbery.

The actus reus of a conspiracy is an agreement between one or more persons to commit a criminal act or to use criminal means to commit a lawful act. Such agreement can be—and often is—established circumstantially. This would likely be viewed by a judge or jury as just such a case. Damaris and Quentin appeared to be working together to draw Kenyatta into a trap and, at the very least (as they may also have intended to kill him), to take his money from him at gunpoint. Or, at least, so a judge or jury could conclude. (They had already taken his cocaine, but not forcibly.)

In addition, to establish the mens rea of conspiracy, the prosecutor must prove the alleged conspirators' intent to agree with each other to commit the crime, and the intent to commit the crime itself. In this problem, a finding by a judge or jury that Damaris and Quentin agreed to engage in a criminal plan to rob Kenyatta satisfies as well the requisite intention on the part of both of them to commit that particular criminal offense. And, just as with proof of the actus reus, Damaris' and Quentin's intent to agree with each other to commit this robbery would appear to be established circumstantially given the prior planning necessary to execute this pretextual sale of cocaine and resulting trap.

The remaining question is whether or not either Damaris or Quentin committed an overt act. In a majority of jurisdictions, the existence of a criminal conspiracy requires proof of the commission by at least one of the co-conspirators of an "overt act" tending to demonstrate the seriousness of the conspirators' purpose. In this case, Quentin's act of drawing Kenyatta out of the car and into the trap through his false statements is more than adequate to establish the existence of an overt act.

Accordingly, Damaris and Quentin are likely to be found guilty of conspiracy to rob Kenyatta. Hence, answer (a) is correct, and answers (b) and (d) are incorrect.

Unilateral/Bilateral Issue: Damaris

If Quentin's attempted abandonment defense did succeed—which is unlikely, as previously discussed in the answer to Question 18–1, above—that result might have led to beneficial consequences for Damaris.

Traditionally, conspiracies were "bilateral," consisting of an agreement between two or more persons to commit an unlawful act or a lawful act by unlawful means. In many jurisdictions today, however, following the lead of the Model Penal Code, conspiracies are now "unilateral." In a unilateral jurisdiction, the act of a single person who believes—rightly or wrongly—that he or she is agreeing with another person to commit a crime is a sufficient showing to establish a conspiracy.

The significance of this distinction in this case is that if these events took place in a bilateral jurisdiction and if Quentin had been found not to have been a co-conspirator and acquitted, then Damaris would also have been not guilty of conspiracy as there was no additional person with whom he conspired. If these events took place in a unilateral conspiracy jurisdiction, in contrast, Damaris would still be guilty of conspiracy even if Quentin abandoned it and was acquitted because Damaris' culpability for conspiracy would not depend upon anyone else's culpability. Hence, answer (c) is incorrect because Damaris could be found guilty of conspiracy to rob Kenyatta if this is a unilateral conspiracy jurisdiction, whether or not Quentin's attempted abandonment defense did succeed.

[Portions of this question were taken from State v. Wiley, 880 So. 2d 854 (La. App. 5 Cir. 2004). You might also consider looking at that decision to see how that court handled some of these issues.]

[For additional discussion of these subjects, see John M. Burkoff, ACING CRIMINAL LAW, Chapts. 8 & 13(D)(1)(West)]

Answer 18–3: The correct answer is (c).

Attempted Murder: Damaris

For Damaris, the actus reus element of attempted murder is easily satisfied. By shooting at Kenyatta, Damaris clearly took a substantial step—the actus reus test in a majority of jurisdictions—toward committing the crime of murder. And in minority jurisdictions which use some form of proximity test instead (how close did the actor come to completing the crime?), Damaris' act of shooting at Kenyatta was just as clearly an action coming close enough to the commission of the crime of murder to suffice to establish that element as well. How much closer can you come to killing someone than to shoot them in the face?

Moreover, the prosecution should be able to easily establish the mens rea element of attempted murder with respect to Damaris on these facts. The mens rea of any attempt crime is the defendant's intent to commit the specific crime that was the alleged criminal objective of the attempt. In this case, Damaris aimed and shot a pistol at Kenyatta, wounding but not killing him. The intent to commit a specific crime—murder—can be established circumstantially. It appears clear from these events that

Damaris intended to shoot and to kill Kenyatta. The fact that he failed to do so—that he only managed to wound him—is irrelevant to the attempt analysis. Hence, answer (b) is incorrect, and ipso facto, answer (d) is also incorrect.

Accordingly, in the absence of a tenable affirmative defense (discussed below), Damaris is likely to be found guilty of attempted murder arising out of his shooting of Kenyatta.

Self Defense: Damaris

Damaris' defense counsel might try to raise a self-defense defense. But such a defense is highly unlikely to be successful in these circumstances. While a person is sometimes justified in using unlawful force against another person in self defense, the use of force in self defense is only justified where the person using it was not an aggressor and where he or she used it to protect himself or herself while reasonably believing that he or she was threatened with the imminent use of unlawful force by another person and that the use of responsive force was necessary to repel that threat or attack.

In these circumstances, Damaris has not satisfied the required elements necessary to make out a good defense of self defense. First of all, Damaris might well be viewed as the aggressor in this encounter. Even though Kenyatta shoved him against a wall before Damaris pulled out his gun in response, the shove was itself in response to the perceived trap arranged by Damaris and Quentin that Kenyatta perceived—reasonably—appeared calculated to seriously hurt or kill him.

However, if the fact-finder finds instead that Kenyatta was the aggressor in these circumstances due to his initial shove of Damaris, Damaris would then have had the right to respond to that shove with the use of unlawful force against Kenyatta.

But, whoever is deemed to have been the aggressor, Damaris would not have had the right to respond to Kenyatta's shove by using a gun—deadly force—against him. Firing a pistol at another person is the use of deadly force. In order to use deadly force in alleged self defense—as Damaris may claim was the basis for his action after being shoved—a person must be responding to the use of deadly force against himself or herself.

The use of deadly force is not justified in response to the use of merely unlawful, but not deadly, force. That is exactly what occurred here. Damaris used deadly force when he was only threatened by Kenyatta's act of shoving him against a wall. i.e. deadly force was never directed against Damaris by Kenyatta. Hence, answer (a) is incorrect.

As a result, Damaris cannot successfully make out a self defense defense with respect to the attempted murder charge. Since the attempted murder charge against Damaris can otherwise be made out, as discussed above, answer (c) is correct.

[Portions of this question were taken from State v. Wiley, 880 So. 2d 854 (La. App. 5 Cir. 2004). You might also consider looking at that decision to see how that court handled some of these issues.]

[For additional discussion of these subjects, see John M. Burkoff, Acing Criminal Law, Chapts. 7 & 14(A) (West)]

Answer 18–4: The correct answer is (d).

Attempted Murder: Quentin

Quentin did not fire a weapon at Kenyatta. He cannot, as a result, be found guilty of the crime of attempted murder directly. But the common law distinctions between parties to a crime—principals in the first degree, principals in the second degree, accessories before the fact, and accessories after the fact—have been abrogated by statute in the great majority of jurisdictions. With one exception—accessories after the fact—the categories of principal and accessory are said to have "merged." Accordingly, if the prosecution can establish that Quentin was complicit in this crime, then he can be convicted of the attempted murder of Kenyatta just as if he was a principal.

To be convicted as an accomplice in these circumstances, the prosecution must prove the mens rea of complicity, namely that Quentin intended to assist Damaris in killing Kenyatta and that he intended that Damaris actually kill Kenyatta.

The mens rea of complicity is often established circumstantially, although mere presence at the scene of a crime is never enough to establish it. In this case, Quentin was present when Kenyatta was being taken into what appeared—after the fact—to have been a trap intended to rob and/or hurt him. But Quentin was not present when the actual shooting took place. Quentin, who was hiding in a doorway, apparently had a change of heart about what he and Damaris were planning to do to Kenyatta—rob him? kill him?—and he had fled from the scene. Certainly there is sufficient circumstantial evidence, however, based upon these facts from which a judge or jury could conclude that Quentin both intended to assist Damaris in killing Kenyatta and that he intended that Damaris actually kill Kenyatta. (The significance of Quentin's act of apparently abandoning his complicity is discussed below.) The fact that Kenyatta was only wounded and not killed is irrelevant. Hence, answer (b) is incorrect.

Moreover, to be convicted as an accomplice, an accused must also have actively assisted another person in the commission of a crime. In this case, it is clear that Quentin rendered just such active assistance. He tricked Kenyatta into thinking that Damaris (or someone else) was going to buy his cocaine, and he drew Kenyatta out of his vehicle and into the baited trap through his false statements to Kenyatta when Kenyatta called him on the phone to see what was happening.

Accordingly, the appropriate actus reus for accomplice culpability is clearly present in these circumstances and there is a good chance that, absent a tenable defense (see below), Quentin could be found guilty of being an accomplice in Damaris' attempted murder of Kenyatta.

Conspiracy/*Pinkerton*: Quentin

If Damaris and Quentin are found to have conspired together to rob Kenyatta, Quentin's complicity in the attempted murder offense may be established in another way, i.e. independent of an accomplice-liability analysis. In many jurisdictions, co-conspirators are held criminally responsible for the reasonably foreseeable actions of their co-conspirators undertaken in furtherance of the conspiracy. This rule is called the "*Pinkerton* Doctrine" after a well-known Supreme Court decision applying it to federal criminal law.

In this case, if Quentin is found to have agreed with Damaris to rob Kenyatta at gunpoint, certainly it would appear clear that the subsequent shooting and wounding of Kenyatta by Damaris during the robbery attempt that was the subject of the conspiracy was reasonably foreseeable. Accordingly, on this ground independent of the law relating to accomplice liability, Quentin might well be found guilty of attempted murder. Hence, answer (c) is correct.

Abandonment: Quentin

Quentin will likely seek to defend himself against the attempted murder charge by claiming that he abandoned the attempt before the crime actually occurred. Most jurisdictions recognize that it is a valid defense to an attempt charge that the accused voluntarily and completely abandoned or renounced the intended criminal objective before it was committed.

To establish a good abandonment defense, however, Quentin would have to prove that his decision not to continue in the conspiracy was a result of his internal decision not to persist in the criminal conduct at issue. Abandonment is not a good defense when it is motivated, for example, by external changes in the circumstances of the crime which increase the risks of apprehension or motivate the accused to postpone the crime until a better time or to target another person.

In this case, Quentin may be able to successfully defend himself against the attempted murder charge on the basis of abandonment. A judge or jury might reasonably conclude that, while he was waiting in hiding, Quentin simply thought better of his original plan to harm Kenyatta along with Damaris and that he sought to avoid its completion when he suddenly popped out of the doorway and yelled: "I just can't do it. Run, Kenyatta! Get the f* * * outta here!" There is no obvious evidence on these facts that Quentin engaged in this action because the events that had already taken place either increased the risks of going ahead with the plan or because he decided instead to target another person.

Accordingly, an abandonment defense might succeed for Quentin with respect to this particular charge. Hence, answer (a) is correct, and the most accurate answer is answer (d) as both answers (a) and (c) are correct.

[Portions of this question were taken from State v. Wiley, 880 So. 2d 854 (La. App. 5 Cir. 2004). You might also consider looking at that decision to see how that court handled some of these issues.]

[For additional discussion of these subjects, see John M. Burkoff, Acing Criminal Law, Chapts. 6(A) & 8(F) (West)]

Answer 18–5: The correct answer is (d).

At common law and in a minority of jurisdictions today, a person commits a criminal assault when he or she intentionally places another person in actual and reasonable fear of an imminent battery. A battery at common law and in a minority of jurisdictions today is committed when a person intentionally touches another person against the other person's will, thereby injuring him or her. In a majority of jurisdictions today, the separate common law offense of battery has merged into the criminal offense of assault. Accordingly, in those majority jurisdictions, an assault is committed when a person either intentionally places another person in actual and reasonable fear of an imminent battery or intentionally commits a battery.

In either event, whether the facts set out in this problem occurred in a minority or majority jurisdiction, Mark would have a good defense to a charge of criminal assault upon Elizabeth. While Elizabeth was clearly afraid that he might be trying to assault her—and reasonably so since she had no idea who he was and he was running after her—Mark did not act intentionally. He was simply trying to tell Elizabeth that she had dropped something. Of course, in hindsight and using common sense, Mark should have simply called out to her, rather than running after her and scaring her. But, however stupid his well-intended response may have been, since his actions were not intended to place Elizabeth in fear of a battery or to commit a battery upon her, he is not guilty of assault. Hence, answer (b) is correct, and answer (a) is incorrect.

Moreover, Mark might add, with respect to his act of falling on top of Elizabeth, that action in and of itself could not establish an element of a criminal offense because it was not a voluntary touching. An act is voluntary if it is a product of a person's free will, manifested by a corresponding, external body movement. An act is involuntary if it is *not* a product of a person's free will, manifested by a corresponding, external body movement. Since Mark only fell on top of Elizabeth because he slipped on the slippery ground, then this act was involuntary, and the resulting touching would not constitute an element of a merged assault offense that included battery. Hence, answer (c) is correct.

Because answers (b) and (c) are both correct, and answer (a) is incorrect, answer (d) is the most accurate answer.

[For additional discussion of these subjects, see John M. Burkoff, Acing Criminal Law, Chapts. 2(A) & 10(A) (West)]

Answer 18–6: The correct answer is (b).

Mark is clearly not guilty of the attempted rape of Elizabeth even though he fell right on top of her without any clothes on other than his raincoat.

A sex offense—like rape—is an assault crime with the additional element of proof of the accused's commission of a specified sexual act. In some American jurisdictions today, the crime of rape is defined as sexual intercourse with another person where the accused has used or threatened the use of force on the victim to accomplish that sex act. In other jurisdictions, a person commits rape when he or she has sexual intercourse with another person without that other person's consent. At common law, *both* of these elements—the use or threat of force *and* the absence of the victim's consent—were elements of the crime of rape. While Mark clearly used force on Elizabeth and while he did not have her consent to engage in any sort of touching of her person, there was no relevant sex act committed here. At common law and in most jurisdictions today, commission of the crime of rape requires proof of vaginal penetration of the victim by the accused, however slight. Such penetration did not, of course, occur in this situation.

But Mark is charged with *attempted* rape, not rape. Mark could be convicted of *attempting* to rape Elizabeth even if he did not touch her at all, let alone engage in sexual penetration. Hence, answer (c) is incorrect.

To establish the commission of an attempt, the prosecution must prove (1) the accused person's intent to commit the specific crime that was the actor's alleged criminal objective and (2) the accused person's commission of an act beyond mere preparation aimed at accomplishment of that objective. In this case, the prosecution can prove neither of these elements.

Most significant, Mark simply did not possess the intention to commit any assaultive act—including a sex act—on Elizabeth. On this ground alone, there is no attempted rape. Hence, answer (b) is correct, and answers (a) and (d) are incorrect.

Moreover, albeit parenthetically, there is no evidence on the facts of this problem that Mark met any of the various tests that jurisdictions use to gauge the commission of an act beyond mere preparation sufficient to establish an attempt, e.g. proximity to the commission of the actual crime, or the taking of a substantial step toward its commission. Mark did not come close to actually committing the crime of rape, and there is no evidence at all that mark took any step—let alone a substantial step—toward commission of that specific crime.

The chances of a successful defense of Mark against the attempted rape charge are, accordingly, extremely high.

[For additional discussion of these subjects, see John M. Burkoff, ACING CRIMINAL LAW, Chapts. 7 & 11 (West)]

Answer 18–7: The correct answer is (b).

The actus reus element of attempted murder is easily satisfied. By throwing a large rock at Kerry's head, Mark likely took a substantial step—the actus reus test in a majority of jurisdictions—toward committing the crime of murder. And in minority jurisdictions which use some form of proximity test (how close did the actor come to completing the crime?), Mark's act of heaving the rock at Kerry was likely an action coming close enough to the commission of the crime of murder to suffice to establish that element as well. Hence, answer (c) is incorrect, and ipso facto answer (d) is incorrect as well.

However, the prosecution will not easily be able to establish the mens rea element of attempted murder on these facts. The mens rea of any attempt crime is the defendant's intent to commit the specific crime that was the alleged criminal objective of the attempt. In this case, the objective alleged by the prosecution is murder, so the prosecution would have to show that Mark actually possessed the specific intent to kill Kerry (who he thought was Elizabeth).

That will be exceedingly difficult to establish. Mark did heave a large rock at Kerry. But he did it to "teach her a lesson," to hurt her perhaps, but not necessarily to kill her. Although the intent to commit a specific crime can be established circumstantially, it would appear unlikely here that a judge or jury would conclude that Mark intended to kill Kerry—as opposed to simply hurting or scaring her—by throwing a rock at her. Hence, answer (b) is correct.

Accordingly, Mark is likely to have a very good defense to the charge of attempted murder. Hence, answer (a) is incorrect.

[For additional discussion of this subject, see John M. Burkoff, Acing Criminal Law, Chapt. 7 (West)]

Answer 18–8: The correct answer is (a).

Involuntary manslaughter is an unintentional killing committed without malice. The mens rea showing required for involuntary manslaughter is commonly gross (often called "criminal") negligence. Gross negligence is an objective element which is satisfied when the accused *should have* been aware of a substantial and unjustifiable risk that death or serious bodily injury might occur as a result of his actions. Unlike a recklessness element, to establish gross negligence, the prosecution does not have to establish that the accused was actually aware of this risk and "consciously" disregarded it.

In this case, a judge or jury would likely conclude on these facts that Mark—even recognizing that he did not intend to kill Kerry or anyone else—*should* have been aware of a substantial and unjustifiable risk that death or serious bodily injury might occur as a result of his act of heaving a large rock at Kerry. Certainly it can be persuasively argued that anyone should realize the high degree of potential risk that might result from the commission of such a serious assaultive act, particularly where the rock is large (as here) and it strikes someone in the head (as here). Hence, answer (a) is correct, and ipso facto answer (d) (None of the above) is incorrect.

However, if this jurisdiction requires a showing of recklessness in order to establish involuntary manslaughter, it is less likely—although not impossible—that the prosecution would be able to establish that. To prove that Mark acted recklessly, the prosecution would have to show that he consciously disregarded a substantial and unjustifiable risk that he was placing someone in danger of death or serious bodily injury. The key inquiry in these circumstances is the "consciousness" element, i.e. did Mark *actually* realize and disregard the risk that throwing a large rock at Kerry could result in death or serious bodily injury? Certainly a judge or jury might reasonably answer this question either way, i.e. that Mark did in fact actually realize and disregard just such a risk, or that he did not. Hence, since it is not clear that the prosecution could establish a recklessness element, answers (b) and (c) are both incorrect.

Answer 18–9: The correct answer is (d).

Mark threw a rock at Kerry, not at Robert. The rock that Mark threw struck Kerry between her eyes, rendering her unconscious and sending her careening into John, who then roller bladed over Robert, killing him. Given this extremely unlikely (except on law school exams) chain of events, was Mark really the requisite cause of Robert's death?

To establish causation, the prosecution must prove both that: (1) Mark's conduct actually caused Robert's death; and (2) Mark's conduct was a legally sufficient cause of the death. The former test is easy to satisfy; the latter is much more difficult.

Actual—so-called "but for"—causation is easily established on these facts. But for Mark's actions in throwing the rock at Kerry causing her to crash into John causing him to roll over Robert's head, Robert would not have been killed. It's as simple as that. Hence, answer (a) is correct.

But the answer to the question whether Mark's action was a proximate cause of Robert's death is far less clear. A judge or jury might well deem it reasonably foreseeable that throwing a large rock at someone's head might result in serious injury to or the death of that person. But, is it reasonably foreseeable that the resulting blow would cause a bizarre chain of events that led to the death not of the person struck, but of someone else?

In Model Penal Code terms, the question would be whether Robert's death was "too remote or accidental" from Mark's action of throwing the rock to justify the imposition of criminal sanctions? This is, of course, a question for the fact-finder, the judge or jury hearing the case. But certainly a reasonable jury might well conclude that the resulting death in these highly unusual circumstances was too remote or accidental from Mark's triggering actions to find him guilty of involuntary manslaughter. Hence, answer (b) is correct.

Hence, a defense to this charge stressing the absence of criminal causation might well be a successful one. Hence, answer (c) is correct, and answer (d) (All of the above) is the most accurate answer since answers (a), (b), and (c) are all correct.

[For additional discussion of this subject, see John M. Burkoff, Acing Criminal Law, Chapt. 5 (West)]

Answer 18–10: The correct answer is (c).

It is very likely that Zeke will be convicted of statutory rape for having had sexual intercourse with Mindy, a fifteen-year old girl.

Statutory rape is sexual intercourse with a minor who is below a specified age. Statutory rape is committed whether or not the minor who engaged in the act consented to it or not. Accordingly, since the age of consent in this jurisdiction is sixteen years old and since Mindy is only fifteen, Zeke is guilty of statutory rape despite the fact that Mindy engaged in the sexual activity with him freely and voluntarily. Hence, answer (b) is incorrect.

Zeke may try to argue, however, that he did not possess the mens rea required to establish the crime of statutory rape as he mistakenly believed—and reasonably so, as she looked like she was nineteen—that Mindy was over sixteen years of age. But there is no express mens rea element in this offense. It is typical for the crime of statutory rape to be defined as a strict liability offense. In the absence of another statute creating a reasonable mistake of fact defense to this crime or a court decision finding such a defense to exist implicitly (a minority position), Zeke cannot defend himself against these charges by trying to establish that he was acting pursuant to a reasonable, mistaken belief that Mindy was at least sixteen years old. Hence, answer (a) is incorrect.

In some jurisdictions, moreover, conviction of statutory rape also requires proof of a specified age gap between the accused and his or her victim. The difference between Zeke's and Mindy's ages is eleven years. Typically, the statutory gap element used for statutory rape is only four years or so. Hence, this is unlikely to be a good defense for Zeke. Hence, answer (d) is incorrect.

Accordingly, it is extremely likely that Zeke will be convicted of statutory rape of Mindy on these facts. Hence, answer (c) is correct.

[For additional discussion of this subject, see John M. Burkoff, ACING CRIMINAL LAW, Chapt. 11(F) (West)]

Answer 18–11: The correct answer is (a).

The prosecution should be able to easily establish the mens rea element of attempted statutory rape with respect to Zeke. The mens rea of any attempt crime is the defendant's intent to commit the specific crime that was the alleged criminal objective of the attempt. In this case, based upon such facts as the nature of their on-line chats and the fact that he was carrying condoms, there is no question but that Zeke intended to have sexual intercourse with Lola and that, if this jurisdiction's statutory rape statute has an age-gap requirement, Zeke could not use that as a defense since he believed that she was fifteen (*see* Answer 18–10, above). Hence, answer (b) is incorrect, and ipso facto answer (d) is incorrect as well.

Meeting the actus reus test for attempt could be a difficult matter for the prosecution, depending upon the jurisdiction. However, in a majority of jurisdictions—just like this one—the Model Penal Code's test applies, and the prosecution must prove that the accused took a "substantial step in a course of conduct planned to culminate in ... commission of the crime." In this case, the "substantial step" test is easily satisfied. Zeke made clear his intention to have sexual relations with Lola in their on-line postings and, beyond that, he actually traveled to the apartment where he was to meet her to engage in such activity. Zeke was, moreover, carrying condoms, assumedly to be used in the sexual activity. Clearly, actions of this sort are substantial steps on the part of Zeke. Hence, answer (c) is incorrect.

Parenthetically, in a minority of jurisdictions (not this one), various forms of proximity tests are used instead of the substantial-step test to assess the existence of the actus reus of attempt. Tests of this sort focus on the question of how close the actor actually came to commission of the criminal act in question, as opposed to looking at how far he or she had gone (like the Model Penal Code—and majority—approach). In a jurisdiction using a test like this, it is not likely that Zeke would be found to have satisfied this element. He came nowhere near to completing the act of statutory rape. For one thing, he wasn't even *really* trying to have sex with a minor at all as Ralph (posing as Lola) was forty-two years old.

Accordingly, in the absence of a tenable impossibility defense (a possibility discussed below), Zeke is likely to be found guilty of attempted statutory rape. Hence, answer (a) is correct.

[For additional discussion of these subjects, see John M. Burkoff, Acing Criminal Law, Chapt. 7 & 11(F) (West)]

Answer 18–12: The correct answer is (a).

As a prefatory matter, while sexual assaults at common law were only recognized when males assaulted females, that is no longer the case. Hence, answer (b) is incorrect.

The prosecution should be able to easily establish the mens rea element of attempted statutory rape with respect to Mindy. The mens rea of any attempt crime is the defendants' intent to commit the specific crime that was the alleged criminal objective of the attempt. In this case, it appears that Mindy intended to have sexual intercourse with Lola. However, although there is no explicit indication of this in the facts, if *only* Zeke actually intended to have sexual intercourse with Lola, Mindy's intention would nonetheless clearly appear to have been to act as Zeke's accomplice in the commission of this crime. Hence, at the very least, Mindy's intention was to assist Zeke in the commission of this crime. Hence, answer (d) is incorrect.

However, if this had been a jurisdiction where conviction of statutory rape also requires proof of a specified age gap between the accused and his or her victim (*see* Answer 18–10, above), the prosecution would not have been likely to be able to convict Mindy. There is no difference between Mindy's and Lola's (had she existed) ages. If any gap at all was required by law for culpability, Mindy would not have met it. However, in this jurisdiction—as in many jurisdictions—there is no age-gap requirement in the statutory rape statute. Accordingly, the fact that we are dealing with two putative fifteen year olds is irrelevant.

Meeting the actus reus test for attempt could be a difficult matter for the prosecution, depending upon the jurisdiction. However, in a majority of jurisdictions—just like this one—the Model Penal Code's test applies, and the prosecution must prove that the accused took a "substantial step in a course of conduct planned to culminate in ... commission of the crime." In this case, the "substantial step" test is easily satisfied. Mindy made clear her intention to have sexual relations with Lola in their on-line postings and, beyond that, she actually traveled to the apartment where he was to meet her to engage in such activity. Zeke was, moreover, carrying condoms, assumedly to be used in their sexual activity with Lola. Clearly, actions of this sort are substantial steps on the part of Mindy. Hence, answer (c) is incorrect.

Parenthetically, in a minority of jurisdictions (not this one), various forms of proximity tests are used instead of the substantial-step test to assess the existence of the actus reus of attempt. Tests of this sort focus on the question of how close the actor actually came to commission of the criminal act in question, as opposed to looking at how far he or she had gone (like the Model Penal Code—and majority—approach). In a jurisdiction using a test like this, it is not likely that Mindy would have been found to have satisfied this element. She came nowhere near to completing the act of statutory rape. For one thing, she wasn't even *really* trying to have sex with a minor at all as Ralph (posing as Lola) was forty-two years old.

Accordingly, in the absence of a tenable impossibility defense (a possibility discussed below), Mindy is likely to be found guilty of attempted statutory rape. Hence, answer (a) is correct.

[For additional discussion of these subjects, see John M. Burkoff, ACING CRIMINAL LAW, Chapts. 7 & 11(F) (West)]

Answer 18–13: The correct answer is (b).

Zeke—and Mindy—may try to argue that they cannot be convicted of attempted statutory rape because it was impossible to commit that crime in these circumstances since "Lola" was not really a minor. Indeed, she did not really even exist. This is different from the argument that Mindy may make in a jurisdiction with a statutory age-gap requirement, set out above in Answer 18–12, because in such a jurisdiction, what Mindy intended to do was not a crime (due to the lack of an age gap). What Zeke intended to do *was* a crime because he was outside the age gap. But, in any event, impossibility is not likely to be a good defense for Zeke.

Today, in the great majority of jurisdictions, following the Model Penal Code approach as this jurisdiction does, impossibility is not a good defense to any attempt crime. That is to say that it is not a good defense to a charge that an accused person attempted to commit a particular crime where—because of circumstances unknown to that person—he or she could not have actually committed that crime in these circumstances.

More specifically, in this case, it is not a good defense to the crime of *attempted* statutory rape that the intended victim was not actually under sixteen years of age. Hence, answer (b) is correct. And answer (c) is incorrect as it was not Zeke's intention to have sex with Ralph, a forty-two year-old man above the age of consent; rather it was his intention to have sex with a fifteen year-old girl, below the age of consent.

Nonetheless, in a small minority of jurisdictions, the old English rule is still followed that distinguishes between "factual impossibility," which was not considered a valid defense to an attempt crime, and "legal impossibility" which was considered to be a valid defense:

Factual impossibility was said to exist when the actual facts, unknown to the accused, made the commission of the crime he or she intended impossible. Legal impossibility was said to exist when the accused engaged in actions which did not satisfy the elements of the attempt crime charged due to the unknown factual circumstances.

The problem with this distinction is that the very same actions can be categorized as factual or legal impossibility depending on just how the factual circumstances are viewed. Using this approach in this case, if Zeke intended to have sexual intercourse with a girl under sixteen years of age (as is the case here) but failed simply because the victim was not under sixteen, that could be viewed as factual impossibility, and this is no defense to an attempt charge. But the same facts can also be deemed to be legal impossibility as Zeke attempted to engage in conduct where it was impossible to commit statutory rape (because the victim was not under sixteen, although he thought that "she" was).

In any event, since most jurisdictions today reject any application at all of the impossibility defense in attempt cases, it is not a good defense for Zeke that he is faced with the charge of attempted statutory rape, when he actually intended to have sexual intercourse with a person who was really over the age of sixteen. Hence, answer (a) is incorrect, and ipso facto answer (d) is incorrect as well.

[For additional discussion of this subject, see John M. Burkoff, Acing Criminal Law, Chapt. 7(E) (West)]

Answer 18–14: The correct answer is (a).

Zeke and Mindy may try and argue that they are not guilty of the crime of attempted statutory rape in these circumstances because they were entrapped.

Proof of an accused person's entrapment by the government is a complete defense to criminal charges. But there are two entirely different types of entrapment tests being used in the United States today. The federal courts and some states—like this one—use a "subjective" entrapment test. This is a test which asks whether the accused was predisposed to commit the crime charged, i.e. it focuses on the accused person's subjective state of mind.

Many other states use instead an "objective" entrapment test. The objective test focuses on the government rather than on the accused. It asks whether the government agents involved in the transaction encouraged or assisted the accused in committing the crime charged in an outrageous fashion.

Under either test, a law enforcement agent's act of merely giving the accused the opportunity to commit a crime is not enough, in and of itself, to establish entrapment. Moreover, the government's use of an undercover agent is not enough, in and of itself, to establish entrapment.

Under the subjective entrapment approach, Ralph's on-line overtures to Zeke and Mindy were clearly not enough to establish an entrapment defense in these circumstances. Zeke and Mindy were undoubtedly predisposed to engage in criminal conduct: sexual intercourse with a minor. They knew (or they thought they knew) that "Lola" was underage. But they eventually agreed to have sexual relations with her anyway. The fact that they initially refused to have sex with her, but eventually acquiesced is not enough to establish entrapment. It is extremely likely, accordingly, that a judge or jury would find that Zeke and Mindy were predisposed to commit this crime, and that Ralph, acting as Lola, merely gave them the opportunity to commit it. As a result, an entrapment defense would not be likely to succeed for Zeke or Mindy in a subjective entrapment jurisdiction. Hence, answer (a) is correct, and answer (c) is incorrect.

Moreover, answer (b) is incorrect because it is an application of the wrong entrapment test in this jurisdiction, an objective rather than a subjective test. As a result, answer (d) is ipso facto incorrect as well.

Accordingly, Zeke and Mindy are not likely in these circumstances to be able to successfully defend against these charges by using an entrapment defense in a subjective entrapment test jurisdiction.

[For additional discussion of this subject, see John M. Burkoff, Acing Criminal Law, Chapt. 15(D) (West)]

Answer 18–15: The correct answer is (d).

Zeke and Mindy may try and argue that they are not guilty of the crime of attempted statutory rape in these circumstances because they were entrapped.

Proof of an accused person's entrapment by the government is a complete defense to criminal charges. But there are two entirely different types of entrapment tests being used in the United States today. The federal courts and some states use a "subjective" entrapment test. This is a test which asks whether the accused was predisposed to commit the crime charged, i.e. it focuses on the accused person's subjective state of mind.

Many other states, like this one, use instead an "objective" entrapment test. The objective test focuses on the government rather than on the accused. It asks whether the government agents involved in the transaction encouraged or assisted the accused in committing the crime charged in an outrageous fashion. Hence, answer (c) is correct.

The fact that the entreaty to commit a crime came in an on-line solicitation is simply irrelevant. That does not serve, in and of itself, to make the government conduct outrageous. Hence, answer (b) is incorrect.

Under either test, a law enforcement agent's act of merely giving the accused the opportunity to commit a crime is not enough, in and of itself, to establish entrapment. Moreover, the government's use of an undercover agent is not enough, in and of itself, to establish entrapment.

The question to be asked in an objective jurisdiction like this one is: how outrageous was Ralph's conduct here? Again, just as in a subjective jurisdiction, Ralph's actions in merely providing Zeke and Mindy with an opportunity to commit this crimes by lying to them about his age and gender and interests on-line is not enough to establish entrapment in and of itself.

It seems highly unlikely that a reasonable jury would find that Ralph's conduct in chatting with Zeke and Mindy and repeatedly asking them to engage in sexual relations with "her" was outrageous. He merely gave Zeke and Mindy the opportunity to engage in criminal activity. They eventually accepted that opportunity to commit a crime. As a result, an entrapment defense is not likely to succeed for either of them in an objective entrapment jurisdiction. Hence, answer (a) is correct.

Accordingly, Zeke and Mindy are not likely in these circumstances to be able to successfully defend against these charges by using an entrapment defense in an objective entrapment test jurisdiction. Because answers (a) and (c) are both correct and answer (b) is incorrect, answer (d) is the most accurate answer to this question.

[For additional discussion of this subject, see John M. Burkoff, Acing Criminal Law, Chapt. 15(D) (West)]

Answer 18–16: The correct answer is (d).

Olander is not guilty of the crime of battery.

At common law, a battery was committed when a person intentionally touched another person against the other person's will, thereby injuring him or her. The common law definition of battery continues to apply in this jurisdiction. Olander did not commit a battery on Yasmin for two reasons.

First, he did not touch her. Hence, answer (c) is correct, and answer (a) is incorrect.

Second, he did not injure her. Hence, answer (b) is correct.

As a result, on these facts, Olander is not guilty of the crime of battery. Because answers (b) and (c) are both correct and answer (a) is incorrect, answer (d) is the most accurate answer.

[For additional discussion of this subject, see John M. Burkoff, Acing Criminal Law, Chapt. 10(A)(1) (West)]

Answer 18–17: The correct answer is (d).

Strict liability offenses do not require proof of any mens rea at all. It makes no difference, as a result, whether the Johnsons knew, should have known, or did not know that any of the party guests were underage. Hence, answer (a) is incorrect.

Whether or not to include a mens rea element in a criminal offense is a legislative judgment. All that courts are empowered to do is to determine the legislative intention with respect to the mens rea element where the statute is otherwise silent. Where courts have determined that an otherwise silent statute is in fact a strict liability offense, that interpretation is binding in the absence of legislative amendment of the statute. Since that is precisely what occurred in these circumstances, answer (b) is incorrect.

Answer (c) is also incorrect as it concludes that the Johnsons were not guilty of violating this statute because they did not act negligently. Negligence in the criminal law is an objective concept, i.e. to be negligent, the accused *should* have been aware of a risk that the criminal conduct in question would occur. But what the Johnsons should have realized is irrelevant in the face of a strict liability statute. Hence, answer (c) is incorrect, and answer (d) is correct.

[For additional discussion of this subject, see John M. Burkoff, Acing Criminal Law, Chapt. 3(B) (West)]

Answer 18–18: The correct answer is (b).

In a majority of jurisdictions, the fact that an accused was intoxicated or drugged at the time he or she committed the criminal act in question is deemed to be a defense—negativing the mens rea element—if but only if the crime was a specific intent crime. Intoxication or drugged condition is not a defense if the crime was a general intent (or strict liability) crime. Hence, answer (b) is correct, and answers (a) and (c) are incorrect.

Moreover, in jurisdictions that recognize an intoxication or drugged condition defense, the fact that someone had been drinking or using drugs at the time of the crime is not sufficient, in and of itself, to make out the defense. An accused must establish that he or she was so deeply intoxicated or drugged that he or she did not possess the mens rea necessary to establish the charged offenses. Hence, answer (d) is incorrect, and ipso facto answer (e) is incorrect as well.

[For additional discussion of this subject, see John M. Burkoff, ACING CRIMINAL LAW, Chapt. 3(C) (West)]

Answer 18–19: The correct answer is (d).

Lucinda is not guilty of the crime of soliciting Eldon to murder her parents.

The mens rea of the crime of solicitation is the intent to promote or facilitate the commission of a specific crime to be undertaken by another person solicited to commit it. It is not clear from these facts whether Lucinda truly possessed this intent.

But what is clear is that the requisite actus reus did not exist. The actus reus of solicitation is the act of commanding, encouraging, or requesting another person to commit a particular crime, murder in this case. But, significantly, a person's actions are not the crime of solicitation where they consists only of obviously hollow threats, joking, or bragging. In this problem, there is no evidence that Lucinda was seriously soliciting Eldon to commit this crime. Neither of them ever took a single step toward committing this crime, other than this one-time conversation. Hence, answers (b) and (c) are correct, and answer (a) is incorrect.

Accordingly, on these facts, Lucinda did not commit the crime of criminal solicitation. Since answers (b) and (c) are both correct and answer (a) is incorrect, the most accurate answer is answer (d).

[For additional discussion of this subject, see John M. Burkoff, ACING CRIMINAL LAW, Chapt. 9 (West)]

Answer 18–20: The correct answer is (c).

Allison does have a good duress defense to the possession of narcotics charge.

Duress may be used as a defense to a criminal charge when an accused person has been coerced by another person's unlawful threats into committing a crime because he or she reasonably believed that the other person would subject him or her or a third party to death or serious injury imminently if he or she did not commit that crime.

That is exactly what occurred in these circumstances. Denzel kidnaped Allison's child as a means of forcing her to commit a crime—obtaining illegal narcotics—which Allison did because she believed that Denzel would otherwise imminently harm her child. Certainly, in these circumstances, with her young child at risk, her belief that Denzel might carry through with his threat if she did not procure the cocaine was a reasonable one. Hence, answer (b) is incorrect, and ipso facto answer (d) is incorrect as well.

The unlawful threat that must be established in order to support a duress defense must be a threat that a reasonable person could not be expected to resist. In this case, a reasonable person should not be expected to resist a threat aimed at his or her small child's safety by a likely crack addict. Hence, answer (a) is incorrect.

Accordingly, Allison has a tenable duress defense to the charge possession of narcotics in these circumstances. Hence, answer (c) is correct.

[For additional discussion of this subject, see John M. Burkoff, ACING CRIMINAL LAW, Chapt. 15(A) (West)]

Answer 18–21: The correct answer is (c).

Patricia does not have a good self defense argument in these circumstances.

Self defense is a complete defense. A person is sometimes justified in using unlawful force against another person when he or she is acting in self defense. But the use of force in self defense is only justified where the person using it was not an aggressor and where he or she used it to protect himself or herself while reasonably believing that he or she was threatened with the imminent use of unlawful force by another person and that the use of responsive force was necessary to repel that threat or attack.

In this case, Patricia was not the initial aggressor, Gizem was, so that element of an entitlement to self defense is satisfied. Since Patricia was not the aggressor, answer (b) is incorrect because she is not disqualified from defending on this ground due to an aggressor status.

It does not appear, furthermore, that Patricia could reasonably have believed that it was necessary at the moment she stabbed Gizem to act in order to repel Gizem's continuing attack on her. She had already been shoved onto the floor, and the facts do not indicate that the attack was continuing or that it was necessary to repel it.

In any event, however, even if Patricia had satisfied both of these self defense elements, it would only have entitled her to use *unlawful force* against Gizem, not deadly force. Deadly force is force which creates a substantial risk of causing death or serious bodily harm. The use of a firearm or knife are classic examples of deadly force.

In order to use deadly force in self defense, a person must be responding to the use of deadly force against himself or herself. The use of deadly force is not justified in response to the use of unlawful, but not deadly, force. That is exactly what occurred here. Gizem used unlawful force when she accosted Patricia by shoving her to the floor. As a result, even assuming that the assault was continuing, Patricia was entitled to use unlawful force against Gizem in response to that attack. But she was not entitled to use deadly force—such as the use of a knife—against Gizem because Gizem had not used or threatened the use of deadly force against her. Hence, answer (a) is incorrect.

Accordingly, Patricia does not have a good self defense argument in these circumstances due to the fact that she responded to Gizem's assaultive force with deadly force. Hence, answer (c) is correct, and answer (d) (None of the above) is ipso facto incorrect.

[For additional discussion of this subject, see John M. Burkoff, ACING CRIMINAL LAW, Chapt. 14(A) (West)]

Answer 18–22: The correct answer is (c).

This is not a good defense for Rudolfo. A mistaken belief that a criminal act is not criminal is not a good defense. Ignorance of the law is simply no defense. The mens rea element of "knowingly" in the new statute applies only to the action proscribed therein, i.e. the possession of an exotic pet like a bear. Rudolfo clearly knew that he possessed a bear. Knowledge of the fact that such possession was a criminal act is not an element of the offense. Hence, answer (c) is correct, and answers (a), (b), and (d) are all incorrect.

[For additional discussion of this subject, see John M. Burkoff, ACING CRIMINAL LAW, Chapt. 4(B) (West)]

Answer 18–23: The correct answer is (b).

A criminal act must be committed voluntarily. If an accused person shows that his or her actions were "involuntary," no crime has been made out. An act is voluntary if it is a product of a person's free will, manifested by a corresponding, external body movement. Conversely, an act is involuntary if it is *not* a product of a person's free will, manifested by a corresponding, external body movement. If Anne can establish that her act of losing control of her car and hitting a pedestrian was strictly a result of the unanticipated, epileptic seizure rather than the product of her conscious free will, this act was involuntary and no crime was committed. Hence answer (b) is correct, and ipso facto answer (d) is incorrect.

Whether or not the criminal offense was a strict liability offense does not change this answer. The act (actus reus) element is different from the criminal intent (mens rea) element. An accused has not committed a voluntary criminal act if he or she has acted involuntarily whatever the requisite criminal intent element required, i.e. the fact that the mens rea element is satisfied has no bearing on the question whether the actus reus element has been satisfied. Hence, answer (a) is incorrect, and ipso facto answer (c) is also incorrect.

[For additional discussion of this subject, see John M. Burkoff, ACING CRIMINAL LAW, Chapt. 2(A) (West)]

Answer 18–24: The correct answer is (c).

Gary does not have a good defense-of-property defense to an attempted murder charge in these circumstances.

In most jurisdictions, the use of *non-deadly* force is held to be lawful when the person using it reasonably believes that it is necessary to use it to prevent or terminate an unlawful trespass or the unlawful carrying away of that person's property.

Gary was the owner of the rocker, and since Morris and Janine were driving away with it when he acted and since they did not respond to his yelled demand for its return, it would appear that it was indeed necessary to use force in order to successfully terminate their unlawful removal of his property. Hence, answer (b) is incorrect, and ipso facto answer (d) is incorrect as well.

However, Gary was not entitled to use *deadly* force—such as shooting at someone with a rifle—to retrieve his property. Because he used deadly force instead of mere unlawful force in this instance, the defense of property does not apply to this charge. Hence, answer (c) is correct, and answer (a) is incorrect.

[For additional discussion of this subject, see John M. Burkoff, ACING CRIMINAL LAW, Chapt. 14(C) (West)]

Answer 18–25: The correct answer is (d).

In most jurisdictions—like this one—a murder charge can be mitigated to voluntary manslaughter where defense counsel can establish the existence of an "imperfect defense." An imperfect defense is a protective defense—like self defense or defense of others—where the accused honestly believes that he or she needed to kill for self-protection or to protect others, but that belief was unreasonable. That is—arguably—exactly what occurred in this case.

A killing is justified when the person committing the killing act acts in self defense. The use of deadly force in self defense—such as the use of a gun—is justified when a person (not an aggressor) uses it for self-protection when attacked by another person who he or she reasonably believes is threatening him or her with the imminent use of deadly force, and deadly force is necessary to repel that attack. Moreover, a person is entitled to use force not only to defend himself or herself, but to defend third parties who are being threatened by others as well.

Today, some jurisdictions apply an "alter ego" rule in this situation, permitting a person to use the same level of force against someone attacking another person that the person being attacked would be permitted to use. At common law, this approach was used but the defense was limited to the defense only of close relatives, including spouses. Other jurisdictions today—a majority—extend the availability of this defense of others defense to situations where the person using defensive force honestly and reasonably believes that it is justified and necessary under the circumstances, whether or not that assessment is actually correct.

Under either test, if Johnny honestly and reasonably believed that the pedestrian in front of him was about to be shot and killed, he would have had the right to defend that person with his own use of deadly force. That would have been a complete defense.

As stated by the facts, that is exactly what Johnny believed, namely that someone was trying to shoot at the pedestrian in front of him. The question is: was this belief reasonable? If it was reasonable, he has a complete defense to this charge.

But if the fact-finder concludes that his belief was unreasonable—a likelihood, perhaps, on these facts—then Johnny nonetheless has a valid mitigating defense when charged with murder. Hence, answer (a) is correct, and answer (c) is incorrect. Moreover, this imperfect defense mitigates the offense to voluntary manslaughter. Hence, answer (b) is correct as well.

Accordingly, since answers (a) and (b) are correct, and answer (c) is incorrect, answer (d) is the most accurate answer.

[For additional discussion of this subject, see John M. Burkoff, Acing Criminal Law, Chapt. 14(D) (West)]

CHAPTER 19
MULTIPLE CHOICE EXAM #3

Answer 19–1: The correct answer is (d).

The elements of common law larceny—today merged into a more inclusive theft offense in most jurisdictions—are the wrongful taking and carrying away of personal property in the possession of another with the intent to convert it or to permanently deprive its possessor of the property. Although not charged directly with this crime, Mitt and Hillary clearly committed it. They grabbed jewelry that they knew belonged to Johnna and they ran away with it.

Mitt and Hillary have instead been charged with conspiracy to commit this criminal offense. The actus reus of a conspiracy is an agreement between one or more persons to commit a criminal act or to use criminal means to commit a lawful act. Such agreement can be—and often is—established circumstantially. This is likely to be viewed by a judge or jury as just such a case. Mitt and Hillary looked at each other in apparent accord when they saw the jewelry spill out of Johnna's purse, and then they acted—simultaneously—to grab it and run away. Accordingly, there is some solid, albeit circumstantial, evidence that the two of them agreed to engage in this criminal activity. Hence, answer (a) is incorrect.

To establish the mens rea of conspiracy, the prosecutor must prove the alleged conspirators' intent to agree with each other to commit the crime, and the intent to commit the crime itself. In this problem, the crime was actually committed so the latter mens rea element is clear. And, just as with proof of the actus reus, Mitt and Hillary's intent to agree with each other to take Johnna's jewelry for themselves would appear to be established circumstantially. Hence, answer (b) is incorrect.

The remaining question is whether or not Mitt and Hillary committed an overt act. In a majority of jurisdictions, the existence of a criminal conspiracy requires proof of the commission by at least one of the co-conspirators of an "overt act" tending to demonstrate the seriousness of the conspirators' purpose. In this case, the action each of them took in actually seizing the jewelry and running away is more than adequate to establish an overt act. Hence, answer (c) is incorrect.

Accordingly, because answers (a), (b) and (c) are all incorrect, answer (d) is correct.

[For additional discussion of this subject, see John M. Burkoff, ACING CRIMINAL LAW, Chapt. 8 (West)]

Answer 19–2: The correct answer is (d).

Proof of Murder

To support a conviction for second degree murder, the prosecution must establish that the person accused of the crime, acting with malice, committed a killing act that caused the death of another person. Clearly Ron committed a killing act here when he shot and killed John with a semi-automatic weapon.

Malice is also easy to establish on these facts for Ron. "Malice" refers to a particularly heinous ill will on the part of a killer. It is often presumed where a person has killed another person by using a deadly weapon, e.g. a gun or a knife, on a vital part of the victim's body. In Ron's case, that is exactly what happened here. Ron shot John with a semi-automatic weapon.

As to the requisite causation element necessary to convict someone of a homicide offense, to establish causation here, the prosecution must prove both that: (1) Ron's conduct actually caused the criminal result; and (2) that his conduct was a legally sufficient cause of the criminal result.

More than one person or event can be the actual ("but for") cause of the same criminal result, even if the people act or the events occur independently. Ron is definitely a but-for cause of John's death. But for Ron's shooting at John, John would not have died from gunshot wounds.

Ron's act of shooting John was also a proximate cause of John's death in that the relationship between Ron's conduct and the resulting death was legally sufficient as closely enough related to justify criminal culpability. It is certainly reasonably foreseeable that shooting someone with a semi-automatic weapon might lead to that victim's death. Moreover, in Model Penal Code terms, Ron's conduct in mortally wounding John was not "too remote or accidental" from John's resulting death to justify the imposition of criminal sanctions. Hence, answer (b) is incorrect.

Accordingly, unless Ron has a good defense, the chances of success in defending him against this second degree murder charge are extremely low.

Ron's Defenses

Ron might argue that he was provoked into shooting John and, hence, that he is entitled to a mitigating provocation defense that would reduce his culpability to voluntary manslaughter. A provocation defense requires the accused to prove that he or she acted on the basis of a sudden, intense passion resulting from a provocation by the victim which was so serious that it would create such a passion in a reasonable person.

In this case, it appears clear that this defense will not succeed for Ron. While Ron may have been intensely passionate as a result of being struck by the bicycle that he thought was a poisoned spear, in fact he had not been provoked at all by John or Barack, the victims of his gunfire. Additionally, being struck by a bike would not likely be viewed by a judge or jury as a provocation so serious that it would create such an intense passion in a reasonable person. Hence, answer (c) is incorrect.

However, Ron's unreasonable reaction may give rise to another potential defense for him: imperfect self-defense. Ron does not have a good self-defense defense. While a person is sometimes justified in using unlawful force against another person in self defense, the use of force in self defense is only justified where the person using it was not an aggressor and where he or she used it to protect himself or herself while reasonably believing that he or she was threatened with the imminent use of unlawful force by another person and that the use of responsive force was necessary to repel that threat or attack.

In these circumstances, Ron clearly did not satisfy the required elements necessary to make out a good defense of self defense. He could not have reasonably believed that it was necessary to fire his weapon indiscriminately as a response to being struck by a bicycle. And it was clearly unnecessary for Ron to use force against John (or Barack) in order to repel the threat of an attack.

Moreover, in order to use deadly force in self defense—as Ron did by firing his weapon—a person must be responding to the use of deadly force against himself or herself. The use of deadly force is not justified in response to the use of merely unlawful, but not deadly, force. That is exactly what occurred here. Ron used deadly force when he was only struck by a bicycle, i.e. deadly force was not directed against him.

However, in most jurisdictions, Ron could nonetheless mitigate murder to voluntary manslaughter if he can establish the existence of an "imperfect defense." An imperfect defense is a protective defense—like self defense—where the accused honestly believes that he or she needs to kill for self-protection or to protect others, but that belief is unreasonable. Obviously, Ron's belief that the bicycle was a poisoned spear was unreasonable. In fact, it was so unreasonable that Ron might well be viewed as insane (see discussion below). In some jurisdictions, a person claiming that he acted because of a mental disease or defect is deemed not to be eligible to raise an imperfect defense.

But whether or not this is such a jurisdiction, Ron cannot make out the other elements of a valid self-defense defense in any event, as discussed above. In particular, he cannot establish that it was necessary for him to use force against John—deadly or not—in order to repel the threat of an attack. As a result, Ron's imperfect self-defense claim would not be likely to succeed. Hence, answer (a) is incorrect.

Finally, Ron's defense counsel may try to defend against this second degree murder charge by claiming that Ron was insane when he shot John. Some jurisdictions do not permit a defense of insanity. If this is one of those jurisdictions, insanity is obviously not a good defense.

In those jurisdictions that do have an insanity defense—a majority—the most commonly used test is the two-pronged *M'Naghten* test. If this jurisdiction uses both prongs of that test, counsel would have to establish either that Ron was suffering from such a mental disease or defect as not to know the nature and quality of the act he committed or that if he did know, he did not know that what he was doing was wrong.

As to the "nature and quality of his act"—the so-called cognitive prong of *M'Naghten*—Ron did not meet this test. He clearly understood that he was shooting his weapon in response to the perceived attack on him. He knew just what he was doing, i.e. that he was firing his weapon. In a jurisdiction that uses only this first *M'Naghten* prong as its insanity test, any attempt at an insanity defense on Ron's part would most certainly fail.

With respect to the second prong of *M'Naghten*—the so-called "moral incapacity" test—a jury might reasonably decide this issue either way. Most likely, a jury would find that Ron was aware that shooting indiscriminately was wrong, but that he thought that he was justified in shooting in these circumstances because he thought that he was acting for reasons of self-protection. Or a jury might find that Ron's mental disorder was so severe that he did not even realize that shooting indiscriminately like this was wrong. If the jury reached either conclusion and this jurisdiction uses *M'Naghten*—or only the moral incapacity prong of *M'Naghten*—as its insanity test, Ron's insanity defense might well succeed.

There is no indication in the facts of this problem suggesting that Ron acted in response to an irresistible impulse. This would be relevant if this jurisdiction was one of the few that adopted that supplementary test to *M'Naghten*.

Additionally, if this jurisdiction has adopted the Model Penal Codes' insanity test instead of using *M'Naghten*, Ron's defense counsel would need to establish that at the time of this shooting, as a result of his mental disease or defect, Ron lacked substantial capacity either to appreciate the wrongfulness of his conduct or to conform his conduct to the requirements of the law. In these circumstances, as with the moral incapacity prong of the *M'Naghten* test and for the same reasons, a judge or jury might reasonably decide this issue either way. Certainly, a reasonable judge or jury might well conclude, for example, that Ron's mental disorder—the irrational fear that he was being attacked—resulted in his inability to adhere to the dictates of the criminal law.

Accordingly, Ron's chances of being found not guilty by reason of insanity depend on the specific test for insanity used in this particular jurisdiction, if any, and the fact-finding of the jury. Because answers (a), (b) and (c) are all incorrect, as discussed above, the correct answer is (d), none of the above.

[For additional discussion of these subjects, see John M. Burkoff, ACING CRIMINAL LAW, Chapts. 12(A)(2), 12(B)(1), 14(A) & 15(C)(1) (West)]

Answer 19–3: The correct answer is (e).

Proof of Murder

To support a conviction for second degree murder, the prosecution must establish that the person accused of the crime, acting with malice, committed a killing act that caused the death of another person. Clearly Ron committed a killing act here when he shot and killed John with a semi-automatic weapon (*see* discussion in Answer 19–2). *But* Barack merely ran into a bicyclist, knocking him to the ground. That action which only in the most indirect sense—see causation discussion below—led to the death of John would likely not be deemed sufficient to constitute a killing act on Barack's part. Hence, answer (a) is correct.

Malice is easy to establish on these facts for Ron (*see* discussion in Answer 19–2), but once again, not for Barack. "Malice" refers to a particularly heinous ill will on the part of a killer. It is often presumed where a person has killed another person by using a deadly weapon, e.g. a gun or a knife, on a vital part of the victim's body. In Ron's case, that is exactly what happened here. Ron shot John with a semi-automatic weapon.

In Barack's case, as there is neither presumptive nor express malice. Malice sufficient to support a murder conviction may instead, however, be implied from the circumstances. In many jurisdictions, it can be implied from an accused person's act of gross recklessness or actions undertaken with extreme indifference to the value of human life. In this case, it is not likely that a judge or jury would find that implied malice existed on Barack's part, as there is no evidence that Barack acted with gross recklessness or with extreme indifference to the value of human life when he ran into John's bicycle. There is no evidence, for example, that he was reckless because he *consciously* disregarded a substantial and unjustifiable risk that death or serious bodily injury might occur as a result of his indifference. He did not intend to run into the bicycle at all and even if he should have realized that a bike might be in his way, it is unlikely in the extreme that he would have consciously realized that he was taking such a grave risk by running into it. Hence, answer (c) is correct.

As to the requisite causation element necessary to convict someone of a homicide offense, to establish causation here, the prosecution must prove both that: (1) that Barack's and Ron's conduct actually caused the criminal result; and (2) that their conduct was a legally sufficient cause of the criminal result.

More than one person or event can be the actual ("but for") cause of the same criminal result, even if the people act or the events occur independently. Both Barack and Ron are definitely but-for causes of John's death. But for Barack smashing into John on his bicycle and the bicycle subsequently striking Ron, Ron would not have shot at John (or at Barack). Similarly, but for Ron's shooting at John, John would not have died from gunshot wounds.

Ron's act of shooting John was also a proximate cause of John's death in that the relationship between Ron's conduct and the resulting death was legally sufficient as closely enough related to justify criminal culpability. It is certainly reasonably foreseeable that shooting someone with a semi-automatic weapon might lead to that victim's death. Moreover, in Model Penal Code terms, Ron's conduct in mortally wounding John was not "too remote or accidental" from John's resulting death to justify the imposition of criminal sanctions.

In contrast, Barack's act of running into John's bicycle which ultimately led to the unlikely shooting of John by Ron was *not* a proximate cause of John's death in that the relationship between Barack's conduct and the resulting death was *not* closely related enough to justify criminal culpability. It was not reasonably foreseeable that running into a bicycle would lead to someone else shooting the bicyclist (and others) with a semi-automatic weapon leading to the victim's death. Similarly, in Model Penal Code terms, Barack's conduct in running into John on his bicycle was simply "too remote or accidental" from Ron's actions leading to John's resulting death to justify the imposition of criminal sanctions on Barack. Hence, answer (b) is incorrect.

Moreover and parenthetically, Barack cannot be convicted of second degree murder as Ron's accomplice. The common law distinctions between parties to a crime—principals in the first degree, principals in the second degree, accessories before the fact, and accessories after the fact—have been abrogated by statute in the great majority of jurisdictions. With one exception—accessories after the fact—the categories of principal and accessory are said to have "merged." Accordingly, if the prosecution can establish only that Barack was complicit in this homicide crime, then he can be convicted of that same homicide offense.

To be convicted as Ron's accomplice here, the prosecution must prove the mens rea of complicity: that Barack intended to assist Ron in killing John and that he intended that Ron actually kill John. Although this mens rea is often established circumstantially, mere presence at the scene of a crime is never enough to establish it. In this case, Barack's mere presence at the scene is all that the prosecution can establish. Hence, the appropriate mens rea is lacking and Barack cannot be found guilty of being an accomplice to Ron's homicide offense.

Furthermore, to be convicted as an accomplice, an accused must also have actively assisted another person in the commission of a crime. And—just as with proof of mens rea—mere physical presence at the scene of a crime is not enough to establish that such a criminal act occurred. Once again, on these facts, Barack's mere presence is all that the prosecution can establish. Hence, the appropriate actus reus is also lacking and Barack is not guilty of being an accomplice to a homicide offense on this independent ground as well. Hence, answer (d) is correct.

Accordingly, the chances of success in defending Barack against this second degree murder charge are extremely high for all of the reasons described in answers (a), (b), (c), and (d). Hence, answer (e) is the most accurate answer here as it includes "all of the above."

[For additional discussion of these subjects, see John M. Burkoff, Acing Criminal Law, Chapts. 5, 6(A) & 12(A)(2) (West)]

Answer 19–4: The correct answer is (b).

To establish commission of a possessory offense, the prosecution must prove that the accused was aware of his or her possession of a contraband item to a degree sufficient to be able to exercise control over it, and that he or she acted knowingly and voluntarily in possessing it. Obviously, Barack could not be convicted of possession of marijuana as the substance that he actually possessed here was not a contraband item. It was a blend of tobacco, oregano, and garlic powder, not marijuana.

But a person can be convicted of *attempting* to possess a contraband item even if the item he or she actually possessed was not contraband. Hence, answer (a) is incorrect.

To establish the commission of an attempt, the prosecution must prove (1) the accused person's intent to commit the specific crime that was the actor's alleged criminal objective and (2) the accused person's commission of an act beyond mere preparation aimed at accomplishment of that objective. In this case, the prosecution can prove neither of these things.

Although it is true that Barack said "[d]on't be taking my weed, man!" when police officers seized the substance that he was smoking—and "weed" is a common slang term for marijuana—there is no clear evidence here that in using the word "weed," Barack actually intended to possess marijuana, or anything other than the mixture that he did in fact possess. Hence, answer (b) is correct, and answer (d) is incorrect.

Moreover, there is no evidence in this problem that Barack met any of the various tests that jurisdictions use to gauge the commission of an act beyond mere preparation, e.g. proximity to the commission of the actual crime, or the taking of a substantial step toward its commission. Barack came nowhere close to actually committing the crime of possession of marijuana and there is no evidence at all that he took any step—let alone a substantial step—toward commission of that crime. Hence, answer (c) is incorrect.

Accordingly, the chances of success in defending Barack against these charges are extremely high.

[For additional discussion of these subjects, see John M. Burkoff, ACING CRIMINAL LAW, Chapts. 2(B) & 7 (West)]

Answer 19–5: The correct answer is (c).

Mitt and Hillary are clearly guilty of assault. At common law and in a minority of jurisdictions today, a person commits a criminal assault when he or she intentionally places another person in actual and reasonable fear of an imminent battery. A battery at common law and in a minority of jurisdictions today is committed when a person intentionally touches another person against the other person's will, thereby injuring him or her. In a majority of jurisdictions today, the separate common law offense of battery has merged into the criminal offense of assault. Accordingly, in those majority jurisdictions, an assault is committed when a person either intentionally places another person in actual and reasonable fear of an imminent battery or intentionally commits a battery.

In either event, whether the facts set out in this problem occurred in a minority or majority jurisdiction, Mitt and Hillary committed a criminal assault. They intentionally placed Fred in actual and reasonable fear of an imminent battery when they sought to—and did—topple him off of his scooter and onto the ground. Hence, answer (a) is incorrect.

In fact, Mitt and Hillary committed an actual battery (which, in most jurisdictions, again, has merged with the assault offense) when they intentionally pushed Fred off his scooter to clear their path, resulting in his broken nose. Hence answers (b) and (d) are incorrect, and answer (c) is correct.

[For additional discussion of this subject, see John M. Burkoff, ACING CRIMINAL LAW, Chapt. 10(A) (West)]

Answer 19–6: The correct answer is (a).

Defense counsel is not likely to be successful in defending Hillary against this possession charge. To establish commission of a possessory offense, the prosecution must prove that the accused was aware of his or her possession of a contraband item to a degree sufficient to be able to exercise control over it, and that he or she acted knowingly and voluntarily in possessing it. Hillary was clearly in possession of contraband: marijuana. The question is: did she *know* that she possessed marijuana? When they were taken from her by the police, she (and Mitt) yelled at them not to take their "tobacco-oregano-garlic powder smokes."

Did Hillary really think that was what she possessed? Or did she simply say that to try and cover up her crime? It should go without saying that what a suspected criminal says is not always the truth. And tobacco-oregano-garlic powder cigarettes are not a common item for anyone to possess, despite the fact that Barack was actually found to have possessed them. (Did Barack and Hillary inadvertently exchange their smoking material?) In any event, if a judge or jury believes that Hillary was actually unaware that the hand-rolled cigarettes found on her person were marijuana, then she has a good defense to this charge. Hence, answer (a) is correct, and ipso facto, answer (d) is also incorrect. In the more likely case that a judge or jury does not believe this, however, he does not have a good defense.

The same analysis applies to Mitt, except that he has a further defense that he can make as well, namely that—unlike Hillary who had it on her person—he was not actually in possession of this marijuana. But contraband items may be possessed by more than one person, i.e. "jointly," where more than one person is found to have been aware of its existence and to have exercised control over it. Mitt's argument that he was not in possession of the marijuana—that he was unaware of its existence and did not exercise control over it—is weakened by the fact that he referred to these hand-rolled cigarettes as "our ... smokes" when they were taken from Hillary. Nonetheless, he can make the same arguments that Hillary makes with respect to his lack of knowledge that these cigarettes actually contained marijuana rather than a tobacco-oregano-garlic powder mixture. Hence, answer (b) is incorrect, and ipso facto, answer (c) is also incorrect.

[For additional discussion of this subject, see John M. Burkoff, ACING CRIMINAL LAW, Chapt. 2(B) (West)]

Answer 19–7: The correct answer is (a).

For Tyrone, the actus reus element of attempted murder is easily satisfied. By shooting at Marco, Tyrone clearly took a substantial step—the actus reus test in a majority of jurisdictions—toward committing the crime of murder. And in minority jurisdictions which use some form of proximity test (how close did the actor come to completing the crime?), Tyrone's act of shooting at Marco was just as clearly an action coming close enough to the commission of the crime of murder to suffice to establish that element as well. How much closer can you come to killing someone than to wound them with gunfire? Hence, answer (c) is clearly incorrect.

Moreover, the prosecution should be able to easily establish the mens rea element of attempted murder with respect to Tyrone on these facts. The mens rea of any attempt crime is the defendant's intent to commit the specific crime that was the alleged criminal objective of the attempt. In this case, Tyrone aimed and shot at Marco, wounding but not killing him. The intent to commit a specific crime—murder—can be established circumstantially. It appears clear from these events that Tyrone intended to shoot and kill Marco. The fact that he failed to do so—that he only wounded him—is irrelevant to the attempt analysis. Hence, answer (b) is incorrect.

Accordingly, in the absence of a tenable affirmative defense, Tyrone will be found guilty of attempted murder arising out of his shooting of Marco. Hence, answer (a) is correct, and ipso facto answer (d) (None of the above) is incorrect.

[Portions of this question were taken from McKee v. State, 280 Ga. 755, 632 S.E.2d 636 (2006). You might also consider looking at that decision to see how that court handled some of these issues.]

[For additional discussion of these subjects, see John M. Burkoff, ACING CRIMINAL LAW, Chapts. 7 & 12(A)(1) (West)]

Answer 19–8: The correct answer is (b).

To support a conviction for murder, the prosecution must establish that the person accused of the crime, acting with malice, committed a killing act that caused the death of another person. There is no question here that a killing act existed. Tyrone clearly shot Jeffrey with a gun.

Malice is also easy to establish in these circumstances. "Malice" refers to a particularly heinous ill will on the part of a killer. Malice is often presumed where a person has killed another person by using a deadly weapon, e.g. a gun or a knife, on a vital part of the victim's body. That is exactly what happened here. Tyrone shot Jeffrey with a gun, hence, presumptively, he acted maliciously. Hence, answer (a) is incorrect.

Tyrone is not charged simply with murder, however. He is charged with first degree murder in Jeffrey's death. To support a conviction for first degree (premeditated) murder instead of "mere" murder, the prosecution must also establish—in addition to the elements discussed above—that Tyrone had the specific intent to kill Jeffrey, premeditating and deliberating about the killing act. A conviction for such premeditated murder requires proof of the accused person's actual, prior thought and reflection about the particular killing act in question. This will be difficult to prove.

In many jurisdictions, "no time is too short" for a person to premeditate and deliberate a killing. In this case, there would seem to have been adequate time for premeditation under the rules in effect in any jurisdiction. After arguing with Marco, Tyrone challenged him to go get his guns. And Marco did just that, walking to his car to retrieve them and then returning to confront Tyrone. All of that took time. As a result, Tyrone would appear to have had enough time to think about just what he planned to do.

But an adequate amount of time is a necessary but not a sufficient requirement for a finding of premeditation and deliberation. There must also be sufficient evidence that the accused *actually* premeditated and deliberated the killing. There is little or no evidence in this factual pattern that Tyrone premeditated killing Jeffrey, as opposed to Marco. If the judge or jury finds Tyrone's post-arrest remarks to be credible, he never intended to kill Jeffrey. Jeffrey simply—tragically, even to Tyrone—got caught in the crossfire.

A judge or jury could, of course, conclude that Tyrone's comments about the accidental killing of Jeffrey were not credible. In that event, a first degree murder conviction would result in the absence of a tenable affirmative defense. On the other hand and, in these circumstances, probably more likely, a judge or jury could find instead that Tyrone did not intend to kill Jeffrey at all, but that he was accidentally shot during the course of the gun fight. If a judge or jury concluded that, Tyrone would likely still be guilty of murder, but not first degree murder, the charge that has been brought against him by the prosecution. Hence, answer (b) is correct, and answer (c) is incorrect. Additionally, because answer (b) is correct, answer (d) (None of the above) is ipso facto incorrect as well.

[Portions of this question were taken from McKee v. State, 280 Ga. 755, 632 S.E.2d 636 (2006). You might also consider looking at that decision to see how that court handled some of these issues.]

[For additional discussion of this subject, see John M. Burkoff, ACING CRIMINAL LAW, Chapt. 12(A)(1) (West)]

Answer 19–9: The correct answer is (b).

As to the requisite causation element necessary to convict someone for a homicide, to establish causation, the prosecution must prove both that: (1) Tyrone's conduct actually caused Jeffrey's death; and (2) that Tyrone's conduct was a legally sufficient cause of Jeffrey's death.

Actual—so-called "but for"—causation is easily established on these facts. But for Tyrone's actions in shooting at Marco with his gun, Jeffrey would not have been shot and killed. The fact that the shooting may have been accidental is irrelevant. Hence, answer (a) is incorrect.

Tyrone's action was also a proximate cause of Jeffrey's death. There is no question but that the relationship between Tyrone's conduct and Jeffrey's subsequent death as a result of his gunshot wounds was legally sufficient to justify Tyrone's criminal culpability. It is certainly reasonably foreseeable that engaging in a shoot-out with another person (Marco) might result in serious injury to or the death of that other person or to other persons caught in the crossfire. Moreover, for the same reason, in Model Penal Code terms, Tyrone's conduct in shooting at Marco when Jeffrey was standing in the vicinity was clearly not "too remote or accidental" from Jeffrey's resulting death to justify the imposition of criminal sanctions. Hence, answer (c) is incorrect.

Accordingly, a reasonable fact-finder could—and likely would—find that Tyrone "caused Jeffrey's death. Hence, answer (b) is correct, and ipso facto answer (d) (None of the above) is incorrect.

[Portions of this question were taken from McKee v. State, 280 Ga. 755, 632 S.E.2d 636 (2006). You might also consider looking at that decision to see how that court handled some of these issues.]

[For additional discussion of this subject, see John M. Burkoff, Acing Criminal Law, Chapt. 5 (West)]

Answer 19–10: The correct answer is (e).

Voluntary manslaughter is an intentional killing that has been mitigated from murder, usually because the accused was found to have been reasonably provoked by the victim. This provocation defense requires the accused to prove that he or she acted on the basis of a sudden, intense passion resulting from a provocation by the victim which was so serious that it would create such a passion in a reasonable person.

In this case, Tyrone was obviously upset by Faye's act of throwing him out of her apartment and by Marco's comments ("chill out") on the situation. But the first degree murder victim was Jeffrey, not Marco or Faye. Hence, a provocation defense is inapplicable to this prosecution as the provocation in question was not from the victim who is the subject of this particular charge. Hence, answer (c) is correct, and answer (a) is incorrect.

Moreover, while a judge or jury might well conclude that Tyrone's state of mind supported a finding of intense passion, it is not likely that a judge or jury would find this impassioned state sufficient to entitle him to a provocation defense (even if Jeffrey had not been the victim) for at least two additional reasons.

First, Tyrone's action in shooting Marco was not "sudden." Passion sufficient to mitigate murder to voluntary manslaughter is viewed as having dissipated as a matter of law where the killing act occurred after a reasonable cooling-off period has passed. In this case, a judge or jury could reasonably conclude that there was sufficient time for Tyrone to have cooled off after Marco left the yard to return to his car to get his guns. This action clearly took some time and may be viewed as a reasonable cooling-off period. Hence, answer (b) is correct.

Second, traditionally, the rule has been that a person's provocative words alone were never enough to establish an adequate and sufficient provocation defense, mitigating murder to manslaughter. Accordingly, Marco's comments to Tyrone to "chill out" would not have been an adequate provocation to support mitigation to voluntary manslaughter in a jurisdiction following this rule.

But the proposition that words alone are not enough to provoke has been abrogated in many jurisdictions. Nonetheless, even in a jurisdiction that takes that position (words can be enough), it is quite likely that a judge or jury would conclude that Marco's comments to Tyrone were not sufficiently serious that they would create an intense passion in a reasonable person. All Marco said to Tyrone was "chill out," hardly fighting words to a reasonable person. Hence, answer (d) is correct.

Accordingly, for both of these reasons—the possible existence of an adequate cooling-off period and the fact that these events were likely not sufficiently serious that they would create an intense passion in a reasonable person—a mitigating provocation defense offered by Tyrone, trying to reduce the attempted murder charge to attempted voluntary manslaughter, would also be unlikely to succeed. Since answers (b), (c), and (d) are all correct and answer (a) is incorrect, answer (e) is the most accurate answer to this problem.

[Portions of this question were taken from McKee v. State, 280 Ga. 755, 632 S.E.2d 636 (2006). You might also consider looking at that decision to see how that court handled some of these issues.]

[For additional discussion of this subject, see John M. Burkoff, Acing Criminal Law, Chapt. 12(B)(1)(a) (West)]

Answer 19–11: The correct answer is (c).

Tyrone's defense counsel might try to argue that he should not be found guilty of first degree murder because he was intoxicated when he acted. Tyrone is not likely, however, to be successful in making such a defense.

In a majority of jurisdictions, the fact that an accused was intoxicated or drugged at the time he or she committed a criminal act is considered to be a valid defense, but only if the crime (1) has a specific intent mens rea element, and (2) the intoxication or drugged condition is so extreme as to negative that element.

First degree murder is considered a specific intent crime because the actor's intention went beyond the assaultive conduct being committed and included the further intention that that conduct result in the death of the victim. (The same is true, parenthetically, of the crime of attempted murder where the mens rea is the specific intent to kill.) Because first degree murder is a specific intent offense, intoxication or drugged condition can be a viable defense in the appropriate circumstances. Hence, answer (b) is incorrect, and ipso facto answer (d) is also incorrect.

But even though intoxication may be a defense to this charges in the appropriate circumstances in most jurisdictions, it is not likely that a judge or jury would find that Tyrone was sufficiently intoxicated in this particular case that he could not have possessed the appropriate mens rea required for these offenses. Tyrone retained sufficient motor control to walk and to handle a gun. He had also somehow managed to get to Faye's apartment from the club where they had been. More significant, Tyrone was able to speak coherently to Faye, Marco, and Jeffrey. There is, accordingly, no obvious indication from these facts that Tyrone was so extremely intoxicated that he could not possibly possess the intent to kill. Hence, answer (c) is correct, and answer (a) is incorrect.

[Portions of this question were taken from McKee v. State, 280 Ga. 755, 632 S.E.2d 636 (2006). You might also consider looking at that decision to see how that court handled some of these issues.]

[For additional discussion of this subject, see John M. Burkoff, Acing Criminal Law, Chapt. 15(B) (West)]

Answer 19–12: The correct answer is (d).

Tyrone's defense counsel might also try to raise a self-defense defense. But it is highly unlikely to be successful in these circumstances. While a person is sometimes justified in using unlawful force against another person in self defense, the use of force in self defense is only justified where the person using it was not an aggressor and where he or she used it to protect himself or herself while reasonably believing that he or she was threatened with the imminent use of unlawful force by another person and that the use of responsive force was necessary to repel that threat or attack.

In these circumstances, Tyrone is not likely to be viewed as having satisfied the required elements necessary to make out a good defense of self defense, primarily because he might be viewed as the aggressor in this encounter. It was Tyrone who told Marco that he (Tyrone) was already armed and that Marco should go get his guns. There is no question but that Tyrone clearly started this whole series of events. If the fact-finder views these facts in this way, a self-defense defense will not be successful for Tyrone since he was the aggressor.

On the other hand, there is another way to look at these facts. After being told to go get his guns, that—leaving to go get them—is just what Marco did. Marco then withdrew—albeit to go to his car to arm himself—and he subsequently returned with a gun in each hand. A judge or jury might conceivably view these events as establishing that Marco, having left and then returned, then became the aggressor. If the fact-finder views these facts in this way, then Tyrone would have the right to respond to Marco's threatened, imminent use of deadly force against him with his own use of deadly force, assuming that the fact-finder concludes that it was necessary for Tyrone to respond in that fashion to defend himself.

But that is not the end of the matter necessarily. In some jurisdictions, however, a person who is faced with the use of deadly force against him or her has the obligation to "retreat" if he or she can do so safely, rather than to respond with the use of deadly force. If this is not a retreat jurisdiction and if Marco is viewed as the aggressor, then Tyrone had the right to respond to Marco's threatened imminent use of deadly force against him with deadly force. Hence, answer (a) is correct.

If this jurisdiction does use the retreat doctrine, there is an exception to that rule when the person using defensive deadly force is acting in his or her own home. In that case, such a person does not have an obligation to retreat. In the present circumstances, the facts make clear that Tyrone had just been thrown out of Faye's home, that he had returned her key to her, and that he was standing on her porch when these events took place. Since this was no longer Tyrone's home, no exception to the retreat doctrine would apply. Hence, answer (b) is correct.

Moreover, a retreat obligation only applies when the person who is subject to it can leave the area in complete safety. Could Tyrone leave safely when he was faced with Marco who had a gun in each hand? The answer to that question depends on how the fact-finder views these facts. If the judge or jury concludes that Tyrone started these events and could have ended them safely simply by leaving at this point, then any retreat obligation that might exist would persist. To the extent, however, that a judge or jury concludes instead that Tyrone could no longer leave safely when faced with Marcos standing there with a gun in each hand, any applicable retreat obligation would no longer apply. Hence, answer (c) is correct.

Since answers (a), (b) and (c) are all correct, answer (d) (All of the above) is the most accurate answer.

[Portions of this question were taken from McKee v. State, 280 Ga. 755, 632 S.E.2d 636 (2006). You might also consider looking at that decision to see how that court handled some of these issues.]

[For additional discussion of this subject, see John M. Burkoff, Acing Criminal Law, Chapt. 14(A) (West)]

Answer 19–13: The correct answer is (c).

Faye neither committed a killing act with respect to Jeffrey nor did she fire a weapon at Marco. She cannot, as a result, be found guilty of either of these charges directly. But the common law distinctions between parties to a crime—principals in the first degree, principals in the second degree, accessories before the fact, and accessories after the fact—have been abrogated by statute in the great majority of jurisdictions. With one exception—accessories after the fact—the categories of principal and accessory are said to have "merged." Accordingly, if the prosecution can establish only that Faye was complicit in these crimes, then she can be convicted of both of these offenses.

To be convicted as an accomplice in these circumstances, the prosecution must prove the mens rea of complicity: that Faye intended to assist Tyrone in killing Jeffrey and Marco and that she intended that Tyrone actually kill them both. This will be virtually impossible for the prosecution to establish.

Although the mens rea of complicity is often established circumstantially, mere presence at the scene of a crime is never enough to establish it. And in this case, Faye was not even present when the shootings took place. She had left the front porch and gone into a back bedroom. It is true that Faye said before she left the scene: "Kill each other for all I care. Go ahead! Good riddance!" This fact is the most damning fact that the prosecution can use against her. But, even if Faye really meant what she said—even if she truly intended that Tyrone kill Marco (and vice-versa)—Faye expressed no intention at all with respect to the killing of Jeffrey, and there is no evidence at all that Faye actually *intended to assist* Tyrone in killing either Jeffrey or Marco. Hence, answer (c) is correct, and answers (a), (b), and (d) are all incorrect.

Moreover, albeit parenthetically, to be convicted as an accomplice, an accused must also have actively assisted another person in the commission of a crime. Once again, Faye was not only not present at the scene, but—other than her sarcastic verbal encouragement that Tyrone and Marco shoot each other—she did nothing that could be construed as an act of active assistance. Accordingly, the appropriate actus reus for accomplice culpability is not present in these circumstances and there is very little, if any, chance that Faye could be found guilty of being an accomplice in Tyrone's killing of Jeffrey and the attempted killing of Marco.

Finally, for the same reasons that apply to Tyrone's actions, if Faye somehow could be found guilty of these offenses as an accomplice, she would not be likely to be able to defend herself successfully on the basis of intoxication. Although she had also been drinking heavily, there is no obvious indication from these facts that Faye was so extremely intoxicated that she could not possibly have possessed the intent to kill.

[Portions of this question were taken from McKee v. State, 280 Ga. 755, 632 S.E.2d 636 (2006). You might also consider looking at that decision to see how that court handled some of these issues.]

[For additional discussion of these subjects, see John M. Burkoff, Acing Criminal Law, Chapt. 6(A) & 15(B) (West)]

Answer 19–14: The correct answer is (a).

Defense counsel is not correct. Les did in fact commit an assault on Monica.

At common law and in a minority of jurisdictions today, a person commits a criminal assault when he or she intentionally places another person in actual and reasonable fear of an imminent battery. A battery at common law and in a minority of jurisdictions today is committed when a person intentionally touches another person against the other person's will, thereby injuring him or her. In a majority of jurisdictions today, the separate common law offense of battery has merged into the criminal offense of assault. Accordingly, in those majority jurisdictions, an assault is committed when a person either intentionally places another person in actual and reasonable fear of an imminent battery or intentionally commits a battery.

In either event, whether the facts set out in this problem occurred in a minority or majority jurisdiction, Les has committed a criminal assault. He intentionally placed Monica in actual and reasonable fear of an imminent battery when he put the cats in Monica's bedroom, knowing that she had an actual and deep-seated fear of them. In fact, the fact that she had this fear was precisely *why* he released the cats in the bedroom.

Monica's actual fear was a given, and certainly such an actual fear on her part would be likely to be deemed reasonable in these circumstances, particularly when she was awakened so precipitously out of a deep sleep by creatures she feared. The fact that these were just cats, not tigers or some other fearsome animals, is irrelevant, as is the fact that Monica was—other than being deeply frightened—otherwise unharmed. In any event, answer (a) assumes the reasonableness of Monica's fear. Hence, answers (b) and (c) are incorrect, and ipso facto answer (d) is incorrect as well.

Accordingly, on these facts, Les has committed a criminal assault on Monica. Hence, answer (a) is correct.

[For additional discussion of this subject, see John M. Burkoff, ACING CRIMINAL LAW, Chapt. 10(A) (West)]

Answer 19–15: The correct answer is (a).

Santonio is not likely to be able to defend himself successfully with this omissions argument.

It is true that a person's omissions—mere failures to act—are not ordinarily held to be culpable at criminal law. But the exception to that general rule is that an omission is treated as a criminal act when the person failing to act had a legal duty to do so. A classic legal duty of this sort is where a contractual obligation exists.

In this case, Santonio was employed as a crossing guard and, hence, had the contractual duty to look out for children who sought to cross at the intersection where he was employed. As a result, Santonio's negligent failure to perform this contractual duty resulting in the death of little Rosa does expose him to criminal responsibility for his inaction. Hence, answer (a) is correct, and answers (b), (c) are incorrect. Answer (b) is incorrect because the existence of a familial relationship is irrelevant to this contractual duty exception to the omissions rule. Moreover, because answer (a) is correct, answer (d) (None of the above) is also incorrect.

[For additional discussion of this subject, see John M. Burkoff, ACING CRIMINAL LAW, Chapt. 2(D) (West)]

Answer 19–16: The correct answer is (b).

It may be possible to prosecute Olivier as well as Olivier's and Olivia's corporation, depending on exactly what Olivier's role was with respect to the distribution of the tainted fudge sauce, i.e. whether or not he had the power to prevent this activity.

Corporations may be held criminally responsible—just like individuals can be—for their criminal actions. But a corporate officer is not usually held vicariously responsible for the corporation's criminal acts unless that officer was directly involved in the criminal activity. As Model Penal Code § 2.07 (6)(a) provides, for example, "[a] person is legally accountable for any conduct he performs or causes to be performed in the name of the corporation or an unincorporated association or in its behalf to the same extent as if it were performed in his own name or behalf."

Accordingly, in this case, in order to prosecute Olivier for distributing tainted food products, if this jurisdiction follows the majority—and the Model Penal Code—approach, the prosecutor would need to establish that Olivier was directly responsible for such distribution, either personally or through acts that he caused other people in the corporation to perform, whether or not he actually knew about or ratified those acts. Hence, answer (c) is incorrect, and ipso facto answer (d) is incorrect as well.

Moreover, if Olivier is prosecuted for this offense, he may possess a "powerlessness" defense. The Supreme Court has ruled that, although corporate officials may be subject to criminal responsibility for their corporation's criminal offenses, they possess a "powerlessness defense" where they can show that they did not possess the actual power and control to keep the criminal activity in question from taking place. *U.S. v. Park*, 421 U.S. 658 (1975). If Olivier can establish his powerlessness over the distribution of the tainted peanut products, he cannot be found guilty of this criminal offense. Hence, answer (b) is correct, and answer (a) is incorrect.

[For additional discussion of this subject, see John M. Burkoff, ACING CRIMINAL LAW, Chapt. 6(B) (West)]

Answer 19–17: The correct answer is (d).

This is not a good defense for Elvira. Period. A mistaken belief that a criminal act is not criminal is not a good defense. Ignorance of the law is simply no defense. It does not matter whether the statute is or is not strict liability, or whether it includes any particular mens rea element. Hence, answers (a), (b), and (c) are all incorrect, and answer (d) (None of the above) is correct.

[For additional discussion of this subject, see John M. Burkoff, ACING CRIMINAL LAW, Chapt. 4(B) (West)]

Answer 19–18: The correct answer is (b).

Elvira would have a good defense if she can convince a jury that she honestly and reasonably believed that she was not driving in a passenger car and the statute's mens rea element requires purposeful conduct. This is a mistake of fact defense.

Whether this is a good defense or not for Elvira depends on the mens rea element of the possession of narcotics statute under which she has been charged. If the offense is strict liability, for example, she has no defense as mistake of fact is a mens rea defense and a strict liability crime has no mens rea element. Hence, answer (a) is incorrect.

If the offense does have a mens rea of purposefulness and if Elvira can convince a jury that her mistaken belief was honest and reasonable (as the facts state), that is a good defense. As Model Penal Code § 2.04(1)(a) provides, for example, in relevant part, "[i]gnorance or mistake as to a matter of fact ... is a defense if ... the ignorance or mistake negatives the purpose ... required to establish a material element of the offense." Hence, answer (b) is correct, and answer (c) is incorrect.

[For additional discussion of this subject, see John M. Burkoff, ACING CRIMINAL LAW, Chapt. 4(A) (West)]

Answer 19–19: The correct answer is (a).

In a majority of jurisdictions, the fact that an accused was intoxicated or drugged at the time he or she committed the criminal act in question is deemed to be a defense—negativing the mens rea element—if but only if the crime was a specific intent crime. It is not a defense if the crime was a general intent (or strict liability) crime. Hence, answer (c) is incorrect.

Typically, a crime is deemed to be general intent when the mens rea requires only the intent to do the act that causes the harm, e.g. punching someone as an assault. Accordingly, since assault is a general intent crime, there is no intoxication defense. Hence, answer (a) is correct, and answers (d) and (e) are incorrect.

Moreover, in jurisdictions that recognize an intoxication or drugged condition defense, the fact that someone had simply been drinking (or using drugs) at the time of the crime is not sufficient, in and of itself, to make out the defense. An accused must establish that he or she was so deeply intoxicated or drugged that he or she did not possess the mens rea necessary to establish the charged offenses. A small amount of alcohol—one beer here—is simply insufficient to negate the mens rea required for any criminal offense. Hence, answer (b) is also incorrect.

[For additional discussion of this subject, see John M. Burkoff, ACING CRIMINAL LAW, Chapt. 3(C) (West)]

Answer 19–20: The correct answer is (d).

Some jurisdictions do not permit a defense of insanity. If this had been one of those jurisdictions, insanity would obviously not have been a good defense for Kenosha.

In those jurisdictions that do have an insanity defense, the most commonly used test is the two-pronged *M'Naghten* test, the test that is used in this jurisdiction. This jurisdiction uses both prongs of that test (some jurisdictions do not) since the problem refers to the *M'Naghten* test, rather than merely to one part of it. As a result, Kenosha's defense counsel would have to establish that she was suffering from such a mental disease or defect as not to know the nature and quality of the act she committed (the so-called cognitive prong of *M'Naghten*) or, if she did know, that she did not know that what she was doing was wrong (the so-called "moral incapacity" test). Hence, answer (c) is correct.

Moreover, answer (a) is correct because Kenosha could make out a good insanity defense even if she knew the nature and quality of her act, as long as defense counsel could establish that she did not know that what she was doing was wrong. And answer (b) is correct because even if Kenosha knew that kidnaping was a crime, she would have a good insanity defense as long as defense counsel could establish that she did not know the nature and quality of her actions in these circumstances.

Since answers (a), (b), and (c) are all correct, answer (d) (All of the above) is the most accurate answer.

[For additional discussion of this subject, see John M. Burkoff, ACING CRIMINAL LAW, Chapt. 15(C) (West)]

Answer 19–21: The correct answer is (c).

In a jurisdiction that has a criminal conspiracy offense in its crime code, Arn, Elliot, and Russ are guilt of conspiracy to commit robbery. Robbery is a more serious offense than theft, and focuses on the use or threat of violence or force when a theft of property is committed.

Whether it is a unilateral or a bilateral conspiracy jurisdiction, the actus reus of conspiracy is an agreement between one or more persons to commit a criminal act or to use criminal means to commit a lawful act. Such agreement can be—and often is—established circumstantially. This is just such a case. Arn's, Elliot's, and Russ' actions in accosting Necia appeared choreographed. One held a gun on her, while the other two each grabbed an arm and then took a piece of her property by force. Accordingly, there is clear, albeit circumstantial, evidence that Arn, Elliot, and Russ had agreed to engage in this criminal activity. Hence, answer (a) is incorrect.

To establish the mens rea of conspiracy, the prosecutor must prove the alleged conspirators' intent to agree with each other to commit the crime, and the intent to commit the crime itself. In this problem, the crime was actually committed so the latter mens rea element is clear. And, just as with proof of the actus reus, Arn's, Elliot's, and Russ' intent to agree with each other to rob Necia—to take her property by force or threat of force—is clearly established circumstantially. Hence, answer (b) is incorrect.

Accordingly, Arn, Elliot, and Russ are each guilty of the criminal offense of conspiracy to commit robbery. Hence, answer (c) is correct, and, and answer (d) is incorrect ipso facto.

[For additional discussion of this subject, see John M. Burkoff, Acing Criminal Law, Chapt. 8(C) (West)]

Answer 19–22: The correct answer is (a).

Dolan is likely to be convicted of the rape of Ellen.

In some American jurisdictions today, the crime of rape is defined as sexual intercourse with another person where the accused has used or threatened the use of force on the victim to accomplish the sex act. In other jurisdictions, a person commits rape when he or she has sexual intercourse with another person without that other person's consent. At common law, *both* of these elements—the use or threat of force *and* the absence of the victim's consent—were elements of the crime of rape. Whichever form of rape statute is used in this jurisdiction, Dolan is likely to be convicted of rape.

If this jurisdiction has a rape statute with a use-of-force element, it is likely to be deemed satisfied on these facts by a judge or jury since Dolan dragged Ellen forcibly behind the bushes and ripped off her clothes, and then kept her from leaving by laying on top of her. As soon as he rolled off of her, she left to report the incident. Furthermore, the fact that Ellen did not resist him physically is irrelevant. Under the common law, a victim needed to resist to the utmost before a rape prosecution could succeed but this requirement has been eliminated in the United States. Hence, answers (b) and (c) are both incorrect.

Moreover, in a jurisdiction where the rape statute does not have a use-of-force element but does have an absence-of-consent by the victim element instead, Dolan will clearly be convicted of rape as well. Consent to sexual activity is effective only if it is freely and voluntarily given by a competent person. In this case, Ellen clearly indicated to Dolan that she did not want to have sex with him. The fact that she may have been willing to have sex with him for $200—if this was, in fact, not just a joke on her part—is simply irrelevant. The absence of consent does not have to be verbal. It can be—and often is—inferred from a person's actions. Ellen never indicated to Dolan that she freely and voluntarily consented to have sexual intercourse with him at that time. In fact, everything she said and did made clear exactly the opposite. Hence, there was no consent, and answer (d) is incorrect.

Accordingly, Dolan is likely to be convicted of the rape of Ellen. Hence, answer (a) is correct.

[For additional discussion of this subject, see John M. Burkoff, Acing Criminal Law, Chapt. 11(A & B) (West)]

Answer 19–23: The correct answer is (b).

Tia cannot defend herself successfully with this omissions argument.

It is true that a person's omissions—mere failures to act—are not ordinarily held to be culpable at criminal law, i.e. they are not actions. But the exception to that general rule is that an omission is nonetheless treated as a criminal act when the person failing to act had a legal duty to act. A classic legal duty of this sort is where the "status relationship" of parent-child exists. A parent has the duty to protect his or her child from harm.

In this case, Tia was Rosa's mother. Hence, she had the parental duty to protect her child from danger. No statute needed to exist or to be enacted to create this duty. As a result, Tia's criminally negligent failure to perform her parental duty by not protecting Rosa from Eduardo's beating is an action exposing her to criminal responsibility for the death of her daughter. Hence, answer (b) is correct, and answers (a), (c), and (d) are incorrect.

[For additional discussion of this subject, see John M. Burkoff, ACING CRIMINAL LAW, Chapt. 2(D) (West)]

Answer 19–24: The correct answer is (d).

It is possible that Paulie will be convicted of involuntary manslaughter in the death of Josiah, but it is more likely that he will not be convicted.

Involuntary manslaughter is an unintentional killing committed without malice. The mens rea showing required for involuntary manslaughter is commonly gross negligence. Gross negligence is an objective element which is satisfied when the accused *should have* been aware of a substantial and unjustifiable risk that death or serious bodily injury might occur as a result of his actions. Unlike a recklessness element, to establish gross negligence, the prosecution does not have to establish that the accused was actually aware of this risk and "consciously" disregarded it. Nor is there a malice element as part of involuntary manslaughter. Hence, answer (c) is incorrect.

In this case, it is possible that a judge or jury would conclude on these facts that Paulie should have been aware of a substantial and unjustifiable risk that death or serious bodily injury might occur as a result of his use of old tires. On the other hand and more likely, it is also possible that a judge or jury might conclude the opposite, that Paulie should not have been so aware. There is no legal obligation or duty on a driver to purchase newer tires with better safety features, including enhanced skid resistance. Hence, answer (a) is incorrect.

Accordingly, while it is possible that Paulie will be convicted of involuntary manslaughter in the death of the pedestrian, it is also possible—if not likely—that he will be acquitted of this charge. Hence, answer (d) is correct.

Moreover, in either event, there is no assumption of the risk defense in criminal law. Hence, answer (b) is incorrect.

[For additional discussion of this subject, see John M. Burkoff, ACING CRIMINAL LAW, Chapt. 12(B)(2) (West)]

Answer 19–25: The correct answer is (d).

Alton is not guilty of the crime of soliciting Ed to assist him in committing a burglary.

The mens rea of the crime of solicitation is the intent to promote or facilitate the commission of a specific crime to be undertaken by another person solicited to commit it. It is not clear from these facts whether or not Alton truly possessed this intent.

But what is clear is that the requisite actus reus did not exist. The actus reus of solicitation is the act of commanding, encouraging, or requesting another person to commit a particular crime, complicity in a burglary in this case. But, significantly, a person's actions are not the crime of solicitation where they consists only of obviously hollow threats, joking, or bragging. In this problem, there is no evidence that Alton was seriously soliciting Ed to commit this crime. Indeed, nothing ever happened after the fact to indicate that Alton really meant to seriously gain Ed's services in committing a criminal act.

Accordingly, on these facts, Alton did not commit the crime of criminal solicitation. Hence, answer (c) is incorrect. Answers (a), (b), and (d) are all correct, and the most accurate answer is answer (d) since both (a) and (b) are correct.

[For additional discussion of this subject, see John M. Burkoff, ACING CRIMINAL LAW, Chapt. 9 (West)]

SOME FINAL ADVICE

The most important source of information about Criminal Law you can and should use is what your professor has said in class. If your professor has explained to you a particular rule of law and a study aid—*any* study aid—suggests a different rule, use what your professor said on the exam, not what the study aid says. The criminal law rules in different jurisdictions vary widely.

If you have access to them, take a look at your Criminal Law professor's old, multiple choice questions. How does he or she phrase his or her questions? What does he or she tend to examine about? How many answer options does he or she tend to give you, and do they include multiple possibilities (e.g., All of the above, None of the Above, etc.)? Be prepared! Don't be surprised!

Whether or not your exam is going to be open-book, make sure to pay special attention to your own class notes in preparing to take any law school exam. Don't rely on a study aid—*any* study aid, even *this* wonderful study aid—as your principal source of information.

Discussions with other students in and outside of study groups can be useful, but when you think you know the right answer to a question and someone in the group—or the whole group!—thinks otherwise, don't necessarily assume that you are wrong. You may well be right. And, sometimes, given the different rules in different jurisdictions, you may both—or all—be right!

Find out whether your professor deducts points for wrong answers on multiple choice exams. If he or she does not, then make sure that you do not fail to at least make a "best guess" in answering *every* question. If you're not sure what the right answer is, start by eliminating the listed answers that appear to be clearly wrong. If you're going to have to guess, make it an "educated guess."

Be very sensitive to how much time you have been given to complete the exam. If you have one hour to answer twenty-five multiple-choice questions and they are each worth an equal amount of points, then don't spend ten minutes on one of them. Do the math ... you have less than 2 ½ minutes for each question in that case ... and you may well want to save a little bit of time to look over your answers to some of the more difficult questions after you have finished the last question! Allocate your time wisely!

Make sure that you read both the factual scenario given and the possible answers *carefully*. In multiple choice questions, the correct answer can easily turn on the way only one, single word has been used (or not used) in the factual statement or in the answers themselves. Don't skim. Read everything carefully!

In answering exam questions, focus only on the areas of criminal law that were actually covered in your Criminal Law class. Your professor is not very likely to be asking you a question that touches upon a subject area you may have read about in a study aid or in another course (Torts?), but that he or she did not cover in class.

Get some sleep during your exam preparation. In fact, why don't you consider treating a good night's sleep every night during the exam period as part of your exam preparation? You won't be sorry.

Finally and importantly: Calm down! Chill! Be cool! Your frame of mind is at least fifty percent of the battle!

ANSWER SHEET

A B C D E	A B C D E	A B C D E	A B C D E	A B C D E
1 ① ② ③ ④ ⑤	6 ① ② ③ ④ ⑤	11 ① ② ③ ④ ⑤	16 ① ② ③ ④ ⑤	21 ① ② ③ ④ ⑤
A B C D E	A B C D E	A B C D E	A B C D E	A B C D E
2 ① ② ③ ④ ⑤	7 ① ② ③ ④ ⑤	12 ① ② ③ ④ ⑤	17 ① ② ③ ④ ⑤	22 ① ② ③ ④ ⑤
A B C D E	A B C D E	A B C D E	A B C D E	A B C D E
3 ① ② ③ ④ ⑤	8 ① ② ③ ④ ⑤	13 ① ② ③ ④ ⑤	18 ① ② ③ ④ ⑤	23 ① ② ③ ④ ⑤
A B C D E	A B C D E	A B C D E	A B C D E	A B C D E
4 ① ② ③ ④ ⑤	9 ① ② ③ ④ ⑤	14 ① ② ③ ④ ⑤	19 ① ② ③ ④ ⑤	24 ① ② ③ ④ ⑤
A B C D E	A B C D E	A B C D E	A B C D E	A B C D E
5 ① ② ③ ④ ⑤	10 ① ② ③ ④ ⑤	15 ① ② ③ ④ ⑤	20 ① ② ③ ④ ⑤	25 ① ② ③ ④ ⑤

A B C D E	A B C D E	A B C D E	A B C D E	A B C D E
1 ① ② ③ ④ ⑤	6 ① ② ③ ④ ⑤	11 ① ② ③ ④ ⑤	16 ① ② ③ ④ ⑤	21 ① ② ③ ④ ⑤
A B C D E	A B C D E	A B C D E	A B C D E	A B C D E
2 ① ② ③ ④ ⑤	7 ① ② ③ ④ ⑤	12 ① ② ③ ④ ⑤	17 ① ② ③ ④ ⑤	22 ① ② ③ ④ ⑤
A B C D E	A B C D E	A B C D E	A B C D E	A B C D E
3 ① ② ③ ④ ⑤	8 ① ② ③ ④ ⑤	13 ① ② ③ ④ ⑤	18 ① ② ③ ④ ⑤	23 ① ② ③ ④ ⑤
A B C D E	A B C D E	A B C D E	A B C D E	A B C D E
4 ① ② ③ ④ ⑤	9 ① ② ③ ④ ⑤	14 ① ② ③ ④ ⑤	19 ① ② ③ ④ ⑤	24 ① ② ③ ④ ⑤
A B C D E	A B C D E	A B C D E	A B C D E	A B C D E
5 ① ② ③ ④ ⑤	10 ① ② ③ ④ ⑤	15 ① ② ③ ④ ⑤	20 ① ② ③ ④ ⑤	25 ① ② ③ ④ ⑤

ANSWER SHEET

A B C D E A B C D E A B C D E A B C D E A B C D E
1 ① ② ③ ④ ⑤ 6 ① ② ③ ④ ⑤ 11 ① ② ③ ④ ⑤ 16 ① ② ③ ④ ⑤ 21 ① ② ③ ④ ⑤

A B C D E A B C D E A B C D E A B C D E A B C D E
2 ① ② ③ ④ ⑤ 7 ① ② ③ ④ ⑤ 12 ① ② ③ ④ ⑤ 17 ① ② ③ ④ ⑤ 22 ① ② ③ ④ ⑤

A B C D E A B C D E A B C D E A B C D E A B C D E
3 ① ② ③ ④ ⑤ 8 ① ② ③ ④ ⑤ 13 ① ② ③ ④ ⑤ 18 ① ② ③ ④ ⑤ 23 ① ② ③ ④ ⑤

A B C D E A B C D E A B C D E A B C D E A B C D E
4 ① ② ③ ④ ⑤ 9 ① ② ③ ④ ⑤ 14 ① ② ③ ④ ⑤ 19 ① ② ③ ④ ⑤ 24 ① ② ③ ④ ⑤

A B C D E A B C D E A B C D E A B C D E A B C D E
5 ① ② ③ ④ ⑤ 10 ① ② ③ ④ ⑤ 15 ① ② ③ ④ ⑤ 20 ① ② ③ ④ ⑤ 25 ① ② ③ ④ ⑤

A B C D E A B C D E A B C D E A B C D E A B C D E
1 ① ② ③ ④ ⑤ 6 ① ② ③ ④ ⑤ 11 ① ② ③ ④ ⑤ 16 ① ② ③ ④ ⑤ 21 ① ② ③ ④ ⑤

A B C D E A B C D E A B C D E A B C D E A B C D E
2 ① ② ③ ④ ⑤ 7 ① ② ③ ④ ⑤ 12 ① ② ③ ④ ⑤ 17 ① ② ③ ④ ⑤ 22 ① ② ③ ④ ⑤

A B C D E A B C D E A B C D E A B C D E A B C D E
3 ① ② ③ ④ ⑤ 8 ① ② ③ ④ ⑤ 13 ① ② ③ ④ ⑤ 18 ① ② ③ ④ ⑤ 23 ① ② ③ ④ ⑤

A B C D E A B C D E A B C D E A B C D E A B C D E
4 ① ② ③ ④ ⑤ 9 ① ② ③ ④ ⑤ 14 ① ② ③ ④ ⑤ 19 ① ② ③ ④ ⑤ 24 ① ② ③ ④ ⑤

A B C D E A B C D E A B C D E A B C D E A B C D E
5 ① ② ③ ④ ⑤ 10 ① ② ③ ④ ⑤ 15 ① ② ③ ④ ⑤ 20 ① ② ③ ④ ⑤ 25 ① ② ③ ④ ⑤

ANSWER SHEET

A B C D E	A B C D E	A B C D E	A B C D E	A B C D E
1 ① ② ③ ④ ⑤	6 ① ② ③ ④ ⑤	11 ① ② ③ ④ ⑤	16 ① ② ③ ④ ⑤	21 ① ② ③ ④ ⑤
2 ① ② ③ ④ ⑤	7 ① ② ③ ④ ⑤	12 ① ② ③ ④ ⑤	17 ① ② ③ ④ ⑤	22 ① ② ③ ④ ⑤
3 ① ② ③ ④ ⑤	8 ① ② ③ ④ ⑤	13 ① ② ③ ④ ⑤	18 ① ② ③ ④ ⑤	23 ① ② ③ ④ ⑤
4 ① ② ③ ④ ⑤	9 ① ② ③ ④ ⑤	14 ① ② ③ ④ ⑤	19 ① ② ③ ④ ⑤	24 ① ② ③ ④ ⑤
5 ① ② ③ ④ ⑤	10 ① ② ③ ④ ⑤	15 ① ② ③ ④ ⑤	20 ① ② ③ ④ ⑤	25 ① ② ③ ④ ⑤

A B C D E	A B C D E	A B C D E	A B C D E	A B C D E
1 ① ② ③ ④ ⑤	6 ① ② ③ ④ ⑤	11 ① ② ③ ④ ⑤	16 ① ② ③ ④ ⑤	21 ① ② ③ ④ ⑤
2 ① ② ③ ④ ⑤	7 ① ② ③ ④ ⑤	12 ① ② ③ ④ ⑤	17 ① ② ③ ④ ⑤	22 ① ② ③ ④ ⑤
3 ① ② ③ ④ ⑤	8 ① ② ③ ④ ⑤	13 ① ② ③ ④ ⑤	18 ① ② ③ ④ ⑤	23 ① ② ③ ④ ⑤
4 ① ② ③ ④ ⑤	9 ① ② ③ ④ ⑤	14 ① ② ③ ④ ⑤	19 ① ② ③ ④ ⑤	24 ① ② ③ ④ ⑤
5 ① ② ③ ④ ⑤	10 ① ② ③ ④ ⑤	15 ① ② ③ ④ ⑤	20 ① ② ③ ④ ⑤	25 ① ② ③ ④ ⑤

ANSWER SHEET

A B C D E A B C D E A B C D E A B C D E A B C D E
1 ① ② ③ ④ ⑤ 6 ① ② ③ ④ ⑤ 11 ① ② ③ ④ ⑤ 16 ① ② ③ ④ ⑤ 21 ① ② ③ ④ ⑤

A B C D E A B C D E A B C D E A B C D E A B C D E
2 ① ② ③ ④ ⑤ 7 ① ② ③ ④ ⑤ 12 ① ② ③ ④ ⑤ 17 ① ② ③ ④ ⑤ 22 ① ② ③ ④ ⑤

A B C D E A B C D E A B C D E A B C D E A B C D E
3 ① ② ③ ④ ⑤ 8 ① ② ③ ④ ⑤ 13 ① ② ③ ④ ⑤ 18 ① ② ③ ④ ⑤ 23 ① ② ③ ④ ⑤

A B C D E A B C D E A B C D E A B C D E A B C D E
4 ① ② ③ ④ ⑤ 9 ① ② ③ ④ ⑤ 14 ① ② ③ ④ ⑤ 19 ① ② ③ ④ ⑤ 24 ① ② ③ ④ ⑤

A B C D E A B C D E A B C D E A B C D E A B C D E
5 ① ② ③ ④ ⑤ 10 ① ② ③ ④ ⑤ 15 ① ② ③ ④ ⑤ 20 ① ② ③ ④ ⑤ 25 ① ② ③ ④ ⑤

A B C D E A B C D E A B C D E A B C D E A B C D E
1 ① ② ③ ④ ⑤ 6 ① ② ③ ④ ⑤ 11 ① ② ③ ④ ⑤ 16 ① ② ③ ④ ⑤ 21 ① ② ③ ④ ⑤

A B C D E A B C D E A B C D E A B C D E A B C D E
2 ① ② ③ ④ ⑤ 7 ① ② ③ ④ ⑤ 12 ① ② ③ ④ ⑤ 17 ① ② ③ ④ ⑤ 22 ① ② ③ ④ ⑤

A B C D E A B C D E A B C D E A B C D E A B C D E
3 ① ② ③ ④ ⑤ 8 ① ② ③ ④ ⑤ 13 ① ② ③ ④ ⑤ 18 ① ② ③ ④ ⑤ 23 ① ② ③ ④ ⑤

A B C D E A B C D E A B C D E A B C D E A B C D E
4 ① ② ③ ④ ⑤ 9 ① ② ③ ④ ⑤ 14 ① ② ③ ④ ⑤ 19 ① ② ③ ④ ⑤ 24 ① ② ③ ④ ⑤

A B C D E A B C D E A B C D E A B C D E A B C D E
5 ① ② ③ ④ ⑤ 10 ① ② ③ ④ ⑤ 15 ① ② ③ ④ ⑤ 20 ① ② ③ ④ ⑤ 25 ① ② ③ ④ ⑤

ANSWER SHEET

A B C D E A B C D E A B C D E A B C D E A B C D E
1 ① ② ③ ④ ⑤ 6 ① ② ③ ④ ⑤ 11 ① ② ③ ④ ⑤ 16 ① ② ③ ④ ⑤ 21 ① ② ③ ④ ⑤

A B C D E A B C D E A B C D E A B C D E A B C D E
2 ① ② ③ ④ ⑤ 7 ① ② ③ ④ ⑤ 12 ① ② ③ ④ ⑤ 17 ① ② ③ ④ ⑤ 22 ① ② ③ ④ ⑤

A B C D E A B C D E A B C D E A B C D E A B C D E
3 ① ② ③ ④ ⑤ 8 ① ② ③ ④ ⑤ 13 ① ② ③ ④ ⑤ 18 ① ② ③ ④ ⑤ 23 ① ② ③ ④ ⑤

A B C D E A B C D E A B C D E A B C D E A B C D E
4 ① ② ③ ④ ⑤ 9 ① ② ③ ④ ⑤ 14 ① ② ③ ④ ⑤ 19 ① ② ③ ④ ⑤ 24 ① ② ③ ④ ⑤

A B C D E A B C D E A B C D E A B C D E A B C D E
5 ① ② ③ ④ ⑤ 10 ① ② ③ ④ ⑤ 15 ① ② ③ ④ ⑤ 20 ① ② ③ ④ ⑤ 25 ① ② ③ ④ ⑤

A B C D E A B C D E A B C D E A B C D E A B C D E
1 ① ② ③ ④ ⑤ 6 ① ② ③ ④ ⑤ 11 ① ② ③ ④ ⑤ 16 ① ② ③ ④ ⑤ 21 ① ② ③ ④ ⑤

A B C D E A B C D E A B C D E A B C D E A B C D E
2 ① ② ③ ④ ⑤ 7 ① ② ③ ④ ⑤ 12 ① ② ③ ④ ⑤ 17 ① ② ③ ④ ⑤ 22 ① ② ③ ④ ⑤

A B C D E A B C D E A B C D E A B C D E A B C D E
3 ① ② ③ ④ ⑤ 8 ① ② ③ ④ ⑤ 13 ① ② ③ ④ ⑤ 18 ① ② ③ ④ ⑤ 23 ① ② ③ ④ ⑤

A B C D E A B C D E A B C D E A B C D E A B C D E
4 ① ② ③ ④ ⑤ 9 ① ② ③ ④ ⑤ 14 ① ② ③ ④ ⑤ 19 ① ② ③ ④ ⑤ 24 ① ② ③ ④ ⑤

A B C D E A B C D E A B C D E A B C D E A B C D E
5 ① ② ③ ④ ⑤ 10 ① ② ③ ④ ⑤ 15 ① ② ③ ④ ⑤ 20 ① ② ③ ④ ⑤ 25 ① ② ③ ④ ⑤

ANSWER SHEET

A B C D E	A B C D E	A B C D E	A B C D E	A B C D E
1 ① ② ③ ④ ⑤	6 ① ② ③ ④ ⑤	11 ① ② ③ ④ ⑤	16 ① ② ③ ④ ⑤	21 ① ② ③ ④ ⑤
A B C D E	A B C D E	A B C D E	A B C D E	A B C D E
2 ① ② ③ ④ ⑤	7 ① ② ③ ④ ⑤	12 ① ② ③ ④ ⑤	17 ① ② ③ ④ ⑤	22 ① ② ③ ④ ⑤
A B C D E	A B C D E	A B C D E	A B C D E	A B C D E
3 ① ② ③ ④ ⑤	8 ① ② ③ ④ ⑤	13 ① ② ③ ④ ⑤	18 ① ② ③ ④ ⑤	23 ① ② ③ ④ ⑤
A B C D E	A B C D E	A B C D E	A B C D E	A B C D E
4 ① ② ③ ④ ⑤	9 ① ② ③ ④ ⑤	14 ① ② ③ ④ ⑤	19 ① ② ③ ④ ⑤	24 ① ② ③ ④ ⑤
A B C D E	A B C D E	A B C D E	A B C D E	A B C D E
5 ① ② ③ ④ ⑤	10 ① ② ③ ④ ⑤	15 ① ② ③ ④ ⑤	20 ① ② ③ ④ ⑤	25 ① ② ③ ④ ⑤

A B C D E	A B C D E	A B C D E	A B C D E	A B C D E
1 ① ② ③ ④ ⑤	6 ① ② ③ ④ ⑤	11 ① ② ③ ④ ⑤	16 ① ② ③ ④ ⑤	21 ① ② ③ ④ ⑤
A B C D E	A B C D E	A B C D E	A B C D E	A B C D E
2 ① ② ③ ④ ⑤	7 ① ② ③ ④ ⑤	12 ① ② ③ ④ ⑤	17 ① ② ③ ④ ⑤	22 ① ② ③ ④ ⑤
A B C D E	A B C D E	A B C D E	A B C D E	A B C D E
3 ① ② ③ ④ ⑤	8 ① ② ③ ④ ⑤	13 ① ② ③ ④ ⑤	18 ① ② ③ ④ ⑤	23 ① ② ③ ④ ⑤
A B C D E	A B C D E	A B C D E	A B C D E	A B C D E
4 ① ② ③ ④ ⑤	9 ① ② ③ ④ ⑤	14 ① ② ③ ④ ⑤	19 ① ② ③ ④ ⑤	24 ① ② ③ ④ ⑤
A B C D E	A B C D E	A B C D E	A B C D E	A B C D E
5 ① ② ③ ④ ⑤	10 ① ② ③ ④ ⑤	15 ① ② ③ ④ ⑤	20 ① ② ③ ④ ⑤	25 ① ② ③ ④ ⑤

ANSWER SHEET

A B C D E　　A B C D E　　A B C D E　　A B C D E　　A B C D E
1 ① ② ③ ④ ⑤　6 ① ② ③ ④ ⑤　11 ① ② ③ ④ ⑤　16 ① ② ③ ④ ⑤　21 ① ② ③ ④ ⑤

A B C D E　　A B C D E　　A B C D E　　A B C D E　　A B C D E
2 ① ② ③ ④ ⑤　7 ① ② ③ ④ ⑤　12 ① ② ③ ④ ⑤　17 ① ② ③ ④ ⑤　22 ① ② ③ ④ ⑤

A B C D E　　A B C D E　　A B C D E　　A B C D E　　A B C D E
3 ① ② ③ ④ ⑤　8 ① ② ③ ④ ⑤　13 ① ② ③ ④ ⑤　18 ① ② ③ ④ ⑤　23 ① ② ③ ④ ⑤

A B C D E　　A B C D E　　A B C D E　　A B C D E　　A B C D E
4 ① ② ③ ④ ⑤　9 ① ② ③ ④ ⑤　14 ① ② ③ ④ ⑤　19 ① ② ③ ④ ⑤　24 ① ② ③ ④ ⑤

A B C D E　　A B C D E　　A B C D E　　A B C D E　　A B C D E
5 ① ② ③ ④ ⑤　10 ① ② ③ ④ ⑤　15 ① ② ③ ④ ⑤　20 ① ② ③ ④ ⑤　25 ① ② ③ ④ ⑤

A B C D E　　A B C D E　　A B C D E　　A B C D E　　A B C D E
1 ① ② ③ ④ ⑤　6 ① ② ③ ④ ⑤　11 ① ② ③ ④ ⑤　16 ① ② ③ ④ ⑤　21 ① ② ③ ④ ⑤

A B C D E　　A B C D E　　A B C D E　　A B C D E　　A B C D E
2 ① ② ③ ④ ⑤　7 ① ② ③ ④ ⑤　12 ① ② ③ ④ ⑤　17 ① ② ③ ④ ⑤　22 ① ② ③ ④ ⑤

A B C D E　　A B C D E　　A B C D E　　A B C D E　　A B C D E
3 ① ② ③ ④ ⑤　8 ① ② ③ ④ ⑤　13 ① ② ③ ④ ⑤　18 ① ② ③ ④ ⑤　23 ① ② ③ ④ ⑤

A B C D E　　A B C D E　　A B C D E　　A B C D E　　A B C D E
4 ① ② ③ ④ ⑤　9 ① ② ③ ④ ⑤　14 ① ② ③ ④ ⑤　19 ① ② ③ ④ ⑤　24 ① ② ③ ④ ⑤

A B C D E　　A B C D E　　A B C D E　　A B C D E　　A B C D E
5 ① ② ③ ④ ⑤　10 ① ② ③ ④ ⑤　15 ① ② ③ ④ ⑤　20 ① ② ③ ④ ⑤　25 ① ② ③ ④ ⑤

†